The Fate of Difficulty
in the Poetry of Our Time

The Fate of Difficulty in the Poetry of Our Time

✦

Edited by Charles Altieri
and Nicholas D. Nace

NORTHWESTERN UNIVERSITY PRESS
EVANSTON, ILLINOIS

Northwestern University Press
www.nupress.northwestern.edu

Printed in the United States of America

10   9   8   7   6   5   4   3   2   1

ISBN 978-0-8101-3606-9 (cloth)
ISBN 978-0-8101-3605-2 (paper)
ISBN 978-0-8101-3607-6 (e-book)

Library of Congress Cataloging-in-Publication data
are available from the Library of Congress

CONTENTS

Part Three: Addressing the Multiple

POEMS

Introduction

✦

Charles Altieri and Nicholas D. Nace

The difficulties found are seldom ever the difficulties looked for, as the editing of this collection has proven. In focusing on the idea of difficulty in contemporary poetry, we at first expected to engage with poems that ennoble modes of complexity, density, indeterminacy, opacity, and abstraction. Such an expectation has, after all, been common in recent critical engagements with self-consciously "innovative" poetry. Yet this way of proceeding sets one up to find precisely what one expects to see, namely the present manifestation of established lineages defined by well-known difficult poets of the past.[1] We soon realized in working on this project that we had to alter our expectations. For one thing, we wanted to be guided by how a sense of difficulty seems to inhere in specific poems, without recourse to the clustering of poets as exemplars or inheritors of certain schools, movements, or techniques. When we follow this approach, the concept of difficulty expands over a messy terrain. Looking at the field from this vantage, we found that the expectations we held onto were seriously limited and limiting.

We started with the idea that we would feel less frustrated in our approach to the work of relatively young contemporary poets if we could figure out how, precisely, they approached the compositional role of difficulty in a manner different from their modernist predecessors and even from influential postwar poets such as Bishop, Merrill, O'Hara, Creeley, Ashbery, and Plath. So we invited twenty-six of the critics and poets we most admired to take up this topic in essays of no more than five thousand words. Our understanding of difficulty at the start was quite formal—a matter of how poets organized languages of poetry—and therefore our assumption was that the internal physics of difficult poems could be laid bare through a variety of close reading that intensely focuses on their organization (the approach offered in Altieri's contribution to this collection). We wanted to know how contemporary poets deploy difficulty in their linguistic and lyric structures. And we wanted to know how particular contemporary understandings of difficulty differed from one another as means of challenging and rewarding readers skeptical of modernist difficulty as largely the construction of cultural capital. We did not ask at all about difficulties engaging the nature of social life or even of engaging various groups of readers, since we now realize that we assumed all relevant readers were devoted to impersonal acts of reflection and judgment focused through attention on the authorial activity. Furthermore we did not ask sufficiently general questions about why difficulty might be a central concern for the study of poetry. Nor did we ask about the joy of difficulty, though we assumed such a complex emotion existed.

Our blindness set us up to encounter substantial surprises. The first surprise was that our authors did not choose some of those we thought the most interesting younger contemporary poets. But our disappointment turned into considerable pleasure as we read about poets whom we did not know or did not take sufficiently seriously before encountering our contributors' essays. More importantly, the variety of work our contributors explored almost completely transformed our sense of our topic. What we had to come to call "comparative difficulty studies" was a far richer and more telling approach to contemporary poetry than we had imagined. The essays challenged many of our core assumptions and, in doing that, provided what we think are fresh and compelling perspectives on how contemporary poets engage their cultural situations.

Here we can offer an initial overview of what these essays accomplish by invoking distinctions proposed long ago by the late M.H. Abrams.[2] He suggested that we clarify how each theoretical argument handles four specific topics, conceptualized almost as if they were points on a compass. The two most obvious topics involve how the theory conceives of the basic roles of author and of audience in the production of literary artifacts. Granted—or so we thought. But Abrams suggested, too, that we must specify what attributes of the construction of the work are central to the theory and how these attributes make possible distinctive relations to the world beyond the text. Understanding the fit between work and world was where fundamental assumptions about authors and audiences began to get complicated.

Before reading these essays, we tended to imagine authorship in poetry as a kind of mastery, bringing the intensity of personal engagements with situations into a kind of order that would provide structure for passion and intensity for the work of mind. But most of these essays stress the ways that authors acknowledge the limited nature of such mastery.[3] They emphasize a level of authorship that does not offer confessional sincerity as a badge of authenticity but instead makes visible a sense of struggle that precludes any stable identity position. Rather than stress the authority earned by craft, these writers seek from the audience an intimacy with their own confusions and tensions about the position of a writer. Most contemporary poets want to share a condition more than they want to instruct and to delight, even if this sharing is based not on an inner life so much as on painful encounters with structures that organize social reality. We began to notice that such desires tend, in our time, to require considerable space for articulation. For many poets who approach issues of authorship, difficulty takes place less in short lyric or anti-lyric forms than in longer book-length works.

Our biggest surprise was how these goals mobilized concerns for audiences within this poetry. In fact we were forced to realize that we had not thought much about audiences at all, assuming as we did that a work, especially an experimental work, constructed its audience on and by its own terms. The work tried at once to appeal to the aesthetic judgment of its implied audience and, at the same time, to engage the best contemplative selves of that audience so that readers might provisionally identify with the author's interests in making this particular aspect of an imagined world. But essay after essay here proposes a very different sense of audience. The audience becomes a set of agents who are assumed to be suspicious of language because it seems to function less as a vehicle of discovery than as a mode of interpellation imposing on audiences control and conformity. That suspicion of language accompanies a profound uneasiness about social position—whether it be the position of privileged white professional or the position of imaginary rebel obsessed with the inadequacies of the dominant social order. And most important, we had to recognize that many of our poets do not either assume or construct an audience but assume a position of need that invites the audience to participate creatively in the space marked out by the poem.[4] The divided author needs to have not only the presence of a sympathetic audience but also hope that the writing can help form communities capable of modifying the social conditions that generate the desire in the first place.

We will see that work and world, Abrams's other basic constituents for theorizing about literature, are dialectically constituted in relation to these transformations of the roles of author and audience. How could the work be unified and offered up for contemplative impersonality when the author endures the kinds of anxieties and traumas that are experienced as forces blocking any hope of coherent self-understanding? Yet these anxieties and traumatic elements are not alleviated by confessional strategies and appeals for empathy and toleration. Rather they are mostly created by the social negotiations necessary for living under corporate capitalism—difficulties like pervasive economic injustice, exponentially increasing destruction of the environment, and rampant challenges to any kind of trust in the motives of others or in the capacity of the writer to offer coherent and telling self-descriptions. It was astonishing to us how the visible consequences of the world produced by late capitalism seem to preoccupy almost all the poets studied in this book. One need not be revolutionary to feel the trivializing of distinctive subjective concerns that occur when one faces the naked consequences of corporate power.

We were tempted to organize this introduction—and to some extent this book—in terms of Abrams's categories.[5] But while we find these terms immensely helpful in generalizing about the situation of contemporary poetry, they do not seem sufficiently precise or flexible to capture the range of what we most appreciate in these essays. So we have structured the book in terms that we think capture the different emphases of the particular essays. There are four large sections: (1) essays that posit historical stages as the preferred ground for appreciating questions about difficulty facing contemporary poets; (2) essays that elaborate what Judith Goldman calls "difficult affect as it originates in the social" often taking "radically mimetic forms that maintain fidelity both to that disfiguring difficult affect and to the cultural logic that generates it"; (3) essays that clarify how awareness of cultural differences and cultural boundaries partially shapes these affective conditions and create somewhat new demands on our practices of reading; and finally, (4) essays that grapple with how the modifications in our culture's ways of processing information demand new modes of attention to how writing can be understood as productive technology, with special emphasis on the challenges posed by conceptual poetry.

I. Continuities

The opening section is in many respects not typical of the rest of the book because it is more concerned with continuities than with discontinuities, at least in terms of how difficulties are presented within various poetic traditions. We begin with Langdon Hammer's fascinating account of the difficulty of correlating intimacy and sociality because this offers a microcosm capturing our sense of how our poets face the problem of hearing voices from the past that they now find alienating and disturbing because of the voices' distance from our social realities. Yet Hammer shows how Srikanth Reddy's rendering of Kurt Waldheim—the U.N. Secretary General whose Nazi past was revealed while he was in office—produced a voice from which it is in fact difficult to dissociate ourselves. Waldheim shares a good deal of how we might represent our own denials of uncomfortable political realities while piously claiming to speak for humanity. So the composite voice formed by erasure and reappropriation cannot be dismissed as anyone's idiosyncratic and troubled expression. It is too abstract for that, and that abstraction itself becomes terribly intimate because we try to ward off the identifications that in fact come too close to our own ways of thinking to dismiss outright. Hammer carefully traces the modulations of voice in each of the three parts of Reddy's *Voyager* (2011) and their attendant methodologies. Here we can only note that the modulations themselves become aspects of the difficulty of this poem's inquiry into who really is speaking and who can escape this mode of speech.

There is nothing more traditional for English poetry than the sonnet. As Al Filreis shows, this relation to tradition offers a telling occasion by which poets can define their own sense of now occupying a very different world.

He chooses an intricate poem by Laynie Browne to stage the complex sense of presence Browne realizes by reworking for contemporary consumption John Donne's sonnet "I am a little world made cunningly." This reworking manages to acknowledge, by reduction and transposition, all that has grown sodden in the sonnet tradition while bringing out what can still be cunning about it. Browne's compression and linguistic recasting effectively dramatize how formal issues can still have a significant presence despite their self-conscious withdrawal from the scene of writing. (For example the poem reminds us of how sonnet compression can be intensified yet more.) And she develops her own mode of Donne's sense of vitality by treating as sacred all the terms of dailiness that for Donne provided terms of belief. But as she cuts formally, she also erases the abstractness of belief, with the effect that the choices in the present must carry all the burden of significance. Browne's recasting of tradition and bringing difficulty to the fore establish the possibility of living imaginatively, simply in the cunning of immediate creativity in dialogue with tradition.

Aaron Kunin's essay on Jacqueline Waters offers a unique rendering of how the contemporary continuities with modernist ideologies of poetry can provoke fresh and unexpected twists in sensibility. Kunin presents Waters as continuing the modernist suspicion of rhetoric that demanded "difficulty" as a kind of purification ritual making sure that the poem did not invoke popular bromides or yield to common bourgeois interests. But what happens when the quest for difficulty becomes a part of the problem rather than an aspect of a feasible solution? What if the pursuit of difficulty seems now itself driven by rhetorical concerns at least as much as concerns to break through into more "authentic" and less corrupted modes of speaking? If Waters's difficulty is, as Kunin suggests, "with difficulty itself," how can she dignify poetry as breaking from standard ideological and rhetorical frameworks so that it can afford significant models of active, self-aware sensibility? Kunin in fact provides strong motives for Waters's commitments to judgment, intelligence, and toleration. Waters registers the delusory features of social speech without quite opposing them because she is more interested in cultivating a spirit of tolerance that allows audiences to listen for what passions take on such malformation. The poetry, if we can locate it, is in the challenge of listening to efforts at social positioning (a more concrete notion than "ideology") that stress attitudes dispelling temptations for approval as well as disapproval. What matters is purifying capacities for the crowd to listen effectively without self-righteousness, because no one enjoys freedom from the need to position one's linguistic acts.

Charles Altieri's essay on Geoffrey G. O'Brien develops a third—and more formal—contrast with modernist accounts of difficulty. It argues that O'Brien represents a radical change from modernist ideals of pursuing something like the internal coherence of organic form because the contemporaries he most cares about insist on undoing any objective coherence that the poem might have as text. For O'Brien, what holds the text together is always a work in progress, always something dependent on an individual reader's choices, which prompt an awareness of their own partiality. If the central figure for the modernists was metaphor, at least in the sense that it has the capacity to set up a logic of integrative possibilities, the central imaginative resource for O'Brien seems to be how enjambment requires the reader to wonder momentarily how the poem can continue—so that reader becomes aware of what he or she must exclude as well as include to produce a desired coherence. And enjambment calls attention to the power of grammar that makes us hover between options. So O'Brien can fuse an intensive and emphatic sense of formal compositional relations with a version of politically significant agency in a world where opportunities for fully self-aware decision making do not abound.

John Wilkinson's essay on Andrea Brady's "The Husband" comes next because it offers a complexly textured close reading with more appreciation of traditional ideals than Altieri's essay. However, Wilkinson does not just offer close reading. He shows how the invitation to close reading is itself another kind of political act because it displays and honors the possibility of restoring a language of aesthetic experience in a literary culture often obsessed with ethical and political earnestness. The language of difficulty in his view is too easily absorbed into those modes of earnestness, so that we lose the capacity to honor particular acts of mind—in this case an act of mind that replaces a generalized obligation to be difficult with a celebration of the craft it takes to establish "virtuoso tonal management" of domestic values. And then, by invoking Kant on the aesthetic, Wilkinson shows how such craft can plausibly imagine an appreciative response that binds audience members to the awareness of a universal dimension of their pleasure.

Finally, we conclude this section with Michael Clune's essay on Aaron Kunin's poem "First." Although it has the scope to fit anywhere in the volume, we place it here because we like its symmetry with Kunin's own essay. And we think that Clune's quite general discussion of difficulty clearly fits well as a summary of the pressure the past imposes on how we think about difficulty in the present. Clune shows how Kunin's distinctively contemporary self-consciousness manages to satisfy long-standing ideals of what difficulty can make possible. The primary difficulty here is the need to make compelling the question of "firstness"—or how origins and originality can be woven together—while also establishing a plausible perspective capable of dealing in secular terms with what had been the domain of theology. Clune initially distinguishes questions of difficulty from questions involving obscurity, which several critics here point out often comprise little more than an effort to establish social capital. Then he separates sharply two different kinds of value that difficulty can foreground. First there is the kind of difficulty stressed by Russian formalist critics such as Viktor Shklovsky. Instances of this difficulty stress the demand on language to produce estrangement as its means of staging surprisingly fresh attitudes toward a stale world. Think about the strange appropriateness of Prufrock's representing the evening as "spread out against the sky / like a patient etherized upon a table."[6] But surprise fades, and this level of originality soon becomes indistinguishable from cliché. Not so with Clune's second kind of difficulty, which serves as a rhetorical means of developing a situation that is intrinsically difficult to understand. Here the sense of having overcome difficulty provides a measure of significance for whatever clarity the poem can win.

The example of Shklovsky helps negatively because it reminds us that none of the other essays even mention estrangement. Perhaps deliberate acts of local estrangement seem an absurd project when the poets grapple with such total estrangement from their culture and from the language through which they might be expected to set things right. But the example of difficulty overcome as a measure of truth—or difficulty partially overcome as a measure of the recalcitrance of truth—seems a useful reminder of why poetry still affords a powerful vehicle for realizing all of the different ways author, audience, work, and world can be asked to function.

In the case of Kunin's "First," the will to confront difficulty leads him to treat firstness as a fundamentally conceptual problem requiring resources beyond the typical ken of lyric poetry. This means that the poem has to manifest its estrangement from any Romantic or psychological account of origins. And that estrangement, common to contemporary poetry, leads Kunin to uncommon reflections on the appropriateness of physics rather than biology as our most effective framework for thinking about firstness—both in general terms and in the somewhat chilling sense that creativity itself must be submitted to models of explanation that do not include intentionality but see actions as simply phenomena that instantiate laws. So Kunin ends up sharing with the other poets addressed by this collection an obsession with the necessity of self-consciousness haunted by a perspective that insists on the impotence of such states. But there is a strange consolation here. "First" also reminds us that there is a primary condition for negotiating difficulty—a will not to let the supplementary materials necessary for establishing what the poem is about determine the actual force of the particular act the poem makes present. If difficulty is present, it must remain a vital condition of our reading that is not explained away by the contexts it elicits.

II. Troubled Affects

The rest of our essays lead us into very different intellectual atmospheres. Difficulty resides as much in the social and personal situations rendered by the poems as in anything one might say about the rendering. Our second category consists of essays that emphasize the kinds of troubled affects that precipitate the lack of affective resolution fairly common in contemporary poetry. We subdivide this into two groups because there seems a significant distinction between, on the one hand, poems exploring the powers and limits of deploying intimacy to reach some kind of communal bond and, on the other, poems that directly express responses to trauma. In fact, the basic source of trauma is often the impossibility of finding any contemplative space not already divided, and in some way intolerable, because of how social conditions infiltrate the personal.

The poets studied in this section are tormented by the fact that a separate aesthetic realm cannot be invoked, whether on Wilkinson's Kantian terms or on more pragmatic grounds. Nor, in fact, can these poets achieve any believable universal that transcends differences. The best these poets can imagine is appealing to a community that finds its bond in acknowledging differences. It is hard to imagine a richer or more sensitive account of this situation than Siobhan Phillips's essay on Juliana Spahr's "switching" and its careful placement of the poem within Spahr's writings on poetics. Phillips sees much of Spahr's work as asking a simple question: Why in the Romantic tradition is the desire for intimacy always focused on the position of the one expressing affect rather than on the interlocutor? For Spahr it proves possible to imagine otherwise and ground the possibility of community directly in the ways that the poet reaches out for the participation of her readers. Then we can project the expressive activity itself as not so much the presentation of a psyche as opening that psyche to its place in shareable social situations.

Our emotions about war and injustice simply are not matters of isolated inwardness. So by refocusing our ways of imagining how lyric subjects develop expressive activity, we can redefine what kinds of emotions might now be most pressing—as causes of anxiety and as possible confirmations of a community suffering from similar problems. But Phillips and Spahr recognize that these possibilities are rife with difficulty—not just in establishing genuine intimacy but also in locating means by which other subjects with their own anxieties might be open to that which is potentially shareable within the subject's expressive acts. This is where "switching" elaborates a useful and perhaps necessary strategy. Because we do not have any stable sense of social bonds, the best the poet can do on most occasions is to switch constantly between the expressive and the collective aspects of experience in the hope that audiences will find their identification with the collective in adapting to that necessity.

Michael Davidson's commentary on Jena Osman's "The Beautiful Life of Persona Ficta," from her volume *Corporate Relations* (2014), provides another aspect of investigative poetics. Davidson concentrates on the difficulty of having to adjust to poetry that is based not on lyrical impulses but rather on deep and persistent threats to all of the beliefs on which lyricism has been based. Now the relation between intimacy and sociality is reversed. Rather than bring intimacy to social and communal aspects of our imaginings, the force of particular social rhetorics, in Osman's view, threatens to absorb any significant role for intimacy. Osman develops a grimly playful rendering of "how legal analogical reasoning threatens the lyrical voice by altering our sense of what persons are." Under these conditions, perhaps poetry can "do political work, not by shouting down the opposition or by demonizing bad practices but by exploring and framing the productive means" by which the "master ventriloquist called Capital" labors to construct social identities. But this project can work only if Osman can successfully face another difficulty. She needs to have her version of investigative poetics avoid the somber righteousness of cultural critique. She accomplishes this by working with analogy and constructing a world—painfully like the actual world—in which analogy takes on formative power and renders subjectivity as a mode of puppetry. Then corporations can be actual persons, and worse, persons tend to make judgments in the ways corporations and law courts do. Yet by exposing those tendencies, writing can move to end them—or at least restrict them by exposing their powers of contamination. In Osman's work, Davidson sees some hope in poetry's capacity to expose various forms of depersonalization.

Ben Lerner is concerned with similar cultural transformations of lyric voice, but his approach, being more general, proves more attentive to the variety of roles of poetry in contemporary culture than Davidson. He asks how we can continue to value the writing of poetry when its Romantic core, based as it is on ideals of intense personal expression, has been substantially disrupted by critiques of inwardness and constructive mastery that begin in poststructuralist thinking but now seem part of the fabric of our imaginative lives, even as literary culture distances itself from both that form of thinking and the Language poetry that elaborated its consequences for creative work. As both poet and novelist, Lerner finds an instructive example in poets like Spahr, Maggie Nelson, and Claudia Rankine, who investigate how prose might perform much of the traditional work of poetry without relying on the traditional building blocks of lyric, which have become unstable and even "shameful" in their dependencies on traditions of expressivist poetics. Prose seems suited to the challenge posed by Ron Silliman's projections about "the new sentence" without Language poetry's commitment to having difficulty be a force for frustration by directly "undermining the assumption of univocality and spokenness conventionally associated with the lyric." Prose also might escape the self-congratulatory rhetoric of social critique that many conceptual writers in their own way seek to avoid.

The poets exploring how prose might do much of the work of lyric stress its openness to intimate phenomenological fluctuations without having to carry the burden of overt formal intricacy and the aspects of self-consciousness inseparable from that kind of authority. Or, to put the case somewhat differently, prose manages to erase expectations formed through discourses about difficulty while providing aspects of challenge for the complicated interrelationships that seem born of the writer's subject matter rather than of the writer's will. Relying on prose invites us "to think of lyric as a reading practice as much as a writing practice." In this version of reading, the ostensibly "shameful" attributes of the mode (e.g., an egotistical, asocial inwardness) can be replaced by a collaborative effort on the part of reader and writer to overcome the "loneliness" basic to Claudia Rankine's recent poetry. And Maggie Nelson's *Bluets* (2009) marvelously naturalizes the emphasis on song, so basic to traditions of lyric, by locating the music sheerly in what can be described and shared so long as one attends to how prose opens itself to the natural world.

At this point our essays shift attention from the plights of lyric voice to the plights defined by the overall affective modes contemporary poets tend to emphasize. Several of our authors stress the difficulty of readers being asked to adapt to truly direct assertions of trauma that ultimately cannot be located only in the individual psyche offering confessions of its plights. Some of these assertions are focused on threats from the social world, others on desperate incapacities to find resources adequate for handling those threats. Whatever the causes, such poetry has as its primary task separating plausibly felt emotion from the rhetorical invocation of emotions to seduce audiences.

Judith Goldman's complexly learned essay on Ariana Reines's "RENDERED," from Reines's book *The Cow* (2006), presents our most radical immersion in modes of affect such as disgust, which in the past had been largely limited to satire but now seem inextricable from the struggles of lyric to find anything that can even approach conditions for singing. One aspect of Reines's strength, and of her difficulty, is her insistence that significant affect derives not from the personal psyche but from sheer impersonal description of what cannot be quite internalized because it is so alienating—such as the facts about how cows are treated, then metaphorized into forms of disgust with women, then become factors in how women abject themselves to accord with these descriptions.

Another strength, and another source of difficulty, is Reines's capacity to echo Stein's undoing of the material world while forcing Stein's exuberance to confront the figures of the slaughterhouse and, more generally, the abjected stance of feeling that the psyche's powers are undergoing severe malformation. The major difficulty that this essay poses for us, and for the growing amount of contemporary poetry anchored in such details, is the question of whether any "hope" at all can emerge from what Goldman calls the "sink poetics" of waste and "leakage" that this book makes present. For Goldman there is a source of "hope" in the straightforward vitality of the effort to characterize the enormity of this leakage, as if critical consciousness totally liberated by its capacity to tell the truth may generate some kind of productive excess encouraging possibilities of resistant action. But we wonder whether that mode of resolution is largely a process of learning to love one's disease simply because it alone can produce an active sense of identity.

Cary Nelson's essay on Atsuro Riley's twenty-six-section book-length narrative poem *Romey's Order* (2010) makes a superb counterpart to Goldman's.

The affective dilemmas embodied in Reines's and Riley's texts are very similar, but the means of elaborating them could not be more different. Whereas Reines locates affect largely in our expected responses to discursive practices that dominate social life, Riley is intensely concrete, offering a carefully indirect and unidealized bildungsroman of sorts that fleshes out conditions of impoverished rural life in South Carolina.

Riley's story is decidedly not an account of triumph over rural narrowness. Instead it seems as if the oppression deepens and generalizes as Romey ages and gains experience. Because Nelson tracks that aging process so carefully and concretely, he can show how Riley relies on shifting contexts that, as Romey ages, generalize his sense of impotence. But the efforts to generalize also call into question any sense that there are right judgments of what remains implicit and tantalizing. So even though the dramatic process is traditional, the interpretive process cultivates difficulty because it invites us to take pleasure in the momentary shifts of sensibility and significance without worrying about developing a true and unified interpretation. For Romey what matters most as an interpretive process is the music of the wordplay, as if this could help him gain a "sense of a protective retreat, a way of wrapping himself in that river bend home and keeping the world at bay." This may not be revolutionary, but it does give poetry the possibility of consolation, which seems only a vague hope in Reines's more abstract emotional landscape.

There is no consolation whatsoever in Myung Mi Kim's *Penury* (2009). Joseph Jonghyun Jeon shows that where any exuberance might arise in this book, Kim shuts it down because she is intensely concerned with the delusory effects of theatricalized feeling. Paranoia runs all through Kim's book. It is the one psychological state whose insights cannot bring satisfaction but instead intensify the need for intricate defenses. The prevalence of paranoia reminds us that many of the difficulties made familiar by Language poetry remain in Kim's more recent work. But these difficulties are not taken as conditions of language so much as defenses against the seductions of believing that poetry can defend itself against the multiple traps set by the culture's appeals for affective identifications. *Penury* does not seek unity on any level; rather it insists on a constant tension between "clues to what we might call meaning" and the strident frustration of any "interpretative enterprise." So the book turns to figures of war in which fear and anxiety become not so much refusals of healthy experience as necessary "forms of intelligence." This is what it means to feel always "targeted" by what might seem at first innocuous invitations to experience. Yet this tension becomes a dynamic affective field in its own right—setting "evocative and even heartbreaking" details of word, phrase, and image against an unrelenting opaqueness where we might expect generalization from those details. Difficulty is at once a source of frustration and a desperate relief from even greater violence. Yet in literalizing and dwelling in a diasporic position, Kim can at least establish a position "from which to witness more pernicious and global forms of encoding."

III. Addressing the Multiple

Some of our most interesting essays emphasize a range of cultural difficulties that stem from the need to negotiate boundary crossings in order to respond fully to the complexities of American social life. These difficulties involve three primary concerns: the authorial choices deciding the kinds of information and codings that can address multiple audiences; the invitations to audiences to see themselves choosing in ways that resist assumptions bred into culturally dominant classes; and capacity of the work's language not only to accept diversity but also to adapt it for lyrical purposes. These essays fall into two subcategories—those involving straightforward difficulties of negotiating racial differences and those investigating, and often celebrating, the linguistic diversity that poets manage to address in innovative ways.

Brian Reed's essay on Sherwin Bitsui's *Flood Song* (2009) offers what we see as an exemplary self-conscious inquiry into the degree to which a white critic can both acknowledge the cultural differences an indigenous poet depends on and find his way into what he must recognize will remain beyond his grasp. A reading of Bitsui inattentive to authorship is likely to produce a lyric version of standard devices that make the poem a typical version of indeterminate surrealist gestures made for a contemporary marketplace. Such a reading will inevitably fail to motivate the indeterminacies or test the degree to which they could make sense if one knew the appropriate context. More importantly, such a reading would fail to engage an author who might envision ownership of the poem as a crucial aspect of its meaning, and may define ownership as structuring the poem at least in part through terms of "culturally specific information." So Reed's essay tells a fascinating story of attempting to do the research that may narrow that information gap while learning to exercise restraint over the critical desire to "force intelligibility" where one has "no right to expect it."

This discovery process only deepens Reed's sense of his own limited capacity to cross cultural boundaries. But in the process he comes to appreciate why Bitsui and other poets might foreground difficulties to develop attitudes that simultaneously preserve the right to mean in accord with native values and try to engage audiences in why those values might be significant. The significance itself, however, must achieve difficult balances: the critics rendering the poem meaningful cannot allow it to be translated into the dominant culture without substantial loss, since such translation is likely to reinforce the universalist ambitions of readers oriented by Western academic traditions. Bitsui's ideal non-Indigenous readers would be those who recognize and accept the gap between cultures, in part because of what they can experience in the poem.

The very first sentence of Nadia Nurhussein's essay on Douglas Kearney's "The Miscarriage: A Minstrel Show" dramatizes a striking difficulty in negotiating diversity: "Why try to express the trauma of miscarriage through the comic-grotesque lens of blackface minstrelsy?" There can perhaps be no sharper threat to liberal consensus politics than to flaunt blackface as a means of staging a narrative of miscarriage. Who could remain at ease or keep a single attitude in encountering this kind of text? Yet Nurhussein shows how Kearney brilliantly builds on this discomfort, in part by treating this text as the basis for performance. As Nurhussein puts it, "Kearney writes *through* the minstrel show, and ironically intensifies the poem's pathos and intimacy as a result."

Kearney's "writing through" develops an intriguing balance among disgust, embarrassment, and the author's unembarrassed and aggressive delight in the wordplay that the medium makes possible. Yet white audiences probably cannot take ownership of these devices. So they also are likely to be made even more uneasy by the power of the medium to address miscarriage than they are by the miscarriage itself. The associated sufferings produced by the miscarriage must be regarded as transcultural if not universal. But the white audience is likely to find its discomfort with the medium blocking them from the medium's capacity to foreground the odd intimacies connected with anxieties about gender identity. So this audience is likely also to both recognize and envy the ways the performance allows some comic distance from the pain of actual loss. Surely such an audience will not be able to move from that recognition to use sentences like "I ain't see'ed no seeds by your fanny."

Jeanne Heuving's lucid account of Tisa Bryant's *Unexplained Presence* (2007) offers what might be considered a further development of coming to terms with all that blackface has come to signify. Heuving shows how Bryant asks us to re-see Africanist presences in film as well as visual and literary art in order to move beyond their interpellation in white scripts. Bryant, however, does not so much wish to critique white privilege or stereotypes as to assert and describe black presences. For Bryant, aesthetic illusions are one of the most potent modalities of the misrepresentation of black persons, but also one of the most powerful means of correcting them. Heuving's essay raises the question of what audiences can do with the recognitions Bryant's text forces upon them. And, more elementally, what does a face marked by its blackness, but not reducible to its racial identity, become as it emerges from a history always already inscribed racially and in racist ways?

The unsettling power of Bryant's poetics of "talking the seen" is sharply presented in Heuving's account of what Bryant does to, and does with, James Schlesinger's *Darling* (1965), starring Julie Christie, who is positioned as a paragon of white female beauty. Bryant, attentive to "doubling" throughout *Darling*, expends considerable energy on the scene when a black man produces "what amounts to a kind of whiteface of Diana." As the black man emerges from a crowd, we see how "Diana and her doppelgänger are dramatically and visually intertwined through their unusually pronounced cheekbones, thick lips, and toothy smiles. But while Julie Christie's teeth are perfect, the doppelgänger's crooked, prominent teeth, by comparison, are grotesque." Now we have two faces irreducibly different, and irreducibly determined by their worlds, in a haunting display of inescapable mirroring, in which the possibility of mutuality is sorely in question. The political gets subsumed into the ontology of what faces display when isolated from explanatory contexts. And the aesthetic ontology gets subsumed into a different level of politics where we have to wonder why and in what ways our seeing these faces in Bryant's text will enable us to renegotiate social orders.

Evie Shockley develops an intense close reading of the section "In/somnia" of Tonya Foster's book-length poem, *A Swarm of Bees in High Court* (2015). This reading demonstrates that any audience can engage the difficult language of that poem. But it also substantiates the claim that in fact nonblack audiences tend to miss much of the dynamic linguistic play in experimental black poetry. These audiences might mistake—as "noise" or "interference"—the modes of signification that gave bite and intricacy to that poetry: "Simple until proven difficult was the presumption that most frequently informed approaches to work by African American authors over the past century. Simply protest. Simply derivative. Simply vulgar. Simply black. Simply simple." Perhaps the most striking feature of this quotation is the utterly convincing simplicity of the claim that the charge of simplicity stems from ignorance of how certain kinds of difficulty might matter.

Shockley makes her case for Foster through a close reading of how her linguistic intricacy both captures the tensions that make for insomnia and suggests a power to control those tensions that may help explain how the entire domain of sleep and dream can become a significant resource for adapting what becomes apparent only when the light of reason begins to fade. The analysis of linguistic mobility "destabilizes the terms of racial essentialism while simultaneously destabilizing the presumption that no collective or productive concept of 'blackness' can exist without that ground."

So Shockley helps us see how the close reading of one experimental poet's creative refashioning of speech patterns opens into the possible reconsideration of the ways in which generations of poets deployed difficulty. And along the way she provides a highly effective response to the problem of how poetry can be intimate and still address "communal experiences in a collage aesthetics that calls its various potential readers to meet each other in the difficult, always-be(e)ing-made space of the commons." By imagining this poem as the voice of Harlem's "various incommensurate relationships between part and whole," Foster evokes an intimacy that is directly of and for a particular "aesthetic commons": while the idea and ideal of universality is typically a mere chimera, speaking simultaneously to, as, and for a community is a plausible possibility, especially when that community historically grounds its identity in part on playing the kinds of language games that find the unity in disjunction.

Shockley's essay could easily be placed in our second subdivision because of her attention to the specificities of black language and her sense that cultivating its differences from mainstream speech brings both a specific literary history and a specific social identity into new modes of audibility, and hence visibility. But we have reserved this section for the kinds of difficulty caused by, and elaborated within, poetry that insistently calls for multilingual modes of awareness. Such poetry may be considered inherently critical of any single linguistic frame because such a frame would produce aggressive defensiveness against the challenge posed by demands for flexibility and consciousness of social limitation. But for us the most interesting feature of this set of essays is their refusal to be content simply with critique. Their subject matter affords a concrete and compelling opportunity to display the positive forces diversity can afford.

Our first essay in this section is one of our more subtle ones. Roberto Tejada's analysis of "Voice Activation" by Rosa Alcalá does not so much celebrate diversity as provide a concrete analysis of the cultural dangers involved when we settle for any one language or the technologies that reinforce it. There is no way not to cite at least segments of the passage from Alcalá on which Tejada works:

> This poem, on the other hand, is activated by the sound of my voice, and, luckily, I am a native speaker. Luckily, I have no accent and you can understand perfectly what I am saying to you via this poem. I have been working on this limpid voice, from which you can read each word as if rounded in my mouth, as if my tongue were pushing into my teeth, my lips meeting and jaws flexing, so that even if from birth you've been taught to read faces before words and words as faces, you'll feel not at all confused with what I say on the page. But maybe you'll see my name and feel a twinge of confusion. Have no doubt, my poem is innocent and transparent.

Here the major source of difficulty is in specifying the kind of power that voice activation cannot acknowledge. This poem is driven by the sound of the speaker's voice—perhaps as an avant-garde conceptualist gesture. But it soon reveals itself as also a technological product that contradicts aspects of what we learn must be her actual voice. The poem we hear may have no accent because of technological remastering. Yet the person we hear has a distinctive Spanish accent, so we begin to doubt all of the recording's assertions. They are what technology demands, not what the person would say if she could speak without technology. And once we realize this, we also start to attend to the strange physicality of the passage, as if the repression of the actual voice made it present simply in its eagerness to break through what constrains it. As Tejada puts it, "An ostensibly stable surface gives the lie to a protean performance." And "the other language" perhaps begins to divide the world into languages "of the other." There emerges a linguistic struggle between efforts at silencing and the possibility of rebellion born of those efforts at repression.

Yet the poem has, in the customary sense, asserted nothing. And there are no modernist strategies manipulating diction or syntax or structure. Even the irony here does not create either distance or sympathy. It simply functions as an index that we have to read the poem otherwise and interpret that otherwise in relation to an "indeterminacy" that struggles to escape, at least indirectly, the power of technology and the even greater power of the majority culture to trust in a technology that ensures its hegemony will survive unchallenged. Yet challenge there is, because, once the veneer is fractured, every gesture has a manifest and latent content. Because the poem's mode of presentation as poem so thoroughly contradicts the poem's presentation in the form of voice activation, we have to begin to credit how multiple voicings might take place even under the scrutiny of technological authority. And then what seemed an initial difficulty in fully believing the voice we hear generates a potential to believe in the power of the voice we infer. Difficulty manages to challenge authority without ever saying anything that would present itself as self-congratulatory historical criticism.

Lyn Hejinian makes just the opposite kind of case for "Paolo's Lust," poem 25 in Paolo Javier's *60 lv bo(e)mbs* (2005), which stresses the exuberant sense of "noise" encouraged by multiple linguistic frameworks. Most modernist difficulty is associated with asceticism, in the spirit of Flaubert. Javier writes in the spirit of *Finnegans Wake*, with a vivacious defying of coherence that "while generating mischief keeps the reader's attention darting. And for the attention to find what it's looking for, it has to leap." But such leaping, we discover, is not quite Joycean. Javier's leaping is less to complex internal elements and underlying patterns of allusion than to a plethora of "referential details that direct the reader as much to things outside the poem as to things in it." That is, each of the languages speaking to and through each other in Javier's text does what language is supposed to do. Only they do so with an exuberance that makes it seem all the parts of language were participating in a kind of free flow of attention constantly adapting emotionally to shifts in focus.

Hejinian sees this functioning of language in Javier's text as the combination of two drives—"hypersignification" and "oversignification." The former foregrounds the "possibility to link to further . . . referential sites and systems." So it is a matter of how language is oriented directly to "multiple areas of significance." *Oversignification* refers instead to the properties of language itself as performed in the work. Oversignification allows Javier to break from the model of lyric as privacy overheard (on which Hejinian is very precise) to stress the multiplicity of the signifying activity in the poem as it engages the world: "Value is situated not in inner meanings but in the extroverted, manic outward cast of the poetry." It is not quality but quantity of signification that matters; the greater the number of references, the richer—and perhaps wilder—the relevance. The conjunction between these two forces produces a difficult but revealing model of how lyric can engage the political. *Hypersignification* is the space in which the anger and the woe get concentrated because of what the Philippines has suffered under imperialism. Oversignification becomes lyric's means of engaging what historical narrative insists upon. Javier calls this particular form of overdetermined connoting a process of "fishing" that continually opens up possibilities for transforming anger into the production of an "enormous sonic momentum," linking destruction to love and pain to the elaboration of how humans might "innovate each other as subjects."

This section concludes with Jennifer Scappettone's elaborate and lovingly detailed commentary on how concerns for difficulty change as modernist "cosmopolitan," multilingual concerns yield to the "subaltern" poetics of "polyglot poetry." This poetry is represented by LaTasha N. Nevada Diggs's *TwERK* (2013), a text that makes one think Antonio Gramsci could be reborn in Harlem and given a sense of rhythm. Where the cosmopolitan poet sends those engaged by the multiple languages to "annotations and, inevitably, institutions to accrue knowledge that might begin to make them adequate to the poetry," Diggs's version of subaltern poetics turns to what becomes a highly multivalent figure of "twerking," which, before it became subject to appropriation, was popularized in New Orleans's bounce music in the 1990s but likely draws from various dance forms long popular across Africa, from Côte d'Ivoire to Kenya. Poetry then rivals dance—in its "muscular alteration of measure" and its explorations of how measure can activate nondiscursive embodiments of meaningfulness that are also enticements to participation in an emerging communal space. This space brings blackness as background into conjunction with the forms of doubleness carried by active "code-switching."

Here we cannot go into Scappettone's very useful contextualizing of Diggs—through Gramsci's political model of the subaltern's resistance to hegemony and through Teresa Cha's foundational exploration of subaltern possibilities in developing intercultural ways of reading. Instead we will dwell for a moment on how Scappettone's essay emphasizes the concrete difficulties of twerking the language into a sense of "networking" "the languages and lingos of globalization, transnational capitalism, and information overload deliriously, but never without critiquing them." She points out how "metro-multilingopollonegrocucarachasblahblahblah," which initially seems homage to Eliot's *The Waste Land*, changes course by focusing on a cockroach whose physical ugliness is transformed into its elegant Spanish name, *la cucaracha*, which in turn restores the situation to song. And this move then warrants a half-playful return to the logic of Eliotic allusion in the figure of Pentecost and its celebration of the apostles learning to speak in tongues. But while this allusion requires learning, it immediately shifts to self-reference in the poem's own network of intricate tonguings. So the difficulty is less in tracking down the reference than in understanding how to preserve its openness to surface transformations so there can be the actual construction of possible communities bonded by the modes of participation Diggs elicits. The Harlem audience would not miss the reference to the Pentecostalist religion whose rituals are not far in intent and in action from the "ecstatic" working of this poem.

IV. Rhetorics of Information

The final mode of difficulty emphasized by some of our essays is that posed by the efforts of poets to address changes in information technology and, more generally, in ways of thinking that presuppose very different kinds of values from those shaping most of twentieth-century American poetry. Bob Perelman pays attention to information technology in order to establish an ethical dimension for focusing on the literal and seemingly innocuous process of computer transcription by the means of optical character recognition (OCR) software. Because his focus is poetry, the ethical lies mostly in the limitations and errors of the technology—whether noisily, as Javier would have it, or oracular, in that the failures of many procedure-based poems end up revealing larger truths. His focus is on how Rachel Zolf's *Janey's Arcadia* (2014), which documents the settler colonialism of Manitoba, dramatizes through OCR distortion the issue of recognition so as to enable a form of difficulty at the level of sheer legibility. The variety of interaction with prior texts in Zolf's project requires our distinguishing the fascination with error from satire, although the project lapses into satire when it merely demonstrates the comic fallibility and indifference of digitization. This fascination turns out to be highly political, though Zolf's use of distortion has no single stable political valence.

Our difficulties in reading Zolf's text hinge on recognition errors in the process of representing text, which turn reading into an opportunity to witness a process strikingly like settlers' inability to recognize the rights and personhood of indigenous people. Sometimes surface error signifies ethical certainty (something we instantly recognize is false), and sometimes what is instantly legible can present ethical or factual truth, such as the undistorted passages naming and mourning murdered indigenous women. As Zolf presents the colonialist violence, religious cant, and sexual predation of the settlers, there is no more ethical ambiguity than there is in Dante's presentation of the sinners in *The Inferno*. The difference is that Zolf uncouples systematic relations between surface and depth, what we see and how we take it, through the processes of recognition, unrecognition, and re-recognition. And the process of recognition in this case yields identification when Zolf describes herself as "settler Rachel Zolf." She is not using OCR from a vantage of ethical purity to diagnose a corrupt past; rather, she is of the OCR world, as are we reading this book that asks us to recognize our contemporary situation.

Lytle Shaw's subject, Lisa Robertson, develops a more capacious ethical framework for close attention to the negotiation of information. For

Robertson the very idea of negotiating information has to stress the entire circuit—producer, recipient, and the directedness oriented by the encounter. On this basis her collection of essays *Nilling* (2012) is probably the most important twenty-first-century document in poetics because it powerfully establishes a critique of identity thinking that skewers traditional ideals of expression as the communication of an inner coherence to a stable audience open to being shaped by what authorial genius can construct.[7] Shaw takes a distinctive stance toward Robertson's thinking because he is less interested in her critique of identity thinking per se than in the power of that critique to sponsor a version of historical inquiry that breaks sharply with the modes of critique shaping historicist work for the past three decades. In many of her poems, exemplified here by portions of *R's Boat* (2012), Robertson replaces the expressive project with an activity of research that can emphasize how both poet and audience become very nearly co-creators of the significance of various kinds of information. For example, research into the history of how popular uprisings emerged can show not only the limitations of the historical agents but conditions of possibility for reorienting the affinities the imagination might draw between past and present, as well as between surface and depth—not least because surface, when imaginatively treated, can provide its own texture of implication. Those possibilities depend not on ideas so much as on the life of the poetic line that engages an audience in concrete dialogue with the research project. And that life in turn can mobilize—once again—genres such as epic, based now not on constructed narrative but on conditions of engagement with large-scale concerns of the culture.

Geoffrey G. O'Brien offers a more concrete synthesis of this section's two basic concerns: how poets handle our situatedness within vast amounts of information and how the conceptualists develop models for mobilizing existing information in the service of loosening that information's constraints on our perception. The increase in information virtually requires poets to seek new ways to think about indeterminacy and decision making. For O'Brien, this situation also entails focusing on how thoroughly new experiments in form, or new forms bred of experiment in other disciplines, "capture a new, vast, and alien space of reading and viewing" while projecting a self-reflexive aspect of the present moment (in reading and in living) that "can resist easy consumption while imitating it." His essay on Kevin Davies's *Lateral Argument* (2002)—in the context of Davies's more comprehensive volume *The Golden Age of Paraphernalia* (2008)—tries to show how thoroughly "the provisional forms of vulnerable storage" can generate and interpret forms capable of taking on aspects of content vital to contemporary life. The primary need, and Davies's primary achievement, is to adapt forms that guarantee continuous and unstable movement for the mind. Form need not be static, and need not have as its primary role to establish unity, although in Davies's case the unity is actually constituted by the irreducibility of movement along particular self-modifying paths. To appreciate all this, we need simply to adapt a critical language sufficiently abstract to generate its own principles of content having nothing to do with ideals of organic unity that have mystified discussions of form for more than two centuries. Theory becomes not a matter of discerning truth so much as weighing comparative approaches to container theory.

"Bundling" is Davies's and O'Brien's basic concept for the work that form does—in Davies's poetry and in everyone's life now that we have entered the information age. We will not presume to summarize O'Brien's dense yet playful account of the intricacies of Davies's use of rules attuned to traditional formal measures by adapting them to the language of units of information. It must suffice to outline O'Brien's general argument. Container technology becomes basic to poetry when poets conceive their task as the evocative bundling of bits of information so that the work implicates more capacious senses of reality. Poems should be seen then as primarily modes of storing information that make certain actions possible or solicit particular modes of activation. Then poems need not be organized as statements or dramas but can become miniature structures that themselves occupy positions in the world because of the work of containment they perform and encourage. The effect of such attention is that "we don't know what we're in, we only know where we are." And the significant difficulties such positions pose are less about the emotions or ideological conditions than about our panic when these traditional modes of organizing critical discourse no longer seem necessary or effective. We would do well to adapt to seeing ourselves as bundlers, juggling various kinds of bundles and trying to limit our concerns to how the flow of information allows gatherings rather than how it might reflect foundations and truths and principles. Such formations have exposed themselves as highly abstract ways of bundling that are both prone to error and inclined to imposing stasis on the one primary fact of our lives—that they are always flowing and flown, and so both comic and tragic at once: "The poem is a telling argument about digital aimlessness, its first ode and parody, hard to read and easy to surf. The argument consists in the lateral passage backward and forward across these experiences in the place we must be." And the goal is the radiance established by our awareness of this motion as a kind of contained freedom.

Our final section centers on conceptual writing, which has, in the decade and a half since its rise along with digital humanities, afforded poetry's most intense and public engagements with the unexamined issues at the core of poetic production. Many of O'Brien's remarks on information culture could be invoked to frame our essays explicitly on conceptual poetry, indubitably the greatest source of uneasiness, and hence of a kind of difficulty, for many readers of contemporary poetry because of its antiexpressive embrace of what are often the less noble aspects of the information age. While some of conceptualism's practitioners—Kenneth Goldsmith most prominently—have indeed argued that an actual reading of a conceptual work is inessential to our intellectual engagement with it, the authors here demonstrate the value of seriously and attentively reading such work. By closely reading that which often claims to lie beneath the minimal level of interest needed to engage even a surface reading, our final group of critics manages to identify and to clarify a more humane strand in conceptual poetry that is less interested in "unoriginal genius" than in ways genius can adapt what seems an unpromising impersonal ground for endless irony.

Nicholas D. Nace elaborates a somewhat controversial, strictly formal concept of lyric to show how Vanessa Place's "First Stone" brings significant social force to the process of conceptual appropriation. Critics tend to challenge the propriety of Place's ways of taking over the texts of others. But Nace takes a different approach. He asks what emotional fields are activated by Place's putting appropriated texts in new and troubling contexts. Many of Kenneth Goldsmith's conceptual projects prior to 2015 use a self-consciously boring textual transcription as a kind of *lorem ipsum* that, when contained by a different form, enables an awareness of the intellectual and affective dimensions of our engagement with a textual incarnation that has little to do with its content. Place, however, works dangerously in the reverse direction, presenting—in what might seem at first a satirical gesture—inflammatory material in seemingly phlegmatic forms that can reveal, but not manage, the political dimensions of their new intelligibility.

In Place's "First Stone" we have what appears a lyric although it is composed of nothing more than jokes made at the expense of Muslims, all taken from a website called Sickipedia, where texts trade on their very capacity to offend.[8] Reframing such decidedly unowned cultural material as what appears to be a lyric involves very little labor for Place, though coming to terms with this fact simultaneously requires an acknowledgment that the ministrations of line break and stanzification are all that is needed to transform discrete jokes into what seems to present something capable of eliciting feelings associated with lyric experience. (Determining degrees of closeness and distance in relation to lyric is part of the pleasure of negotiating Place's texts.) Nace argues that the trace of lyric invites readers to see the form as inviting them to accept her poem as a bid for triumphing over intolerance through voice while enabling them simultaneously to reject the demotic nexus of intolerance out of which its words issue. But the more one looks at the jokes as such, the more they appear not to be inherently intolerant. The very adaptability of these jokes to the lyric form ultimately shows just how much context can affect our reading of the subtleties of tone and how the most basic conventions of poetic presentation automatically confer a politics grounded in the poet's self-image as an opposing force to intolerance. Yet this ease of contextual switching does not quite reconcile Nace to any idea of transfiguration. There remains a strange emotional turmoil because the tone of these jokes retains their offensive qualities. So in reading we almost have to recognize how difficult it is to find a tone that incorporates Muslims into American literary life and conventions without falling into the blindnesses of either smug multiculturalism or jocular reinforcements of unbelonging.

While likewise concerned with ethics, Dee Morris's essay is a more straightforward and generalized account of the challenges much conceptual poetry poses to readers whose model of experiment in poetry comes from the major modernists. Her topic is Divya Victor's *Hellocasts* (2011), a copying of sections of Charles Reznikoff's documentary passages from his 1975 multivolume *Holocaust*, put into Hello Kitty™ formats. Her focus is on how contemporary conceptual poetry poses severe problems for readers who take their understanding of experiment in poetry from the great modernists who prepared intricate texts to read into. A good portion of conceptual poetry presents texts copied from public records that we are intended to read as products of the world that produced or tolerated the immense "gap" between deeds and the documents establishing responses and justifications for these deeds. There is no significant author function involving self-expression or original genius. There is only quotation, where even what authorial purpose there might be is displaced into what fascination the documents might produce. And because there is no art object to treasure, these conceptual pieces can be transformed into other art venues such as performances.

Morris summarizes three major differences between conceptual poetry and high modernist work. Conceptual poetry tends to position the text as "a catching and casting of the stocks, flows, and vectors of information" rather than imagining expressive functions or attempts to disclose specific insights; it tends to see itself as part of an ongoing cultural conversation involving social attitudes; and as part of that conversation the work aims to have its documentation become a provocation not to participation but to putting the audience into a troubling "state of obligation." Focusing on Robert Fitterman's and Victor's engagements with the Holocaust, Morris shows how there is inescapable ethical force to what we are asked to read, even if, or perhaps because, we cannot quite figure out how to discharge that obligation.

Finally, we close with two delightful essays staging the possible significance for poetry of engaging the rhetorics of information technology and finding its own space within those rhetorics. Jennifer Ashton threatens to give conceptual poetry a good name by her superb reading of "One-Line Poem" from Guy Bennett's *Self-Evident Poems* (2011). Here we can reproduce the poem in its entirety: "This is it." Ashton is interested first in the difficulty in these hermeneutical times of having readers not dismiss such obviousness but elaborate the possible reasons why a poet might think obviousness itself can play an important role in aesthetic and social matters. After all, it has been a basic dream of almost all serious artists since at least 1900 that artworks be self-evident in the sense that they be proof of the literal states of presence possible for the kinds of engagement they have with the actual world. "This is it" is a perfect realization of what Michael Fried has called "art as objecthood."

But there are many varieties of self-evidence: some are banal, present as detritus, and some are engaging, present for their mode of vitality. The further difficulty Ashton faces is in showing readers that Bennett's poem is of the second kind. She addresses this by a playful yet careful analysis of the resources of grammar that Bennett summons in this poem. *This* is a marvelous grammatical operator because in English it is the primary way we both point to particulars and announce what occupies the mind, as the bridge between the actual and our judgments. We point by *this*. But we cannot help pointing both to the poem on the page and to the reading of it that occurs in mental space. What verb is more elemental than the copulative, and more capable of producing a bridge between the pointing and what satisfies it as a stable object? Yet that stable object is the intricately indefinite pronoun *it*, which also does triple duty in referring to the existence of the self-evident object, to the poetry that this self-evident object has become, and to the place the object occupies in the mind. This reading then allows Ashton to make important historical claims for this demonstration of self-evidence in poetry because Bennett's achievement contrasts sharply with the emphases in Language poetry and most conceptual poetry on the responder's position rather than on the object.

We have left Marjorie Perloff's essay to conclude the collection, in part because it makes a forceful case for a kind of conceptual poetry whose difficulties reside in learning to adapt lyric to our new modes of gathering information and in part because we just love how she shows that relying on technology is by no means incompatible with rich and expansive human feeling. Her subject is a new book-length poem by Craig Dworkin entitled *The Pine-Woods Notebook* (2018). Perloff calls this poem a "conceptual lyric" because it addresses Ponge's *Le carnet du bois de pins* (1947) in such a way as to revise "our expectations of what 'nature poetry' is and can be in the twenty-first century." Just look at what she shows Dworkin accomplishing in his opening line: "The pitch of the pines on the ridgeline thickens, bewitching." There is evocative description. But this is not the core of the poem's power. Rather that power resides in the many ways that its manifest qualities justify the judgment that this pitch is "bewitching." Think of "the intricacy of internal rhyme (*pitch*/*bewitch*; *pine*/*line*), the alliteration of hard stops (*p*; *k*) and fricatives (*tch*), the assonance of short *i*'s, as well as the tight metrical form (from iamb and anapest to trochee)." And think of how this sonic filling out of the space of the pines is complemented by intense verbal play—not dramatically evoked but provoking exciting affects by its sense of what an online dictionary can provide.

The difficulties created here are not difficulties of recognizing underlying forces, negotiating complicated syntax, attuning to knotted subjective states, or decoding allusiveness. Rather than problems with vertical relations, we have problems becoming aware of the horizontal reach of what Dworkin's language implies and the various sites it leads us to, much like how oversignification functions in Javier's poetry. But Dworkin is much more subtle and more lush. Notice, for example, how it is not the pines that generate the bewitchment but their "pitch." How can *pitch* not attract its sonic analogue *bewitch* when all its definitions conjoin so intricately with all the definitions of *pine*? *Pitch* is noun and verb, and as noun it evokes color, texture, and musical tonality. *Pine* is even more dramatically noun *and* verb, as George Herbert long ago demonstrated in "The Collar," a poem that, like many others, is evoked as a kind of byproduct of Dworkin's procedure. As a noun *pine* enlists for the poem both an image and a state of pain and punishment. And as verb it expresses one kind of feeling solicited by the thickening and darkening of the ridgeline. So there is intense affect here. But that affect does not derive from the subjectivity of an expressive author. Feeling derives from sheer pleasure in construction and in discovering analogues made available by power for recall possessed by computers: "Words drive feelings and not the other way round." We have to become listeners and readers in order to see, and we have to see that dreams of synaesthesia may not have died with aestheticism. Dworkin's book, in other words, presents "lyric meditation for the information age," not rejecting but renewing our faith in what language can establish as a domain of attention and affective satisfaction.

As the poets and critics collected here demonstrate, the new tendencies toward difficulty do not originate from precisely the same places as the difficulties of previous generations. Not only is poetry differently and newly self-conscious and skeptical—even of itself—but it responds to new pressures that attenuate most varieties of consensus. The poets discussed here are seldom part of any distinct poetic movement, and the difficulty of their poems proves less a form of cultural capital—as difficulty often was for those in the twentieth century who wished to defy easy accessibility—and more a manifestation of individuality. The poets set their own terms over the course of elaborate projects, most of which take the form of books that establish rules to be followed by constituent poems or parts of poems. These poets have lost faith in the plausibility of traditional ideals of address to a universal audience, evolving in the process ways to respond to increasingly conflicting aspects of social life. They are energized by anxieties about the very possibility of authority, which stems from an uncertainty about how much the constructs of gender and class produce blindness. And they develop forms that must be adapted to the constant flow of information that overwhelms not only the quiet and repeated acts of contemplation that once were taken for granted but also the very notion of legibility itself. Yet for all their tendency to critique, to instruct us about the struggles of contemporary life, these poets also delight, as many of our essays make clear.

In addressing these aspects of difficulty as they emerge through individual poems, the critics here also demonstrate what it is like to write about poetry under cultural circumstances that make any form of reflective life seem at best a private escape from the challenges posed by addressing issues of diversity and economic justice. We believe that this entire book makes the case that by inventively facing an immense range of pressing difficulties, poets continue to show what essential tasks imaginative language can perform in the various social settings the poems invoke.

Notes

1. The most recent example of this tendency is reflected in *Reading the Difficulties: Dialogues with Contemporary American Innovative Poetry*, ed. Thomas Fink and Judith Halden-Sullivan (Tuscaloosa: University of Alabama Press, 2013), which offers substantial argumentative essays, though it focuses mostly on well-established poets who are now frequently discussed as exemplars of their particular movements, such as John Ashbery, Bruce Andrews, Ron Silliman, and Lyn Hejinian.

2. These ideas are most fully developed in M. H. Abrams, *The Mirror and the Lamp: Romantic Theory and the Critical Tradition* (Oxford: Oxford University Press, 1953).

3. For a lively examination of the bitter defensiveness associated with the impossibility of mastery in poetic making, see Ben Lerner, *The Hatred of Poetry* (New York: FSG, 2016).

4. Charles Bernstein offers a comically sincere elaboration of this position of need in his essay "The Difficult Poem," in *Attack of the Difficult Poems* (Chicago: University of Chicago Press, 2011), 3–6.

5. Before turning to Abrams, we were tempted to organize our essay in terms of the four kinds of difficulty defined by George Steiner's essay on difficulty in literature, in *On Difficulty and Other Essays* (Oxford: Oxford University Press, 1978), 18–47. This essay deploys wide and keen learning to distinguish contingent, modal, tactical, and ontological difficulties. The first involves difficulties that can be resolved by research; the second notes difficulties in determining the authorial attitude informing specific choices; the third worries over how writers work out solutions to tensions between the conventionality of language and the demand of insight driving the text; and finally there is the difficulty of determining the nature of person and world in the kinds of hermetic resistance posed by work like the later poems of Paul Celan. We are comforted by the fact that Steiner is even more insistent than we were in the supposition that all writing in essence occupies the same imaginary stage, without the need to specify audiences and ideals of witness for one community in relation to specific other ones.

6. T. S. Eliot, *Collected Poems, 1909–1962* (New York: Harcourt Brace Jovanovich, 1963), 3.

7. Lisa Robertson, *Nilling: Prose Essays on Noise, Pornography, the Codex, Melancholy, Lucretius, Folds, Cities and Related Aporias* (Toronto: Bookthug, 2012).

8. This is probably the place to express our exasperation over the difficulty of establishing any clear meaning of the term *lyric*. There has been excellent recent scholarship on the term, yet the meaning of *lyric* remains difficult to fix. Virginia Jackson, in *Dickinson's Misery: A Theory of Lyric Reading* (Princeton, N.J.:

Princeton University Press, 2005), tells us this is because *lyric* is essentially a historically driven context with no clear foundational meaning, while Jonathan Culler makes a powerful case that the lyric over time consistently returns to the idea and ideal of address to an imagined "you" in the eternal present posited by language intensely aware of its own creative force. See Culler, *Theory of the Lyric* (Cambridge, Mass.: Harvard University Press, 2015). We think that even if there are recurrent traits, there is no way to impose a fixed meaning on a term that can easily be taken to mean only a short construct in lines that do not run to the left margin. Vanessa Place plays on this vagueness by composing what is both lyric and not lyric as one aspect of her interest in the problems created by the instability of our acts of naming.

Part One

✦

Continuities

SRIKANTH REDDY

from *Voyager*

The world is the world.

To deny it is to break with reason.

Nevertheless it would be reasonable to question the affair.

The speaker studies the world to determine the extent of his troubles.

He studies the night overhead.

He says therefore.

He says venerable art.

To believe in the world, a person has to quiet thinking.

The dead do not cease in the grave.

The world is water falling on a stone.

Chapter 1

Voice and Erasure in Srikanth Reddy's *Voyager*

Langdon Hammer

This haunting series of assertions appears on the first page of Srikanth Reddy's long poem *Voyager* (2011).¹ The haunting effect has to do partly with the way each claim stands on a line of its own, emerging from and then echoing in the space that surrounds it. It also has to do with the fact that Reddy's poetry really *is* haunted: every word of *Voyager* has been taken from Kurt Waldheim's memoir of his career as Secretary General of the United Nations, *In the Eye of the Storm* (1985). "The dead do not cease in their grave" indeed.

To be clear: what Reddy is doing is not what modernist poets like Pound or Moore or Eliot do when they sample sources. Their borrowings most often involve a complete syntactic unit, a phrase or a sentence or more; the quoted speech is marked as such; and it's set inside the language of the poem quoting it, with the result that the distinction between the two texts, the one quoted from and the one doing the quoting, is more or less preserved. Here Reddy takes apart his source text bit by bit, at times isolating lexical units as small as a preposition or an article, to build new statements altogether—and *all* of his words come from Waldheim. The voice is therefore a weird composite, the triangulated expression of two authors that belongs to neither one precisely.

In this way *Voyager* presents a novel and I think distinctly contemporary instance of poetic difficulty. These opening lines require a reader to ask that basic discussion-starting question posed by the New Criticism: Who is speaking? But it is not a question that can be settled: even here, although far more troublesome passages await us in the poem, it could be asked of every sentence. And behind it, I'll suggest, are a number of other, rather odd questions: What is it like to be the speaker of a poem, or at least the speaker of a poem such as this? How does it feel when the central feeling expressed is an absence or (better) a dislocation of feeling? And along with these come questions about other sorts of coherence: How does one sentence (or how does one word or phrase) follow from another? What is the operative logic in a given sequence? What do Reddy's lines add up to? Later I will work through answers to these questions by looking carefully at the lines quoted above. But the results will be of primarily local use because *Voyager* resists stable resolution as we move from one page to the next.

The difficulty of deciding who is speaking in *Voyager* is further compounded by the fact that each of its three main sections, or "books," explores a distinct genre and formal plan. How the whole poem fits together is another difficulty, then, and a major one. *Voyager* is not a poem with a beginning, middle, and end, but a poem that begins and ends three times. Each iteration amounts to a particular event, a new reading, if you like, of *In the Eye of the Storm*. Which means that we must approach the poem as simultaneously an act of writing and an act of reading.

The poem's technique, usually called "erasure," is described quite explicitly in Book 2. "I began to cross out words from his book on world peace" (23), Reddy writes, referring to Waldheim and *In the Eye of the Storm*. Then he says again: "I had to cross out his world anew. This history is the effect of that curious process" (25). The process of "crossing out" Waldheim's book is represented graphically elsewhere in *Voyager* when Reddy includes a bit of crossed-out text. In the poem's epilogues (there are three, one for each book and the erasure that created it), crossing out takes over: here Reddy prints the epilogue to Waldheim's memoir three times, striking through line after line of text, leaving only a few scattered words for readers to assemble in new sentences. A number of paratextual references call attention to the technique: Reddy mentions his erasure of Waldheim's text in his acknowledgments; a blurb from Marjorie Perloff calls attention to Waldheim and the erasure technique on the back cover. Moreover, the method can be studied on a website to which the acknowledgments direct us, where Reddy has posted examples of his writing process.[2]

I'll say more about the method and its implications shortly. What is Reddy doing when he applies it to *In the Eye of the Storm*? With its notorious falsification of Waldheim's service as a Nazi SS officer who was in a position to be aware of, if not more directly involved in, war crimes committed by the German military in Greece and Yugoslavia, the memoir is not a promising starting place. There can be little point in arraigning Waldheim and exposing his self-representations as lies: that's been done, and by scholars and journalists better equipped to do it than a poet.[3] But Waldheim's culpability is not the essential issue in *Voyager*. Rather, in Reddy's poem Waldheim comes to stand for a general failure of humanistic ideals and democratic leadership, stretching beyond National Socialism and the Second World War to the democratic regimes that dominate the world today.

Or, because Reddy's engagement is specifically with Waldheim's language, it would be more accurate to say: Waldheim comes to stand for a failed way of speaking. Using Waldheim's words, as he does everywhere in *Voyager*, Reddy sums up the case with irony and sympathy too: "This man, legend states, likely knew of the mass execution of groups of people as a capable officer required to collect and analyze data, prepare reports, conduct investigations, and otherwise facilitate operational projects in the last world war. At the time, however, he did not express concern at this action. To a degree this is understandable. His voice failed" (21).

That failure of voice is complex. It involves two stages of denial and two silences, the second repeating while also covering up the first, as, over the decades, Waldheim first failed to speak against the "mass execution of groups of people" going on around him and then failed to speak of that wartime failure of protest. Moreover, Waldheim's failure was never a matter of saying nothing. Both silences were disguised by the fluent speech of a bureaucrat: "a capable officer" collecting and analyzing data, and then an international statesman recalling his actions on the world stage. Those roles and the discourses proper to them, no matter how distant from each other in style and function, are joined in the moral history of one man's voice.

Engaging with that history, Reddy tries to get inside Waldheim's voice, to anatomize, appropriate, and reformat it, and ultimately to rescue something from its ruins. Reddy seems interested specifically in the irony that this man whose voice conspicuously "failed" during the Second World War should have become a general "spokesman for humanity" in the postwar era. The role is epitomized by the message from Waldheim carried aboard the Voyager interstellar space probes launched by NASA in 1977. Speaking as the Secretary General of the United Nations, Waldheim offers "greetings on behalf of the people of our planet": "We step out of our solar system into the universe seeking only peace and friendship, to teach if we are called upon, to be taught if we are fortunate. We know full well that our planet and all its inhabitants are but a small part of this immense universe that surrounds us and it is with humility and hope that we take this step."[4]

The human collective unmarked by difference that Waldheim speaks for in this laughably vacuous message is as much a fantasy as the alien being he addresses. But Reddy takes his poem's title from the Voyager mission, and to that extent, he takes it very seriously. (Perhaps the poem is a machine bearing its record of life on earth into uncharted space?) Nor is Reddy ridiculing Waldheim when he describes him as "a man who by some quirk of fate had become a spokesman for humanity, who could give voice to all the nations and peoples of the world, and so to speak, the conscience of mankind." Waldheim's role as a spokesman for "all nations and peoples" descends from an Enlightenment ideal that is as much poetic as political. It is memorably articulated by Wordsworth: "In spite of difference of soil and climate, of language and manners, of laws and customs: in spite of things silently gone out of mind, and things violently destroyed; the Poet binds together by passion and knowledge the vast empire of human society, as it is spread over the whole earth, and over all time."[5]

There is no mention of Wordsworth in *Voyager*. But I think Reddy's poem asks by implication whether a vision of poetry such as this can be recovered and refashioned for our time—in spite of the global history of political oppression, torture, and genocide, "in spite of things gone silently out of mind, and things violently destroyed," which is the repressed subtext of Waldheim's memoir. Reddy grasps *In the Eye of the Storm* as a grotesquely failed poem from which he will attempt to create a new and truer one. Humanity, he seems to say, goes on needing people who will try to speak for it.

Reddy's ambivalent attitude toward Waldheim as spokesman has a parallel in the complex effects of his erasure technique, although the point of that technique appears simple enough on the face of it. The idea of a representative speaker implies in poetry a first-person lyric voice valued for originality and authenticity, invention and sincerity. (Again Wordsworth is a model.) The constraint Reddy works with throughout *Voyager*—his choice to use only Waldheim's words and maintain the order in which they appear in the memoir—flies in the face of that idea: here is a long poem made entirely of someone else's language.

Erasure literalizes, and so brings inescapably to mind, the truism that books are made out of other books. Precedents include the "treated" books of Marcel Bloodthaers, who blacked out the words of Mallarmé's *Un coup de dés* (1969), highlighting the poem's spatial arrangement, and Tom Phillips, whose work in progress, *A Humument* (begun in 1966), is made out of an obscure nineteenth-century novel. Ronald Johnson's visionary redaction of *Paradise Lost*, *Radi os* (1976, reprinted in 2005), and Jen Bervins's *NETS* (2004), based on Shakespeare's *Sonnets*, are other examples. Once an eccentric strategy, erasure has become a familiar practice, as inviting to intellectual younger poets as the sestina was thirty years ago. Along with other types of found text, it is a period-defining technique for an era when the conventions of lyric autobiography have been challenged by the antiexpressive, citational, procedural writing endorsed in Marjorie Perloff's *Unoriginal Genius: Poetry by Other Means in the New Century* (2010).

In particular, *Voyager* shares a good deal with the "uncreative writing" on exhibit in Craig Dworkin and Kenneth Goldsmith's *Against Expression: An Anthology of Conceptual Writing* (2011). But in Reddy, as opposed to conceptual writers like Dworkin and Goldsmith, the rejection of a Romantic, expressive poetics is not at all complete or programmatic. He is curious, rather, as to how erasure, this technique so associated with today's critique of poetic voice and its allied values, once it is put to work on a manifestly "failed" voice, might generate a voice (or voices) with new expressive properties. So although Reddy himself uses it "for lack of a better word," the term *erasure* hardly captures what he is doing.[6] It implies silencing a voice rather than appropriating and reanimating it, and it calls to mind negation and aggression rather than collaboration. (Reddy has said he feels "profoundly indebted to Waldheim as a literary collaborator")[7]

To be sure, negation and aggression are part of the approach. This is emphatically so when Reddy draws a line through Waldheim's words in his

9

Human Rights and Wrongs

One of the most regrettable consequences of the schism between the developing countries and those of the industrialized Western democracies was the deep divide that opened up in the interpretation of what constituted human rights. This is particularly to be lamented because the United Nations will go down in history as the first international organization to concern itself in a sustained and serious way with the rights of all human beings.

In its preamble the UN Charter reaffirmed 'faith in fundamental human rights, in the dignity and worth of the human person, in the equal rights of men and women and of nations large and small'. That principle was codified in the Universal Declaration of Human Rights of 1948. This was no more than the first step in a lengthy journey. The UN can accept a reasonable share of the credit for imprinting this concept of human rights on the consciousness of mankind. It is the principal agency for focusing world attention on the gravest violations of such rights, but even now it has only just begun to grapple with the problem of applying its proclaimed standards when they are most flagrantly disregarded.

It would be unreasonable to expect more in a world still dominated by sovereign nation states. The Charter established forty years ago persists to the present day. On the one hand members pledge themselves 'to take joint and separate action in co-operation with the Organization to promote universal respect for and observance of human rights and fundamental freedoms for all without distinction as to race, sex, language or religion'. On the other, the organization is not authorized 'to intervene in matters which are essentially within the domestic jurisdiction of any state ...' This provision is too often used to override any specific human rights obligation a state may have accepted. When the organization seeks to induce members to observe universal standards, it moves into a delicate and often inflammatory area of activity.

134

HUMAN RIGHTS AND WRONGS

Implementation, inevitably, will continue to lag far behind good intentions. Since the United Nations is not a world government, it could hardly be otherwise. The organization has nevertheless succeeded in encouraging member states to accept voluntarily binding legal obligations to apply accepted standards of human rights within their territories. The general provisions of the Universal Declaration were elaborated in 1966 in legally binding 'covenants', one on civil and political rights and a second on economic, social and cultural rights. It had taken eighteen years to reach even this stage. The covenants were to come into effect when ratified by thirty-five states and it took another ten years before, with my encouragement, the necessary number of ratifications was secured in 1976. The number has continued to grow but as I write I have to note to my great regret that less than half the total membership has adhered to the covenants. There have been some curious anomalies. The Soviet bloc states have found it possible to ratify, but the United States, normally in the forefront where human rights are concerned, has not so far adopted either of them.

The covenants were carefully drafted to allow considerable flexibility in their application and reflected the situation at the time they were drawn up in the sixties, at the climax of the de-colonization process and the creation of so many new independent states. The first article of each covenant proclaimed, in identical terms, the rights of all peoples to self-determination and the free disposal of their natural wealth and resources. The language was significant and lies at the root of the present differences of interpretation. It reflected the desire of the emerging states to emphasize their sovereignty and challenged the Western democratic view that a sound human rights structure must of necessity be based on the inherent civil and political rights of the individual. The Third World countries assert that such rights, preserved in isolation, merely sanction and perpetuate privilege and exploitation. Of what use is the right to vote, they ask, if a person is starving or the right to free expression if he is illiterate? Millions of people in Africa and Asia die of hunger and starvation and are deprived of education and economic progress. Their problem is survival, and they are less exercised by violations of individual human rights whether it be in totalitarian or authoritarian regimes. It is this appearance of double standards that exasperates and alienates the West.

The inter-relationship between economic and social rights on the one hand and civil and political rights on the other finds continuing expression in every UN declaration and resolution over the years. The Third World majority has consistently emphasized the former at the expense of the latter. Their priority has been the promotion of collective rights: opposition to racial discrimination, anti-colonialism, full sovereignty over

135

[Handwritten annotation:] And this history is the effect of that curious process.

Figure 1.1. Worksheet from stage 1 in Reddy's erasure process. Note that Reddy ignores the chapter break in Waldheim's memoir as a unit of organization for his poem.

three epilogues. Those nine canceled pages highlight the defacement of text that underlies Reddy's process throughout the poem. Yet there's more to that process. On his *Voyager* website, Reddy divides the work of composition into three steps and gives samples of each. First, he marked up the text of *In the Eye of the Storm*, circling and underlining words and phrases (fig. 1.1). (He worked not on a bound copy of the book but on photocopies: it was always the text, rather than the physical object, that he was concerned with. This focus distinguishes his project from, among other practices, book art.) Then, in the process of selecting words, he "deleted language from the book, like a government censor blacking out words in a letter from an internal dissident," as he puts it on the website (fig. 1.2). This is the moment of "erasure" proper. Finally, he closed the space between selected words to create new syntactic and reconfiguration structures, introduced punctuation, and made choices of format and prosody, integrating what he had preserved of the memoir in a text of his own making. So the process included acts of cancellation, preservation, and reconfiguration.[8]

Figure 1.2. Worksheet from stage 2. The sentence "This history is the effect of that curious process" follows "I had to cross out his world anew" in *Voyager*, Book Two (25).

On the one hand, this is a highly constrained, rule-driven means of writing poetry, binding the poet's choice of words to a specific external lexicon. On the other hand, the freedom Reddy permits himself is notable. After all, the lexicon he draws on is a 268-page book. And while he confines himself to Waldheim's words and the order in which he finds them, he crosses out as many pages as he likes before selecting the next word or phrase; he changes the grammatical function of words and phrases when he wishes; and he freely creates his own rhythms and images, inventing personages, place names, and a great deal more. The poem is not an attempt to write poetry "for" Waldheim as if it were some kind of dramatic monologue; there is never an issue of verisimilitude. From this perspective, Reddy's method looks less like a refusal of "originality" than a peculiarly elaborate means of achieving it.

Guiding each erasure, as I've said, were decisions about the genre and prosody Reddy would employ. In Book 1, he daringly eliminates the grammatical basis of Waldheim's memoir—the first-person pronoun—to create a different sort of text entirely, made up of sequences of impersonal prose statements, ten to a page. The question seems to be, can Waldheim's text, despite itself, be made to yield a philosophy, an impersonal discourse of truth we can apply to the ongoing violence of our world? Reddy's model is the propositional structure of a text like Wittgenstein's *Tractatus*, to the famous first sentence of which ("The world is everything that is the case") the start of *Voyager* alludes: "The world is the world." Wittgenstein's reasoning, however, is parodied more than emulated in the statements that follow, which involve a critique of the official rationality embedded in Waldheim's prose and perhaps a critique of rationality as such, viewed as the will to order the world intellectually. Let's look back now at those opening lines to examine that critique and the interpretive difficulties it entails: Who is speaking? How does one claim follow from another?

The initial tautology does not at first seem like the start of any train of thought. It expresses a simple, seemingly irrefutable realism, a rationality based on common sense: the world is the world we all know, *QED*. But the poem immediately throws that idea into question. Though presented as another statement of fact, the second sentence's abrupt defense of the first makes it feel like a warning: if we deny that the world is the world and claim that it is "a" world, implying that other worlds, or at least other accounts of this one, are possible, we will violate the rules of legitimate thought and be judged out of bounds, beyond reason. The second sentence now makes the first appear less simple and assured and more like an attempt to forestall objections that we didn't know had been raised but are already present by implication, motivating the poem to start with. What counts as "reason" seems brittle and easily disturbed: an official picture of the real, held in place by rhetorical force.

As if to acknowledge that weakness, the third sentence allows that our definition of what is "reasonable" must be stretched far enough "to question the affair." That's a significant adjustment: rather than reason in the abstract, Reddy has introduced the pragmatic category of the reasonable, a matter of social consensus more than logic or principle. There is a modulation in diction too audible in the puffed-up assertiveness of "nevertheless," the hedging, stilted elegance of the conditional ("it would be"), the vagueness and euphemism of "to question the affair." The last word resonates because the controversy precipitated by *In the Eye of the Storm* is known as "the Waldheim affair." Here, as so often in *Voyager*, Reddy precisely catches the tone of official muddle and obfuscation. This is highly self-conscious speech, attempting to manage the impression it makes through carefully counterbalanced weights and measures, the cumulative effect of which is to say nothing concrete, nothing particular, and in that respect, nothing at all.

It's tempting to identify the speaker "who studies the world to determine the extent of his troubles" as Waldheim himself, emerging as a character in the poem. But "the speaker" is pointedly unspecific. He is a *rückenfigur* whom we encounter as an outline without face or identity, engaged in meditation on the world, possibly of the sort the poem itself is engaged in, as if Reddy had taken a step back to show us the person speaking the poem's opening lines. That term—*the speaker*—neatly holds together political and poetic models of representation: we use it to indicate the leader of a democratic assembly and the voice in a poem. Both operate by means of convention and formal arrangement; and both are suspect as frayed, if not failed, ideals, masking particular biases and interests behind the claim to representativeness. To reassert his authority in the face of these "troubles," the speaker appeals to logic ("therefore") and the traditions of high culture ("venerable art"). But the repetition of "he says" makes his discourse seem like a matter of rote, without specific content or point. That the speaker is male is important and not a surprise.

Having moved over the space of a few lines from propositional reasoning to description of a man thinking, Reddy suddenly reverts to a proposition: "To believe in the world"—to be able to say, "The world is the world" with simple confidence—"one has to quiet thinking." "Reason," as we suspected, turns out to require the suppression of thinking. But why does thinking threaten our belief in the world? Reddy answers the implied question by mentioning the dead who "do not cease in the grave." To think is to enter into the silences in the historical record and there, as in a burial ground, to encounter the "disappeared" and "silent," all the people murdered in the wars that have shaped the map of nations, our picture of the world as it is.[9] "The dead do not cease" because, precisely in their silence, they clamor for expression and recognition.

Their restless condition is refigured when this series of statements ends by revising the first. The world is not the world; it is "water falling on a stone." Instead of tautology, we have a metaphor. It implies that the world is not a noun but a participle, not a static fact but an ongoing event. A collision of opposites, unstoppable and ungraspable, it is not to be accounted for by rational propositions moving in series toward a conclusion, in the form of a proof. To represent it truly, a text would have to be more like an explosion, or a fire.

The page of poetry I've just been describing is like a debate within a mind, or between two minds, or perhaps within a discourse attached to no mind in particular that is pushed forward, forced this way and that, by the pressure of facts that threaten its claim to reason and mastery, as Reddy deconstructs the rationality of Waldheim's writing to see what thoughts it represses and what other ways of thinking it might make available. That deconstruction works by disassembling sentences and assembling new ones from the scattered parts. Its halting, probing rhythms are a record of Reddy's experience as a reader of Waldheim's memoir, and they reproduce a version of that experience for his reader.

Erasure, Reddy has commented, "became like a form of reading, or detection. Which made me feel . . . that writing is itself a form of reading" ("The Weight of What's Left [Out]"). To examine his compositional process on his website is indeed to observe someone reading—or perhaps learning to read?

That is, as he marks up his source text, pointing up parts of speech, attending less obviously to "content" than to grammar and syntax, circling or underlining words and phrases to return to, Reddy behaves like the student of a foreign language, diagramming a text to absorb what he can for practical use.

The interesting turn is that the foreign language Reddy uses the memoir to learn is English. Importantly, *In the Eye of the Storm* is an English-language work, not a translation of Waldheim's native German.[10] Only that's not precise enough: what Reddy is trying to "learn" is no one's native tongue. Only acquired through long training and acculturation, it is the contemporary language of power, of bureaucracy and business, the idiom of expert rationality familiar to us from press conferences, policy statements, media interviews, and the like. This is a variety of English as exchangeable and placeless as the architecture of corporate offices and airport hotels; it aspires to the prestige and authority of universal reference that any merely national language by definition lacks.

The special contemporaneity of Reddy's poem and much of the difficulty it involves reflect his engagement, through Waldheim's memoir, with a specific postwar phenomenon: the rise of English as the default public discourse of global elites. What are the qualities of that discourse? Franco Moretti and Dominique Pestre have tracked the evolution of one variant—which, echoing Orwell's *1984*, they call "Bankspeak"—by undertaking a quantitative linguistic analysis of the World Bank's annual reports since 1950.[11] What they describe is suggestive though scarcely surprising: from the 1970s onward, the language of the World Bank's reports has grown increasingly abstract. This development is reflected in, among other features, the proliferation of nominalizations—nouns, usually Latinate ones, made out of verbs. Absorbing and obscuring the actions they refer to, the nominalizatons in these reports tend to blur reference to concrete political and economic realities, and make human subjects disappear. Along with this abstraction comes an indeterminacy of time and place that Moretti and Pestre demonstrate also on the levels of grammar and rhetoric.

Their research seeks to get inside the linguistic operations of the "management discourse" that dominates the world economy (in which the noun *management* is among the most frequently used) to call attention to its construction and analyze its repressed logic, in more or less the same way that Orwell, insisting on the concrete effects of state policy and war, approaches political and military propaganda in "Politics and the English Language." With pen and ink rather than computers and graphs, Reddy does something similar to *In the Eye of the Storm*. But the World Bank's annual report is not the same thing as a statesman's memoir. As opposed to Moretti and Pestre, Reddy is concerned with a literary question: How does a bureaucratic discourse affect the one who inhabits it? Is it possible, and if so, what is it like, to experience the world subjectively in language that turns human subjects into abstractions and makes them disappear?

These questions emerge forcefully in Book 2 of *Voyager*. In Book 1, Reddy's daring move was to remove Waldheim's first person. In Book 2, daring now in an entirely different way, Reddy restores Waldheim's "I" and uses it to speak about his own experience, according to the conventions of autobiography. In blocks of prose, one to the page, Book 2 offers lyric introspection of a type found in a private journal or memoir. The nature of the world—and of world-making—is in question again, but this time the point of view is highly personal. For instance: "As a child, spelling out *world* was to open a world in myself, private and byzantine, with mountains by a pale, fragile sea, the coast stretching southwards in the curtained evening hours" (23). Or again: "In my office a globe was set up, less a world than a history of imperialism and corruption. I used to search that poor political patchwork in the period leading up to my tenure" (25). Reddy's use of *In the Eye of the Storm* to describe (or seem to describe) the inner world of his childhood or his daily life "in the period leading up to my tenure" is a remarkable feat. But it's not a naturalistic illusion he is going for. Rather, his prose is calculatedly impersonal (the use of the passive voice in "was to open" or "was set up"), not at all colloquial ("private and byzantine," "pale, fragile sea," "the curtained evening hours"), and subtly fragmentary in grammar (the intransitive use of *search*). These effects keep reminding us that Reddy's sentences are made out of quotation and echo with the odd formality of their source.

They also underline a certain stitched-together quality in Waldheim's writing that is easy to overlook, given its smooth contours and appearance of rational control. Yet, on inspection, Waldheim's not-quite-idiomatic idioms give his style the feeling of an acquired language, meticulously spoken. The foreword to *In the Eye of the Storm* begins this way:

> This is not a book of memoirs in the ordinary sense, nor is it a comprehensive account of events during my term of office as Secretary General of the United Nations. Had I embarked upon either task, it would have taken me far beyond the confines of this present endeavor.
>
> Instead I have attempted to offer some insight into my background, actions, and aspirations. Without dwelling upon the routine and frustrations that are also the hallmarks of any arduous career, I have described those events and episodes which I feel bear some significance for the course of history. (*In the Eye of the Storm*, vii)

There is perfect confidence in this writing; nothing ruffles its surface. Yet phrases like "had I embarked upon either task," "far beyond the confines of this present endeavor," or "the hallmarks of any arduous career" feel as though they have been cut out of a thesaurus and taped in, one after another. Put that diction together with the studied casualness of "offer some insight into" and the self-regarding modesty of "bear some significance for the course of history," noting the strategic vagueness of both phrases,[12] as well as the fact that the author's feelings, if not missing, are prim and disciplined, and you have a good sense of Waldheim's prose style throughout *In the Eye of the Storm*.

Probably the style interests Reddy because Waldheim's voice, unlike Milton's or Shakespeare's (the canonical poetic sources for Ronald Johnson's and Jen Bervins's erasures), is a mode of official expression, not simply prosaic or subliterary but generic. The sound of a person comes through, but it is the sound of a person struggling to make himself present—and to conceal himself too, a person struggling to sound statesmanlike *and* intimate, trying to project personality in a formal idiom that is a little too weighty, a little inexact, and in those ways not fully controlled, despite the effort to control it. The style is the product of a patient, incomplete effort to construct a plausible speaker. Reddy makes the point concisely in Book 1: "He wrote formally in private" (13). Or better still: "Kurt Waldheim is a formal negotiation" (15).

By adapting this style to describe his own experience, Reddy experiments with a provocative overlay of perspectives. Already in Book 1 the ambiguous identity of "the speaker" had been a way to play with this idea. "He had a professorship at the university and had been out of contact with his personality as a result" (8), Reddy writes, and his readers who are university professors can laugh—at the idea that being a professor puts one in danger of losing touch with one's personality and at Reddy's impersonal phrasing of the idea. It doesn't matter whom *he* refers to precisely: Waldheim, Reddy, or no one in particular. For no one in the generic, representative role of a "speaker" is quite himself. Even a professor-poet like Reddy, despite the content of his work and the freedoms he enjoys, occupies a position on a continuum with other bureaucratic roles, all of which entail some objectification, some submission to an institutional identity and official function, separating a person and his personality. That condition is expressed in Reddy's style, derived from Waldheim's.

The glimpses that Reddy gives of his life in the university include reflections on the obsessive activity of erasing Waldheim's memoir: "To cross line after line out of his work seemed to me a slow and difficult process that verged on the ridiculous" (23). He wrote *Voyager* over a six-year period (2003–09) during which the United States invaded Iraq and Afghanistan. In Book 2 Reddy comments on those wars and the protests they stirred: "As I write these lines, people with pictures of people killed in action run through New York's traffic-choked streets, rising to the spirit of the occasion, while I, sitting in my second-floor office connected to various communication cables, maintain control over some very unruly emotional forces" (30). In contrast to the demonstrators who are "rising to the spirit of the occasion" (a strange phrase in this context), Reddy tries to control his emotions (or no: "some very unruly emotional forces" is more controlled and impersonal than that). He remains tethered to his "second-floor office" by the "various communication cables" that are supposed to connect him to the world outside. He is not so unlike a young "capable officer" busy collecting and analyzing data while "the mass execution of groups of people" goes on elsewhere.

Dryly, with implications for himself as much as Waldheim, Reddy notes: "It was difficult to see how to stop the activities of the government" (25). The passive construction ("it was difficult") and Latinate euphemism ("the activities of the government") with which Reddy sums up his situation belong to a neutral, professorial mode of speaking that comes with his office and communication equipment. That idiom uncomfortably reproduces features of the official discourse of the government itself. In its flatness and impersonality and its careful imprecision, Reddy's autobiographical writing merges with a general discourse of power that, perhaps especially when fluently spoken by persons in authority (that is, by designated "speakers"), involves an observable, deliberate caution, a testing of words, meant to manage and defuse potentially explosive or flammable contents, conveying self-possession while also suggesting the difficulty of achieving it (and therefore pointing to the opposite).

As an act of reading, Reddy's erasure explores that process of searching for words, probing Waldheim's style for its feints and fissures, even as it writes another version of them, entailing its own careful searching. The activity sets Reddy against Waldheim and forces on him a partial identification with Waldheim too. This passage is the climax of Book 2:

> To cross scenes out of a text would not be to reject the whole text. Rather, to cross out a figure such as ~~to~~ *carry out* ~~programmes they approve~~ *the* ~~various regional economic commissions and inter-governmental~~ *bodies* sometimes increases the implications. I had hoped to voice my unhappiness in the world thus. More and more, it seems to me the role of the Secretary General in this book is that of an *alter ego*. In a nightmare, Under Secretaries General, Assistant Secretaries General, and other officials of rank reported directly to me. I was given an office and a globe. But I wondered why the forest just beyond the window seemed so cold when it was, to be sure, rapidly burning. (31)

"Carry out the bodies": the phrase (sentence fragment or imperative?) first appeared in Book 1 (10). Here Reddy shows us the erasure process by which he created it. The words he crosses out could have come from any World Bank annual report analyzed by Moretti and Pestre. The concrete is recovered, as Orwell would wish, when Reddy excavates "the bodies"—the dead—from the ponderous bureaucratic jargon that obscured their fate. Or perhaps "carry out the bodies" is an encoded order instructing who can read it not to recover and speak for the dead, as Reddy tries to, but to get them off the scene and hide them better. Either way the point holds. Murder is embedded in the muddling, boring rhetoric of bureaucratic authority.

In voicing his "unhappiness in the world" by erasing Waldheim's voice, Reddy has drawn closer to him, rather than the opposite. The "role of the Secretary General in this book," in *Voyager*, seems to be "that of an *alter ego*." Which is not surprising: that is what a poetic speaker is supposed to be. The twist is that Waldheim serves in this way because his "I" is an alter ego, an effigy, from Waldheim's own point of view. Reddy can identify with Waldheim as he speaks of himself in his memoir not because he sincerely articulates deep sentiments we all share but because his alienation from himself in discourse, his mendacity and obscurity, which we feel in the stilted, slightly unnatural quality of his prose, models the power of professional identity and bureaucratic function to modify anyone's speech and thinking—which Reddy feels as a professor who has been "given an office and a globe." The mediated condition of his perspective makes for a paradoxical knowledge: the window of the professor's office shows him the world and bars him from it. The trees out there are as numerous and indistinct as "groups of people": a forest of data, waiting to be analyzed. Although it "seems so cold" to him, he knows very well that the wood is on fire.

That image disturbingly captures the sensation of cognitive dissonance—call it the feeling of not-feeling—when there is a disjunction between what we know to be the case and what we can fully admit into consciousness, which is to say, what we can both state and feel. The effect involves a curious lyricism whereby self-expression is routed elaborately through a text that voices the muted, inaccessible feelings of another man. Reddy voices a very personal "unhappiness in the world" by erasing—but in the process, absorbing and reanimating—someone else's voice, which is itself the product of "a formal negotiation," a kind of writing involving a painstaking process of analysis and selection we might just as well call "reading." In this way Reddy revisits and redefines Waldheim's role as spokesman: the "I" of *In the Eye of the Storm* turns out to be transferable to Reddy and to that extent representative, as the speaker of a lyric poem is supposed to be. But again it is not the unity of a self and its expression but the distance between them in his case that makes Waldheim available as an alter ego for Reddy.

Books 1 and 2 of *Voyager* are a preface to Book 3, which is more than twice the length (eighty pages) of the other two combined. Book 3 presents a Dantesque dream vision in which the first-person narrator descends into the past, is brought before a distinctly bureaucratic council in "an abandoned fortress" (39), and compelled to tell his life story. The narrator of Book 3 is addressed as "Waldheim" (45). But surely Reddy, having successfully contrived to make Waldheim speak for him in Book 2, is now speaking for

Waldheim. What precisely would that mean? In the strange discursive space constituted by the poem, Reddy is making Waldheim face, and making himself feel what it would be like for Waldheim to face, everything his account of the world repressed. There is perhaps nothing so extraordinary about this: Reddy is putting words to what Waldheim was silent about, as others have done in their engagements with the Waldheim affair. But the trick is that these are Waldheim's words; and, by using them, what Waldheim could not admit to knowing and feeling, Reddy and his reader can.

Notes

1. Srikanth Reddy, *Voyager* (Berkeley: University of California Press, 2011), 3. Further page references to *Voyager* appear in parentheses in the text.
2. The website link given in *Voyager*, tiny.cc/voyagermethod, is no longer live. However, Reddy's process still can be seen under Voyager at www.srikanthreddy poet.com/books.
3. For an introduction to the controversy, see the newspaper and magazine obituaries following Waldheim's death in 2007. *The Waldheim Report* was produced for the Austrian state by the International Commission of Historians (Copenhagen: Museum Tusculanum, University of Copenhagen) in 1993.
4. See "The Golden Record" page on the Voyager website, http://voyager.jpl. nasa.gov/spacecraft/goldenrec.html.
5. William Wordsworth, "Preface to Lyrical Ballads," in *Complete Poetical Works*, ed. Henry Reed (Philadelphia: Porter & Coates, 1851), 666.
6. Reddy, "Note on the Process" (www.srikanthreddypoet.com/books).
7. Reddy quoted in Andrew King, "The Weight of What's Left [Out]: Six Contemporary Erasurists on Their Craft," http://www.kenyonreview.org/2012/11/erasure-collaborative-interview/.
8. The three dimensions of *aufheben* in the Hegelian dialectic. Reddy doesn't make anything of that connection. But he is likely to be familiar with Hegel's radical descendant, Walter Benjamin, and Benjamin's "Theses on the Philosophy of History," where the concept is invoked to describe the work of the materialist historiographer who "blasts open" the official historical record (Walter Benjamin, *Illuminations: Essays and Reflections*, trans. Harry Zohn [New York: Schocken, 1968], 262–63).
9. The cover of *Voyager* is a detail from an altered book by Brian Dettmer called *Prevent Horizon* (2008): a road atlas of the United States that has been cut up in irregular patterns and hollowed out, converting the flat surfaces of the map into a series of planes, creating shadows and depth, bringing disparate places into disorienting configurations, and seeming to move ever inward, rather than outward, where the horizon usually points.
10. *In the Eye of the Storm: The Memoirs of Kurt Waldheim* was published by Weidenfeld and Nicolson (London) in 1985. *Im Glaspalast Der Weltpolitik* (In the Glass Palace of World Politics), the German version, appeared the same year

from Econ (Düsseldorf/Vienna) in a translation from the English by Johannes Eidlitz and Gunther Martin.

11. Franco Moretti and Dominique Pestre, "Bankspeak: The Language of World Bank Reports," *New Left Review* 92 (March–April 2015).

12. On the ways Waldheim confusingly represents the generic status of his memoirs in the English version of the foreword, see Jacqueline Vansant, "Political Memoirs and Negative Rhetoric: Kurt Waldheim's *In the Eye of the Storm* and *Im Glaspalast Der Weltpolitik*," *Biography* 25, no. 2 (2002): 343–62.

LAYNIE BROWNE

6/14 Donne Sonnet

I am a liturgy worsted made cupidity
Of elixir, and angelica spumone

I am a minute orb made subtly
Of rudiments, and innocent goblin

I am a little live oak made cupbearer
Of Elizabethan and angstrom sprawl

Chapter 2

✦

Rewriting the Sonnet's Cunning:
On Laynie Browne's *Daily Sonnets*

Al Filreis

Worsted is a noun, finely woven wool. But encountering it in the first line of this seemingly difficult poem by Laynie Browne, one might read or hear the word as an adjective (modifying *liturgy*) or, somehow, a verb (the opposite of *bested* or *to best*).[1] Can the speaker herself be—or at least be *like*—a religious formulary? If the "I" of "I am" is meant to refer to the maker of these odd lines, can some of our immediate trouble with this nonsense poem be resolved by understanding her as a writer whose practice is so closely woven and so finely wrought that in itself it discloses a certain amorousness or even rapacity? Still, the first line of the poem does yield little in the way of conventional semantic sense.

Facing difficult reading at the level of a line, the readerly eye typically pulls back. If word-by-word reading fails, what can be seen? An uncomplicated view of all three brief stanzas: a reader readily beholds the visual and also the grammatical parallel frameworking in and around the triad of couplets:

	I am	an	A	B	made	C
e.g.	I am	a	liturgy	worsted	made	cupidity

	Of	X,	and	Y	Z
e.g.	Of	elixir,	and	angelica	spumone

There is some sort of formulary here after all. Perhaps these lines evince a cunning harmless magic, made by the rudimentary "innocent goblin" revealed in line 4.

Browne's "6/14 Donne Sonnet" (2007) retains the "rudiments" of the fourteen-line sonnet, not its fundamentals or first principles so much as its underdeveloped or unactualized parts. The poem offers 42.8 percent of the traditional form. Is it incomplete? Whatever John Donne as Laynie Browne's predecessor had once greatly achieved, Browne in re-encountering such achievement has left more than half of the effort (as it were) undone. And since, moreover, she works just Donne's first two lines, rewriting them thrice to make three couplets, it could be said that the poem is actually *two-fourteenths* of Donne's original cunningly prosodic feat. Does a "fractional sonnet" (Browne's term of art[2]) claim implicitly—in implicitly carrying the literary-historical weight in the very fact of the towering sonnet form—that it cannot or need not equal? Beyond incompleteness, might *fractional* also suggest the connotation of *fractious*—partisan, unruly, refractory?

Browne's least unruly first line ("I am a minute orb made subtly" of the second stanza) derives apparently without difficulty from John Donne's "I am a little world made cunningly." This is the opening of one of the most famous of Donne's nineteen "holy sonnets"—an Italian or Petrarchan sonnet written sometime between 1609 and 1611 and published in the second edition of Donne's *Poems* (1635). Here are this sonnet's almost regular fourteen lines:

> I am a little world made cunningly
> Of Elements, and an Angelike spright,
> But black sinne hath betraid to endlesse night
> My worlds both parts, and (oh) both parts must die.
> You which beyond that heaven which was most high
> Have found new sphears, and of new lands can write,
> Powre new seas in mine eyes, that so I might
> Drowne my world with my weeping earnestly,
> Or wash it, if it must be drown'd no more:
> But oh it must be burnt; alas the first
> Of lust and envie have burnt it heretofore,
> And made it fouler; Let their flames retire,
> And burn me O Lord, with a fiery zeale
> Of thee and thy house, which doth in eating heale.[3]

The holy verse, addressed to God, identifies the beseeching penitent writer as formed of equal parts basic and pure. As God's creation, the poet is exactly as cleverly made as the poem, *his* creation, a world in itself thus indicative of miracles far beyond its self-making—an alignment, initially at least, that befits Renaissance microcosmology. The poet handles this convergence of ingredients well until his capacity for sin begins to reveal the compositional fracture of divinely contrived selfhood. God has an imagination far greater than seems indicated by the division. It far outreaches the poet's fancy, despite his canny attempts at expressing faith. God, superpoetic, is said to "write" new lands and sea, such that the world of the poem, telling the tale of such creative capacity, will pale by comparison even as it proceeds toward its own cunning perfections. So in the crisis of faith enabled by the difference between thematic fracture and formal completion, the poet-penitent drowns and then burns in the narrative. Poet, it turns out, is elemental more than angelic. His lines must bear a talent for beholding earth, water, and apocalyptic cleansing fire. The poem as an expressive thing survives a test of faith, despite the lingering unrhymed *retire*, as it reaches the sweet concord of its last couplet: *zeale/heale*. Yet the final prospect of healing, after a great agonistic split between content (poet as sinner fails again) and form (poet as poet manages deftly), only seems warranted if one stipulates the first analogy between creation and creativity.

For a number of reasons we will now explore, Laynie Browne cannot get past that first stipulation. Because Donne's presumption seems to require a concept of balance and of intelligent design (simply pondering, which requires great time and patience) and a tone of confidence (about what a poet means when she or he begins with the portentous theological or confessional "I am"), she must keep working through the problem—by amending through variation, investigating through replacement. In the first round:

Little → *liturgy*
world → *worsted*
cunningly → *cupidity*
elements → *elixir*
angelic → *angelica*
sprite → *spumone*

Browne's method is apparently some sort of nonintentional alphabeticism, what might be called lexical rhyming. *Worsted* is not far down alphabetically from *world*, so using one against the other is a kind of harmony. And yet they are, as it were, semantic worlds apart. Or are they? Is the world constituted of rough material deftly woven? Proximity could allege a strange or radical synonymity. Browne has indicated that she sought to gamify the poetic act of choosing words, using a dictionary to make "N+7" substitutions (more about this later). Donne's words, chosen by design to indicate integral and then misaligned humanity and holiness, are altered in Browne's composition to the realm of quotidian vocabularistic hodgepodge. Her terms—or, rather, the terms she selects—produce counterintuitively an effect more *ordinary* than Donne's, even if some word choices represent upgrades (*elements* → *elixir* is a theme-denying replacement; *little* → *liturgy* nonintentionally undermines Donne's faux diminution).

A momentous, overarching substitution is to be found in the title of the whole conceptual project Browne was undertaking at the time she wrote "6/14 Donne Sonnet" as an unfinished exercise. The project, and the book published from it, given the title *Daily Sonnets*, descends too from Donne's *Holy Sonnets*. There is an additional epoch-defining substitution: *Holy* → *Daily*. So how to mark the move from holy to daily? Is daily truly less holy? Notwithstanding the poem's final atomic-scaled "angstrom sprawl," it is true that "6/14 Donne Sonnet" tells of no drowning sinners, nor presents calls for self-immolation in orthodox prosody. Browne's uncreativity spares her nonsonnet from such theological drama and irony. Yet among the daily sonnets are magical Hebraic amulets, set there unironically to protect the others from all transgressions ("poetry from *The New Yorker*" and, for the children who frequently appear in the poems, "Spiders on the potty").[4] While this strain of Jewish mysticism is not obviously present in "6/14 Donne Sonnet," it operates in its kabbalistic abecedarianism and in its very refutation of things cunningly made: "This sonnet is sent without cunning," Browne writes in "Protector #2: Your Personal Amulet," "to cull a particular phrase from your lips."[5] Experimental dailiness, distinct from metrical canonical holiness, discloses a perhaps even greater disjunction than (and a spiritual crisis just as wrenching as) that felt by Donne's skillful sinful speaker. With "the bumpiness of days passing," Brown observes—as every day she composes compromised, incomplete pieces instead of the extraordinary, cunning masterpiece—"time is unhinged."[6]

Of *Daily Sonnets* overall Browne has written that such poems are "a collaborative experiment in time."[7] Some were collaboratively composed with her two then-small children. (The book is dedicated "to Benjamin and Jacob, my daily sonneteers, investors of the 'real time sonnet' and 'dailiness.'")[8] Some sonnets in the series are collaborations with "the daily news" and some with other poets: aside from Donne, there are Bernadette Mayer, Norman Fischer, Lisa Jarnot, Rainer Maria Rilke, Lee Ann Brown, Aristotle, Ted Berrigan, Elizabeth Robinson, Jordan Davis, and Leo Tolstoy. Opposites otherwise in their attitudes toward the sonnet as a form, Mayer and Donne are vital guiding spirits for Browne's project, for they both in particular conceive of the sonnet as not just marking time but making it. Aligned with Browne in her rediscovery of poetic form as a harried parent, and generally as a mentor, Mayer similarly "think[s] of the modern sonnet as an increment of time within a frame,"[9] having invented a radical poetic secularity for exploring possibilities of a supreme fiction. But Donne, premodern and of course intensely devout, perfected the holy sonnet as a form of momentary holiness "in which," as A. J. Smith in *Metaphysical Wit* has put it, "every moment may confront us with the final annulment of time."[10] One of the putative difficulties of understanding, not to mention appreciating, Browne's "6/14 Donne Sonnet" is the disjuncture between the Christian, piously upright, male calculatedness of the original, and the beleaguered, Jewish, feminist extemporizing of the appropriation. If Browne deploys metaphysical wit at all, it is in the *concept* on behalf of which the poem is an instance or exponent. Yet Browne seeks a twenty-first-century version of the famed John Donne experience of temporal annulment. "This is a wake up and discover another year disappearing tactic," she writes.[11] "As a parent of two small children I invent time in order to work. Thus the one-minute sonnet." Like a sonnet composed in sixty seconds, or one made as a rough or free translation without subsequent revision, or from words a child cannily utters at the moment of writing, "6/14 Donne Sonnet" investigates the daily influx of poetic moments. Whereas the holy sonnet aims to make the extraordinary ordinary—intense religious experience discerned as a person's experience—the daily sonnet through experimentation seeks to make the ordinary extraordinary. The writer of a stanza form always first and foremost cited for its conventional number of lines did not compose a work falling an entire octave short to achieve canonical greatness—neither greatness of spirit, nor that of poesy. Rather, "6/14 Donne Sonnet" signals the writing and reading of sonnets as essentially a quotidian habit or practice, endemic in the time-stamping of daily routine and in the fractioning of calendar, measures of effort, and other fictive arrangements. Charles Alexander has noted that a person, like the day, "is a divided concept, within time, finding time, inventing time."[12]

Time is also the existential iteration, the attempt. *Try again one more time*. Three times in the case of our poem.

> I am . . .
> I am . . .
> I am. . . .

No conjunction, *and* or *but*, is given to indicate that a second or third time succeeds where the previous failed. Browne on the contrary insists on the so-called false start. It is implicated in life's physical (and hardly just conceptual) difficulties, for the poem does not achieve even half of its official aim when "someone else literally [is] pulling you out of your chair. Writing in your sleep, or falling face first (exhaustion) into the keyboard while writing."[13] Barely overcoming exhaustion, "6/14 Donne Sonnet" asks not that readers excuse the bone-weary parent for her aesthetic inadequacy, but rather that we not defer art's exploration of the unknown until the moment when leisure, comfort, solitude, physical wholeness, and freedom from mundane human responsibility render its beauty in accordance with standards once set by those who never operate without such conditions—and that we consider what writing the keyboard might produce at moments when life's difficulties transform the poet's falling face into authorial hand or keyboarding fingers. To be sure, as Browne explicitly reported to this author, when asked about John Donne: "I love his vast range from wit, to erotic, to pious."[14] "6/14 Donne Sonnet" is not a reformation or repudiation but an offering of fresh means of reading the holy sonnet as, in the words of Donne scholar William Zunder, "represent[ing] a turning to God as a resolution of *life's difficulties*."[15] *Daily Sonnets* makes a liturgy of ordinary complaint—as if the winner of television's sexist *Queen for a Day* refused gifts of new automobile, exotic vacation, and double-sized freezer, and chose to exploit the cultural mode of daily lament as that which properly inherits the sovereign art. In a reversal of secularization, Donne's *little* in Browne's hands—or her tired falling face—becomes *liturgy*, resisting all diminution while affirming cunning. The unknown is not God but the making of a poem, improvised time.

Improvisation—not of words, as in the case of "6/14 Donne Sonnet," but of
method—derives from the writer's sense of the writing body and from a will-
ingness to experiment. "No one knows exactly what they are setting out to
do because poetry is a living transmission whose evolution is linked to other
bodies in time," as Browne has written in an essay titled "On the Elasticity
of the Sonnet and the Usefulness of Collective Experimentation." And: "I
approach all writing as the unknown. I am constantly returning to the ques-
tion: can I do something I haven't done?"[16]

Browne has thematized difficulty. In "6/14 Donne Sonnet" she attempts
to draw out Donne's original sense of "life's difficulties" to emphasize that
by this late point in literary history we no longer easily discern them, owing
to the overpowering canonicity of his sonnet as sonnet. What is needed is
"elasticity" in the conception of what gets to count as sonnet. Following
Mayer, Browne certainly sympathizes with the modernist jeremiad against
the sonnet as an imperial poetic force inhibiting freedom and newness. Fol-
lowing William Carlos Williams's detestation ("Forcing twentieth-century
America into a sonnet—gosh, how I hate sonnets—is like putting a crab
into a square box"),[17] Bernadette Mayer often similarly excoriates the son-
net. "How serious notorious and public a form," she wrote in a prefatory
statement for her collected *Sonnets*, disclaiming the tradition that seeks
"the solution to a problem or an ending to an observation in one brief
moment."[18] In 2014 Mayer responded to a novice's question about whether
she should begin writing traditional forms before trying to experiment, by
saying, simply, "No." Yet almost immediately after issuing the strong nega-
tive, and after further comic, sardonic remarks on the obstructionism of the
sonnet tradition, Mayer performed one of her own daily sonnets, "You jerk
you didn't call me up."[19] Closely following Mayer's desire to teach appren-
tice poets the pleasures of experimentation as an integral part of her poetic
practice, Browne's "On the Elasticity of the Sonnet" was written to empower
writers who feel enjoined by lack of time. She offers two recommendations:
first, realize that like poetry, "life is already a time-based experiment"; and
second, that although the model of a single great canonical sonnet, such
as "I am a little world made cunningly," seems inimitable, write a series or
sequence of poems. The experimental sequence will emphasize the notion
that a poem is only an iteration or étude. "While you begin to write son-
nets," Brown advises, "I invite you to think about writing series of sonnets.
One reason I like to think in series and sequences is that it tends to pull us
out of the problem of preciousness."[20] Notwithstanding the contorted accu-
sation of cruelty in his crab conceit ("You've got to cut his legs off to make
him fit"), Williams's main concern for the avant-garde writer was that he or
she avoid preciousness, thus avoiding both insularity and cleverness in one
strategy. Donne's "little world made cunningly" was after all that of a witty
coterie.

"6/14 Donne Sonnet" is an instance in which Browne sought to evacuate cunning and to empty metaphysics of conscious wit. It might have been written directly in response to one of her own twenty-nine recommended "Sonnet Experiments"—these having been modeled closely on Mayer's much-sampled list of experiments.[21] "Try writing a sonnet in an unlikely circumstance," Browne urges in one suggestion of her own. "Try writing upon waking or before sleep" is another. "Write a mock historical sonnet." "Write a fractional sonnet, for instance, one-half sonnet, 6/14th sonnet, one-and-one-half sonnet, etc. Experiment with the number of lines written, implied, missing, added. How does this change the form and the intent of form?" "Use a chance operation to rewrite or create a new version of a sonnet by yourself or anyone else."[22]

Readers of "6/14 Donne Sonnet," far from necessarily being excluded by the semantic confusion, might be liberated from conventional line-by-line discernment of story or narrative sense to an awareness of varied methods. The first couplet, as we have noted, replaces key terms with alphabetically proximate words—the result of some sort of chance operation using a dictionary. (Browne has confirmed this: "the chance operations I used are variations on N+7 dictionary games.")[23] The second couplet,

> I am a minute orb made subtly
> Of rudiments, and innocent goblin

replaces *little* with *minute*, *world* with *orb*, *cunningly* with *subtly*, and so on. Mere uncreative synonymizing, it would seem. And yet as a kind of bland paraphrase this "experiment" underscores and perhaps satirizes the way in which Donne's puzzle-like conceits made him the superstar exemplar during the heyday of the New Criticism, when the method of close reading eschewed mere paraphrase and deemed it interpretive "heresy." The substitutions deliberately relinquish rhyme and meter while only retaining sense, precisely defying the traditional formalist's definition of poetry as writing that says what it says mainly by way of how it is said. The *being* of a great poem inhered in tone derived from diction, the density of word choice, etcetera, while a poem that merely *means* will likely lack such complexity. And yet how complex is the second couplet! Browne, following Mayer and others, believed that writing can and in some sense *must* always be a form of translation, produced by substitutive operations even when it is not the result of specific aleatory process.[24] The second couplet of "6/14 Donne Sonnet" concedes and actually affirms critical heresy, ignoring the valorization of creativity and at the same time standing as a kind of English-to-English translation.[25] We are led to ask, as "Sonnet Experiments" advises, how does "I am a *minute orb* made *subtly*" "change the form and the intent of form"?

So readers of the first and second couplets, able to compare against the Donne original, can come at least roughly to recognize which operation of chance is operative. But the third couplet defies easy discernment.

> I am a little live oak made cupbearer
> Of Elizabethan and angstrom sprawl.

There is actually not much about the first couplets that is random. Determined by a choice of operation, they are not arbitrarily constructed even as the sense of the lines seems indiscriminate. But our fractional sonnet ends suddenly with little of its operation apparent. However does one go from *world* to *live oak*? Perhaps Browne applied what we might call an "N+0" process to the word *little* (translating it as itself) and then employed some variation of "N+7" on *little* a second time to produce *live oak* in an accidental substitution for *world*. *Elizabethan* would follow in any dictionary from *elements*, of course, but that supposedly disjunct replacement makes perhaps too much historical and cosmological sense, such that it encourages us to miss or mourn the loss of Donne's *world*. Does "6/14 Donne Sonnet" conclude with an instance of *The Elizabethan World Picture* gone awry, its strictly divine hierarchical and constrained chain of being providing a life balance that even the holy sonnet, a recipe of confusions of element and angel—uncannily of *elixir* and *angstrom*—cannot itself achieve? There is great cosmological sense to Browne's poem, to its aleatory chain of being, from methodogical coherence to chaotic "sprawl," as it moves from alphabetical substitution to paraphrasal heresy to the breakdown of even the nonintentional rule.

Reading Laynie Browne's harried, hasty knock-off returns us to John Donne's original with a keener sense of the model's irregularities and a greater awareness of cupidity underlying pious cunning. For one thing, as a Petrarchan instance of the tradition, "I am a little world made cunningly" invokes the association of the sonnet with cupidity. While God's order is strictly maintained, it is a literary history that has been upset. While his love poems in *Songs and Sonets* happen to include not a single formal sonnet, his devotional poems, of which Browne's choice of model is the classic instance, embrace the Italian form conjuring traditions of earthly love. Browne's goal in choosing Donne is to advocate the stanza form as itself capable of carrying meaning forward, leaving thematics and semantics entirely aside. The interconnectedness of secular and sacred experience is honored and emphasized in *Daily Sonnets*, not satirized. By aligning Donne as a collaborator with the likes of Bernadette Mayer and Ted Berrigan and Lee Ann Brown, she moves his work toward a community of artists for whom the traditional poem cannot contain life's "real difficulties"—for whom running out of time and space to write *becomes* the time and space of the poem. It presents an incommensurate convergence, yet when one considers the fractional value of Browne's never getting past the significance of Donne's initial complaint, it becomes easier, not more difficult, to see the unusual structure of the model. For in truth the urgency of Donne's complaint about his own sin in "I am a little world made cunningly" causes him to overflow the limits of the octave by a line, "leaving," as one critic put it, "only five [lines, not six] for the mediator's petition to God."[26] The poem would have been seen as an overt violation of the traditional octave—just as heretical as, in her time, Browne's omission of the octave altogether, which can be understood as part of an effort to revive awareness of poems' spatial and temporal constraint, foregrounding its inventiveness. Insofar as Browne's daily sonnet is only as supposedly difficult now as Donne's holy sonnet was in its day, difficulty need not necessarily indicate progress but does require a troubling of cunning.

Notes

1. A recording of Browne performing the poem is available at PennSound: https://media.sas.upenn.edu/pennsound/authors/Browne-Laynie/3-11-09/ Browne-Laynie_11_Six-Fourteenths-Donne-Sonnet_Contemporary-Writers-Series_Brown-University_3-11-09.mp3.

2. Laynie Browne, "On the Elasticity of the Sonnet and the Usefulness of Collective Experimentation," in *Poets on Teaching: A Sourcebook*, ed. Joshua Marie Wilkinson (Iowa City: University of Iowa Press, 2010), 100. The term appears in a recommended list of writing experiments.

3. *John Donne: The Divine Poems*, 2d ed., ed. Helen Gardner (Oxford: Oxford University Press, 1978 [1952]), 13.

4. Laynie Browne, *Daily Sonnets* (Denver: Counterpath Press, 2007), 37.

5. Browne, *Daily Sonnets*, 34.

6. Browne, *Daily Sonnets*, 157.

7. Browne, *Daily Sonnets*, 157.

8. Browne, *Daily Sonnets*, title page.

9. Browne, *Daily Sonnets*, 158.

10. A. J. Smith, *Metaphysical Wit* (Cambridge: Cambridge University Press, 1991), 133.

11. Browne, *Daily Sonnets*, 158.

12. Charles Alexander, review of Laynie Browne's *Daily Sonnets*, "Chaxblog," March 5, 2007, http://chaxpress.blogspot.com/2007/03/daily-sonnets-by-laynie-browne.html (accessed April 2, 2015).

13. Browne, *Daily Sonnets*, 157.

14. E-mail from Laynie Browne to Al Filreis, January 19, 2015.

15. William Zunder, *The Poetry of John Donne: Literature and Culture in the Elizabethan and Jacobean Period* (Sussex: Harvester Press, 1982), 94; emphasis added.

16. Browne, "On the Elasticity of the Sonnet," 96.

17. Linda Wagner, ed., *Interviews with William Carlos Williams* (New York: New Directions, 1986), 30.

18. Bernadette Mayer, "Note on Sonnets," in *Sonnets* (New York: Tender Buttons Press, 1989), 119.

19. Bernadette Mayer, videorecorded discussion at Kelly Writers House, Philadelphia, October 21, 2014, http://jacket2.org/content/bernadette-mayer-writing-traditional-forms.

20. Browne, "On the Elasticity of the Sonnet," 95.

21. "Bernadette Mayer's List of Journal Ideas," ed. Charles Bernstein, PEPC Library, http://www.writing.upenn.edu/library/Mayer-Bernadette_Experiments.html.

22. Browne, "On the Elasticity of the Sonnet," 97–99.

23. E-mail from Browne to Filreis, January 19, 2015.

24. See Rachel Zucker, "Poetry as Translation and Radical Revision," in Wilkinson, *Poets on Teaching*, 120–22.

25. Conceiving of writing as English-to-English translation encourages writers "to write outside their habits or beyond their perceived formal, substantive, or aesthetic limitations" (Jen Hofer, "Two Dozen English-to-English Translation Techniques," in Wilkinson, *Poets on Teaching*, 114).

26. A. C. Partridge, *John Donne: Language and Style* (London: Andre Deutsch, 1978), 134.

JACQUELINE WATERS

The Tax

It was anxiety that led me to love—an unsituatedness
That made me fear rest
And hate sleep—now I sleep
That I take no final faith
In what I gathered: the ideas I had
And set about testing
Like who can pull
Another up, a complexion like
A boiled root, suggestions you found
In other people's mouths
Or thought up yourself
Then fought for and stored, counting out an allotment
High enough to seem gracious, low enough to save

The sun rose or the sun sank behind a bank
Of broken clouds. If waiting is patience
Waiting to be recognized, then destiny
Is a little sarcastic, which is how I described
Blake's *Tyger, Tyger* poem in 10th grade English
For which the teacher
Mocked me—it turns out
Blake meant it, was sincere about it, and no one suggested
SARCASTIC was just one of the very few words I had, like, in my
    vocabulary
Like people have the word DRY for wine
Because it sounds sophisticated and gives you a chance
To tell your server what you like
And you can buy a wine card
With a list of words
Like OAKY or BROAD
So you can be
Even more sophisticated
About what you'll tolerate
In this life. What did I mean? SARDONIC? AGHAST? Or just
Blake was smarter than our class
So he had a right
Not to be direct—like

A poet is a clown
In a good way
The purpose
Is to entertain people
You can be more smart than funny
Perhaps not even
Funny at all

And if something is to be a commodity and a currency
At once, like gold, or a feeling, then it's got to be subject to laws
Affecting both, though I can say
It being one
Unfits it for being the other: love
Is a feeling and I LOVE YOU
Its expression, but I LOVE YOU
Begets an I LOVE YOU back, or it falters
As it its harbor
Fails to find. I LOVE YOU
Is what I trade you, a thing
And I try not
To drive down the value
Of a thing. Implicit love
Can be described
But not remanded
And if ever it multiplied
To take away
That currency power
Its allegiance to barter
Well then I would just be cheated

She said I never wear panties
Even when I'm playing a cold city
As though panties
Were for warmth
What she's doing
Is a trick if you
Think about it
The knack
Of coupling sensations
That pass from top to bottom
Like the best sensation
May be one you know you can remove, an unpleasant
Film on your fingers
After you use them
To mix some meal: you know you can

Wash, you know you're just tolerating
Something that can be relieved—and maybe that's
The notch that unbelief
Yields in the structure's foundation: they *are* structures
These arrangements: living together
Sleeping alongside, staying awake while the other one sleeps. You have
To care! Be the sun
Shining through a watery cloud, or the cloud
Creased to be a white veil
Since where you believe you have power you don't
And where you do you refuse to wield it

But I don't know should people
Who show a little doubt
In what they do
Always lose? Who wants to be
Reassuring all the time it'd be
Like a job. And it's so
Public too it's not
Like we won't ever have much
To go on about
That's the best part
About being gone
Rosy hill, buck-colored dale, heaving
Old enemies over: nothing
Owned, just borrowed
One soul from another in the throes
Golden throes
Ones meant to make the most
Of an exchange
Picked out of the air, like a flower
Cut out from some pot, just to let
This impression fall away
Without considering
What you are letting it fall away from

Chapter 3

Trouble with Difficulty:
Jacqueline Waters's "The Tax"

Aaron Kunin

Jacqueline Waters is not an especially difficult writer. Her poems are characterized by a rare clarity of thought—a virtue that I associate more with really good criticism than with poetry. Few are the poems that provoke the exclamation, "If only I could always think this clearly!"

Her difficulty, if she has one, is with difficulty itself:

>. . . destiny
>Is a little sarcastic, which is how I described
>Blake's *Tyger, Tyger* poem in 10th grade English
>For which the teacher
>Mocked me—it turns out
>Blake meant it, was sincere about it, and no one suggested
>SARCASTIC was just one of the very few words I had, like, in my
>   vocabulary
>Like people have the word DRY for wine
>Because it sounds sophisticated and gives you a chance
>To tell your server what you like
>And you can buy a wine card
>With a list of words
>Like OAKY or BROAD
>So you can be
>Even more sophisticated
>About what you'll tolerate
>In this life. What did I mean? SARDONIC? AGHAST? Or just
>Blake was smarter than our class
>So he had a right
>Not to be direct—

Discernible in this stanza is a traditional concept of poetic difficulty. Blake's poetic wisdom gives him "a right / Not to be direct." Figures of speech say and unsay, or say without saying. Schemes of rhythm and rhyme use words for sound effects rather than argument. Or the sound effects determine the shape of the argument. Poetic diction favors archaic, distressed forms such as the *y* in *tyger*. In his study of obscure vocabularies in poetry, Daniel Tiffany has argued that poetry is indiscriminate in its search for diction, finding sources in the cant of criminal underworlds as well as the approved extraordinary language of elite literary traditions.[1] In short, any location of culture will do, as long as the meaning of the words is sufficiently obscure. A relationship to tradition can be faked; further, a traditional vocabulary acquires a new layer of artifice by dint of its circulation in poetry. The forced archaism of *tyger* is a blatant example of the fakery that Tiffany celebrates.

In "The Tax," Waters finds obscurity in a surprising place: a tenth-grade English classroom, where the word *sarcastic* sits uneasily in the mouth of a student who is not quite sure of its meaning. Although the student recognizes Blake's right to complexity in language, she does not affirm that he exercises it in "The Tyger." Instead she seems to endorse the interpretation of the high school English teacher: "It turns out / Blake meant it, was sincere about it," as though Blake's catechism of questions without answers had been written from innocence rather than the contrary state of the human soul. The teacher, a figure of enlightenment, demands direct expression from students and assumes it in canonical works of literature. Further, like a real Augustan critic of poetry, the teacher responds to indirect, imprecise, or simply pretentious uses of language with unforgiving mockery.

Curiously, Waters, although a poet herself, does not seem to view Blake as her colleague. Blake is "smarter," and his special intelligence comes with special rights that Waters does not dream of claiming for herself. She does not seem to identify with the teacher either, although she endorses the teacher's expertise. Instead, when she creates a surrogate for herself within the poem, she puts herself in the position of the humiliated student: unlike Blake, incapable of the free expression of art, and unlike the teacher, incapable of the disciplined language of school.

Writing with a vocabulary of "very few words" of whose meaning she is innocent, she finds an unlikely path to poetic obscurity. The high school student who uncertainly mouths, "Sarcastic?" is similar to the first speakers of human language, who, according to Giambattista Vico, were also the first poets, because they had to use their "very few words" to refer to a variety of concepts. In her innocence, by substituting one obscure meaning for another, the high school student invents a trope.

Is this the language of an elite? Perhaps Tiffany would say that any obscure vocabulary, regardless of the social rank of those who understand it, must be elitist, merely by virtue of its obscurity to anyone outside its community. As a student in high school, Waters does not know the meaning of the word *sarcastic*; it is "just one of the very few words I had, like, in my vocabulary." Then, and perhaps now, she does not know the meaning of "The Tyger." The former obscurity substitutes for the latter obscurity. She uses a word without having a clear sense of its meaning to interpret a poem without having a clear sense of its meaning.

Perhaps there is another sense in which the speaker of "The Tax" has a superior relationship to language. Ford Madox Ford wrote in a memoir of Christina Rossetti that "exaggerations really pained her." (In Ford's anecdote, when he casually mentions that "hundreds of people" would like Rossetti to be poet laureate, "she pinned me down until she had extracted from me the confession that not more than nine persons had spoken to me on the subject.")[2] This pain, which might be called the pain of difficult language, is the subject of Waters's poem.

I do not mean to suggest that Waters is a new Rosetti. Waters uses the language of rights to designate the poet's freedom to convey simple meanings using unnecessarily complicated expressions, "a right / not to be direct," whereas Rosetti condemns such complications in the name of moral right. The absence of a sense of righteousness differentiates Waters's attitude toward language from Rosetti's and, even more, from that of Laura Riding, in whose work the condemnation intensifies and finally overwhelms the act of composition.

The name of the historical passage from Rosetti to Riding is modernism, and according to Ford, Rosetti's attitude toward poetic diction is essentially modernist. Rosetti demands the exact rendering of impressions in language. This attitude differentiates her from contemporaries such as Ruskin, who uses the vague adjective *golden* several times on a single page of *Sesame and Lilies* only for its impressive sound. Rosetti looks forward to modernist precision and to the difficulty of finding particular expressions to convey particular experiences. For example, Ford's younger colleague Stephen Crane invented the word *squdgy* to describe the greasy grip of a bottle in *Maggie: A Girl of the Streets*. Waters turns away from the project of modernism and from the difficult language that belongs to other poets by right but that she disclaims. She has in common with Rosetti only a sensation of pain around this language.

The real subject of "The Tax" might appear to be love, not pain. At the center of the poem is an expression of love, "I LOVE YOU," which looks clear enough but turns out to be difficult to interpret, both "a commodity and a currency." The declaration "I LOVE YOU" is an example of what the speaker calls "an allotment": "Suggestions you found / In other people's mouths / Or thought up yourself / Then fought for and stored." In other words, allotments are a demonic aspect of language. They might come from inside ("thought up yourself") or outside ("other people's mouths"), but in neither case are they freely chosen personal expression, unless one has the right of the poet to say "tyger" or "squdgy." Waters isn't going to invent a new language every time she opens her mouth. She sticks with the words allotted to her.

Allotment, as it happens, has an interesting history as a problem for definition:

When "the Act to facilitate the provision of Allotments for the Labouring Classes" was before the House of Commons in 1887, a well-known member for a northern constituency asked the Minister who had charge of the measure for a definition of the term *allotment* which occurred so often in the bill. The Minister somewhat brusquely told his interrogator to "look in the Dictionary," at which there was, according to the newspapers, "a laugh." The member warmly protested that, being called upon to consider a measure dealing with things therein called "Allotments," a term not known to English Law, nor explained in the Bill itself, he had a right to ask for a definition. But the only answer he received was "Johnson's Dictionary! Johnson's Dictionary." . . . The real humour of the situation, which was unfortunately lost upon the House of Commons, was, that as agricultural allotments had not been thought of in the days of Dr. Johnson, no explanation of the term in this use is to be found in Johnson's Dictionary.[3]

For Irene Tucker, this story, which she quotes from Murray, illustrates the difference between the text of the dictionary and how it's used—something the dictionary is good for other than reading. In certain situations, such as parliamentary debates, it can be useful to make the meanings of words less definite (212–13). Similarly, for Waters, *allotment* is a technique of speaking without being responsible for the meanings of words.

Now let's return to the painful feelings of the speaker in "The Tax." Behind love is anxiety—"it was anxiety that led me to love"—and in front of it fear, hate, and doubt are massed. What is the speaker afraid of? What keeps her awake at night? Like Rossetti, she has a horror of needlessly complex language. When she encounters hyperbolic, ignorant, and imprecise usage in others, she judges their expressions harshly. She fears the potential rhetorical power of these expressions. What if they affect her without her knowing that she is affected? Even more, she fears that she may be guilty of similar unjustifiable complexities.

The high school student who hears sarcasm in Blake's song is like the adult in the bar who orders a "dry" wine. Both adjectives, *sarcastic* and *dry*, are motivated by a wish to "sound sophisticated." The speaker in the poem rejects the possibility that these are primary qualities; the sarcastic tone and the dry flavor are not properties in the song and the wine. She does not even take seriously the possibility that she in her student days and the imaginary drinker might sincerely be trying to describe their own perceptions. They are just trying to impress other listeners or survive social situations with the only words they have for reading and drinking. The problem does not go away when you add another vocabulary word. The terms of art for distinguishing nuances of flavor in wines (and by implication, the esoteric vocabulary of literary studies) do not represent knowledge of primary qualities, or self-knowledge of aesthetic experience, just a way to appear "even more sophisticated / About what you'll tolerate / In this life."

The surprising implication of the comparison between high school student and drinker is that the latter merely sounds more sophisticated than the former but is not actually any more sophisticated. In Blake's terms, the drinker remains on the side of innocence. The drinker is older and has a greater vocabulary but no developing precision of impression or expression. Rather than becoming smarter, one grows more tolerant.

The concept of tolerance is a complicated one, although Waters expresses it, as usual, in clear, abstract language. The fourth stanza provides two examples of this kind of tolerance:

> Like the best sensation
> May be one you know you can remove, an unpleasant
> Film on your fingers
> After you use them
> To mix some meal: you know you can
> Wash, you know you're just tolerating
> Something that can be relieved

How does "an unpleasant / film" become, through tolerance, a superior mode of pleasure? In this calculus of pleasures, there's the simple pleasure of keeping one's fingers clean, and then there's the greater pleasure, "the best sensation," of leaving the fingertips a bit dirty and knowing all along that one can clean them. This is the complicated pleasure that ancient Stoicism cultivated of enjoying one's superiority to passing bodily sensations by choosing how one responds to them. By the same logic, the speaker may "fear rest / And hate sleep" because she would prefer to make sleep an elective state.

Ideally one would be able to choose one's feelings as easily as putting on a garment or leaving it off:

> She said I never wear panties
> Even when I'm playing a cold city
> As though panties
> Were for warmth
> What she's doing
> Is a trick if you
> Think about it
> The knack
> Of coupling sensations
> That pass from top to bottom

The speaker lives in a society corrupted by sneaky rhetorical manipulation, the "tricks" and "knacks"—tropes, as they are called in the study of poetry—for which she must always be vigilant. Here, in what appears to be an interview with a rock star, she zeroes in on a misleading suggestion about the function of undergarments, which she dismisses with sarcastic mockery: "As though panties / Were for warmth." While castigating this ambiguous speech, the "trick," for the rhetorical power it might wield, she also admires the position of the rock star who wields it, who by tolerating an unpleasant sensation of cold demonstrates a Stoic imperviousness to manipulation.

Thus the speaker arrives at the startling conclusion that love talk should be regulated:

> And if something is to be a commodity and a currency
> At once, like gold, or a feeling, then it's got to be subject to laws
> Affecting both, though I can say
> It being one
> Unfits it for being the other: love
> Is a feeling and I LOVE YOU
> Its expression, but I LOVE YOU
> Begets an I LOVE YOU back, or it falters
> As it its harbor
> Fails to find.

This isn't a love poem. Instead of saying, "I love you," the speaker puts the declaration "I LOVE YOU" under glass. This apparently simple expression turns out to have the same suspicious tendency to exaggerate and overcomplicate as the tricks and knacks of figurative language. The speaker calls for regulation—taxation, even—of this utterance, because it functions not only as description but also as coercion: "I LOVE YOU / Begets an I LOVE YOU back." Thus the speaker can never fully trust that her sleeping partner's affection is not the result of her rhetorical manipulation. Her own feelings must be examined for signs that they are the result of someone's tricks.

Like Rosetti, Waters experiences pain when she encounters imprecise language, and this experience makes her suspicious of all figures of speech. These tricks might be nothing more than unmotivated projections of poetic intelligence. But I said earlier that Waters is not a new Rosetti. She might have more in common with Ford. In a familiar genealogy of modernism that Ford mediates, poets distress diction, exaggerate figures, and push the limits of their medium in response to the pressures of modern life. The different genealogy that, according to Ford, begins in Rosetti's poetry, reacts against Victorian vagueness and modernist difficulty and seeks the greatest possible precision.

What is Ford doing in these two intertwined literary histories? He has a lot of sympathy for Rosetti. The pain he experienced when he heard the Victorian, superpoetic diction of Pound's early poems is well documented. Hearing words that he never heard spoken outside of poems, he rolled on the floor, clutching his head and moaning.[4] One complicating factor is the undeniably Victorian style of some of the diction in Ford's prose. Think of the sentences in Ford's and Conrad's novels that go, "It is all a darkness." "It is all a vagueness." Like Pound, Ford never eliminated the Victorian slush from his product. A more telling complication is that Ford's vocabulary includes both Rosetti's precise language and Ruskin's vague one. Waters is similar in that, for one thing, she coincidentally uses the very word, *golden*, that marks Ruskin's vagueness and sonority: "Nothing / Owned, just borrowed / One soul from another in the throes / Golden throes." Like Ford, Waters values precision but does not drop the vague poetic language entirely; she incorporates it in the mode of judgment.

This procedure implies a fundamental optimism about human intelligence. Waters may not think she is as smart as Blake, but this assessment does not lead to despair. Decades later, she is still trying to work out the problem. Even surrounded by anxiety, fear, doubt, and hate, she has a sense that people can solve problems by thinking and talking about them honestly. She puts her whole intellect into her judgments of minor tricks of language and gives other people a lot of credit for their intelligence while describing her own rather modestly.

In this way, Waters establishes a newly superior relationship to language. She can't select or discard the vocabulary she has been allotted, but she can establish a different kind of control by tolerating it. She does not exactly practice obscurity; instead, she acts as the judge of other obscurities. For her, the trouble with poetry is its difficulty, and the trouble with difficulty is that it's too easy.

Notes

1. Daniel Tiffany, *Infidel Poetics: Riddles, Nightlife, Substance* (Chicago: University of Chicago Press, 2009).

2. Ford Madox Ford, *Memories and Impressions: A Study in Atmospheres* (New York: Ecco Press, 1985), 64.

3. James Murray, "The Evolution of English Lexicography," quoted in Irene Tucker, *A Probable State: The Novel, the Contract, and the Jews* (Chicago: University of Chicago Press, 2000), 210.

4. Hugh Kenner, *The Pound Era* (Berkeley: University of California Press, 1971), 80.

GEOFFREY G. O'BRIEN

from "Winterreise"

Pulling back the blinds, the other
Ones, the entire play of nowhere
In its proper place, inviolable;
Getting back to a natural posture,
Patient with the newcomers, friends
Of these conditions voices are
The bride of, that really could go
Either way rather than entirely
Where yesterday's sharpness fades
On the branch of having to,
A surprise that doesn't go away,
Carries invisible content out
To lure back even the diffident
Who are an old patience becoming

Chapter 4

✦

Some Contemporary Roles for Difficulty in Geoffrey G. O'Brien's *People on Sunday*

Charles Altieri

I think one of the best ways to approach any body of poetry is to ask what are its characteristic difficulties and how does engaging them define distinctive historical projects on the part of the poets. This begs the question of the many kinds of difficulty possible in poetry—some formal, some involving adapting to troubling emotional and political intensities, some involving finding a voice at all.[1] In fact I am realizing that my own interest in difficulty is emphatically formal—a result of my commitment to self-consciously modernist writing, where one basic question is always why the poet does not offer an easier or immediately clearer presentation of how language can engage the situations that drive them to write.

My modernist heritage gives me a distinctive perspective on difficulty as contemporaries deploy it in constructing their linguistic textures because there are striking contrasts between the different affective and self-reflexive orientations toward the world that underlie this contemporary work. It seems obvious now that modernist poets felt they had to be difficult to combat the large-scale pressures of righteousness, conformity, and market values society had become so good at imposing on social life. Difficulty, then, was primarily a mode of clearing a space for developing modes of agency educated against by an increasingly empiricist and pragmatic culture. Writing had to call attention to the possibility of organizing psyches cultivating different modes of attention that seemed transpersonal and anchored in structures of temporality more capacious than our typical engagement in our practical present tenses. And writing had to present literal and striking constructive powers repressed by the culture's empiricist bent in philosophy and in practical matters. Modernist difficulty sought affiliations with the sense of violence cultivated most obviously by Eliot's apocalyptic sensibility and magazines like Wyndham Lewis's *Blast*.

This is not the case with the kinds of formal difficulty contemporary poetry seems to pursue. These poets no longer dream of improving readers by disciplining them into developing the range of knowledge and eye for complexity that make reading an analogue for experiencing our fullest human potential. Embracing one's contemporaneity now appears inseparable from shedding dreams of any kind of transcendence so that we can accept our situations as limited beings mired in the cultural detritus spawned by an unjust and violent society. Yet even now it is rare to see our more ambitious poets simply accepting the pathos of these conditions. They know their heritage, and they manage to use the challenges in our traditions of lyric poetry to reject mainstream modes of writing that seem content with elaborating immediately recognizable scenes, partially transformed by moments of epiphanic insight. The best and most ambitious contemporaries know that they must deploy difficulty to defamiliarize such submission to the pathos of our lives and make readers realize how fresh imaginative intensities might transform our disposition toward the imperatives lurking within the cultural structures we inhabit. And perhaps the one benefit of the banal discursiveness pervading American culture is that some poets at least have to be difficult just to clear the ground for what they might be saying, and for how the manner of their saying might count as manifesting resistance.

Let me then develop an example of what I see as one influential mode of difficulty developed in the recent work of Geoffrey G. O'Brien by concentrating on the poem quoted at the beginning of my essay. It is the ninth in a sequence of twelve linked fourteen-line poems, titled "Winterreise" in honor of Franz Schubert

Clearly this is poetry fervently dedicated to sonic intensities—verbal music referring to states produced by instrumental music. But just as clearly this poem has a strange sense of otherness virtually built into its DNA. This otherness does not derive from allusion: O'Brien's text is haunted by the history of the sonnet but does not seem to engage any particular text or mythic archetype. In fact one might say that the difficulties here involve primarily the poem's sense of the intricacies of grammar and appositional complication as they cross the desire for plain speech and force enjambment upon it. And perhaps more surprising, O'Brien seems to have no interest at all in binding poetry to perceptual images or to any version of the ideology of image dominant in English poetry since Romanticism. Notice, for example, how the poem begins with an action that could occur in any poem pursuing epiphanic realizations of what can be seen through that window. But perhaps no other poet would so quickly deny the scenic promise of this opening by moving immediately to "the other / Ones," opening on a radically non-scenic "entire play of nowhere." Now we have to ask ourselves what is the proper place of "nowhere" and why is it "in its proper place inviolable." We might also wonder why the modifier "inviolable" comes after "place," the term it qualifies.

We are entering a world where perceiving matters very little, so there is no room for acts of sensitive discovery, typically congratulating the poet for removing what had been blinding. O'Brien wants his poem to establish a site in which the other plays a constitutive role—other to sense, other to common understanding, and other to the kinds of presence of the world to the self that poetry has pursued since James Thompson. As the poem develops, we see that its world depends entirely on the emerging logic that stems from how the writing guides us into what I want to call a sense of constitutive difficulty. Difficulty tests the mind's power to compose against the senses so that it can follow a logic imposed by imagination—a logic, I hasten to add, that establishes a possible home distinctive to engaged reading. Difficulty ends up not so much resisting the world as affording means of enjoying and meditating upon the role of that resistance. And in so doing, the poem recalls a great epoch in Western poetry when the mind sought out analogous difficulties to manifest the values inherent in its differences from the senses. For that poetry the world was less an event or series of events based on emotional encounters given to writerly experience than a construct given point by the reader's capacity to inhabit imaginatively the argumentative resources of language.

John Ashbery has a similar distrust of any image that provides dramatic organization for lyric situations. And O'Brien has strong connections to Ashbery's syntactic waverings and taste for multiple levels of meaning almost free to go in their own directions. Yet he also has very different imaginative priorities. No poet could be less interested in camp than O'Brien is, or in the demotic textures and associations that agglutinate around the poet's attempts to develop lyrical structures. So I will try to show how he deploys aspects of Ashbery ways of staging difficulty for a very different historical project, weaving Ashbery's ambiguities into a sense of continuity with a Renaissance poetry confident in the powers of naked mind to dwell on and in intricate argumentative logic, and always tempered by a compulsion to make language sing as it thinks.

Let me, then, set the stage for O'Brien by talking first about Ashbery's break from any overt equation of the poet's labors with the desire for a coherent dynamics based on the effort to provide a visibly unified experience. There can be little doubt that Ashbery's sentences match those of any modernist for complex syntax capable of evoking fluid and dense aural patterns. But he develops that complexity so as almost to deny the powers of intelligence to impose structure, preferring instead to render states of mind anxious to track their own emerging ambivalences and confusions.

Take as Ashbery's emblem for the goals of his own work the lines concluding "As One Put Drunk into the Packet Boat": "The summer demands and takes away too much, / But night, the reserved, the reticent, gives more than it takes."[2] Night gives the opportunity to organize emotional intensities around what cannot and need not be made lucidly visible. So in stressing what night offers in its reticence, Ashbery can mine the lyrical resources made available by two emphases in his writing. The satisfactions of the enigmatic are the most important feature of this analogue with night. Night does not afford clear outlines. It allows beings to rest in a kind of fullness that has no outside and few means of compelling attention. But that very condition affords many means of soliciting fascination with how unity and rewards for intense concentration can be frustrated and modified. In effect these creatures of night cannot be absorbed within sequential or argumentative thinking. They do not yield meaning so much as auras of possible significance within an unstable yet endlessly suggestive sense of the circulation of levels of meaningfulness that resist specific statement. Put more bluntly, Ashbery wants to embody in language what is suppressed when we embark on quests for clear understanding.

A second, closely related feature of Ashbery's poetry in the 1960s and 1970s is his sharp preference for analogical rather than purely descriptive functions: he elaborates "as" relations of equivalence rather than "is" relations of pure reference.[3] The author seems to be trying to keep up with what continually emerges as between apprehension and projection rather than relying on memory to compose a coherent and integrated set of meanings. As-ness demands capturing the look and feel of what emerges as if it provided invitations to further imaginings not quite under the control of any purposive stance. And more important, rather than idealize the descriptive capacities of language, Ashbery works out something close to an ontology based on recognizing the constant copresence of opposites in multiple dimensions. Approaching the real requires seeing a situation as framed by competing subjective orientations, whose interactions shape what appears as fact. Just think of how much is excluded when we posit propositions stressing only single terms as objects of attention. And the situation becomes even more problematic when we claim sincerity, because we then focus on certain aspects of the psyche and exclude others that may be equally formative in our feelings, rendering the sincerity dangerously close to a stage performance. There is simply no identification or act of naming that does not have to be aware of the incompleteness of any positive distinction, because the phenomenon will also be haunted by its opposite or its negation—at least in matters of the psyche and of how language works in the world. In this regard night's reticence proves amazingly voluble.

O'Brien sees that Ashbery establishes a distinctive role for the reader at odds with modernism's attempts to develop something approaching a master-slave model of dominance. With Ashbery the reader's primary role is to project his or her own sense of "asness" on what the language composes. The reader enters the events of the poem but is invited to explore a series of complex attitudes ranging from cooperation to shifting the fantasy basis for identification to downright resistance. Ashbery does not offer his readers any kind of truth. Instead he offers them the experience of recognizing what is involved when one imagination is stimulated by another and seeks further companionship. Both reading and writing can become completely satisfactory states when audience and author can feel what is involved in saying "now, really now" (CP, 661).

Ashbery poses a challenge that O'Brien eagerly takes up concerning the relation between the ascetic and the effusive. This is Ashbery's conclusion to "And Ut Pictura Poesis Is Her Name":

> The extreme austerity of an almost empty mind
> Colliding with the lush, Rousseau-like foliage of
> its desire to communicate
> Something between breaths, if only for the sake
> Of others and their desire to understand you and desert you
> For other centers of communication, so that understanding
> May begin, and in doing so be undone. (*CP*, 519)

On the one hand, Ashbery recognizes the need to reach understanding—of what the poem engages and of whom the poem engages with. On the other hand, understanding is always a dead end, because it displaces all the drives connected to continuing need with the desire for singularity and with demands for imaginative intensity that build on the sense that one is "really now" attuned fully to one's capacities to be fully present. Summer seeks the satisfactions of understanding. But night, the reserved and the reticent, offers a continuous promise that our imaginations are best fostered when understanding can be undone.[4] Understanding can remain in the background, but only as a dialectical trace sublated by its negation and by the thrill of the ability to make such large-scale negations take the form of another kind of positive content.[5]

I will argue that O'Brien is a master at putting the relation between negation and affirmation in tighter logical formulations than Ashbery typically provides (without losing a commitment to lushness of sound and situation), largely because O'Brien is much more directly attentive to the resources of syntax and lineation than is Ashbery. "Pulling back the blinds" is built on three fundamental challenges to the audience: (1) to process its syntax, (2) to develop sympathy for why the syntax is difficult to process, and (3) to find through the poems' abstractness a route to intense and complicated feeling. Such feelings are probably not available in poems where the imagination concentrates on elaborating relations to a dramatic encounter with what becomes a central image demanding affectively charged interpretation.

The first fact about the syntax is how the single sentence that is the poem unfolds by what seems an intense listening to its own somewhat enigmatic processes. That syntax has the task of defining the "other" that "nowhere" becomes. And the strange relation of the poem to "nowhere" is initially manifest in the two balanced participles governing the opening series of appositions. Syntactically these participles modify "surprise that doesn't go away," which occurs all the way down in the eleventh line. Navigating this sentence seems almost as full of adventure as a boat trip on turbulent seas.

The reader has to recognize the demand to choose and the consequences of the partial erasure that results from each choice. Yet the exercise of that freedom may be necessary if the poem is to resist how all of our conventional orientations toward action are devoted to denying or destroying the "other." Here the goal is to manage to align our reading with the imaginative presence of a specific domain that is "nowhere." After all, there may be no alternative to how stressing musicality in a text situates us within a world of fact, even as it pulls us into a sense of "nowhere" beyond physicality. Just think of the poem as playing major chords with the sounds of *o*, modulated by minor chords carried by the *a*'s.

This thematizing of "nowhere" occurs as a condition of direct experience because *other* here introduces a strong enjambment, with a surprising result that puts the issue of surprise on the table from the first. For I begin to wonder if *other* can ever be without enjambment and still do the work of challenging our tendencies to repeat the same old habits. It is only by completing an emphatically dangling expression that the poem relocates issues of seeing and adapting into a far more intricate imaginative site than the poem seems initially to offer. We learn that these blinds are either constituted by "the entire play of nowhere" or give access to that "nowhere." And then we also realize why these participles evoke human presences but with something close to a zero degree of practical human power. The agency referred to by these participles seems exhausted by their role of defining the scene and eliciting the voice from the "no place" that is the poem. Any more assertiveness would risk encouraging a false confidence in the adequacy of human habits for producing meaning. Then the poem would risk weakening its sense of how this "other" might trouble our standard practices. And the poet might become an unwitting ideologue for bourgeois modes of insisting on making clear and practical utterances.

Enjambment comes to the rescue of surprise, especially in the superb sequence, "Friends / Of these conditions voices are / The bride of, that." The first enjambment here brings out the power of the genitive to limit nouns and yet to expand worlds by specifying relationships of one entity participating in another. The second enjambment intensifies the relational field by first providing a space for the "no space" of metaphor, and then using the genitive in the final position in the line to define voices as fulfillments of what had been an almost empty "Other." As we work out a rationale for the pauses, we must decide on several questions. Are the voices the conditions themselves or the brides of those conditions, bringing them into articulate collusion with the world? Then is *that*'s antecedent *conditions* or *voices*? Finally we have to notice that the one line that is not enjambed, "Where yesterday's sharpness fades / On the branches of having to," resolves on a verb that lacks an expected infinitive. The line that is syntactically incomplete turns out to be semantically painfully complete even with its double meaning. "The branches of having to" could refer to having to fade or having to as a sense of obligation that kills one's openness to possibility. The unenjambed line is woefully all too definitive.

The poem's one sentence finally produces a main clause in lines 11–14—a syntactic surprise about surprise. Here surprise is cast as an alternative to what must fade. And what must fade is inextricably woven into the ways that duty, or "having to," blocks openness to experience. Now the poem's movements resolve into a promise of eventfulness capable of luring back "even the diffident / who are an old patience becoming." Yet the appeal of "nowhere" cannot be cast all in positive terms because that would collapse its otherness into our systematic contrasts between negative and positive. So the poem uses the complexities of grammar to merge negative and positive.

The audience for the surprise can hear in its "patience becoming" the lure of the invisible content. But the poem also emphasizes how those who hear also possess a patience that is resistant to change. The diffident simply become fixed in an "old patience becoming" that is inseparable from the endless repetition of a life governed primarily by a sense of duty. Repetition in time precludes dwelling in this other space. Yet one cannot not hear *patients* in *patience*, although it appears nowhere. So one actually makes "nowhere" appear. And when we engage that hearing, we actually find that the construct "old patients" offers a faint possibility of humans actually becoming something new thanks to the music they begin to hear. This music proves inseparable from the possibility that all these multiple registers of meaning suggest something beyond diffidence and patience, something attuned to "becoming." So while the poem insists on its bleakness, it also strives to overcome that bleakness without quite making the dangerous move of actually allowing itself to believe that change is possible. Perhaps it is the poem that is the ultimate old patient becoming.

I have tried to suggest a path through the poem that makes it a coherent and suggestive experience. But to do this I have deprived the poem of much of its strangeness and almost all of its dynamic drive. To honor those elements fully, we have to speculate on how O'Brien shares Lisa Robertson's concern for the reader as cocreator of what are mere possibilities if we look only to the text. This poem wants to "lure" us back to the space of possibility primarily by reminding us of what is involved in completing what poetry demands of us. That demand seems to arise in the constant surprise of "nowhere." So we find that the categories accounting for the authorial and the readerly roles effectively merge into one correlated set of activities.

Consider, for example, the processes we went through to respond adequately to lines 6 through 10. When we ask what "nowhere" involves, our only clue is the text's own act of imagination weaving together something like construction and deconstruction. The only place such interaction can be "inviolable" is the imagination. In effect authorship and readership live one another's life and have to be prepared to die one another's death. This is how poems fully enter the space that is "nowhere," a space that one composes by choosing, or at least determining, a path through the poem that one knows cannot quite be an objectification of what the writer might have "intended."

Where modernist poetry seems emphatically the performance of the author, O'Brien manages to make a parallel exhibition of control an appeal to (and a demand on) the capacity of readers to observe how they make decisions and so in a sense take ownership of the poem. The reward for honoring these demands is that the poem's serious readers never feel relegated to being passive interpreters of programmed rhetorical gestures or highly plotted epiphanies. Instead readers feel their own decision making as an aspect of the poem's coming to mean anything at all. One has to recognize the degree of control it takes to give up mastery in order to dwell where patient becoming might be possible. And one has to recognize how this "nowhere" derives at least in part from the possibility that language itself need not be used up in referring. It can take on itself the work of producing a constant sense of becoming rather than subordinate itself to the satisfactions of concrete discovery, which rapidly fade into mere understanding. O'Brien's poem does Ashbery one better by composing a process where understanding and the undoing of understanding keep changing places, establishing and mobilizing the possibility that this "nowhere" composed by imagination is also potentially an everywhere in which reading might assume its full powers.

Notes

1. One source of my recognition is recent work on emotional difficulty by Jennifer Doyle, *Hold It against Me: Difficulty and Emotion in Contemporary Art* (Durham, N.C.: Duke University Press, 2013); and by John Emil Vincent, *Queer Lyrics: Difficulty and Closure in American Poetry* (New York: Palgrave Macmillan, 2002). I am also slightly dismayed to find out how much my thinking on difficulty mirrors George Steiner's, in his *On Difficulty and Other Essays* (Oxford: Oxford University Press, 1978.

2. *Collected Poems 1956–1987*, ed. Mark Ford (New York: Library of America, 2008), 427–28 (henceforth abbreviated as *CP*).

3. In my book *Wallace Stevens and the Demands of Modernity* (Ithaca, N.Y.: Cornell University Press, 2013), I oppose the late Stevens fascination with "as" to the investments in "is" powerfully developed in Peter Nichols's *George Oppen and the Fate of Modernism* (Oxford: Oxford University Press, 2007).

4. The only way to temper these abstractions is to demonstrate how a segment of a characteristic Ashbery poem operates. So I have chosen the conclusion to the poem "As We Know" from the 1979 collection of the same name. This poem is careful to separate our typical sense of meaning provided by the understanding from what might be called the meaningfulness potential in tracing how elements and forces come together in privileged moments of consciousness. Here the force of subjectivity consists primarily in the capacity to negotiate opposing forces while holding off the demands for believing in an inner self. For that belief

establishes an alternative locus for one's attention rather than locating value concretely in how experience takes form.

The title "As We Know" evokes first a sense that knowing is a present-tense activity that goes along with other mental processes, like caring or worrying or celebrating. "As" correlates these activities temporally and modally because knowing in this poem ultimately depends on our always adjusting for perspective and occasion. Knowing is a relation less to fixed matter than to the vagaries of manner that occupy consciousness aware of the relations it is negotiating in the present tense. And in the participatory mode of equivalence, reading emphasizes the "we" that becomes possible in correlating how people come to share what knowing can contain.

But the irony in the title's tone of jaded conventionality requires us to be careful in positing what this "we" involves. In one sense of the term *we* is utterly bound by convention. If we stress the knowing, we find ourselves risking any flexibility to adapt to the vagaries of the present tense. Yet there is also a consoling dimension to "as we know" that stresses the idea of coming to know in a manner that allows the first person plural. On this level, knowledge seems to depend on the work writing performs in the present tense, without any overarching plan for readers to realize or, more important, to fear that they have failed to realize in what the other is thinking and feeling.

The more imaginative dimensions of the title depend on our becoming involved in what I am calling "the ontological dimension of equivalence" established by this poem. Consider the opening lines:

> All that we see is penetrated by it—
> The distant treetops with their steeple (so
> Innocent), the stair, the windows' fixed flashing—
> Pierced full of holes by the evil that is not evil,
> The romance that is not mysterious, the life that is not life,
> A present that is elsewhere. (*CP*, 661)

"We" refers primarily to the lovers. But because of the lack of concrete identification, "we" also becomes anyone capable of fleshing out this penetrating "it." That process turns out to involve a series of oxymorons involving "the evil that is not evil" and "the life that is not life."

The basic contrast here seems to play off what can be elaborated in imagination (like erotic desire) against what are typical terms for characterizing disturbing transitions. So we have to ask how we can enter the space characterized by such oxymorons. Here the poem suggests that flexibility about how the self is constituted becomes a crucial virtue. This repeated *you* offers a marvelous parallel to the oxymoronic since we have to identify it as an address to a romantic partner, but we cannot stop with this specific reference. In one direction *you* vacillates into addressing the self; in another it invites the reader to share the range of intensities that anchor the details of the speaking. Then bringing life to these details produces in itself all the alternative we need to more abstract versions of *I* that are armored against how imagination can complicate its existence.

All this ambiguity ultimately functions to sustain a somewhat new vision of the kind of satisfaction lyric can produce. We need only to reflect on how this poem renders the shift from background context to the capacity for fully invested speech in the present:

> The light that was shadowed then
> Was seen to be our lives,
> Everything about us that love might wish to examine,
> Then put away for a certain length of time, until
> The whole is to be reviewed, and we turned
> Toward each other, to each other.
> The way we had come was all we could see
> And it crept up on us, embarrassed
> That there is so much to tell now, really now. (*CP*, 661)

This poem stages a fusion of opposites that is quite different from the organicist ideals shaping much of twentieth-century poetry. For when the speaking reviews the whole, the particular synthetic shape taken by this whole simply does not matter. What does matter is how the speaking develops an appreciation of all that can be gathered into the present tense. This appreciation occurs as the proliferation of pronouns settles into forming a "we." And "we" takes on power as it learns to identify with the transition from "now" to "really now." Here romance plentitude arises not from anything heroic the individual agents might perform. Rather it arises because the speaking can find a new relation to time, which had been seen in the poem only as the enemy of any kind of bliss deriving from treating home as a place "to get to, one of these days." By the end of the poem *we* dissolves into an affirmation of the difference between that ordinary time and the kind of time that can warrant the adverb *really*. It is not important what details allow that new sense of reality so long as the agents feel the difference from the kind of time that simply passes. "Really now" can be asserted without reference to any specific images because it refers to a state of mind rather than an object of attention. "Really now" affirms the possibility that there can emerge a charged sense of the present tense where "telling" can replace reviewing and the moment itself can replace any need for meaning at all beyond all that it takes for the telling to constitute a sense of plenitude. If that "now" could be represented in terms of images, we would destroy the sense of reality that matters most for romance—the sheer telling to someone who wants to hear precisely that activity.

5. I suspect that Ashbery is too diffident to make any claims to knowledge of these Hegelian figures for the work of imagination. But the second part of *Three Poems*, "The System" (*CP*, 280–317), makes it abundantly clear he is no stranger to dialectical thinking.

ANDREA BRADY

The Husband

Inhale. Never to die happier and posting
this tenuous climax for dry futures, but here
intaglio skins never shed this resin etching
or series of gelatine prints all screwed into
the particular faces of the infants: demand
fostered by infusion of its negatives. Never to feel
that anxiety, all but dying squeezed out
of the decorator's tip into ripples, never to ask
for anything less than a box of matches
all laced in black diamonds in a pavé setting;
never to ask if I have to take my socks off,
never to open the lungs again unaccompanied.
All are there, all the mathematical animals
the subtracting monkeys and the interrogational
anteater with his electric probe: all around the house
scraping, scraping, all bent on escaping back into
the garden to use its fantastic implements.
Notice that snapped rosemary branch, some trodden
hyacinth and the patch of chlorosis. We are never
alone, we cannot exclude
the terrific persons or the index of leading shares
but how solitary one could have been, thinking so.
Even this shelter negating so many, so much
damage by exposure—she couldn't last it—and what
it contains leaks from some unsealed windows, some white
caught by some surveillance van working for the council.
The house which is warm boxlike paid for the house
of our children and our faithfulness, our marriage.
Comes down to one. Down to one, and in that one cove
and one ability and one constant streaming signal
make another one, at least another one. One
or two, or two and three
confused, narcissistic, appealing, right
turning faces the morbid animals, the straight tree
sipping its sap as a prognostication,
the crunching credit, the credit monsters relying
all on each other eating some and paying some others,

turning into the house, turning towards the windows,
holding up the couple. Holding the child up, the look out.
We will stay here until we die and never collapse
in awe at our great fortune, to subtract from all
the some who might help or hinder who defer our credit
rating, to elicit the negative and keep the image
blinding in its white heat against the irradiated night:
so absolute the fidelity to the track, the cut, the original,
do you hear a noise? It is nothing, the safe house
is bound in weather, we can rest in it together. We are
together, the continuum is our happiness, our troubles
the condition of possibility without retreat: no, no less
than everything, put on
the all in one, we being some who resound
in one range in the house knocking like a cooker, sing, chose
what one we want and wearing that to death. Exhale,
that can be your contribution to the world
the dangerous commerce. Sung twice over. We can do this,
let's do this, together. Look, there. Hear it? There. Exhale then,
    do it now.

Chapter 5

✦

The Dark Looks of "The Husband"

John Wilkinson

Why anyone might be drawn to one poem or poet rather than another, especially if a work does not set out to seduce through conforming to widely held standards of attractiveness, continues to be a puzzle. What comes to hand, if not to notice, may arrive through friends and therefore be, as the TSA puts it, "pre-approved," but that doesn't dispose to much beyond a casually appraising glance. What am I looking for? What will detain me and set me to work for my pleasure? Thus to expand the question smuggles in some assumptions at the start. The assertion that beauty cannot be recognized through contemplation but demands engaged work is contestable. But what quality, emergent through the notorious and incessant distractibility of the contemporary reader, can induce a conviction that one enigmatic piece of writing should be trusted with otherwise scattered energies? Kant identified poetry as a site of exceptional free play, although this exceptionality relied on a different idea of poetry from the present-day lyric, favoring poems strict in form but vague in tenor; but qualities in a poem causing it to stand forth from page or screen, regardless of whether its political, ethical, or procedural qualities are agreeable, may not be so different now from the late eighteenth century.

The institutional study of literature can look like training in a variety of methods to dodge aesthetic judgment or, more strongly, to contest the possibility of aesthetic judgment regarded as epitomizing "Enlightenment" claims to universal disinterestedness—and needing to be knocked over time and again like a weighted skittle. Such an ambition unites the whole bang shoot from historicism to queer theory, and produces a now notorious cleft (in debates on the future of the humanities, etc.) between the enthusiast's ill-informed judgment and the professional student's informed avoidance of judgment. There was obvious value in the game of skittles when the canonicity of English and American literature was blatantly sexist and racist, but the speed with which new canons of taste have been rustled up on the ruins of the discredited suggests that judgment is an irrepressible drive—leave aside the web activity devoted to fervent advocacy of new novels and collections of poetry. Whether judgment leading to new canons of taste in graduate school is any more aesthetically disinterested than the aesthetic standards shaped by British imperialists for the instruction of the colonized seems disputable. Still, I want to begin with the claim that Kant was right in identifying lyric poetry as the genre offering the greatest potential for aesthetic judgment to be pronounced with full universalizing conviction; so there are poems by John Donne, John Keats, and Frank O'Hara that would lead me to claim that if a contemporary English speaker was unable to respond aesthetically to them, he or she must be disabled with respect to lyric poetry. I make this claim knowing that the work of each of these poets has at different times been despised as offensive to taste. Neither does the probability that empirically the majority of English speakers are disabled vis-à-vis lyric shake my claim. What troubles me is how many who study poetry cultivate and boast of such disability as a badge of goodness in moral, religious, commonsensical, political, or professional terms. But this is nothing new except for its systematic and institutional organization and approval.

A diminishing likelihood of intense encounter with the unprecedented may be compensated by webs of association across a scarcely conscious history of reading and looking. The fact that aesthetic claims are vulnerable should not, however, lead to their abandonment, because that way lies an atomization of human experience more than depressing to accept—it is psychically poisonous. A freedom to feel in ways disconnected from the feelings of people about me is not one I find attractive; to shirk from strong universalizing claims can leave the field to assumptions whose interestedness may be disguised but is nonetheless powerful and escapes the vulnerability attending aesthetic judgments. It is a part of the value of aesthetic judgments that they are questionable, while literary professionalization works to place its adepts beyond question, where errors can be corrected without personal harm except for the blush caused by exposure of a peccadillo.

Here I have selected (or been selected by) a poem by Andrea Brady, a poet I know and like, and therefore my aesthetic judgment is suspect from the start. More, I have written about Brady's writing previously and she has written about mine, so there must exist a basis for mutual recognition that may or may not represent a kinship in poetic practice. If what I recognize in Brady's writing is effectively mine (leaving to one side theoretical questions of authorship), any claim to disinterestedness must dissolve—for narcissism figures as the typical pathology of the lyric poet. Such narcissism is likely to be most pronounced in the first phase of encounter with a poem, but this is tricky, for writing that I recognize as akin to mine is liable to repel me. Therefore if actuated by narcissism, what looks back at me must not resemble my image; it must be something like my way of looking but from a different or occluded face. Indeed, that may be a condition for allure; deep affinity breaking through a very different countenance. What looks out and what returns the look may, however, belong to a kind of looking no one would want to meet in ordinary social encounter. There may be a category error in the charge of narcissism if such looks start from somewhere prior to, outside, or other than the constituted self.

I have lived with "The Husband" for some time, so I can know that my claim for it does not reflect a transient passion. Like anyone else I can be influenced by friendship and by identification and by the workings of an unconscious desire to fulfill my intellectual choices in a contrived spontaneity. And that's before I start to bracket (so far as that's imaginable) my race, gender, orientation, or more broadly my situated intellectual and affective formation. How can I possibly form an aesthetic judgment that could be the basis of a universal claim? This is not what has come to be thought of as difficulty in poetry; while readers have become adept in at least the theoretical framing of poetry resistant to paraphrase, aesthetic judgment presents new difficulty. Both the extreme of situatedness ascribed politically to poet and reader and its negative counterpart in language speaking itself put aesthetic judgment under severe pressure.

Nonetheless, I wish to explain to myself and to others why I think "The Husband" is not only a formidably good poem but one of those unusual poems that can actuate a full aesthetic encounter. Why leave aesthetic judgment to the conservatism that enforces answerability to "timeless" aesthetic principles as the basis for success in art? It is necessary, against this shibboleth, unceasingly to question the basis for a judgment without succumbing to total contingency. Such a proceeding is difficult but worth trying for a complicated poem. The cleft between enthusiast and scholar has enticed poetry to seek scholarly approval by a performance of repeatedly dissolving any claim to aesthetic value as though such a performance were itself a satisfactory substitute for aesthetic value; or has led to poetry that is belligerently stupid. "The Husband" is a poem by a scholar-poet whose poetry is not intimidated by her scholarship, her feminist activism, or her theoretical sophistication, nor does it belie any of those competencies and commitments. Ethical and rational judgment can be part of what a poet does without becoming a substitute-formation for poetry.

Hölderlin wrote that "the concept of judgment already contains the concept of the reciprocal relation of object and subject to each other, as well as the necessary precondition of a whole of which object and subject are the parts."[1] What this rather Platonic formulation implies, and what is implied in Kant's assertion that beauty is most disinterestedly visible in another human face, is that aesthetic judgment is based upon encounter, an encounter that leads to immediate recognition. But the beauty in another's face (by contrast with sexual attractiveness) is not a quality of immediate recognition; we are aware of false fronts and may be especially suspicious of kinds of beauty that approach too closely to a cultural ideal. "The reciprocal relation of object and subject to each other" requires at least two phases: a look that offers the promise of reciprocity, being an initial event, and a subsequent experience of reciprocity at work. The mutual regard need not be candid; it can

be clouded, intermittent, sly, or sidelong. One proposition is foundational
here: the obscure can be only passingly beautiful, whereas the enigmatic can
be inexhaustibly beautiful (this is so of visual art also, but the case would
be more difficult to make). And this substantially clarifies the question of
productive difficulty. The reason is that in lyric poetry the enigmatic is a
condition of language's event; whereas the obscure contrives an external cov-
ering and, because it modifies the art object's situation, agitates for the object
to be brought to light. It pimps for an idea. The obscure solicits appreciation
of its situating and of the situatedness of the beholding subject, it courts
the light of reason; obscurity leads to conceptual poetry, having worked
through a calculatedly resistant objectivism, acts of displacement of found
things, the deployment of unstitched collaged materials, and so on. Char-
acteristic of obscurity is its promotion of the rhetoric of questioning: What
does this poem, this artwork, have to say about heteronormativity? Or rep-
resentation? The darkness of the enigmatic by contrast lies in its unfolding,
although the origin of unfolding cannot be identified except as primal void
or uncommunicative core, defying heuristics. This is the dark light of which
the psychoanalyst W. R. Bion writes, and which for Lacan is the Real; what
has hitherto been obscured in light glows in the body of darkness that forms
between the poem and its reader, initiated by the beam of darkness discerned
in the poem. Shall I respond to the poem's dark looks? No, I cannot, not this
"I" I am, unless I can be effaced by its dark looks.

So writing about "The Husband" requires a distinction between the event
of encounter with the poem, necessarily a reconstruction, and a reading of
the poem detached from the temporality of encounter. I knew I was being
looked at. Dark looks are different from glances. They are *meaning* looks
but not necessarily accusatory, even if I might feel accused by the strange and
estranging title "The Husband." "Are you the husband, then? Better come
along with me!" But such guilty thoughts are suspended; indeed, as Bion
admonishes, memory, desire, and understanding must be suspended to meet
the dark look—it may be that aesthetic encounter facilitates what cannot be
achieved by taking thought and willing such suspension. But it is difficult
nonetheless.

I read "The Husband" first on its appearance in *Notre Dame Review*, hav-
ing already decided to teach Brady's work in a London course for Chicago
students and hoping to impress them by persuading the poet to visit the class.
None of this explains why when I read this poem I experienced an upwelling
of uncontainable feeling. What reading produced was a rare but immediately
recognizable embodiment of imaginative thought and feeling that seemed
to occupy my breast not as "my" response but as a being for which my self-
hood had been merely a host, fighting to be released from my body in order
to be united with the aesthetic object/subject. Yes, this is a negative of *Alien*,
where an ecstatic self is given birth. Simultaneously the poem gathers into a
physical presence struggling from the plane of the page. Such a voluminous

condensation has eventuated for me in front of a painting by Roger Hilton or Joan Mitchell, for example, or out of a few seconds of a song.

Nothing I can write is likely to make this description seem anything but disproportionate to "The Husband," because accountancy can never track the conditions for the eventuality of aesthetic experience, any more than meteorology can be spot on in its predictions. This poem storms; it is dark and exhilarating. I cannot show the storm in the light. All I can do is show what might gather into this event radiating from the word *together*—misleadingly, since I am tracking precursors in a poem returned to again and again. However, the evanescence of the aesthetic event is not its definitive attribute; what aesthetic experience offers is exactly a repeatable evanescence—for otherwise its universalizing burden would fail even in my own isolated and atomized time of being. Not only would I be unable to effect a social exchange in an aesthetic claim, but I should also be unable to sustain a sense of my continuous subjectivity. Here a distinction needs to be made in conformity with my suggestion that aesthetic judgment entails two phases. The first phase I have described, but what is repeatable will not be a disturbance in the solar plexus—rather an emanation whose shape is recognized again and again while restaged in a shifting configuration.

What follows will have the quality of bathos because it ex-plains, that is, it takes the fullness of an event and reduces it to a two-dimensional map. It risks abandoning the aesthetic modality of thought and feeling to return to the modality of the good: and why this poem is good would be susceptible to critical accountancy. Here goes, and there comes into view. The impossible ambition will be to return *here*, to the aesthetic encounter.

How could a poem be entitled "The Husband"? The suppression of the possessive, "my husband," "your husband," makes the word *husband* a structuring device, which might be traced back philologically—a husband is one who inhabits a house. Looking at this poem, perhaps the husband is to be found within.

Between its first command, "Inhale," and its last, "Exhale then, do it now," this poem might be an auscultation. Therefore it lasts through one stanza, except that this poem cannot be a stanza, it's a house. It would challenge any breath; the lines are mostly long and becoming longer, and the sentences, extending in regular propulsive syntax, are exceptionally long. Some sentences consist of lines enjambed toward gasps, with a single word at the start of a successor line followed by a comma for breath.

I frequently love Brady's poems for their huge cadence, the feeling that their breaths can include everything, a comprehensive generosity. "Everything" pulls assemblages and miscellanies into billowing containers. This generosity, this sweep, is such that I can accept without anxiety much that I fail to comprehend; the house contains lumber, children's stuff, quite a lot of sex, and syntax blunders through it all without being too concerned whether anything is in its right place. I have to work quite hard to settle the meaning of the first six lines if I want to, and the phrase "demand / fostered by infusion of its negatives" is a dodgy moment threatening a deployment of the important and political-sounding rhetoric familiar in recent British dissident poetry. (Brady is American but lives in London and has strong and tense relations with so-called "Cambridge" and "Sussex" poets and poetry.) The subsequent reference to "that anxiety" attending the possibility of having children or another major decision in life can also reflect on the full stop and pause following the rhetorical flourish and the succeeding half-line "Never to feel"; as though to clamber out of this house on such a ladder of highfalutin abstractions might escape a mess at the expense of the death of the heart. But really I have only the foggiest idea of what "demand / fostered by infusion of its negatives" means beyond the proposition that the urgency of desire is renewed by the oppressive evidence of lack, along with a suggestion that the envisioning of human futures relies on capture in visual art and photography (so by extension any fixed destiny) that oppresses the living ("all screwed into / the particular faces").

What does *dry* signify in line 2? After the poem has been read once, the adjective begins shifting toward "warm and dry," although first reading might render *dry* as "meager" or "unproductive"; the first sentence of the poem, running through six lines, feels like a wobble stabilizing into attributable meaning but not quite. These lines track an emergence rather than reporting a meaning arrived at before the poem's composition or delimiting a zone for paratactical play. I don't find that repeated readings make clearer sense; what is the second *never* doing syntactically? The opening phrase, "Never to die happier," cues the passage's disorientating effect: "never to die happy" would offer a bleak, unambiguous negative, but the comparative could imply that things are as good now as they ever will be. Strong affirmation is counterbalanced, though, by the phrase's negative template. The second sentence sustains this strong version of ambiguity up to the semicolon; does *tip* indicate a mess, as in "left the room a tip," or a precise application through "the decorator's tip," as of grouting or anaglyptic, or of cake frosting? And might "the decorator's tip" propose also, not to put too fine a point on it, the husband's penis? *Tip* and *ripples* hint at *nipples*, and the following lines are unmistakably sexy even before interpretation chases them down. "Never to ask / for anything less"; is what is asked for here quirky, trivial, modest, extravagant, or teasingly suggestive of female sexual pleasure, that particular "box of matches"? But after the semicolon everything changes; sex becomes domestic.

The poem then has already swung from its first enigmatic emergence to a sexual preparation for domestic life in what will become "the safe house"; asking whether such safety, supported by others' more expensive credit, might be criminal. At this point an affinity with Denise Riley's poems of domestic life appears, although Riley's poems are more continuously ambivalent, catching the writing and comprised and discomposed self within a complicated setting and syntax. Such an achievement is continuously perilous, and next to Riley's highly strung high-wires, Brady's poem might seem too accepting of compromise. The rhetoric of both poets modifies the meditative early Prynne style of *The White Stones* drawing on the Coleridge of the conversation poems; but Prynne's domestic settings feel symbolic and tendentious, whereas Riley and Brady regender their spaces, with the poet more responsive than appropriative. Characteristically Riley is alone with her troubled self while Brady accepts her situation within a "we," such that the strange and distancing locutions of *the husband* and *the infants* are absorbed into the *we* that follows the injunction *notice* halfway down the first page. *Notice* here marks a shift from dissociated consciousness to social consciousness and prepares for this strongly marked first *we*. The definitive article will now migrate decisively to "the house."

The journey of this poem leads from an unstable opening with no defined pronouns, no habitable space, to a single "I" relinquishing separate selfhood, to a "we" performed as a voluntary association, a marriage. And this is a "we" that fills a reader's experience of the poem. The poem has built to something that might be received, from never/none, to one, to some, to all. I am glad there is no queasiness or apology for happiness here, once arrived at. It would, given Brady's other writing, have been tempting to apologize for a house "paid for." The financial undergirding of professional class home ownership in London is specified and its politics noticed, "the credit monsters relying / all on each other eating some and paying some others," but nevertheless this poem presents marriage and family life as a wager from which the reservations and self-consciousness of the "I" must be kept distinct. The paid-for house holds the husband, by now "the couple," who are "holding the child up, the look out." That's their lookout, if also their criminal enterprise, guarding the stash. It's the house's lookout and the poem's too, although all looking out "is bound in weather."

By now something extraordinary happens to the negative. No longer "screwed into / the particular faces," the negative can be acknowledged as elicited. From where? The negative image of child raising and domesticity, from the mortgaged bourgeois "safe house"? From negative equity? The ghostly white negative impressing its series of "gelatine prints" returns as the aspiration of the couple, the child, and the house filled with things and activity, "blinding in its white heat against the irradiated night." At the ecstatic moment of fidelity to the imagined, "do you hear a noise?" Yes, but the noise does not interrupt a state of happiness, where blinding can be contained within the "bound." This poem might be retitled "Within Bounds" so long as it is understood that binding (based in iambic pentameters, the rhythm of joined speech) makes such ecstasy repeatable. And that is what the poem discovers: "let's do this, together. Look, there. Hear it? There. Exhale then, do it now." No intelligent lyric poem can avoid such reflexivity—what matters is whether the reflexivity is immanent or external, detached, a function of obscurity staging its knowingness. This enigmatic poem makes a wager on the repeatable evanescence of ecstatic love within marriage, insisting that the boundness/boundedness of marriage and the assembly of a family home are not inimical to ecstatic love within safety and happiness. It can be read, if you like, as an evidentiary riposte to the tendency of younger British (mainly male) poets to go to extremes in yoking ecstatic love to transgression and to trade in contempt for the tenured and the mortgaged, the bound. Their challenge is invited by Brady's poem and by any aesthetic claim for it since this poem embodies a corresponding claim for lyric poetry—to be bound is to embrace and to be embraced in language's physicality, and this is a precondition for aesthetic joy and for social happiness.

This is not a poem that flaunts difficulty. Its lexicon is everyday and domestic, eschewing theoretical and technical language except what passes among the London bourgeoisie. I have argued that difficulty in aesthetic judgment is generic to contemporary lyric poetry (how dare you judge my feelings? or my way of expressing them?); Brady's poem also deals with difficult matter, for marital intimacy and motherhood are expressed publicly against the ideological grain and against a scarcely contained panic squeezing out commas. The need for containment against internal disorder and external surveillance is met by the poem's prosody and contracting and accommodating syntax, as it is by marriage. This is not a compromise but a necessity for psychic survival.

This quick play of a spotlight over a few features of "The Husband" might still seem to leave quite a stretch between Bion's dark light and Brady's domestic bliss in Hackney. But the negative dialectics of this poem enact what Bion describes in theory. It is only once desire, with its violent stamp on the face of the present, is abandoned that its negative image can stand forth from a bound mess as the sponsor of the real. Returning to the poem now, I think it enviably grown up. It is able to contain apprehensiveness, frightening part-objects like "subtracting monkeys," compromise in the present for the sake of the future, a rare celebration of ordinary happiness, some incomprehensibility, all within a contested unity that is a song, inhaling, exhaling, gasping, breathing together. That's what a lyric poem can do when it's not primping itself or denying itself. It's quite an art to restore the aura to marriage and to have imparted prosodically to the hollow language of physical and spiritual self-improvement the affective power of the poem's ending. The difficult conflict the poem must manage on the level of content is audible to the last exhalation in its virtuoso tonal management.

Note

1. Friedrich Hölderlin, "Being Judgement Possibility," in *Classic and Romantic German Aesthetics*, ed. J. M. Bernstein (Cambridge: Cambridge University Press, 2003), 191–92, esp. 192.

AARON KUNIN

First

Mother made me by removing
Her luminous beauty from one
Area of "her" body. Earth
Where "her" foot fell
Cooled and hardened around the dent.
Impression left

"By" a fingernail in "the" skin
"Of" an apple. I never grew
But more "and" "more" "of" "the" beauties
She had "in" "me"
Dwindled. Teeth seeming to lengthen
Showing their roots

As "the" gums recede. Just "a" piece
"Of" "mother" with all "her" treasures
Kept back. On my tongue, "the" edge "of"
"An" unpleasant
Flavor that "I" instinctively
Knew "to" be death.

"A" proud "and" overprotective
Parent "of" "the" "one" thing "she had"
Invented, "she" rather enjoyed
Seeing "her" blood
Go about "in" another shape
"My" sweet "mother."

"Proud" "of" "all" "that" "I" "kept" hidden
Deeply moved, or merely chewing
"I" learned early "to" hear "the" sound
"Of" coughing "with"
Unconcern. "Merely" "a" cut through
Which you may see

"A" short distance into "her" face
"And" that's "her" mouth. Uniformly
Silver, "a" cold color, "in" hair
Green eyes blanched gray

"Where" "I learned" "to" seek happiness
"In" "a" woman's

Glance. "She" burned "through" "the" "earth" when "she"
Divided "her" store "of" "beauties"
"From" "her" substance, "the" remainder
Froze, "and" "she" "froze"
"The" remover. "As" alike "as"
"One" "of the" halves

"Of an apple" "to" "the" other
Could two faces make "a" third "face"
"By" friction "of" "one" "mouth" against
"Another," "could"
"One" "face" split "into" "two" copies
"Of" itself "and"

"I" "their" mirror, now told apart
"By" temperature, "or" "the" notch
"In" "the" ear, "or" "just" "by" pointing?
"Of" "luminous
Beauty," "her" defining feature
Absent "from" your

Composition, "a" seemingly
Casual mention. "I" looked up
"From" "a" fiery outline, "her
Face" held warring
Energies "in" check, sovereign
"And" ecstatic.

"I" would have "enjoyed" saying "that"
"My" forehead was hotter than "her"
Iron, "but," truthfully, "I" guess
"It" wasn't, since
"The" brand "left" "a" visible scar.
"I" love women.

Chapter 6

✦

The Science of Creation:
On Aaron Kunin's "First"

Michael W. Clune

We should distinguish difficulty from obscurity in poetry. The latter refers to a lyric substance that repels understanding. Trying to understand is the wrong orientation to such poems. Daniel Tiffany, in *Infidel Poetics*, has taught us a more rewarding mode of attunement to the curious properties of the incorrigibly obscure text.[1] The verbal circuits of poetic difficulty, on the other hand, describe a winding path to understanding. There are many reasons why a poet might choose to tell the truth slant, but I think there are two strong ones.

The first, or Shklovskian, motive is to reproduce in the artwork the cognitive labor of encountering a familiar image or situation as if for the first time.[2] If he wished to communicate the identity of the emotion, object, or relation he has in mind, the poet might have spoken simply. Difficulty is added as the aesthetic dimension of the poem. *Aesthetic* here signifies the force that returns perception automated by habit to the dawning intensity characteristic of the experience of a new thing. The theory underlying this method is sound. We know from Kant, from neuroscience, and from our own experience that the process of assembling the elements of a new image into a novel whole is hard and that we experience this difficulty as heightened consciousness, intensified perception.[3]

Yet we might well be suspicious of poetic efforts to reproduce the encounter with a new thing by generating challenging verbal representations of familiar things. Part of the problem is that, once one makes difficulty an aesthetic quality, one risks obliterating the distinctions that make some difficult poems magically effective and other difficult poems utterly dull. We lack a good theory of these crucial distinctions. Shklovsky's intuitive judgment seems, like that of most of us, to be in advance of his critical capacity on this score. The absence of such a theory means that different judgments of difficult poems are apt to be dismissed as merely subjective expressions of taste or opinion. Or even worse, difficulty itself comes to stand as an emblem of poetic art. The calculation of a sufficient degree of difficulty replaces the judgment of a given difficult poem's success at reviving the sensorium. At this point the artistic motivation and justification for difficulty has been lost. When this happens to a poetic culture, the entire poetic enterprise is put at risk. Neither Shklovsky nor Kant but Bourdieu becomes the appropriate theorist of an artistic culture that has decayed to the status of a social group.[4]

The varieties of Shklovskian defamiliarization do not exhaust the field of difficult poems. The second strong motive for poetic difficulty is that the poet wishes to communicate an idea or experience that is intrinsically hard to understand. I take Aaron Kunin's "First" as an example of this second kind of difficulty. Shklovsky writes about poems that try to make you see familiar things as if for the first time. Kunin creates a poem that shows us what it is like to come into the world for the first time. The difficulty in the first case is designed to delay the moment when one recognizes the contours of a known event. The difficulty in the second case lies in the effort to communicate the contours of an unknown event. Kunin's difficulty, in other words, consists in placing pressure on familiar terms in an effort to describe an unfamiliar state of affairs. It is the difficulty of an earnest effort to communicate something new. The difference can appear subtle, but it has deep roots and far-reaching implications for the poem's meaning and significance. The successful Shklovskian poem results in intensified experience; the successful poem of the second kind results in new knowledge. Unlike in Shkolvskian defamiliarization, difficulty for Kunin is not pursued for the sake of aesthetic effects difficulty can deliver, but simply because the circuitous route is the most direct route to a difficult knowledge.

We can begin to appreciate the necessity of "First"'s difficulty by putting ourselves in the poet's place and imaginatively reconstructing the decisions that led to the route which lies open before us. Consider the difficulties of writing an original poem, a poem of origins. Perhaps the fundamental resource of lyric poetry—experience—is here foreclosed. Birth and early growth are opaque to our experience, consciousness, memory. No one remembers his or her own birth. The poem's subject absolutely resists the most obvious poetic resource. Further, the poet chooses to deny himself the most obvious recourse for humans faced with the task of describing situations for which experience is inadequate. This is the technique of the third person or, more properly, the *techniques* of the third person. Denied the multiform, ready-to-be-shaped matter of personal experience, the poet might instead have chosen to work with what might appear to *anyone* in the scene of his birth. He might have chosen to see in his birth what *one* might see. His choice not to do so isn't an aesthetic choice, in Shklovsky's sense, but a choice determined by the nature of the knowledge of birth he wishes to express. To see why, we must explore the road he didn't take a little further.

There are two ways of voicing this third-personal *one*. One might express the recognitions of the culture. If one believed in the essential rightness of our culture's representations of birth, one would face the task of fashioning a different kind of poetic defamiliarization, one that aims not at restoring perceptual intensity but at restoring the conceptual force, the insight that lies buried beneath cliché. Take the cultural vocabulary of birth—*miracle, innocence, future*—and subject it to rearrangement, derangement, deconstruction. Or fashion an entirely new vocabulary to communicate the truth these words have become powerless to indicate.

But perhaps one doesn't, after all, feel compelled by our culture's understanding of birth, or by its half-secularized Judeo-Christian ethos. One can see in other than cultural terms. Alternately, the *one* might express the scientific method, which eschews cultural recognitions to present what one might call an ultimately third-personal perspective. The poet might have drawn upon the neutral vocabulary of the organic logic of birth. Given the unparalleled prestige of science as the discourse of knowledge, when one wants today to know how one came into the world, this is the language one is apt to turn to.

"First" eschews this method, not, in my view, because the poet retains a Keatsian distaste for how science "unweaves the rainbow." This poem has nothing against science. It is simply that, in the case of birth, the third-personal perspective indicates *the wrong science*. Not biology, the poem suggests, but physics and geology are the proper sciences of one's *own* birth, of the birth of the poet.

> Earth
> Where "her" foot fell
> Cooled and hardened around the dent.
> Impression left
>
> "By" a fingernail in "the" skin
>   "Of" an apple.

Birth is a process of "earth" "cooling and hardening." The complex and invisible informational dynamics of heredity by which the mother's body shapes the son's are here replaced by the brute logic of "impression." A part of the mother's body stamps itself onto another substance. At another point, the processes of birth are described in terms of the chemical reactions of "burning" and "freezing."

> "She" burned "through" "the" "earth" when "she"
> Divided "her" store "of" "beauties"
> "From" "her" substance, "the" remainder
> Froze, "and" "she" "froze"
> "The" remover.

"First" rigorously adheres to a perspective from which strangely inorganic qualities of the body become manifest. This perspective is that of the poem's first person. It sees something that one doesn't see; it knows something one doesn't know. How does it see this? How does it know it? We can summarize

the preceding discussion and penetrate more deeply into this poem's diffi-
culty by formulating the key question it raises thus: What is the source of
the knowledge possessed by the first person when that knowledge is not of
experience?

The fact that the poem's knowledge of birth is delivered through a first-
personal, lyric voice implies that the source of this knowledge is other than
the sources available to the third person, to *the one*. And this implication can
be quickly confirmed by comparing the facts of life in the poem with the facts
of life as understood outside the poem. Birth, for example, is here rendered
as a process in which the body of the mother "recedes" from the body of the
baby. The mother "removes" her body from that of the baby.

But even this strange paraphrase dulls the strangeness of the poem's lan-
guage. The challenge here is to minimize the interference of what "one"
knows when trying to ascertain what the poetic "I" knows. Kunin's criticism,
signally among contemporary writing, has demonstrated how. Most relevant
in this context is his article on Shakespeare's sonnets, where he patiently
describes the counterintuitive logic of "Shakespeare's Preservation Fantasy."[5]
Attending as no one before him to the sonnets' language, Kunin traces Shake-
speare's several strategies for achieving the preservation of the young man's
beautiful face. Suspending his sense of how sexual reproduction works in the
world, Kunin shows us how, in the poetic space of Shakespeare's sequence,
the young man's sexual organs—and his reproductive power—appear to be
located in his face. Let's try to read Kunin's own poetic account of reproduc-
tion with the same willingness to attend to the strangeness of poetic logic he
displays in his criticism.

> Mother made me by removing
> Her luminous beauty from one
> Area of "her" body.

What recedes when the child is created is not the mother's body but her
beauty. Furthermore, the moment of birth doesn't appear to figure especially
prominently in this recession. "Mother made me." This making is a process
that begins at a moment which might correspond to what one calls concep-
tion and that terminates at the very edge of the child's body, where he tastes
"death."

This recession isn't the only account of the poet's making in the poem.
Unlike the confidence of the initial assertion, that "I" was made by a process
of receding beauty, this second account is speculative, though its speculation
appears rooted in the facial sex Kunin discovers in Shakespeare.

> Could two faces make "a" third "face"
> "By" friction "of" "one" "mouth" against
> "Another"?

Both accounts—the confident and the speculative—stress the possibility of treating biological facts purely in terms of physical dynamics. We noted this displacement at the outset of our investigation. It constitutes the difference between the poem's lyric account of making a person and third-personal, nonlyric accounts. We might therefore further refine our question about the source of the poem's knowledge by asking *why* physical terms are preferred to biological terms.

Imagine the poet, cut off from the resource of personal experience, facing the task of writing an account of his creation. Perhaps the most primitive choice available to him is the choice of the relevant science for describing the creation of the self. And perhaps this choice or revelation comes *before* the decision to write the poem in the first person. Perhaps this choice or revelation dictates the latter decision. I am not the product of biological reproduction, we might imagine the poet realizing. But to write an account of birth in terms of physical dynamics, one can only write in the first person.

What in the way the self looks back upon his creation leads him to reject the common biological account? Why is physics better than biology? *From what perspective* is physics better than biology? The answer may give us a clue as to the nature and source of the poem's knowledge.

The problem is that physics is better than biology from almost every perspective. It's better from a scientific perspective. Biology is the least intuitive of the sciences, the most complex, the latest. No one—other than perhaps H.P. Lovecraft—imagines that the final grand theory of everything will be biological in nature. Philosophers of science describe physics as a more fundamental science than biology.[6] Our intuition is that biology has an ultimately physical origin. But all our efforts to show how biology might emerge from physical or chemical processes are baffled by our incapacity thus far to expand our sample size to two from one. We have no other instance of life than the matrix in which we were born, here, on this planet. Until we discover or invent a second instance of life arising, biology will remain, from a scientific perspective, suspended in air. We can enumerate its irreducible complexities as it revolves, but we can't yet bring it to ground.

Biology is even worse from an aesthetic perspective. The myths of every culture offer a rich trove of efforts to redescribe birth as nonbiological. Beings born from skulls. Beings born from rocks. Biology is also bad from a religious perspective, for reasons similar to the reasons that place it in bad odor scientifically: Where does it start? How does the first birth happen? We might, in the description of creation as a physical process nonetheless intended and directed by the mother, see in "First" a fusion of religious and scientific antipathies toward biology. There must, so goes the religious as well as the scientific intuition, be a nonbiological origin for biology.

Interestingly, the most notable feature of Kunin's form in the book containing "First"—his convention of placing quotation marks around each repetition of a word—bears a strange resemblance to physical speculations about the origins of biology. Daniel Dennett, for instance, argued in *Darwin's Dangerous Idea* that the basic concept of modern biology is the idea of design in the absence of a designer.[7] He understood, however, that for its ground this concept must go beyond—or before—biology. Therefore, toward the end of the book, he offers a startling thought experiment about how the forces of life might have originated through a blind physical process that resulted in the accretion of certain proto-biological forms over time. Rigorously pursued, biology's central idea turns out to be not a biological idea after all, but a physical idea.

I detect in the poem's formal convention a certain resemblance to this bootstrapping, this accretion of order through a blind tendency of certain forms to adhere to other forms. The curious "mechanical" patterning of the poem's latter stanzas by the marks of repetition thus seem to respond to a physical, or geological, logic. It may be best not to push this analogy too far, in that the form's thematic resonance depends on the context established by this *particular* poem, while the convention is deployed across the entire volume of *Cold Genius*. Then again, wouldn't "Cold Genius" be a good name for the slow, blind watchmaker of biology, who eventually turns out to be the glacial artificer of physics?

In any case, the urge to replace biology with something else isn't exhausted by religion, science, or aesthetics. Biology is also objectionable on legal grounds, in the difficulty, for example, of determining a moment when the difference of mother and fetus may be said to be definitively established. Faced with this weakness, people often adopt aesthetic or physical or religious perspectives. The fetus is a person when it's moving. The fetus is a person when it looks like a person. The fetus is and has always been a person.

In short, there are too many reasons to prefer physics over biology to make this preference a useful device for specifying the source of the poem's nonbiological knowledge of birth. So let's begin from the other end. Instead of asking where the poem's knowledge comes from, we will ask what this knowledge enables.

"I love women."

The poem's first-personal knowledge of birth, of the process of his creation, and of the nature of the mother enables him to love women. This is how the poem ends, and the rest of the poem allows it to end this way.

What kind of knowledge will enable a man to love a woman? On what basis can this love be secured? The answer: on the basis of knowledge of one's birth as a physical process. One can love a woman on the basis of realizing that one's own body is the space from which the mother's luminous beauty has receded.

So now we have at last an answer. But we may not yet understand the question that elicits this answer. We may wonder why it is difficult for a man to love a woman. It isn't difficult in practice, as the history of the world makes abundantly evident. It isn't, in other words, difficult for a man to love a woman *for biological reasons*.

But for the one who speaks, the one who thinks, the one who awakes within a poem and says "I," the love of a man for a woman is difficult. Heterosexuality's counterintuitive nature is the corollary of biology's counterintuitive nature. Heterosexuality is less intuitive than homosexuality, *in the same way* that biology is less intuitive than physics. It makes less sense. Plato understood this. But if Plato had access to the poem's science, if Plato knew the poem's description of the creation of man through the recession of the mother's beauty, he might be able to glimpse a flicker of that impossible thing: *philosophical heterosexuality.*

Three final notes:

1. The poem, insofar as it rationalizes female-male heterosexuality, rationalizes by the same logic (love of the mother) female-female homosexuality.

2. The poem leaves unspecified the form the achieved desire of the final line will take. But I think we know that the form of gratified desire will be inassimilable to the postures of biological sexuality. The simplest and most obvious way to imagine the form the poet's love will take is to examine the actual form of the poem. The great poem, as the ancients understood, gives birth to a future.[8]

3. Our discussion provides us with an initial way of characterizing the aesthetic quality of the class of difficult poems exemplified by Kunin's "First." Shklovskian defamiliarization is aesthetic only provisionally. Once one defines art as, in the language of his famous essay, "device," one has defined art in terms of a function, an effect. Nothing restricts this function to art in principle. And in fact, as I've argued elsewhere, among the primary legacies of Shklovskian defamiliarization are works that imagine more effective, nonartistic technologies for achieving something like permanent defamiliarization. Similarly, once one defines art as knowledge, as we have done here, one must ask: Does anything make this knowledge intrinsically aesthetic? Here again, I am tempted to suggest that the aesthetic quality of this knowledge is provisional and lies in the inadequacy of existing discourses when faced with what the poet knows about the relation between birth and love. This is why, for all truly difficult poems of the type exemplified by Kunin, the operation of "applying" existing theory to dispel difficulty is the worst crime a critic can commit. The true difficulty lies not in substituting other terms for the poem's own but in taking what the poem says at face value.

Notes

1. Daniel Tiffany, *Infidel Poetics* (Chicago: University of Chicago Press, 2009).

2. Viktor Shklovsky, "Art as Device," in *Theory of Prose*. Trans. Benjamin Sher (Champaign, Ill.: Dalkey Archive Press, 1991 [1929]).

3. See my *Writing against Time* (Stanford, Calif.: Stanford University Press, 2013), 1–55.

4. Pierre Bourdieu, *Distinction: A Social Critique of the Judgment of Taste* (Cambridge, Mass.: Harvard University Press, 1984).

5. Aaron Kunin, "Shakespeare's Preservation Fantasy," *PMLA* 124, no. 1 (Jan 2009): 92–106.

6. A good, brief overview of the relevant issues is found in Samir Okasha's *Philosophy of Science: A Very Short Introduction* (Oxford: Oxford University Press, 2002).

7. Daniel Dennett, *Darwin's Dangerous Idea* (New York: Simon and Schuster, 1996).

8. Two works that have been especially important to both Kunin and myself on this topic are Hannah Arendt's *The Human Condition* (Chicago: University of Chicago Press, 1998), and Allen Grossman's *The Sighted Singer* (Baltimore, Md.: Johns Hopkins University Press, 1991).

Part Two

Troubled Affects

THE PLIGHTS OF LYRIC

JULIANA SPAHR

from "switching"

In a room we sit around a table.

The table is dark wood.

It has thick legs.

It is a space for gathering with a
boundary of wood.

•

In another room, in a hotel room,
we hurriedly undress.

•

We use the table as a barrier and
we rest our things on it.

We value the table as decorum.

A table that is wood, that is hard.

•

A bed is soft and we, the two
people in the hotel room, run our
hands over each other's bodies
while reclined upon it.

We like the feel of each other's
bodies.

This is pleasure.

This is also speaking.

•

We in the room with the table
speak over the table.

We in the room with the table
gesture.

We debate how to want action.

We point.

We speak of uninvested discourse.

We confess.

We trouble.

We speak to each other in
elaborate patterns of sentences.

We are similar to each other. We
look like each other. We understand
each other even in argument.

•

We who come together with
some difficulty or we who
haven't seen each other for some
time thus desire each other all the
more on the bed in the hotel room.

This desire takes the form of one
person having one leg on one
person's shoulder and the other
leg stretched out and twined
around the other person, moving
back and forth.

•

We gather at the table to hear
opinions.

We gather at the table because we
are uncertain about what is right.

The table is where we go to
speak of uncertainty.

We gather to discuss.

We gather to pass and shuffle
papers.

We gather to use words like ethical re-
sponsibility.

We gather to advocate silence
on issues as we speak out on certain
others.

We gather to wait.

We gather to speak of our own
difficult history.

We gather to read and discuss.

We gather to puzzle.

We gather because we are similar.

We sway and are swayed.

We long for fluency.

We confess.

We trouble.

We speak again of ethical
responsibility.

Or again of uninvested discourse.

We claim rationality.

We claim what is useful or what
is not useful.

We learn.

We exchange.

This is thinking in exchange.

The love of wisdom.

Chapter 7

On Spahr's Poem "switching"

Siobhan Phillips

In 2002 Juliana Spahr coedited an anthology subtitled *Where Lyric Meets Language*. At that time Spahr suspected what now seems true, that the lyric/language opposition is impossible to maintain. It seemed helpful, in the late twentieth and early twenty-first centuries, for putting some limits on the labor of reading poetry. If one kind of poem cares about subjectivity and one kind of poem cares about signification, if one expresses and one investigates, if one has a voice and one has a system—or if one has the absence of the voice and one has the impossibility of a system—then we know *how* each kind of poem is supposed to be difficult. The difficult poem uncovers a fractured, perhaps hidden subjectivity. Or the difficult poem mines unstable, perhaps contradictory semantic codes. These alternatives are useful.

They are also outdated. Lyric/language could be another test of fealty to Stevens or Pound. Another person/program alternative, another reinscription of alienation and systematization, damaged consciousness and mass culture; another paradigm that makes the modern or modernist bargain of defending or reviling a more and more fictional conception of privacy in order to counter or refashion a more and more inescapable systematization of publicity. (That is to say: another capitulation to the logic, ultimately, of confessionalism and the dead end it represented.)

We're left wanting a label for poems that do none of the above—some of which seem the most interesting, and the most valuable, of our current century. Poems that would "retreat from individualism and idiosyncrasy by pointing to heady and unexpected yet intimate pluralisms . . . that help [one] to place [oneself] as part of a larger, connective culture . . . that comment on community and that move lyric away from individualism to shared, connective spaces . . . that reveal how our private intimacies have public obligations and ramifications, how intimacy has a social bond with shared meaning."[1] The difficulty taken up by such poems wouldn't come from the struggle to represent an individual or negotiate an ideology. It would come, rather, from the effort to realize an intimacy—that "social bond with shared meaning."

And then, from concomitant difficulties: how *does* private intimacy become public obligation? How *does* language "reveal" such becoming?

The quotations in the paragraph above are from Spahr's 2002 introduction. Her difficulties with established terms, her desire for a different difficulty than they admit, prepare for the departures and difficulties in her own work.

The poem "switching," from *Fuck You-Aloha-I Love You* (2001) is a good one with which to particularize her statements because the poem seems so simple. Its words are mostly plain and its syntax mostly methodical. "In a room we sit around a table," the poem begins. "The table is dark wood. / It has thick legs. / It is a space for gathering with a boundary of wood." Section break. Next page: "In another room, in a hotel room, we hurriedly undress."[2] Mimetic, objective, these lines avoid both the feeling that would be associated with lyricism and the formal disjunction that would be associated with Language poetry. They don't intend to make us feel or think so much as (eventually) act. The lines of "switching" only begin to seem complicated, in fact, when the poem brings up the most important action of all: "The problem is how to we all together now."[3] "switching" is an instruction manual for a tricky sociality.

Spahr's poetry is plain about these sorts of ambitions. It is anti-Kantian, anti-*Kritik*. In her critical monograph, *Everybody's Autonomy*, she professes openly "a defense of literature . . . in an age of critique."[4] She looks to scholars who "turn away from a work's 'literariness' and towards its collective resonances and uses."[5] *Everybody's Autonomy* analyzes works of poetry by Gertrude Stein, Lyn Hejinian, Bruce Andrews, Harryette Mullen, and Theresa Hak Kyung Cha, but it's not aestheticist autonomy she's after: rather, she seeks autonomy as a "social, political, and cultural" right.[6] Spahr's study is interested in certain kinds of writing that allow or elicit certain kinds of poetic reading—and therefore, by her logic, support and encourage certain kinds of human beings.

How do these two—the reading and the being—connect? It's not entirely clear. *Everybody's Autonomy* first defends texts that, through indeterminacy, allow readerly agency. It then defends readings that produce community. It doesn't explain how the latter results from the former. Demotion of writerly authority—allowing readers to be cocreators—might encourage a sense of equality between writer and reader, but that may or may not manifest as a sense of connection. The reverse seems just as likely. Also the imperative to join the author in a creative project doesn't mean an imperative, necessarily, to join other readers in the same creative project. In fact, the *autonomy* in the title of Spahr's study seems to suggest an individual endeavor of meaning making. Spahr is careful to reject the American ideology of "rugged individualism"[7]—and uses *everybody's* to mitigate the suggestion. But *everybody's* doesn't necessarily do so. It could just as easily universalize free agency. A word like *everybody* is the other side of the coin—a buffalo nickel, perhaps—of the American liberal ideology in a word like *autonomy*. It does not change the currency.

Everybody's Autonomy wants to change the currency. It wants a "semi-autonomy rooted in the community."[8] It wants to engender fellow feeling among small groups of specific people. The book's final pages, in which Spahr describes that aim, join the final paragraphs of her introduction to the anthology—published the following year—in their hunger for "social bonds." My cavil over an inaccurate title seems unproductive, therefore. Especially as Spahr clearly picked her phrase to echo Stein's *Everybody's Autobiography*. And yet that echo is itself clarifying in its obliquities. Stein's art assumes an opposition of individual and collective—"myself and strangers."[9] Stein's very modernist alternation between elitism and populism is another species of the modernist dichotomies of one and many, private and public. Spahr's art resists that opposition. Her work shows the push-pull struggle of contemporary verse against influential modernist forebears. Spahr's poetry obsesses over an intimacy that rarely bothers Stein. The difficulty of Spahr's verse lies, first, in her struggle to evade an outdated—for Spahr's purposes—paradigm.

This struggle is clear in "switching." (Though *Fuck You-Aloha-I Love You* appeared in the same year as *Everybody's Autonomy*, the latter book was begun earlier.) Spahr's poem begins with descriptions of the two opening settings—the first room, where we "gather . . . to hear opinions," where we push papers and make decisions, a place of "ethical responsibility," "uninvested discourse," and "rationality"; and the second room, where bodies touch and twist and interpenetrate, where if "this is also speaking," as Spahr says, the discourse is invested and un-rational.[10] The poem aims to put these two rooms together and make them indistinguishable. In the climactic section, Spahr asks "how to get we here then together in the same room . . . [h]ow to speak around a table as if one leg is on one shoulder and then the other is stretched out or twined around the other person."[11] How to put together, she writes finally and starkly, "the public table thinking" and "the private bed thinking."[12] No answer is forthcoming. No coincidence of consultation and coitus, boardroom and bedroom—public and private—seems possible. Thus the "switching" of the title. Moving between these two realms is a second-best alternative to abolishing their difference. Navigating a modernist poetics is a second-best alternative to moving beyond them. "We switch. We switch from table to bed," the work concludes. ". . . So it is switching."[13]

With this trajectory, "switching" revises both points of *Everybody's Autonomy*. The poem wants connection but understands that connection means overcoming the division between auto- and omni-, between one and everyone. Or rather, "switching" knows that connection means redefining what one and everyone are. The group claimed in these rooms and this poem is a particular one—and, it seems, a problem. For "switching" wants indeterminacy too. But it provides indeterminacy not as a grant to the reader, a license to cocreate, so much as a mimetic admission, an acknowledgment of unease. Spahr does this with her grave deployment of the first person plural, evident as soon as those opening sections, where "we sit around" a table and "we undress" near a bed.

Just for contrast, consider the opening of a different work and space, Stein's "Rooms" from *Tender Buttons*, which advises us to "act so that there is no use in a centre. A wide action is not a width. A preparation is given to the ones preparing. They do not eat who mention silver and sweet."[14] Stein's work examines the kind of people who do certain things, with categories of action and agent that the speaker might analyze; her sentences speak of *they*. Spahr's work worries over a group of people to which the speaker belongs, and for which she/he is responsible; her sentences attempt more and less stable versions of "we." They do so again and again in the sections that directly follow: "We like the feel of each other's bodies. . . . We debate how to want action. / We point. . . . We speak to each other in elaborate patterns of sentences."[15] Whereas *Buttons* asks readers to recognize familiar surroundings in what seem like difficult clauses, "switching" asks readers to perceive the difficulty in what seems like familiar embodiment.

And then to do something about it. To address the problems of "we," wherever we are.

Where should we be? *Fuck You-Aloha-I Love You*, written out of Spahr's time in Hawai'i in the late 1990s and early 2000s, isn't sure. The first poem is "localism or t/here," and the poem preceding "switching," called "gathering: palolo stream," wonders how "a place allows certain things and certain of we of a specific place have certain rights."[16] The grammatical solecism in "certain of we," which replaces what should be the object of a preposition with a nominative form, calls attention to the complementary subjection of a "certain" group denied access to locations necessary for traditional Hawai'ian cultural practices. Spahr suggests that we cannot identify or understand the groups to which we belong unless we understand also the spaces that we occupy (or not)—and vice versa. Ten years later, in 2011's *Well Then There Now*, Spahr begins with the same grammatical-global worry about a situated first person plural, using linguistic improprieties to make her anxiety plain. "Some of We and the Land That Was Never Ours," an updated, cosmopolitan reversal of Frost's "The Gift Outright," asks "what it means to settle. What means it arrangement. To we are all in this world together."[17] The last of these sentences turns its pronoun into an intransitive verb, a way of being. *Well Then*, which begins each of its poems with a latitude and longitude, wants to understand the globe as the largest possible locality. It wants salvation through the largest possible application of "we . . . together."

That togetherness, that social bond: as in her introduction, Spahr here seeks a substitute for—a remaking of—both public and private life. She remains unsatisfied with the second-wave feminist mantra to recognize personal as political.[18] For her, both terms are unsatisfactory. "I tried to think some about public and private in this essay," Spahr writes in a piece from

Well Then There Now called "2199 Kalia Road." "But I could come up with nothing profound to say about it."[19] The profundity would instead be a reorganized "we" that obviates a need for "switching." Or a reorganized "you," obviating the same, which emerges in *This Connection of Everyone with Lungs*, a post-9/11 collection. Here, Spahr musters global togetherness with an encompassing call: "Beloveds, my desire is to hunker down and lie low, lie with yous in beds and bowers, lie with yous in resistance to the alone, lie with yous night after night."[20] The repetition of "beloveds" and "yous" throughout the book would manifest the connection it desires.

The desire is not Steinian. The near comparison for Spahr's pronoun usage may be Claudia Rankine, who exploits the ambiguity of "you" in works like *Don't Let Me Be Lonely* and *Citizen* to diagnose the slippage between personal aggression and political oppression. Rankine's twenty-first-century books, both subtitled *An American Lyric*, are as interested as Spahr's in the juxtaposition of public agenda and private voice signaled in that very phrase.[21] But Rankine's pronouns interrogate the connections and disconnections such words assume, whereas Spahr's would realize the combinations that such words make possible. The further and truer comparison for Spahr may be with the *I*s and *you*s of Walt Whitman.[22] Spahr recalls poems like "Sleepers" or "Crossing Brooklyn Ferry" when her "Poem Written from November 30, 2002, to March 27, 2003" poses desire against destruction. "In bed, when I stroke the down on yours cheeks, I stroke also the carrier battle group ships, the guided missile cruisers, and the guided missile destroyers," she writes.[23] The sense of implication here—"I felt I had to think about what I was connected with and what I was complicit with. . . . I had to think about my intimacy with things I would rather not be intimate with"[24]—is a sense of possibility too. We can undo the separations of militarism with the connections of carnality, Spahr wants to believe. When one is "twined around" another person, in the words of "switching," one takes up a political position. We can love war to death.

Can responsible intimacy be a viable politics? *This Connection* doesn't convince itself. "When I reach for yours waist, I reach for bombers, cargo, helicopters, and special operations," Spahr writes,[25] but she knows that her reach may exceed her grasp: "It makes me angry that how we live in our bed—full of connected loving and full of isolated sleep and dreaming also—has no relevance to the rest of the world," she admits. "How can the power of our combination of intimacy and isolation have so little power outside the space of our bed?"[26] Since Keats (and before), poets have striven to connect the fancies of dreaming to the facts of waking reality. Spahr's version wants to make nighttime companionship into a daytime polity. Yet while overcoming Keats's gap between imagination and reality may be a matter of intellectual conflation, an ultimately Nietzschean leap, overcoming Spahr's gap between love and war seems to require a movement from specificity to abstraction, an ultimately Habermasian negotiation. It is crucial to acknowledge, as Spahr's poem does, that "each of those one-hundred and thirty-six people dead by politics' human hands had parents and children with ties so deep that those parents and children feel fractured now."[27] But to posit that awareness as a solution to political murder is to risk a solution that answers power with affect. Spahr's poem is toughest and most poignant when it registers the *lack* of power in intimate association: "We say our bed is part of everyone else's bed even as our bed is denied to others by an elaborate system of fences and passport-checking booths."[28] Here the effort of "switching" haunts a writer who has moved from that poem's sense of hypothetical experimentation to a later work's sense of actual exigencies. The charge to find a new "public table thinking" remains.

Likewise for "private bed thinking." Spahr's other post-9/11 work exemplifies trouble within the very love that Spahr would make global in *This Connection*. *The Transformation* narrates in prose a life much like Spahr's own in the last part of the twentieth century and the early part of the twenty-first: moving from a teaching position in Hawai'i back to New York, experiencing the unsettled allegiances of dislocations, "asking who they wrote with and why."[29] *With* is not an easy preposition. The three artists that form the book's protagonist also form a romantic unit in which "one of them would move from bed to bed; one would be always coupled; one would be single every other night."[30] This type of "switching," not from public to private but *within* different privacies, doesn't break down the personal/political division that Spahr's poetry tries to overcome. Rather, *The Transformation* complicates any "connection" that might do so. In a time of "troubled and pressured pronouns," the triangle of desire at the center of *The Transformation* can't undo the bar between "an us and a them," as Spahr would like, in part because of complications within "us."[31] In fact, *The Transformation* shuns *we* or *I* or *yous* or *beloveds* for the more distant *they* and *them*, and a sense of remove continues in the book's descriptions of Oahu and Manhattan: "the island in the middle of the Pacific" and "an island in the Atlantic" (Washington is "the city where the government that currently occupied the continent was located").[32] This work can get no closer to the relationships and locations that make up our lives. If "switching" asks where and what are "we," *The Transformation* answers that *they* are nowhere. It ends with a description of human bodies, as if this were the only space people can love or touch or claim.

The corporeal is both a solution to the difficulty—how to realize a public/private intimacy—and a possible evasion of it. (It may be relevant to note that concern over bodily movements in "switching" seems to avoid the *linguistic* alternation of a more potentially divisive "code-switching.")[33] When *The Transformation* ends with a description of pumping blood, it joins the invocation of breathing at the opening of *This Connection of Everyone with Lungs* or the bodily "positioning" in "switching." All are physical. A common vulnerability in physicality may be, finally, our common ground. (This echoes Judith Butler in her book *Precarious Life*, even though Spahr distrusts

Butler's work earlier in *This Connection*.) *The Transformation* concludes on just that vulnerability, in fact, and uses it to find commonality. "Pumped through the aortic valves changes. With grief, with worry, with desire, with attachment, with anything and everything, they began listing, inventorying, recognizing in the hope that a catalogue of vulnerability could begin the process of claiming their being human."[34]

A catalogue of vulnerability may be only a clarification of powerlessness. The "transformation" of the title presents something of the same, a moment in which the writers agreed to "falter over pronouns. They agreed to let them undo their speech and language. They pressed themselves upon them and impinged upon them and were impinged upon in ways that were not in their control."[35] The difficulty in these lines is not quite the difficulty of living an ecstatic global "yous." Here, Spahr's protagonists try to live through the failure to realize the "social bond" they desire. This is an intimacy of common desire—and struggle—*for* intimacy. Spahr doesn't know the end of the process that she sets in motion in *The Transformation*.[36] "If they kept writing," she merely hopes, "others might point them to answers."[37]

Back to "switching," which predicts this uncertain futurity, this difficult spot between management and change that is both a deferral and an activity. This poem is characteristically clear about its doubt: "We are uncertain of action," Spahr declares.[38] The next section abandons *we* altogether: "What I mean to say here is that I am confused." "I" am confused because "I" am "part of a we and then not part of a we," or rather "part of a we and then part of a we."[39] "I" is "lost between two places," has "abandoned sureness."[40] Without sureness, "I" can only express what it wants from these "two places" in a torrent of half-realized clauses and images:

> How to make meaning in invested discourse. To make fluency. To make flourish in both. A wrought iron trellis in both. A place for suspended and dangling by one's hair in both. A place for plastic flashing red light that represents the heart in both. A place for love of nature in both. A place for cloudy, muggy day in both. A place for detailed and intimate writing of graffiti in the steam of the bathroom mirror in both.[41]

With its rushed, almost breathless catalog, the passage prefigures the fervor of the conclusion to *The Transformation* (not to mention many passages of *This Connection of Everyone with Lungs*) and makes clearer the stakes of each: the effort at uniting table and bed, the effort at resisting public/private divisions—the need, that is, for "both, both, both." As if in reaction, the next section abandons definite pronouns altogether, turning to *one* ("Oh one of thinking / Oh one of desiring") before, finally, returning to *we*: "This is the way we learn to thinking," Spahr writes.[42]

The infinitive-gerund of "to thinking" may be this poem's must subtle bit of mimetic difficulty: using linguistic oddities to capture the strange position in which Spahr feels herself and others to be, at the beginning of the twenty-first century. While *to* indicates a sense of prospect, action to come, the gerund indicates a sense of continuity, action ongoing. The same mixture imbues Spahr's "how to" statement-questions, in which she turns propositions into infinitives: "How to not that one is right and the other is wrong. . . . How to this is meaning."[43] If "yous" or "certain of we" stresses the constitution of community, "to this is meaning" stresses the perpetual movement toward it. Aware that we have not yet found our connection, we continue in the mutuality of that awareness. And we remember "what lasts if only for a moment of coming," as Spahr writes in the penultimate section of the poem.[44]

Coming, with its combined suggestion of arrival and sexual climax, raises the question of Whitmanic carnality ("To touch my person to some one else's is about as much as I can stand," Whitman writes in "Song of Myself").[45] The phrase also looks ahead to the beds of *This Connection of Everyone with Lungs* and *The Transformation*. Or even to *Well Then There Now*, which includes Spahr's desire "to end [a] piece with a scene of metaphoric group sex where all the participants were place names, but the minute I attempted to do this I got bogged down in questions of which places would penetrate and which places would be penetrated."[46] Spahr's ideal globe is a place of "impingement," to use the word of *The Transformation*. Her work wonders whether our smaller moments of "switching" are compensation for the failure of this vision—or service toward it. Ethical action, in Spahr, would lie not only in a self-aware "we" but also in putting that "we" in service of a world to come. Are we living in anticipation or resignation? It's difficult, all sorts of difficult, to tell.

Notes

1. Juliana Spahr, "Introduction," in *American Women Poets in the 21st Century: Where Lyric Meets Language*, ed. Claudia Rankine and Juliana Spahr (Middletown: Wesleyan University Press, 2002), 11.

2. Juliana Spahr, *Fuck You-Aloha-I Love You* (Middletown, Conn.: Wesleyan University Press, 2001), 35–36.

3. Ibid., 49.

4. Juliana Spahr, *Everybody's Autonomy: Connective Reading and Collective Identity* (Tuscaloosa: University of Alabama Press, 2001), 9.

5. Ibid., 14.

6. Ibid., 6.

7. Ibid., 14.

8. Ibid., 154.

9. Gertrude Stein, *The Making of Americans* (New York: Dalkey Archive, 1995), 289.

10. Juliana Spahr, *Fuck You*, 38, 41–42.

11. Ibid., 49.

12. Ibid., 53.

13. Ibid., 56–57.

14. Gertrude Stein, *Tender Buttons* (Mineola: Dover, 1997), 43.

15. Juliana Spahr, *Fuck You*, 38–39.

16. Ibid., 19.

17. Juliana Spahr, *Well Then There Now* (Jaffrey, N.H.: Black Sparrow, 2011), 14.

18. I owe this point to a question from Kaplan Harris.

19. Spahr, *Well Then There Now,* 116.

20. Juliana Spahr, *This Connection of Everyone with Lungs* (Berkeley: University of California Press, 2005), 63.

21. Claudia Rankine, *Don't Let Me Be Lonely: An American Lyric* (Minneapolis: Graywolf, 2004); and *Citizen: An American Lyric* (Minneapolis: Graywolf, 2014).

22. In her recent consideration of the first person plural, Bonnie Costello differentiates the "choral" sense of Whitman's "we" and the "more self-conscious" we of modernist poets; here, Spahr again seems to wish to move past the limitations of modernism. See "Lyric Poetry and the First-Person Plural: 'How Unlikely,'" in *Something Understood: Essays and Poetry for Helen Vendler*, ed. Stephen Burt and Nick Halpern (Charlottesville: University of Virginia Press, 2009), 194.

23. Juliana Spahr, *This Connection*, 74.

24. Ibid., 13.

25. Ibid., 75

26. Ibid., 26.

27. Ibid., 39.

28. Ibid., 30.

29. Juliana Spahr, *The Transformation* (Berkeley: Atelos, 2007), 82.

30. Ibid., 15.

31. Ibid., 205.

32. Ibid., 21, 119, 162.

33. I owe this point to a question from Claire Seiler.

34. Juliana Spahr, *The Transformation*, 214.

35. Ibid., 206.

36. Spahr's most recent book, *That Winter the Wolf Came*, continues her meditation on similar questions, especially in the poet's physical desire for collective political action; however, this essay was written before *That Winter the Wolf Came* was published and cannot consider it in depth. See *That Winter the Wolf Came* (Oakland: Commune Editions, 2015).

37. Juliana Spahr, *The Transformation*, 214.

38. Juliana Spahr, *Fuck You*, 46.

39. Ibid., 47.

40. Ibid., 48.

41. Ibid., 53–54.

42. Ibid., 55.

43. Ibid., 50.

44. Ibid., 56.

45. Walt Whitman, *Poetry and Prose* (New York: Library of America, 1982), 55.

46. Juliana Spahr, *Well Then There Now*, 153.

JENA OSMAN

The Beautiful Life of Persona Ficta

a corporation is to a person as a person is to a machine
   friends of the court we know them as good and bad, they too are sheep
   and goats ventriloquizing the ghostly fiction.

a corporation is to a body as a body is to a puppet
   putting it in caricature, if there are natural persons then there are those
   who are not that, buying candidates. there are those who are strong on
   the ground and then weak in the air. weight shifts to the left leg while
   the propaganda arm extends.

a corporation is to an individual as an individual is to an uncanny valley
   the separation of individual wills from collective wills, magic words. they
   create an eminent body that is different from their own selves. reach over
   with the open palm of the left and force to the right while pamphlets
   disengage.

a corporation has convictions as a person has mechanical parts
   making a hash of this statute, the state is a body. Dobson Hobson and
   Jobson are masquerading under an alias. push off with the right foot, and
   at the same time step forward with the left foot. childlike voice complements
   visual cues and contributes to cuteness factor of the contestational robot.

a corporation has likes and dislikes as a body has shareholders
   bound by precedents the spectral then showed himself for what he was,
   a blotch to public discourse. the right foot is immediately brought forward.
   the body flattens toward the deck rather than leap into the air. it is not a
   hop. subversive literature engaged.

a corporation gives birth as a natural human births profit margins
   some really weird interpretations fully panoplied for war, a myth, torso
   breaks slightly forward. the hand is not entirely supine, but sloping from
   the thumb about thirty degrees. head rotation and sonar sensing
   technologies are employed to create believable movement, while allowing
   for only the most limited interaction.

a corporation has an enthusiasm for ethical behavior as a creature has
   economic interests only
   facial challenges. this person which is not a human being. not a physical
   personality of mankind. custom built from aluminum stock.

a corporation is we the people as a person is a cog
   a funny kind of thing, naïve shareholders. where there is property there
   is no personality. take off in full stride. lead leg exaggerates the knee lift
   of a normal stride. cordless microphones, remote control systems, hidden
   tape recorders.

a corporation has a conscience as a body has a human likeness
   forceful lily; so difficult to tell the two apart. paralyze the wheels of
   industry. an insatiable monster, soulless and conscienceless, a fund.

a corporation says hey I'm talking to you, as an individual speaks through
   a spokesperson
   they wear a scarlet letter that says "C" rejecting a century of history. the
   strong over the weak. better armed. supernatural. richer. more numerous.
   these are the facts.

a corporation admires you from afar and then has the guts to approach you
and ask you for your number, as a being activates a cognitive mechanism for
selecting mates
   it is a nightmare that Congress endorsed. mega-corporation as human
   group, the realm of hypothesis.

a corporation warms the bed and wraps its arms around you and just wants
to spoon as a natural human wants to organize profits
   it's overbroad, a glittering generality, a fiction to justify the power of
   the strong invented by prophets of force. there were narrower paths to
   incorporeal rights.

a corporation has upstanding character as a body has photorealistic texture
   the absorptive powers of some prehistoric sponge. there are good fictions
   and bad fictions. can the fiction ever disappear?

Chapter 8

✦

Attended with Trouble:
Jena Osman's "Persona Ficta"

Michael Davidson

Ghostly Visits

Is difficulty the same as ambiguity? The latter has a noble pedigree in literary study, canonized famously in the New Criticism and through William Empson's *Seven Types of Ambiguity*, where the term refers to "any verbal nuance, however slight, which gives room for alternative reactions to the same piece of language."[1] To this extent, ambiguity is a characteristic of all literary language insofar as words are made to function beyond the level of denotation. Henry James's late prose is ambiguous, due to its heavily subordinated sentences, complex deictics, and parenthetical remarks that thwart forward movement. Ambiguity here lies less in equivocal semantics than in the way James's sentences displace or defer meaning in pursuit of what Tzvetan Todorov calls the novel's "absolute and absent cause": the figure in the carpet, the beast in the jungle, the fissure in the golden bowl.

Difficulty, on the other hand, is associated with the hermeneutic labor involved in decoding a work's ambiguity. As the *Oxford English Dictionary* stipulates, difficulty is "not easy; requiring effort or labor; occasioning or attended with trouble." One might say that the "trouble" with individual phrases in James—or in Gertrude Stein or Bruce Andrews—is not in ambiguities in their denotative meaning but in their creation of a rhythm of affect that, like Whitman's rolling cadences or Creeley's heightened enjambment, instantiates a particular voice or mood. The hermeneutic labor involved in decoding difficult modern poetry, for which James is an essential antecedent, often requires understanding the function of a given allusion or idiolect in a work's larger cultural project. When Ezra Pound invokes James in Canto VII ("the old voice lifts itself / weaving an endless sentence") it is through an imitation of the novelist's style:

> We also made ghostly visits, and the stair
> That knew us, found us again on the turn of it,
> Knocking at empty rooms, seeking for buried beauty[2]

Possibly referring to the late story "The Jolly Corner," Pound appropriates James's characteristic references to houses and rooms, but he also uses these lines as one stage in the canto's larger portrayal of cultural decline, for which Jamesian realism ("the house of fiction") becomes a diagnostic tool. The Jamesian reference is part of a sequence of quotations, from Homer and Ovid through Provençal poets and Dante to Flaubert, each one embodying virtues of verbal clarity in contrast to the "beer bottle on the statue's pediment!" that marks modern culture's decline. The Jamesian description of bourgeois room and house is less important than its cultural meaning as a historical stage in mimesis. Poetic difficulty resides in the absent presence—the ghostly matter—of meaning-making systems such as the realist novel.

When it comes to postwar poetry, difficulty is less about obscure allusions or odd juxtapositions of dissimilar materials than qualities of tone and voice. The desultory movement of lines chronicling the poet's associations, observations, and hesitations is an index of psychological response. When Frank O'Hara refers to Bill or "Grace" or "Mike," or the Ziegfield theater, he doesn't really care if one knows who these people or places are; his references do not shore fragments against cultural ruin but rather enact moments of attentiveness that constellate value. Meaning lies not in an individual line or group of lines so much as in the cumulative affective force in the direction of authenticity. Anyone applying New Critical standards to the New American Poetry would find such causality disturbing precisely because its ambiguity is located not in the poem but in the affective realm the poem creates.

Language poetry said good-bye to all that by attacking voice as a register of value. The flatness of *Ketjak* or *My Life* or "China" was difficult not by any ambiguity in its language so much as by its refusal to organize disparate elements into any recognizable voice or cultural thematic. Procedural methods, appropriation, collaboration were deployed to remove words from speakers and return them to the social idiolects, class inflections, and media bytes that reinforce identity. The point was to retrieve language from the "predatory intent" of more confessional modes while making visible the sensuous particularity of language as a complex system. If, to quote Adorno, "what is considered to be intelligible to all is what has become unintelligible," Language poetry, by making work unintelligible as poetry, curiously redeems what is most familiar.[3] Lest this sound like a revision of Russian formalist *ostranenie*, I would add that the familiar includes the systems and institutions that guarantee clarity: classrooms, boardrooms, and significantly for my purposes here, courtrooms.

Jena Osman's "The Beautiful Life of Persona Ficta," sustains Language poetry's interest in social idiolects and the pragmatics of speech acts but engages in a documentary endeavor that subjects poems to an investigative project of which the individual poem is one component. Her difficulty stems from the particular function that a specific rhetorical device—analogy—serves in a juridical and institutional context. The poem's quotation from legal language offers a recognizable verbal surface to the poem, but it also permits Osman to suggest links between aesthetic and social validity.

"The Beautiful Life of Persona Ficta" is *a* poem, but it is not *the* poem. The distinction between indefinite and definite article separates two definitions of poetry, one that designates an integral language unit and another that recognizes integral units beyond the single poem. For Osman the distinction matters since her poetry often consists of large, exploratory works in which individual elements contribute to a speculative endeavor—what Brian Reed calls the "poem as project."[4] I have chosen "The Beautiful Life of Persona Ficta" as characteristic of her poetics generally, but it is only one component of a densely textured documentary work, *Corporate Relations* (2014), constructed out of multiple registers, voices, and appropriated materials. While it is possible to read this individual poem on its own terms, to do so violates its participation in the larger book specifically and in Osman's poetics generally. And this is a problem that vexes the readings of much contemporary poetry whose integral structure is animated by forces beyond the individual poem.

Corporate Relations consists of a set of five variations on U.S. constitutional amendments that protect rights of speech, religion, and citizenship. Since the Industrial Revolution, these amendments—the first, fourth, fifth, sixth, seventh, and fourteenth—have increasingly been used to grant rights of personhood to collective entities such as corporations. Each section is based on foundational court cases that have contributed to corporate personhood. Osman appropriates language from court transcripts and breaks them into fragments, scattering phrases across the page in a seemingly discontinuous manner (more on "seemingly" in a moment). Each section includes a prose summary of the case in question as well as a short lyric that extends the local terms of the case into more general issues of social justice and personal agency.[5] The book is thus composed of several layers that blur the boundaries between poem and essay, lyric and document, private and public voice. Osman's intent is not to aestheticize public discourse but to expose the close proximity of legal and aesthetic judgment. A document that protects free speech may, in fact, contain the ghostly residue of corporate entities that benefit from such protection; a poem that speaks through the voice of legal authority makes visible the agency ghosted by that authority.

"The Beautiful Life of Persona Ficta" appears at the beginning of *Corporate Relations* as prelude to what follows, condensing the book's exploration of what Osman calls a "shaky analogy: If corporations are persons, are persons machines?"[6] The courts recognize two sorts of persons, natural and juridical, the first of which refers to biological, historical individuals and the second to collective units—corporations, partnerships, sovereign states—which may be treated as persons in certain cases. The latter definition of personhood has governed several recent Supreme Court decisions—*Citizens United v. Federal Elections Commission* and, more recently, *Burwell v. Hobby Lobby*—that declare corporations to have the same constitutional rights as persons. The former case involved a conservative group's interest in distributing a film critical of Hilary Clinton during the 2010 presidential race. Citizens United sought injunctive relief from the Bipartisan Campaign Reform Act (McCain-Feingold), which prohibited "electioneering communication" for purposes of political fundraising. Arguing for the majority, Justice Kennedy declared that the First Amendment protects *associations* of individuals as well as individuals and does not prohibit speech based on the identity of the speaker. By this reasoning, corporations have speech rights as individuals, and those rights may be enlisted in the pursuit of political advantage. To prohibit "electioneering communication" would be tantamount, in the majority's opinion, to the banning of books or restrictions on religious freedom. Of course the court's majority decision went far beyond whether a political entity could produce an on-demand video during an election season; it rewrote the rules on campaign financing and gutted all previous finance reform legislation, including McCain-Feingold. Perhaps more ominously, the ruling in favor of nonprofit organizations paved the way for subsequent rulings for for-profit corporations, most recently that involving a chain of hobby stores, Hobby Lobby. In this case, the court argued that a for-profit "closely held" organization may refuse to provide contraceptive devices through its healthcare plan if such provision violates the owners' religious beliefs. In this case, a for-profit entity was granted rights under freedom of religion principles established in the First Amendment.

What does any of this have to do with poetry? How are finance reform, political documentaries, contraception, or healthcare appropriate topics for poetry? This is a little like asking what sovereignty, political intrigue, or deism have to do with Shakespeare's plays, Swift's satires, or Blake's prophecies. More importantly for our topic, how do Osman's formal strategies contribute, as the editors to this volume ask, to "the imaginative power of the work"? Osman provides one answer in a passage in her 1999 book, *The Character*:

> Someone tells me that according to a poetics of difference, there is a need to leave the experimental behind: writers not privileged by the dominant discourse "cannot leave judgment to 'chance.'" But what if the nature of judgment itself is a matter of chance?[7]

If one of the key components of poetry is voice, what happens when that feature is mediated by legal rhetoric? And to extend the analogy, if one of the key components of Kantian aesthetics is the issue of judgment, what happens when disinterestedness is revealed to be the product of gendered, classed, and political interests? In *Citizens United*, disinterested legal judgment was used to divert agency from the individual to the corporation, speech from the individual to the marketplace. Osman observes that a poetics of difference that does not account for the nature of judgment by which such categories are created and sustained does not go to the structural forces that legitimate such categories.[8] Legal judgment and aesthetic practice are linked insofar as they create criteria of value—as in civil rights legislation—by which persons may be granted civil visibility. Despite the blindfold on the female figure of Justice, interested parties make interested judgments. As commentators pointed out, the *Hobby Lobby* decision was made by an all-Catholic, all-male majority in a case involving women's reproductive health. Osman's idiosyncratic textual techniques—documentary, visual, cartographic, archival, performative, digital—permit her to explore fissures in the presumed neutrality of judgment through the means and rhetorics by which policy is secured. In all of her work she deploys what Joan Retallack calls a "poethics" in which poetry asserts its claim to imagine new ways to live and work.[9] Osman plunders newspapers, encyclopedias, science texts, and media images as sources to probe social realties that those texts cannot imagine. She continually asks how poetry can do political work, not by shouting down the opposition or demonizing bad practices but by exploring and framing the productive means that create social identities.

Osman's poem can be read through several poetic subgenres. The tradition that her work most easily resembles is the documentary imperative manifested in poems such as Charles Reznikoff's *Testimony*, Muriel Rukeyser's *Book of the Dead*, Teresa Hak Kyung Cha's *DICTEE*, Mark Nowak's *Shut Up! Shut Down!* and any number of works by Susan Howe. The poem also contributes to a longer tradition of legal poetry that would include several of Shakespeare's sonnets (35, 49, and 134), John Donne's satires (2 and 5), Emily Dickinson's "I read my Sentence steadily," Edna St. Vincent Millay's "Justice Denied in Massachusetts," and more recently, M. NourbeSe Philip's *Zong!* But whereas many poems in this latter tradition use legal rhetoric as metaphor (*Zong!* is the exception), Osman draws on the specifics of the court case to study how legal doctrine contributes to the reifying effects of capitalism. In the case of *Corporate Relations* her focus is on how private speech becomes ventriloquized through forms of public media, producing in the process a puppet or automaton. Her focus on the uncanny speech of this figure has immediate application to poetics, obviously, but she realizes that to claim lyric interiority—or vatic transcendence—does not strike at the heart of how voice is imbricated in social factors that produce it.[10]

Persona Ficta

Thus far I have focused largely on contextual matters rather than text, hoping to frame some of the historical, generic, and political issues that underlie and frame "The Beautiful Life of Persona Ficta." Osman's poem is haunted by what lies outside the text, both within the book it inaugurates and in the world to which it refers. Perhaps it would be better to say that she attempts to render inadequate the putative border between text and context, poem and history. "The Beautiful Life" is about who (or what) speaks and by what agency. Its anaphoric structure, appropriated legal rhetoric, and analogical development mediate—not amputate—the idea of a unitary, centered voice. If *Citizens United* grants speech to a corporation, then it sets a precedent for agency that impacts many forms of communication.[11]

The title, "The Beautiful Life of Persona Ficta," establishes the main premise of the book: if a fictive person such as a corporation can have a "life," then criteria of beauty are passed from Kant's subjective judgment to public consensus. The poem's thirteen strophes or stanzas outline what that "beautiful" life might resemble, for as a fictive person, its beautiful life can exist only as resemblance to something else; as the book's title suggests, it is a "corporate relation." Each strophe begins with an analogy, A is to B as X is to Y, which could be described as the skeletal structure of legal precedent: "a corporation is to a person as a person is to a machine"; "a corporation is to a body as a body is to a puppet." Osman extends these analogies to absurd lengths ("a corporation admires you from afar and then has the guts to approach you and ask you for your number") to expose the generative potential of the analogy itself. Since the court in *Citizens United* generalized from *corporeal* personhood to *corporate* personhood, based on legal precedent, Osman takes the next step and analogizes a nonhuman body into a human. Although her reference is contemporary, she looks back through an avant-garde tradition that extends from the futurist metalized body and Duchamp's bachelor machines to Donna Haraway's cyborg. In such cases, as Dziga Vertov says in Osman's epigraph, "Our path leads through the poetry of machines, from the bungling citizen to the perfect electric man." But Osman sees them less like avant-garde utopian versions of the machinic human than as puppets or automatons manipulated by a master ventriloquist called Capital.

In earlier books, Osman expresses fascination with the inanimate become human, and at the end of *Corporate Relations* she lists a number of classic versions: "Pygmalion's Galatea, Dr. Frankenstein's monster, Olympia in E. T. A. Hoffman's 'The Sandman,' Delibes' Coppelia, Pinocchio . . . etc.": "We are simultaneously attracted and repelled by the cognitive autonomy of our own creations: their immortality, their limited accountability, the impossibility of their imprisonment, their tendency to change citizenship overnight" (73). Freud described the uncanny quality of such figures, whose terror derives not from their strangeness or otherness but from their familiarity. The automaton that speaks, the unexpected mirror reflection, the replicant are unsettling when human agency is diverted onto a nonhuman object. We witness the return of repressed desires in another that resembles

ourselves. For it *is* ourselves that we encounter, a latent version of child-
hood libido and, socially, an atavistic, polytheistic social identity that we
have suppressed. In Osman's poem, this uncanny replicant appears as a
puppet, doll, and robot:

> a corporation is to a body as a body is to a puppet
>> putting it in caricature, if there are natural persons then there are those
>> who are not that, buying candidates. there are those who are strong
>> on the ground and then weak in the air. weight shifts to the left leg
>> while the propaganda extends. . . .
>
> a corporation has convictions as a person has mechanical parts
>> making a hash of this statute, the state is a body. Dobson Hobson and
>> Jobson are masquerading under an alias. push off with the right foot,
>> and at the same time step forward with the left foot. childlike voice
>> complements visual cues and contributes to cuteness factor of the
>> contestational robot. (11)

The analogy that begins each strophe is unpacked in the subsequent prose
as a series of variations on the analogy proposed. Each phrase, ended with
a period, is prosthetic to the fictive body—puppet, robot, automaton, Dob-
son Hobson and Jobson. The phrases are discontinuous like the mechanical
parts that make up the machine, yet there are repeated figures—such as the
dance instructions above or the various references to robots—that offer a
through-line in the poem. Osman wedges her paratactic sequence within her
analogical structure as if to show two incompatible forms of logic battling
for supremacy. If analogy is the formula by which corporations may be con-
verted into private bodies, parataxis renders the components as discrete, inert
parts. To this extent Osman's experimental techniques are in direct, if oppo-
sitional, conversation with the structure of legal argument.

Osman suggests that legal definitions of corporate personhood have an
interpellative function in producing the subjects they presume to represent.
To respond to the siren call of Capital produces the Subject as subject to its
power:

> a corporation says hey I'm talking to you, as an individual speaks through
> a spokesperson
>> they wear a scarlet letter that says "C" rejecting a century of history.
>> the strong over the weak. better armed. supernatural. richer. more
>> numerous. these are the facts. (12)

Osman's variation on Althusser's theory of ideological interpellation is to
suggest that if a corporation can be granted agency, it asserts its authority by

hailing Subjects, never speaking through itself but through a "spokesperson" or representative. Her prose elaboration refers to a latter day Hester Prynne who wears not the scarlet letter of adultery and agency but the C of Corporate Capital. And indeed, there is a relationship between the erotics of the agent and that of the commodity fetish that seduces:

> a corporation warms the bed and wraps its arms around you and just
> wants to spoon as a natural human wants to organize profits
> > it's overbroad, a glittering generality, a fiction to justify the power of
> > the strong invented by prophets of force. there were narrower paths to
> > incorporeal rights. (12)

Attended with Trouble

Gertrude Stein's famous observation that "nothing changes from generation to generation except the thing seen and that makes a composition" has been used to explain why one era's aesthetic difficulty is the next generation's retrospective viewpoint.[12] To skeptics who faulted Picasso's portrait for not resembling her, Stein responded, "It will." Innovative writers create the conditions by which their works will be read, but this hermeneutic circle leaves out the history within which writers themselves are created and that they address. Jena Osman commits herself to the historicity of her creative act, so much so that in all of her books she places herself literally "in the picture," photographing, as she does in *Public Figures*, not only the mounted hero in the public park but the citizens whom he would see from his pedestal.[13] This dual vision, this testing of history for what is said about it and what it produces, is characteristic of Osman's investigative poetics.

Corporate Relations is deeply invested in the links between modern jurisprudence and the production of a new Subject. The *persona iuris* that is Osman's topic achieves a special resonance when juxtaposed to other aspects of modern normalization—Taylorism, Fordism, eugenics, racial science—that we associate with modernization. Marx's model of base and superstructure could hardly accommodate the latter-day forms that these biopolitical regimes represent. By seizing on the analogical structure of legal argument, Osman suggests that there can be no neat separation of economic reality from the structures of legitimation that keep it in place.

To read Osman's difficulty adequately, we must read across it for its inseminating force in the rest of the book. In the process we are encouraged to look more closely at the Bill of Rights, the structure of legal argument, psychological theories of the uncanny, modernism's cult of the machine, and a dozen other topics. What Osman does that the Supreme Court does not is weave these various discursive realms together as intersectional elements in the formation of the modern Subject. Analogy, the rhetorical basis of "The Beautiful Life," allows one element to be compared to something different, the "bearing across" that is the basis of metaphor. By creating a poem based on spurious analogies, Osman makes visible the links between modernist discontinuity and legal authority.

Notes

1. William Empson, *Seven Types of Ambiguity* (New York: New Directions, 1966), 1.

2. Ezra Pound, "Canto VII," in *The Cantos of Ezra Pound* (New York: New Directions, 1973), 25.

3. Theodor Adorno, *Aesthetic Theory*, trans. Robert Hullot-Kentor (Minneapolis: University of Minnesota Press, 1997), 183.

4. Brian Reed, *Nobody's Business: Twenty-First Century Avant Garde Poetics* (Ithaca, N.Y.: Cornell University Press, 2013), 64–65.

5. These relatively autonomous poems represent, as she says in an interview, "the other side of [an] analogy." Caleb Beckwith interview with Jena Osman, *The Conversant*, April 29, 2014, http://theconversant.org/?p=7506 (accessed June 17, 2014).

6. The poem's rather flat, legalistic prose describes the various ways in which corporations can be analogized to persons. Such analogical thinking, as Osman says in a note at the end of *Corporate Relations*, "reanimates age-old ideas of a mind-body split" and instantiates modernist ideas of the body as a machine (73).

7. Jena Osman, *The Character* (Boston: Beacon Press, 1999), 64.

8. The classic instance of this confluence of literary genre and public document would be slave narratives in which the author includes his or her manumission papers as a component of the text.

9. Joan Retallack, "The Poethical Wager," in *The Poethical Wager* (Berkeley: University of California Press, 2003), 21–47.

10. Osman's previous work offers a series of variations on this theme. The poems in *The Character, An Essay in Asterisks, The Network,* and *Public Figures* use research-based and procedural strategies that complicate the usual terms for poetry or, indeed, scholarship. These hybrid texts draw on multiple visual and textual realms, often incorporating technical data from science journals, Supreme Court cases, etymological dictionaries, cartography, and urban history. In *Character* (1999), she uses the periodic table of elements to generate a hypertext work in which each element leads to a short, lyric poem based on its source. In the title poem, footnotes at the end of stanzas lead to commentaries or quotations that offer a cryptic response to the source text. In *Essay in Asterisks* (2004) a series of stage directions for boxing ("Force the opponent's left and lead to the right with the left glove") are interrupted by prose passages dealing with forms of political resistance and critique. In *Network* (2010) Osman studies the twin trajectories of history and etymology by subjecting the names of streets in lower Manhattan to their sources in mercantilism and the slave trade. In *Public Figures* (2012) she photographs public monuments around Philadelphia and then follows

the trajectories of their subjects' eyes back to the world they see. Because the statues she photographs are often of military figures, she suggests the close relationship between public memorials and military might. These books are, as I have indicated, also "projects," based on a balance of historical and archival research and speculation.

11. Much of the failure of the defense by the solicitor general's office rested with the claim that under McCain-Feingold, Congress could ban not only television advertisements but books as well. Samuel Alito seized on this claim, asking the solicitor general, Malcolm Stewart, whether the publication of a campaign biography during an election season could also be banned. Stewart admitted that if the book advocated for a particular candidate, the government could criminalize it. Thus the conservative majority showed how the denial of Citizens United's right to broadcast *Hilary: The Movie* was tantamount to governmental censorship. On Chief Justice John Roberts's influence over the *Citizens United* case, see Jeffrey Toobin, "Money Unlimited," *New Yorker*, May 21, 2012, 36–47.

12. Gertrude Stein, "Composition as Explanation," in *Writings 1903–1932*, ed. Catherine R. Stimpson and Harriet Chessman (New York: Library of America, 1998), 520.

13. This is a very different perspective from Robert Lowell's memorializing of the monument to Robert Gould Shaw in "For the Union Dead," a public art that "sticks like a fishbone / in the city's throat." Robert Lowell, "For the Union Dead," in *The Selected Poems of Robert Lowell* (New York: Farrar, Strauss and Giroux, 1986), 136.

MAGGIE NELSON

from *Bluets*

1. Suppose I were to begin by saying that I had fallen in love with a color. Suppose I were to speak this as though it were a confession; suppose I shredded my napkin as we spoke. *It began slowly. An appreciation, an affinity. Then, one day, it became more serious. Then* (looking into an empty teacup, its bottom stained with thin brown excrement coiled into the shape of a sea horse) *it became somehow* personal.

Chapter 9

After Difficulty

Ben Lerner

Language poetry—and to my mind the best Language poetry was written in prose—was a machine that ran on difficulty. Reading a prose poem deploying what Ron Silliman called "the new sentence" was intended to be an exercise in frustration: the reader attempts to combine the sentences—which are grammatical—into meaningful paragraphs. The sentences are vague enough ("Sentence structure is altered for torque, or increased polysemy/ambiguity") that a logical relation between sentences will always almost seem possible. But the reader discovers as she goes that many successive sentences cannot be assimilated to a coherent paragraph, that paragraphs are organized arbitrarily ("quantitatively," as opposed to around an idea), that no stable voice unifies the text, that her "will to integration"—her desire to produce higher orders of meaning that lead away from the words on the page into the realm of the signified ("a dematerializing motion")—is repeatedly defeated.[1]

The solicitation and then tactical frustration of the reader's will to linguistic integration had an explicitly political object: it was advanced as a kind of deprogramming of bourgeois readerly assumptions. Such difficult prose would teach us that meaning is actively produced, never naturally given; that language is manipulable material, not a transparent window onto reality; that the "speaker" is a unifying fiction more than a stable subject; and so on. These deconstructive strategies were conceived not only as a critique of other writers—for example, lyric, "confessional" poets with their privileging of subjective experience and inwardness; mainstream novelists with their "optical realism"—but as an attack on existing social and political orders that depended upon the smooth functioning of dominant linguistic conventions.

Many of us learned something from the Language poets' taking up of a constructivist vision of the self and its literature: their insistence on language as material, their combination of Russian formalism and various strains of French theory into a compelling reading of experimental modernism. (And many of us learned to appreciate certain texts associated with Language poetry in terms other than and often opposed to those provided by essays like Silliman's "The New Sentence," with its antiexpressive and anti-aesthetic bent). But who among us still believes, if any of us ever really did, that writing disjunctive prose poems counts as a legitimately subversive political practice? Indeed, for many ambitious contemporary writers, disjunction has lost any obvious left political valence. Does the language of advertising and politicians, for instance, really depend on seamless integration? Transcripts of speeches by Bush or Palin or Trump would have been at home in *In the American Tree*. When aggressive ungrammaticality and non sequitur are fundamental to mainstream capitalist media (and to the rhetoric of an ascendant radical right), the new sentence appears more mimetic than defamiliarizing. In this context, "difficulty" as a valorized attribute of a textual strategy gives way to the difficulty of recovering the capacity for some mode of communication, of intersubjectivity, in light of the insistence of Language poets (and others) on the social constructedness of self and the irreducible conventionality of representation.

Language poetry's notion of textual difficulty as a weapon in class warfare hasn't aged well, but the force of its critique of what is typically referred to as "the lyric I" has endured in what Gillian White has recently called a diffuse and lingering "lyric shame"—a sense, now often uncritically assumed, that modes of writing and reading identified as lyric are embarrassingly egotistical and politically backward.[2] White's work seeks, among other things, to explore how "the 'lyric' tradition against which an avant-garde anti-lyricism has posited itself . . . never existed in the first place" and to reevaluate poems and poets often dismissed cursorily as instances of a bad lyric expressivity. She also seeks to refocus our attention on lyric as a reading practice, as a way of "projecting subjectivity onto poems," emphasizing how debates about the status of lyric poetry are in fact organized around a "missing lyric object": an ideal—that is, unreal—poem posited by the readerly assumptions of both defenders and detractors of lyric confessionalism.[3]

It's against the backdrop that I'm describing that I read important early twenty-first-century works by poets such as Juliana Spahr (*This Connection of Everyone with Lungs*), Claudia Rankine (*Don't Let Me Be Lonely: An American Lyric* and, very recently, *Citizen: An American Lyric*), and Maggie Nelson (*Bluets*). I mean that these very different writers have difficulty with the kind of difficulty celebrated by Language poets in particular and the historical avant-garde in general. Their books are purposefully accessible works that nevertheless seek to acknowledge the status of language as medium and the self as socially enmeshed. I read Rankine and Nelson's works of prose poetry in particular as occupying the space where the no-longer-new sentence was; they are instances of a consciously post-avant-garde writing that refuses—without in any sense being simple—to advance formal difficulty as a mode of resistance, revolution, or pedagogy. I will also try to suggest how they operate knowingly within—but without succumbing to—a post–Language poetry environment of lyric shame or at the very least suspicion.

I call Rankine and Nelson's books works of "prose poetry," and they are certainly often taken up as such, but their generic status is by no means settled. Both writers—as with many Language poets—invite us to read prose as a form of poetry even as they trouble such distinctions. Rankine's books are indexed as "Essay/Poetry" and *Bluets* is indexed as "Essay/Literature." *Bluets* is published, however, by Wave Books, a publisher devoted entirely to poetry. Rankine's two recent books are both subtitled "An American Lyric," begging the question of how a generic marker traditionally understood as denoting short, musical, and expressive verse can be transposed into long, often tonally flat books written largely in prose. On an obvious but important level, I think the deployment of the sentence and paragraph under the sign of poetry, the book-length nature of the works in question, and the acknowledgment of the lyric as a problem (and central problematic) help situate these works in relation to the new sentence, even if that's by no means the only way to read them.

Both *Bluets* and *Don't Let Me Be Lonely* open with a mixture of detachment and emotional intensity that simultaneously evokes and complicates the status of the "lyric I." In the first numbered paragraph of *Bluets,* quoted above, a language of impersonal philosophical skepticism—the "suppose," the *Tractatus*-like numbering, the subjunctive—interacts with an emotional vocabulary and experiential detail. The italics also introduce the possibility of multiple voices, or at least two distinct temporalities of writing, undermining the assumption of univocality and spokenness conventionally associated with the lyric. "As though it were a confession"; "it became somehow personal": two terms associated with lyric and its shame are both "spoken" and qualified at the outset of the book—a book that will go on to be powerfully confessional and personal indeed. *Don't Let Me Be Lonely* opens with a related if distinct method of lyric evocation and complication, flatly describing what we might call the missing object of elegy:

> There was a time I could say no one I knew well had died. This is not to suggest no one died. When I was eight my mother became pregnant. She went to the hospital to give birth and returned without the baby. Where's the baby? We asked. Did she shrug? She was the kind of woman who liked to shrug; deep within her was an everlasting shrug. That didn't seem like a death. The years went by and people only died on television—if they weren't Black, they were wearing black or were terminally ill. Then I returned home from school one day and saw my father sitting on the steps of our home. He had a look that was unfamiliar; it was flooded, so leaking. I climbed the steps as far away from him as I could get. He was breaking or broken. Or, to be more precise, he looked to me like someone understanding his aloneness. Loneliness. His mother was dead. I'd never met her. It meant a trip back home for him. When he returned he spoke neither about the airplane nor the funeral.[4]

Throughout *Don't Let Me Lonely* the traditional lyric attributes of emotional immediacy and intensity are replaced with the problem of a kind of contemporary anesthesia—the repression of the reality of death, the leveling of tragedy into another kind of infotainment in a culture of spectacle, the mediation of experience by technologies ranging from television to pharmaceuticals. The problem of the deadening of feeling—the negative image of traditional lyric content—finds its formal correlative in a flat prose in which verse can appear only in citation or paratext, for example, quotations from Celan embedded in the prose, a Dickinson poem reproduced in the notes. Instead of imagining difficult prose as a technology for deconstructing the self, a highly linear and plainspoken account of the problem of the "I" is offered as Rankine attempts to work her way out of social despair: "If I am present in a subject position what responsibility do I have to the content, to the truth value, of the words themselves? Is 'I' even me or am 'I' a gearshift to get from one sentence to the next? Should I say we? Is the voice not various if I take responsibility for it? What does my subject mean to me?"[5] Rankine forgoes difficulty as a strategy for disrupting subjectivity in order to acknowledge the difficulty of calibrating a responsible self socially. We could say that the anti-lyricism of Language poetry is gestured toward in the banishment of the traditional trappings of the lyric—verse itself, musicality, intense personal expression (what Rankine often confesses is a sense of inward emptiness)—but here these lyric strategies are less willfully rejected than made to feel unavailable. And the felt unavailability of the lyric is a result of Rankine's explicit invitation to read her markedly nonlyric materials (essayistic and often flat prose) *as* lyric—to invite us to think of lyric as a reading practice as much as a writing practice in which the ostensibly "shameful" attributes of the mode (e.g., an egotistical, asocial inwardness) are replaced by a collaborative effort on the part of reader and writer to overcome "loneliness."

Bluets explores many of these concerns with related if ultimately distinct means:

> 70. Am I trying, with these "propositions," to build some kind of bower?— But surely this would be a mistake. For starters, *words do not* look like *the things they designate* (Maurice Merleau-Ponty).

> 71. I have been trying, for some time now, to find dignity in my loneliness. I have been finding this hard to do.

> 72. It is easier, of course, to find dignity in one's solitude. Loneliness is solitude with a problem. Can blue solve the problem, or can it at least keep me company within it?—No, not exactly. IT cannot love me that way; it has no arms. But sometimes I do feel its presence to be a sort of wink—*Here you are again*, it says, and *so am I*.

Nelson's "blue bower" evokes not only the actual bird, renowned for how the males construct and decorate "bowers" to attract mates, but also the traditional association of lyric with a metaphorics of birds and birdsong. It further evokes the Dante Gabriel Rossetti (a shamelessly lyric poet if there ever was one) painting of that name, as well as his poem with the received title "The Song of the Bower." To build a "blue bower" out of "propositions" is to cross a lyric and anti-lyric project in the space of prose, implicating and complicating both. It is hard to find dignity in the privacy of the aestheticized bower—indeed, one might be ashamed of such inwardness—and one of the goals of *Bluets* will be to test what part of experience is sharable as a way out of isolation and despair. The color blue functions as the organizing metaphor for both the possibility of intersubjectivity ("15. I think of these people as my blue correspondents, whose job it is to send me blue reports from the field.") and its limits ("105. There are no instruments for measuring color; there are no 'color thermometers.' How could there be, as 'color knowledge' always remains contingent upon an individual perceiver."). Nelson's accumulating "propositions" do not integrate into a "bower," but the relation between sentences and sections has little in common with new-sentence disjunction. As in Rankine's prose poetry, difficulty here is not deployed as a political/poetical tactic irrupting within the norms of prose; instead, the difficulty of finding a defensible, dignified ground for intersubjectivity is narrated explicitly.

The shift from the tactical deconstruction of ostensibly natural narrative or lyric unities to the effort to reconstruct them with a difference is legible in part because *Bluets* foregrounds its relation to avant-garde prose poetry. Nelson's use of Wittgenstein as muse and model, for instance, invites us to position her work relative to new sentence experiments. Silliman not only cited the *Philosophical Investigations* in "The New Sentence" as an important precedent, but Silliman's own *The Chinese Notebook* models the tone and structure of Wittgenstein's philosophical writing. More generally, the work of Marjorie Perloff (*Wittgenstein's Ladder*) and others has made clear how the philosopher's inquiries into language as a form of social practice— and his own peculiar linguistic operations—have been central to scores of experimental ("difficult") writers.[6] If Nelson weren't also the author of volumes of verse, and if Wave weren't the publisher of *Bluets*, my experience of context and thus text would be different: those facts function as a quieter version of Rankine's subtitle, inviting—or at the very least enabling—us to think of poetry as a reading practice as much as a writing practice, and to experience verse techniques as withheld or unavailable in *Bluets* instead of as merely forgone or forsworn.

As in *Don't Let Me Be Lonely*, in *Bluets*, actual verse is exiled to the space of citation: William Carlos Williams, Lorine Neideker, and Lord Byron, among many others, are quoted; line breaks are replaced with slashes. Indeed, Nelson doesn't have much faith in the effects of actual poems: "12. And please don't talk to me about 'things as they are' being changed upon any 'blue guitar.' What can be changed upon a blue guitar is not of interest here." Or: "For better or worse, I do not think that writing changes things very much, if at all" (proposition 183). And yet, the relegation of verse to the virtual space of citation lends it a certain power, displaying it while also insisting that it's nearly out of reach. This allows Nelson's prose to be haunted by the abstract possibility of a poetry it can't actualize, somewhat like the Mallarméan fantasy she at one point describes: "For Mallarmé, the perfect book was one whose pages have never been cut, their mystery forever preserved, like a bird's folded wing, or a fan never opened." Moreover, Bluets—taking its cue (and lifting many of its locutions) from Wittgenstein's attacks on Goethe's Theory of Colors—often refers to outmoded regimes of knowledge or technologies (e.g., the eighteenth-century "cyanometer," which sought to measure the blue of the sky). One begins to wonder if verse—lyric poetry in particular—is another set of defunct measures, outmoded conventions for communicating experience.

Perhaps there is a sense for Nelson (and Rankine) in which poetry isn't difficult—it's impossible. There is faith neither in poetry's power of imaginative redescription (the blue guitar) nor in its practical effects as a technology of intervening in history ("I do not think that writing changes very much"). The subject isn't a dominant bourgeois fiction of inwardness and univocality in need of deconstruction via new sentence difficulty but an avowedly social and linguistic entity deployed over time in the space of writing; expression itself must be constructed, and that process is narrated clearly in a prose that, when read as poetry, makes actual verse present as a loss. Although I believe these authors use the prose poem and the felt absence of verse in fresh and specific ways, I am not suggesting that the logic I'm describing is exactly new. Stephen Fredman and others have suggested that the prose poem arises as a form during periods in which there is a crisis of confidence in verse strategies, and the notion of the lyric being felt as a loss as it becomes prose is at least as old as Walter Benjamin. Here my limited goal is to indicate a few specific ways the new sentence valorization of difficulty can become a frame for a specific kind of accessibility for two important contemporary poets who write primarily in prose.

One can't pretend to contextualize these books without stating explicitly that part of the contemporary dissatisfaction with attacks on narrative and voice as political strategies is that they can serve to mask what is essentially a white male universalism. The rejection of linguistic integration and antiexpressionist attacks on the lyric subject have recently been described by Cathy Park Hong as a symptom of the avant-garde's "delusion of whiteness,"

> its specious belief that renouncing subject and voice is anti-authoritarian, when in fact such wholesale pronouncements are clueless that the disenfranchised need such bourgeois niceties like voice to alter

conditions forged in history. The avant-garde's "delusion of white-
ness" is the luxurious opinion that anyone can be "post-identity" and
can casually slip in and out of identities like a video game avatar,
when there are those who are consistently harassed, surveilled, pro-
filed, or deported for whom they are.[7]

In a related vein, Nelson's own work as a critic has been attuned to how "the
male Language writers' occasionally monomaniacal focus on warring eco-
nomic systems" was both challenged and expanded by women writers inside
and outside of the Language movement itself. In ways I haven't had the space
to explore here, *Don't Let Me Be Lonely* and *Bluets* are engaged with dem-
onstrating how the uncritical acceptance of voice and narrative conventions
as well as their "wholesale" disavowal by certain avant-garde writers can
preserve racist and sexist ideologies. This is by now an old difficulty, echoing
the even older modernism/realism debate—how the emancipatory potential
of poststructuralist strategies quickly cools into a conservatism (or worse)
like the one Cathy Park Hong describes. Out of this abiding difficulty more
complex, accessible prose poetry is likely to arise. How might verse return?
And when and why?

Notes

1. Ron Silliman, *The New Sentence* (New York: Roof Books, 1987), 91.
2. Gillian White, *Lyric Shame: The "Lyric" Subject of Contemporary American Poetry* (Cambridge, Mass.: Harvard University Press, 2014).
3. Arguments about the nature of the lyric, its historical genealogy, or the effi-
cacy of the term more generally are not my concern here; my purpose is to explore
how the conventional association of *lyric* with "brevity, subjectivity, passion, and
sensuality," among other attributes, is evoked and strategically disappointed by
the authors I examine. (I'm quoting from the entry for "Lyric" in *The Princeton
Encyclopedia of Poetry and Poetics*, 4th ed.)
4. Claudia Rankine, *Don't Let Me Be Lonely* (Saint Paul: Graywolf, 2004), 5.
5. Ibid., 54.
6. Rosmarie Waldrop's trilogy, *Curves to the Apple* (New York: New Direc-
tions, 2006), which often lifts Wittgenstein's propositions and submits them to
a process of substitution (e.g., Wittgenstein's "The deepest questions are, in fact,
no questions at all" becomes "The deepest rivers are, in fact, no rivers at all") is a
beautiful example of how Wittgenstein has functioned as (sometimes antagonis-
tic) inspiration and source material for innovative poets.
7. Cathy Park Hong, "Delusions of Whiteness in the Avant-Garde," *Lana
Turner* 7 (2014): 248–53, quote from p. 248. http://www.lanaturnerjournal
.com/7/delusions-of-whiteness-in-the-avant-garde.

LOCATING AUTHENTICITY

ARIANA REINES

From "RENDERED"

LIVESTOCK MORTALITY IS A TREMENDOUS SOURCE OF ORGANIC MATTER. A TYPICAL FRESH CARCASS CONTAINS APPROXIMATELY 32% DRY MATTER, OF WHICH 52% IS PROTEIN, 41% IS FAT, AND 6% IS ASH. RENDERING OFFERS SEVERAL BENEFITS TO FOOD ANIMAL AND POULTRY PRODUCTION OPERATIONS, INCLUDING PROVIDING A SOURCE OF PROTEIN FOR USE IN ANIMAL FEED, AND PROVIDING A HYGIENIC MEANS OF DISPOSING OF FALLEN AND CONDEMNED ANIMALS. THE END PRODUCTS OF RENDERING HAVE ECONOMIC VALUE AND CAN BE STORED FOR LONG PERIODS OF TIME. USING PROPER PROCESSING CONDITIONS, FINAL PRODUCTS WILL BE FREE OF PATHOGENIC BACTERIA AND UNPLEASANT ODORS.

Across her. Across her.
Unending the weight of her I have to be finding out a grammar.
How to be. Opener.
Sawed open. Easy.
Open like a grammar.
A dust of light the air carries.
What is a night upended.
A carcass in which nothing is leftover.
What is a night upended.
Open, a hole where the head disgorges its body.

. . .

PERCOLATING PAN: A TANK WITH A PERFORATED SCREEN THROUGH WHICH THE LIQUID FAT DRAINS FREELY AND SEPARATES FROM THE TANKAGE

Vented into the forge an analogy.
It blew in there because it thought.
It resembled. A sample of influence.
Using a world to build thought out of.
It is a poem of how to be.

Nobody is preceding too much.
And the form, the form,
An implement of several trains
Of thought. Is it worse to say
Otherwise.
Ow my body.

. . .

TALLOW: THE WHITE NEARLY TASTELESS SOLID RENDERED FAT OF CATTLE AND SHEEP WHICH IS USED CHIEFLY IN SOAP, CANDLES, AND LUBRICANTS

Alimenting the world perpetuates it. Duh. Plus "the world" is itself a food. We go outside we stay in. I am going to try to be a girl. Try to transcribe bare sustenance. Reprimand some light on a brass latchkey. So many rents in the air.

THE EMERGENCE OF BSE (bovine spongiform encephalopathy) HAS BEEN LARGELY ATTRIBUTED TO CATTLE BEING FED FORMULATIONS THAT CONTAINED PRION-INFECTED MBM (meat and bone meal).

. . .

It's downers who have to be dragged to the knocker cause they can't even walk down the ramp. They get mashed up or transubstantiated and used to get fed to the ones living in their own shit at feedlots and that's how come thousands more had to be slaughtered and beyond slaughtered destroyed because DESTROY IS BEYOND SLAUGHTER incinerated or liquefied in special vats. The container contains the corpse. Something gets out from under the end. Disease. Brains and shit.

VAGINAL EXPLORATION IS MANDATORY IN EVERY PERIPARTUM, RECUMBENT COW AND MAY LEAD TO DISCOVERY OF A DECOMPOSING SECOND FETUS. DAMAGE TO AND INFECTION OF THE WALL OF THE VAGINA IS COMMON. METRITUS AND AN ASSOCIATED TOXEMIA CAN CONTRIBUTE TO POSTPARTUM RECUMBENCY.

What happens to the world when a body is a bag of stuff you can empty out of it.
Errors, musculatures.

Can I empty language out of me.
What difference does it make how a thing dies. Consciousness. Nobody knows what that is.

. . .

An animal secretes a lot of cortisol if you harass her too much in killing her and this ruins the meat you are trying to turn her into.
If her flesh can be ruined because of how marauded she feels can the air be ruined if she cries out inside it.
Who if I cried out CREAM O LAND
Who if I cried out
Who if I cried out would hear me etc.
What happens to air that has rubbed up against mistrals, miasmas, or worser, nameless winds.
What happens to an air that carries the screams of what is under slaughter.
When she howls it's with her mouth.
When she howls it's with her mouth a tooth missing in it.
Menthol cigarettes and mozzarella cheese, coffee and sour apples.
Ma Ma. MOUTH MOUTH
Mean ME ME everything I can feel inside
What skin. What hair. What eyes, gold tooth. What muscles. What udder. What are hooves. The liver, what liver. What stomach. Horns. Where isn't she. Where isn't she inside her body. Where is she not. Where is she least.
There was a whole body that went before me: it was her.
Stretch marks on her stomacher.
If you want to know what living is do not ask a doctor.
Where am I not in my body, where am I least in it. What could be excised from me most easily.
Where is a living thing not itself. Is her shit any less her.
And moreover, gender.
It is latent in her until it comes out and then it can belong to her.
Because I am too solid I am an apparatus attached to the question.
Where does life exist. What if everything could be as tender and durable as a genital.
I want to found a country where everyone feels.
Universes shooting out of matter so tiny you can only feel it.
How to be liquid how to be gas how to be Freon, music, how to be flesh or inside of flesh that is living and how to be its equal, how not to be less than it, how not to divide the capital from the provinces, how to be.

Chapter 10

✦

"A poem of how to be": Abjection and Biopolitical Capitalism in Ariana Reines's "RENDERED"

Judith Goldman

The control of society over individuals is not conducted only through consciousness or ideology, but also in the body and with the body. For capitalist society biopolitics is what is most important, the biological, the somatic, the corporeal.
—Michel Foucault, "La naissance de la medicine sociale"

Sucking is dangerous. The danger of sucking.
—Gertrude Stein, "Sentences and Paragraphs,"
from *How to Write* (epigraph to *The Cow*)

Even before we begin to read, Ariana Reines's "RENDERED" launches its assault, blasting the reader with text in all caps. On closer inspection, this text is most unpoetic: it has been appropriated from *Carcass Disposal: A Comprehensive Review*, an all-in-one guide to the animal rendering industry, and from entries in *The Merck Veterinary Manual* on treating diseases afflicting factory-farmed cattle. We take in this language, by turns, objectifying, instrumental, abstract, technical, and commercial. It slowly becomes clear that with the graphic bullying of capitalization, "RENDERED" intends to recover, and perhaps to inflict, a sense of the massive violence these words abscond with, as they describe worlds within contemporary biopolitical capitalism that nearly everyone in the United States connects with on a daily basis through the commodity nexus yet rarely sees. Alternating among prose commentary, lyric prose, and lyric poem, Reines responds to her appropriated texts in a language that could not be any further opposed to clinical distance, disinculpating euphemism, hygienic jargon, or sales pitch: "Disease. Brains and shit."; "Sawed open. Easy."; "Is her shit any less her."; "What if everything could be as tender and durable as a genital."; "Ow my body." This scatology, moreover, takes a recognizable form. I offer a brief passage, almost at random, from Gertrude Stein's *Tender Buttons*, "A PIANO": "If the speed is open, if the color is careless, if the selection of a strong scent is not awkward, if the button holder is held by all the waving color and there is no color, not any color."[1] Compare Reines's final lines above: "How to be liquid how to be gas how to be Freon, music, how to be flesh / or inside of flesh that is living and how to be its equal, how not to be less / than it, how not to divide the capital from the provinces, how to be." However different, these agrammatical sentences bear a strong resemblance: paratactical arrangement of phrases, repetition that becomes rhythm, variation on a given syntactical unit.

Myriad difficulties arise before us: How does Reines work with her appropriated material—exactly how does (or how can) her lyric relate to texts so negatingly counterlyrical? In what ways do bodies figure here—what are these bodies to each other, and why is the body as figure so magnified? Why use Stein's form—and how does this use connect with these other concerns? To begin to address these issues, I turn to the excremental component of Reines's writing: difficult in itself, this language will lead us to a further difficulty at the heart of her poem.

"RENDERED" appears in Reines's feminist tour-de-force *The Cow* (2005) and is preoccupied with the human and animal female body and the body's leavings. Like *The Cow*'s other poems, it employs a cacography (shit-writing) that announces its challenge to "abjection," Julia Kristeva's psychoanalytic term for pervasive psychic and social mechanisms of policing, debasement, and violence. As a primordial infantile dynamic, abjection marks the self's use of processes of excretion to demarcate itself as a self proper, by separating itself from and disowning its wastes: "Such wastes drop so that I might live."[2] As Kristeva specifies, abjection is also a violent delineation of self from other that debases the other. In its infantile form, this autonomizing movement involves separation from the mother, an act Kristeva deems a (figurative) "matricide." To abject is thus not just to expel bodily waste to define the self but to disavow the self's dependencies by laying waste to the mother. For Kristeva, as Imogen Tyler notes, "the maternal (and feminine) body" becomes the "primary site/sight of cultural disgust."[3] If it is fixated on waste and on the mother, Reines's "RENDERED" foregrounds and attempts to undo the abjection of gendered bodies *tout court*—from that of the cow to that of the lyric I. Because abjection stems from and produces toxic affect, Reines's primary concern in the poem is this affect and its reciprocally constitutive relation with abjection. Reines uses Steinian form to "translate"—that is, to penetrate and expose—her appropriated texts. While Stein's style is performed to contest objectifying techno-scientific knowledge

("If you want to know what living is do not ask a doctor"), Reines's char-
ismatic inhabitation of Stein's signatures serves especially to express and
elucidate *difficult affect*.

Criticism that focuses on modernist difficulty often foregrounds the *affect*
of difficulty. In *The Difficulties of Modernism*, Leonard Diepeveen suggests
that affect is the very basis on which we think difficulty: "Using their whole
bodies, people react viscerally to difficulty, often with anxiety, anger, and
ridicule. . . . Moreover those affective responses are enmeshed in the standard
ways of conceptualizing difficulty."[4] In *The Trouble with Genius*, Bob Perel-
man similarly notes, "The high modernist text when read naively would be
more likely to produce perplexity, discomfort, and shame. . . . Although it
could easily be argued that this naive reading would be worthless, it would
be more accurate to consider it a constitutive feature of these works." The
affective dynamics of difficulty are indices of a scripted stymieing of reading
that bespeak "the deep split between reader and writer, or between the social
material used by the writer and the forms imposed on it."[5]
    Ariana Reines is not an author one would readily identify with manda-
rinism. Yet not only is her book *The Cow* bound up with historical literary
forms of obliquity, but its aesthetic strategies are meant to rewire the circuitry
of affect and difficulty, to reflect conditions of very contemporary biopoliti-
cal capitalism and the possibilities for lyric within it. Signifying continually
on and through Stein's style, Reines mobilizes the affect of particularly Stei-
nian difficulty.[6] But *The Cow* is less concerned with the traditional negative
affects produced by encountering textual difficulty than with difficult affect
as it originates in the social. Its poems embody radically mimetic forms that
maintain fidelity both to that disfiguring difficult affect and to the cultural
logic that generates it.
    Disarmingly, aggressively honest—vulgar and exquisite—erudite and street-
smart, *The Cow*'s excremental lyrics bear a quality of immediacy even as
they borrow and torque Stein's opaque grammars. Most obviously, Reines's
confrontational scatology contrasts strongly with Stein's anodyne vocabu-
lary.[7] Unlike Stein, Reines obsessively works through a set of tropes—female
sexuality; mothers and mothering; the cultural and biological life of cows;
the industrialized killing of animals and rendering of carcasses; the writing
and social efficacy of poetry—which her poems labor to link up and expound
upon. Reines's postconceptual inhabitation of Stein thus profoundly shifts
the anti- or complexly referential tenor of much of Stein's writing, in turn
redirecting the stakes of Steinian difficulty, such that Stein's form is brought
to bear on and to bear out what Reines frames as capitalism's painfully total-
izing force. We might thus note a (potential) further difficulty of Reines's
strategy: she requisitions for poetry the capacity to assert and perform bold
claims that reach far beyond her representative tropes and materials, an
amplification that is precisely her point.

In fact, over against her strong contrasts with Stein, Reines's most effective tactic in this endeavor is to draw on the experience of the immediate that Stein's writing elicits despite the mediating difficulty of its alien forms. This immediacy arises from Stein's profound iconoclasm, her refusal of calcified, habitual envelopes of meaning. In *How Reading Is Written: A Brief Index to Gertrude Stein*, Astrid Lorange argues that Stein's "obscurity" is *not* descriptive, in either a straightforward or encoded sense. Her texts are expressive of perception and rhythmically attuned to a relational, processual ontology of the world that includes within it her own performative writing as a compositive force: "[Stein] was interested in the *actual process of composing a grammar.*" [8] Reines harnesses for her own purposes the immediacy of Stein's style as essentially affective. That is, by using an expressive Steinianism, she signifies on our recognition of Stein as *writing affect*. Indeed, *The Cow* questions the very order of discourse through language remade as affective medium vis-à-vis Steinian form. Pitched against swathes of hyper-commodified, hyper-instrumentalizing appropriated text, the lyric translations of "RENDERED" subvert the capitalist abuse of language in its representational, yet obfuscating modes of concept, information, and abstraction, toward revealing violent, primal undercurrents and transformative potential within our culture. Reines uses Stein's style to impart, by enacting, the suffocatingly circular, totalizing grammars involved in what she portrays as capitalism's real subsumption of society and nature. Stein's form, too, here expresses the desubjectifying consequences of female abjection in its human and animal modes, all the while underscoring abjection as a made social relation and cultural construct. In turn, it becomes a means of modeling an alternative polity. Reines finally also extends Stein's proclivity for self-discussion and exhibitionism, in courageous confessional discourse whose posture is also cognate with contemporary flatness, elaborating a ruthlessly gendered lyric self.[9]

We should pay close attention to Reines's decisive gendering of the carcass as "her" in the first section of "RENDERED": "Across her. Across her. / Upending the weight of her I have to be finding out a grammar. / How to be. Opener. / Sawed open. Easy. / Open like a grammar." Suggesting both a humanizing of the animal and an animalizing of the human, the weird "her" of "THE TYPICAL FRESH CARCASS" subtly reminds us, as Nicole Shukin theorizes in *Animal Capital: Rendering Life in Biopolitical Times*, that to "animalize" is *"a power that applies in the first instance to the animal itself."* [10] If animalization, vis-à-vis the sinister referential instability Reines's "her" insinuates, involves the abjectification of women, this is because "the force of animalization presupposes the abjection of animals."[11] Piercing through, by mobilizing, layers of figural work that entwine women with beasts to underwrite the targeting of bodies for degradation and violence, Reines's "her" is difficult not to read as also a *human* body despite the bludgeoning referential directive exerted by the appropriated material from *Carcass Disposal* hanging above it.

Of course, this implication of the human in the animal and the animal in the human is due in part to everything preceding this moment in *The Cow* (e.g., from "KNOCKER": "My body is the opposite of my body when they hang me up by my hind legs").[12] Yet the sense of the human in what could otherwise be taken as a scene of animal slaughter and rendering is generated as well by the dislocations of subject and object Reines activates through Steinian form. Contrary to *How to Write*, what is under discussion here is not simply or only grammar proper, but the grammar of the biopolitical economy in a continuous present. While Reines's use of inversion ("Upending the weight of her I have to be finding out a grammar") mimes the inversion of the body on the meat hook, the fragments' ambiguous syntax destabilizes the "I" such that the I seems itself to become the carcass/her. The characteristically Steinian polyptoton—the turns on the word *open*—amphibolizes "Opener": "How to be. Opener." Does the I, qua industrial butcher, take up the position of an "Opener" who dissects "her" to gain knowledge of the grammar of the slaughterhouse? Or is the I herself to become "opener," more open, taking the very place of "her" as the body "sawed open. Easy. / Open like a grammar"? The slippage to which this open grammar of the carcass is prone echoes in the sinuous amphibrachic, then dactylic rhythm of the passage, its rhyme on feminine endings: "Across her. Across her. / Upending the weight of her I have to be finding out a grammar. / How to be. Opener. / Sawed open. Easy. / Open like a grammar."

This fungibility of "her" is staged more spectacularly in the final lyric section of "RENDERED," a response to text lifted from *The Merck Veterinary Manual*'s "Overview of Bovine Secondary Recumbency (Downer cow syndrome)."[13] In this lyric sequence, the expression of "difficult" affect—the affect germane to abjection, to bare life, both animal and human—becomes the means of tropic interchange among its gendered protagonists. The cries of a cow in slaughter ("can the air be ruined if she cries out inside it") are transferred to the lyric I ("Who if I cried out CREAM O LAND"), then to the mother ("When she howls it's with her mouth a tooth missing in it. / Menthol cigarettes"), only to travel back to the now infantilized lyric I ("Ma Ma. MOUTH MOUTH / Mean ME ME everything I can feel inside").[14] Human and animal anguish blur, anguish gives onto babble, suckling on language is as alimentary incorporation of the mother, while Reines underscores the uncanniness of utterance as an externalization of interior feeling. Taking up a familiar Steinian ruminative register that whittles away at existential givens to exert a groundlessness of thought and being, what follows in the lyric is a kind of antiblason that interrogates as it runs together body parts of mother and cow: "What skin. What hair. What eyes, gold tooth. What muscles. What udder. / What are hooves. The liver, what liver. What stomach. Horns. Where / isn't she. Where isn't she inside her body. Where is she not. Where is / she least. . . . / Where is a living thing not itself. Is her shit any less her." The body's waste redeemed as its very essence, gender in turn becomes embraceable through an unlikely affinity constructed for it with shit: "And moreover, gender. / It is latent in her until it comes out and then it can belong to her." It is here that Reines imagines affect as the basis of politics: "I want to found a country where everyone feels." She activates the radical affective, political potential of abjection by reclaiming its ultimate exponents: mothers, cows, cadavers, shit.

Writing in the tenth section of "RENDERED," "I am going to try to be a girl. Try to transcribe bare sustenance," Reines speaks of the difficulty both of internalizing and performing or living feminine abjectification and of bringing the female as bare life to writing. Yet I would like to raise another challenge taken on by the aesthetic politics of "RENDERED" and *The Cow* more generally—the very sense that affect, even *difficult* affect, presents any kind of resistance to contemporary biopolitical capitalism. According to autonomist Marxists such as Antonio Negri, who theorizes the "real subsumption" of human time, labor, and life by capital, all social processes, including and especially the generation and circulation of affect, are captured in circuits of capitalist value and exploitation.[15] Under biopolitical capitalism, particularly as related to societies organized by a postindustrial economy, immaterial labor, and digital culture, *it is human affective capacities and the making of subjects that are directly productive of value.*

In fact, *The Cow* fiercely confronts this issue, but to address how it does so, we need first to engage with how Reines's awareness of capitalism's externalities and its real subsumption of nature inflects her poetic content and form. Like many contemporary works of ecopoetry, *The Cow* embodies what I term "sink poetics": it makes central the "unintended" toxic externalities generated in the production of commodities, yet so often unaccounted for in the market pricing system; it further traces capital's disastrously ineffective containment of such toxins in sinks.[16] A sink poetics, that is, hones in on hazardous wastes disappeared from the scene of economic and other forms of representation; on capitalist strategies for containing (and forgetting) these wastes; and most importantly, on the consequences of *their tendency to leak.* Reines's "RENDERED" attends, for instance, to the "PERCOLATING PAN," the tank that contains offal being rendered, as well as to the seepage of stress hormones into factory-farmed beef: "An animal secretes a lot of cortisol . . . and this ruins the meat you are trying to turn her into." Reines is always focused on difficult affect: in "RENDERED," she inscribes, in a not-quite-figurative manner, the toxic affect of the animal under slaughter as air pollution: "If her flesh can be ruined . . . can the air be ruined if she cries out inside it."

As its use of the rendering industry indicates, *The Cow* is simultaneously fascinated by capitalism's capacity for the horrific, superefficient exploitation of its own wastes. In *Animal Capital*, Nicole Shukin brilliantly theorizes and historicizes rendering as a foundational practice of so-called sustainable capitalism: it appears as an ethical "recycling" of animal offal by converting it into saleable commodities.[17] Contemporary rendering's reanimation of the wastes of factory farming promotes a certain naturalization of capitalism: such closed-loop production seems to make good on the metaphor of "industrial ecology" as the by-products of one industry become the raw materials of another. Indeed, the coupling of factory farm with rendering perfectly crystallizes the ideological fiction of the closed loop: meat industry waste is rendered and fed to cattle, who are then processed as meat, rendered, and fed to cattle. Rendering thus exemplifies and forwards capital's rightful real subsumption or total enclosure of nature.

Reines reflects on how rendering enacts and reinforces the sense that *everything* may be considered a stock of capital in the penultimate section of "RENDERED": "What happens to the world when a body is a bag of stuff you can empty / out of it. . . . What difference does it make how a thing dies." Yet she is obviously obsessed with rendering as part of a demonic industrial loop. "TALLOW" figures the imprisoning, all-encompassing tautology of capitalist production somewhat abstractly: "Alimenting the world perpetuates it. Duh. Plus 'the world' is itself a food. / We go outside we stay in." But the cruel, dreary, dangerous cycle by which cattle are fed to cattle are fed to cattle is also taken on directly from the poem's first section: "A carcass in which nothing is leftover. / . . . Open, a hole where the head disgorges its body." Significantly, in this moving translation of *Carcass Disposal*'s description of how "THE END PRODUCTS OF RENDERING HAVE ECONOMIC VALUE," Steinian repetition and figurative slippage also ramify the sickening circularity that the rendering industry pursues in "PROVIDING A SOURCE OF PROTEIN FOR USE IN ANIMAL FEED."

One of the most interesting poetic arguments to emerge in *The Cow* is that human affective economic services embody a naturalized sink logic similar to that of rendering. Mothering, and the sexual and other servicing of men done by women, is mostly unpaid, gendered labor that, aside from involving the cleaning of more material forms of waste, entails containing and processing others' toxic affect.[18] Reines focuses intensively on sexualized female abjection, on women's status as repositories of male aggression, on the mother as abject container, always framing the hidden costs of this affective labor: "When she howls its with her mouth . . . Stretch marks on her stomacher." Significantly, Reines also raises the issue throughout *The Cow* of the poet's parallel, difficult affective labor of laundering language and the ambivalence surrounding this work. In the poem "NICO SAID EXCREMENT FILTERS THROUGH THE BRAIN. I'S A KIT," Reines states: "Clean the language. Clean it."[19] In "I AM NO PROPHET, I AM AN HUSBANDMAN," writing functions as a filter of waste much like the vat in a rendering plant: "Books are the same as nets / For time shit, sieves that catch an air's leavings."[20] The poet does not simply muck about in the fallout of sanitized capitalist language but must devise alternative means of laundering it. Yet one notes in turn that this aesthetic strategy of poetically processing text from loathsome industrial guides *is itself a form of affective rendering* that serves, even as it would resist, capital.

In "RENDERED," Reines further names the poet's labor as that of specifically materialist figuration, of constructing analogies between like relations really existing in the world: "Vented into the forge an analogy. / It blew in there because it thought. / It resembled. A sample of influence. / Using a world to build thought out of. / It is a poem of how to be." In a later prose poem, "LODGE," Reines indicts her own homological poetic work as too closely mimicking capital's technologies of equivalency: "There is a stupidity in the conflation I am in the act of, cow with cattle car and mother with me, cunt and carcass and book and stomach. But this stupidity, if it belongs to me, is also exterior to me. . . . Signification is incestuous, iterative, autofellating. I am not sure this is living."[21] Here Reines acknowledges her poetics as enjoined to capitalist complicity, in that her analogizing labor, if somehow revelatory of an external truth, nonetheless operates in a manner akin to rendering's "incestuous," tautological logic. Which is to say, Reines strongly implies that the *real subsumption of nature and society entails the real subsumption of lyric.*

If biopolitical capitalism organizes a gendered political economy of affect that it exploits to its own ends, if the wastes of its productive processes reemerge as commodities, if poetry itself is enlisted in affective labor that abets capital even as it mimics its logic, is there any way to escape capital's totalizing force? Part of the difficulty we find in *The Cow* is Reines's reckoning with the nihilism bound up with real subsumption, her lyric persona so often caught between nauseated resignation and outrage pointing to some kind of exit. Hence her fixation on bovine spongiform encephalopathy, a disease that spreads to humans through consumption of meat and the products of rendering and that seems to present an uncontainable vector beyond capitalist capture. In "RENDERED," she writes of downer cows:

> They get mashed up or transubstantiated and used
> to get fed to the ones living in their own shit at feedlots and that's how come thousands more had to be slaughtered and beyond slaughtered destroyed because DESTROY IS BEYOND SLAUGHTER incinerated or liquefied in special vats. The container contains the corpse. Something gets out from under the end. Disease. Brains and shit.

In the hysteron proteron of this passage, effects are given before their cause: though the last lines here detail a disease that "gets out from under the end," it is also noted that capitalism, if hoisted on the petard of its putative industrial ecology, has already had the last word: at first it extended life past life, and it has learned to kill with a death stronger than death—"DESTROY

IS BEYOND SLAUGHTER." The containment solution harkens back to Reines's scathing earlier poem "A CLEANER, SAFER WORLD," based on text from a website selling systems for liquidating infectious carcasses. All the same, if disease has been profitably cordoned and circumscribed, if "container contains the corpse," Reines, by disrupting narrative order, underscores BSE as a sure sign of wrong, even a harbinger of an insoluble catastrophe.

Yet "RENDERED" closes with more hope. Against capital's annexation of life itself, it raises the possibility of life outside the profit mechanism: "How to be liquid how to be gas how to be Freon, music, how to be flesh / or inside of flesh that is living and / how to be its equal, how not to be less / than it, how not to divide the capital from the provinces, how to be." As Reines has asserted all along in *The Cow*, life under real subsumption may not be living. Perhaps poetry's greatest difficulty, as reflected in its equivocal aesthetic strategies, is that it can claim no exteriority to that totalizing condition. But what "RENDERED" nonetheless ultimately reaches toward, with a suddenly exuberant Steinianism, is unexploited, undivided aliveness—toward being "a poem of how to be."

Notes

1. Gertrude Stein, "A PIANO," from *Tender Buttons* (1914), in *Selected Writings of Gertrude Stein*, ed. Carl Van Vechten (New York: Vintage Books, 1990), 467.

2. Julia Kristeva, *Powers of Horror: An Essay on Abjection*, trans. Leon S. Roudiez (New York: Columbia University Press, 1982), 3.

3. Imogen Tyler, "Against Abjection," *Feminist Theory* 10, no. 1 (2009): 82.

4. Leonard Diepeveen, *The Difficulties of Modernism* (New York: Routledge, 2003), xiv. "Many of the terms used to describe difficulty are affective," he states further, "describing what difficulty does to readers" (63).

5. Bob Perelman, *The Trouble with Genius: Reading Pound, Joyce, Stein, and Zukofsky* (Berkeley: University of California Press, 1994), 11–12, 12.

6. Stein's *Tender Buttons* and *How to Write* are cited in Reines's diverse list of sources; it is unquestionably Stein who sets the tonic of the book from the opening epigraph (see above) onward.

7. Though perhaps not with Stein's form: in *Reading Gertrude Stein: Body, Text, Gnosis*, Lisa Ruddick extensively discusses the anality of Stein's rhythm in *The Making of Americans* (noted in Perelman, *The Trouble with Genius*, 133).

8. Astrid Lorange, *How Reading Is Written: A Brief Index to Gertrude Stein* (Middletown, Conn.: Wesleyan University Press, 2014), 104. She makes this case throughout, discussing Stein in relation to Whitehead especially, as well as Deleuze and Karen Barad.

9. On flatness in contemporary poetry, see Hannah Manschel, "Depthless Psychology," *New Inquiry*, July 7, 2014, http://thenewinquiry.com/essays/depthless-psychology/ (accessed July 16, 2015).

10. Shukin, *Animal Capital*, 10.

11. Ibid., 236n32.

12. *The Cow*, 11.

13. "Overview of Bovine Secondary Recumbancy (Downer cow syndrome)," in *Merck Veterinary Manual*, http://www.merckvetmanual.com/mvm/musculo skeletal_system/bovine_secondary_recumbency/overview_of_bovine_secondary_ recumbency.html, last review/revision May 2014 (accessed July 14, 2015).

14. Here the interjection of the New Jersey dairy's brand name is less the content of the cry than an eruption of commercial language into the space of that cry. Reines's frequent use of such all-caps interjections is akin to their proliferation in the work of Hannah Weiner.

15. "Real subsumption" is a complex concept extrapolated from the "Fragment on Machines" in Marx's *Grundrisse*. Negri's key texts include "Value and Affect"; "The Constitution of Time"; *Marx beyond Marx: Lessons on the* Grundrisse; and his trilogy with Michael Hardt, *Empire*, *Multitude*, and *Commonwealth*. My argument here draws on Shukin's excellent discussion and critique of the concept in *Animal Capital*, 75–86.

16. My thinking on sinks has been strongly influenced by Jennifer Gabrys's "Sink: The Dirt of Systems," *Environment and Planning D: Society and Space* 27 (2009): 666–81.

17. I am summarizing arguments Shukin presents in the introduction and first chapter of her book.

18. On women's processing of toxic affect, see Teresa Brennan, *The Transmission of Affect* (Ithaca, N.Y.: Cornell University Press, 2004); on women's hyperexploited reproductive labor, see Silvia Federici, *Revolution at Point Zero: Housework, Reproduction, and Feminist Struggle* (Oakland, Calif.: PM Press, 2012).

19. *The Cow*, 15.

20. Ibid., 23.

21. Ibid., 100.

ATSURO RILEY

Flint-Chant

Once upon a time a ditchpipe got left behind behind Azalea Industrial, back in the woods backing on to the Ashley, where old pitch-pines and loblollies grow wild. A mild pesticide-mist was falling and mingling with paper-mill smell and creosote oil the morning he found it. The boy shook and sheltered in its mouth awhile—*hoo-hoo! hey-O!*—and bent and went on in. It was like a cave but clean. He C-curved his spine against one wall to fit, and humming something, sucked his shirttail. He tuned his eyes to what low light there was and knuckle-drummed a line along his legs.

What the boy called inside-*oku* called him back. He was hooked right quick on the well-bottom peace of the pumicey concrete and how sounds sounded in there, and resounded. Tight-curled as he had to get—like a cling-shrimp one-day, a pill-bug, a bass-clef, a bison's eye; an abalone (*ocean ear!*), antler-arc, Ark-ant, apostrophe another—sure as clocks a cool clear under-creek would rise, and rinse him through, and runnel free. Hanging in a green-pine O outside were sun-heat and smaze and BB-fire and Mosquito Abatement. Inside there were water-limber words (and a picture-noisy nave), shades of shade.

Chapter 11

From Private to Public Worlds: The Evolution of Atsuro Riley's Hyper-Hyphenated Universe

Cary Nelson

This is "Flint-Chant," the opening section or prologue to Atsuro Riley's twenty-six-section book-length narrative poem *Romey's Order*. Romey is the young boy, "eye and voice" of the book, living with his family on a river bend in rural South Carolina. If it ever was an uncompromised rural Eden, however, that day is past. The world that Romey sees and internalizes, the world he shapes in observation and wordplay, is awash in the bric-a-brac of a postindustrial wasteland. And nature itself is a summer swarm of overripe and musty, composted leavings and leave-takings, a mist and ooze of live creatures passing through his world and organic compounds deposited there to stay. "Chokedamp's in it. / Born blackdamp" (33):

> Lure-spoor of brack-beyond:
>
> fox-tracks
>
> *slp thwp* slug-muscles
>
> gristle-snails
>
> coarse boar-hairs;
>
> rumor. (31)

Positioned here in an abandoned pipe redoubt that recalls the similarly abandoned setting of W. S. Merwin's "The Drunk in the Furnace," Romey imagines a stream rising to rinse him clean. And he fashions the pipe into a musical instrument, humming a tune and drumming along his leg to enjoy the hollowed echoes: "Sounds sounded in there, and re-sounded." In addition to the mists and odors that drift in, there are also "water-limber words," because this is a textual setting established in the boy's consciousness, and he lingers over flexible speech that plays out in fluid metamorphosis. Indeed, the poem sequence as a whole is a record of how consciousness is composed of whatever the environment presents to us, including, as Romey discovers when he visits a local fair later in the sequence, "slopes down to low-lying marsh-mire: whiffs of pluff-mud stink and live gnat-pack poison, carnie-cots and -trailers camped on ooze" (28).

Behind an industrial site abutting the Ashley River, a blackwater tidal river rising from cypress swamps, Romey constructs the world above without any of the evaluative judgments readers might make. BB-fire and mosquito abatement are just components of his world to be integrated into his sensory awareness: "A mild pesticide-mist was falling and mingling with paper-mill smell and creosote oil." Of course Riley's authorial humor is also at play here, just as Faulkner's was in *The Sound and the Fury* and *As I Lay Dying*, arguably southern precursors to *Romey's Order*, but for Romey a pesticide-mist is simply what there is.

Riley draws broadly on modernist experimental traditions in the poem sequence—one can hear echoes of Hopkins and Joyce in his wordplay—though *Romey's Order* is not a pure stream-of-consciousness project. There is a third-person narrator alongside Romey throughout. As with other verbally experimental writers, the reader is tasked with puzzling out the meaning of the coinages that saturate the sequence, in this case most frequently in the form of hyphenated words: *Ark-ant, water-limber, pump-monkeyed, nerve-hover, mind-minnows, milk-purling, morning-blood, glow-belling, gloam-knelling, blood-iron, mourn-cranes, clover-kept, calf-patch, drawn-sung, skin-folks, finger-hankered, scorn-brunt, thorn-bined, clamber-mire, itch-moss, fangle-plaited, fret-morass,* and *croodle-field,* among many others. The notes tell us *croodle* means "to make a soft, low-murmuring sound (to coo as a dove); the humming of a tune," but I'm not sure that settles the meaning of "croodle-field." And hyphenated inventions are mixed with other coinages, often in sequences with a joyous and self-conscious celebratory character: "Tremblescent ditch-jellies, globberous spawn-floss. Drupes of / (dapple-clinking) bottle-glass in trees" (44):

> Ore-stope, lode-lamps,
> Turnturbulating crubble-corf and -barrows.
> Trace-tastes of (blast-furnace) harrow-smelt and pour. (33)

Context is generally the key to deciphering meaning here, but the difficulty for the reader, as always, is deciding whether he or she has assigned meaning correctly. Alternatively, as with much experimental writing, you can take pleasure in the connotative and associative play and not worry about whether you have got it right. Close reading traditions can make that a somewhat anxious choice; the drive for some level of certainty remains strong. But for most readers the choice between these two modes of reading is not absolute; we balance one against the other according to preference and training.

Self-reflexive references to verbal invention recur as well, drawing attention not only to the practice of composition but also to readerly self-awareness and difficulty. At one point we get an aside added to a descriptive sequence: "Plus, how to hammer, wire, and jerry homely words" (14). In another passage the textual interplay of sound and sense becomes reflexively performative: "*Romey-boy* . . . he tries saying, slow slurring it long, long, until the word sound goes strange in the air and bends back on itself, like a shell-road or a river" (10). Romey tells himself (and us) to "bind (and try to braid) our river-wrack and leavings" (11), a command that applies both to the kind of perception called for in this bricolage environment of organic and industrial elements and to the verbal invention necessary if one wants to capture it in words. And there are moments of address to the reader that foreground narration: "Have I said yet how mudworms (and flickery mind-minnows) live off leaf-chaff / and blown bark-slough and home-grounds and gravel?" (12).

Romey's parents are a strong presence in the poem, but only as he perceives them, not through the descriptive categories the external world would offer. A jacket comment by Frank Bidart gives us the key social designations: "*Romey's Order* is the world of a young boy growing up in backwoods South Carolina. His father is an ex-soldier, his mother the Japanese wife the father brought home from his time as a soldier." Whether appropriately or not, a difficulty the reader would have had with this experimental text has been eliminated. The book itself only offers oblique clues to knowledge of this alternative order. Thus, through Romey's eyes we see that Daddy "carries tattoos" of a partly military character: "Inked-on anchors and bird's heads, bluegreen as blood-veins" (18). His mother is partly present through her cultural heritage, first in the Japanese diction Romey absorbs; *oku*, in the second stanza above, as the notes at the back of the book tell us, thereby resolving another difficulty the reader would have confronted, is "Japanese: roughly equivalent to interior, a deep place" (53). When Romey describes her it is as he sees her from a tree outside the house where he has perched, adapting his body to the "Y-crotch" of branches in much the same way as he curves his body to fit the "ditchpipe" above: "See that funnel-blur of color in the red-gold glass? —Mama, mainly: boiling jelly. She's the apron-yellow (rickracked) plaid in there and stove-coil coral: the quick silver blade-flash, plus the (magma-brimming) ladle-splash; that's her behind the bramble-berry purple, sieved and stored" (7). As she cooks jelly that bubbles like a volcano on the stove, Romey sees her in fragments, like a bird glimpsed through foliage, though she does get a name—*"KAY" (KAZUE) HUTTO*—as she labels jars of preserved vegetables later in the book.

Romey's house is an equally strong presence, serving as the prime instance of several enclosed spaces—beginning with the pipe—that function as mental extensions and representations of his body. In the opening line of "Picture," the same poem that offers Mama cooking her volcanic jelly, Romey says, "This is the house (and jungle-strangled yard) I come from and carry" (7). He carries the house with him wherever he goes. Anyone who has seen kudzu engulf a southern property will have one meaning of "jungle-strangled" readily in mind, but here a whole cornucopia of insects and vegetation are at issue: "Out here, crickets are cricking their legs. Turtlets are cringing in their bunker-shells and burrows. Once-bedded nightcrawling worms are nerving up through bean-vine-roots and moonvines), —and dew-shining now and cursive." Cursive, the worms instinctively write their way up through the soil in darkness. Meanwhile the house begins to succumb to natural processes: "Blisters cluster over there by the sink, owing to floor-slope and pipe-seep and spring-steady trickling: a mildew-map will sprout, and spread, and blacken there by noon" (17).

Soon "every flying insect with a taste for something spoiled" crowds into Romey's river-bend world, beginning with "a fever-cloud of glassy-eyed iridescent flies": "They were hovering hairnet (and halo-) style above my bald-headed daddy; now they are down-diving and landing, in dark clots and clusters, on his eyebrows, neck-bones, knees" (9). When a trip away from home is in order, much the same process engulfs the family car as it backs out of the driveway: "Every hard in-breath, river-reek and oil-scorch and marsh-gas mingling, our under-chassis (and rear axle, eyeteeth) chuttering due to roots and rain-ruts, our rust-crusting Rambler swerving and fishtailing and near-missing trees" (26). As always with Riley, rhyme and alliteration enrich and enliven his lists and action sequences.

So far at least, the social world most of us know, the public world of historical event, makes itself known here only by way of the detritus of industrial waste. Even the house, built of man-made products, seems well on its way to rejoining nature's preferred mode of animated liquidity. But the family car is on its way to the Blue Hole Summer Fair, and there Romey overhears others remark his status as other:

> *I wonder does her boy talk Chinese?*
> *You ever seen that kind of black-headed?*
> *Blue shine all in it like a crow.* (28)

There too the attractions include booths called "Rebel Yell and Shoot the Gook Down," and his father has a role to play before "bleacher-rows of (cooncalling) men": "And there he is, up in front with some tall man, iron-arming two black-chested boys toward the ring" (29). All this is offered without commentary, but of course the diction goes beyond neutral marking, at least for audiences not part of the community. The ticket-taker's Dixie-flag t-shirt speaks for itself, though the spectacle of two black men boxing before a white audience is hardly unique to the American South.

The visit to the fair and the spectacle of its freak show booths provokes "Filmstrip," a two-page, thin, columnar poem structured by appearances of Bait-boy, wild-man, boot-man, shack-man, belt-man, and *salt-man*, all locals now elevated to the status of oddities. But none of them get orderly descriptions that would make them easily positioned or relegated to pity or condescension. Instead they are embedded in an alliterated and syncopated vertical list that returns us to the knuckle-drummed rhythms of "Flint-Chant." Bait-boy is minnow-naked

(neck to belt)

chigger-bit and calamined:

powder-pinkish chalk-nickels

spackle-scales

nipple-jots like dimes.

Buckets (sperm-teemsome

silversides

(prime) tad-tails

creel-crickets

redworms):

cottonmouthy creek-prong

(marsh-musk,

trailer-husks)

wrong-water swale

(and back-slues)

back

beyond. (30)

We have leapfrogged from the fair to a whole self-reinforcing universe of southern fishing holes and the social world they encompass—and to an unforgettable tour-de-force rhythmic sequence. "Back beyond," indeed, but also pressing into consciousness for readers everywhere. It is all readable, from the "boy" festooned with insect bites and curative lotion to the bait bucket full of critters to the river world teeming with snakes and shadowed with fog, but the music takes up these referents and turns them into a performance as much chant and tongue-twister as social portrait.

Yet the world of historical reference returns nonetheless, notably toward the end of the book in "Scroll," one of several tributes to Romey's Japanese mother. The form this time is the disjunctive, open-form poem preferred by so many postwar American poets. He uses it here to scatter biographical and historical detail across the page in the manner of Ezra Pound, Charles Olson, and Robert Duncan. Especially since the open form versus closed form poetry battles of the 1950s and '60s, of course, it is clear many readers find such open-form difficulties to be opportunities for engagement. They present ambiguities to be resolved; they require readerly investment. Indeed, as with Riley's work, they often provide subtle and complex ways of engaging with history. Here we get glimpses of a life in Japan: "Once upon a summer-quilt, a girl-child. Kazue. . . . Handed—more so as hot hibachi-coal—from cord-mother to (hired) milk-mother to skin-folks, foot of Fuji" (37) interleaved with the South Carolina household, and then suddenly history at its most pivotal enters the poem: "*Shhhh* is the center-sound—and her shelter-hole—in *Hi ro shi ma   mushroom*" and "*Bokugo was this hole we dug we closed ourself inside it.*" *Bokugo*, the notes tell us, is Japanese for underground bomb shelter. The term *oku* (deep place) returns here for the first time since its use in "Flint-Chant." And so Romey's enclosure, the world his wordplay helps him create, gains the sense of a protective retreat, a way of wrapping himself in that river-bend home and keeping the world at bay. Just how we are to take these lines, however, remains ambiguous. Was Kazue in Hiroshima or elsewhere in Japan? Does that shelter and its silence also describe the silence the family has imposed on itself in South Carolina? And how many forgetful and uninterested Americans have long ago acquiesced to national silence about Hiroshima and Nagasaki? Is that self-censuring "*Shh-hhh,*" which is also the poem's final line, though with the number of *h*s increased from four to five, the price Romey and his family pay to accommodate to South Carolina culture and politics? Romey will not tell us. Neither will the narrator. But then they never do. We have moved from readerly uncertainty about the meaning of Riley's verbal inventions to a more fundamental challenge to our moral integrity. If we marginalize the memory of Hiroshima individually and collectively, what does that say about us as a people?

Then it is as if the invocation of Hiroshima opens an outlet for South Carolinian grief in the next poem: "The heard-tell *how her baby'd burned* downrivering and rippling. . . . Brackwater cove-woods by her marsh-yard oak-creaking and -crying. . . . The grieve-mother *Malindy Jean* porch-planking brunt and planging" (40). The choice of Malindy's first name is an allusion to Paul Laurence Dunbar's 1895 poem "When Malindy Sings," in which a melody echoes from the kitchen to the woods. Now it is nature and a mother integrated in sorrow. The poem is titled "Bell," perhaps because its threnody tolls on behalf of the community and because it shows a version of Romey-style enclosure embodying suffering. Malindy has turned the skillet that killed her baby into a bell, hammering it to make her grief echo wide, "The live heft-fact scorch-skillet willow-strung low and hanging. / Her heaving shovel-hafts and oars to make it ring" (40).

The book opened with Romey and his innocent consciousness, which could harmonize and celebrate everything. Now childhood curiosity has begun to meet its adult match. In "Fosterling-Song" on the following page, four lines long, we encounter a foster child's song:

> Hadn't he come to us from County Home
> cleaved to a caul swaddle
> cloth (of coarse croker-sack weave)
> he all the time plucked and wrung? (41)

Croker-sack is a southern term for a burlap bag used to hold frogs that have been caught. It is an emblem of absolute poverty and the near absence of care as a child's clothes. "Hutch," the next poem, reminds us that Vietnam vets are scattered among the South Carolina hollows and lowlands: "*Nary a one of the brung-homes brung home whole*" (42). Returning to the ditchpipes of "Flint Chant" and recalling how Romey in "Picture" can "belly-worry" along a branch to position himself in a tree outside the reach of the tides, "Hutch" recasts this diction for darker ends. Romey, who has perhaps begun to grow up, learns that some crave such retreats to cower in fear:

> *Remembering the Garner twins Carl and Charlie come home mute.*
> *Cherry-bombs 4th of July them both belly-scuttling under the house.*
> *Their crave of pent-places ditchpipes.*
> *Mongst tar-pines come upon this-box thing worked from scrapwood.*
> *From back when it was Nam time I tell you what.*
>
> (43)

In "Box" we get a description of how Romey's mother fertilizes and waters her okra crop so the yard is flooded "like a paddy," turning a favorite southern vegetable into an amalgam of South Carolina and Southeast Asia: "Dark groves rose like Vietnam bamboo. Cars came by to see her camouflage-green stalks going high as the house" (23). We learn that her okra crop is grown from "seeds of the time when her okra-crop grew giant," but we do not know at that point that the Vietnam reference is also a seed planted in the poem that will not bear fruit until toward the end of the book. Until then, "her rice-life now (river-oaked hereabouts)" remains "near-underground" (38). The pointed finger-pods atop the stalks of okra are "not like food but human"; then they become human in "Hutch," as we learn what a more traumatic amalgam of South Carolina and Southeast Asia entails: "*Them days men boys gone dark groves rose like Vietnam bamboo*" (42). Now we have the challenge—or difficulty—of deciding how much trauma to read back into the earlier poem, a difficulty foregrounded by the repetition of phrases from "Box."

I can understand why the reviews of *Romey's Order* emphasize the title character's joy in linguistic invention and the sheer wonder of the world he creates, since all of that confronts the reader immediately upon opening the book, but the narrative arc of the book doesn't end there, and the demands on the reader are not limited to taking pleasure in Romey's and the narrator's wordplay. For those readers who follow *Poetry*, where most of the individual segments were gradually published separately prior to the book being issued, the linguistic inventiveness was altogether textual, not linked to Romey's world. Encountered separately, "Drift-Raft" is simply a brief imagist poem; in the book it is about Romey listening to the sounds his house makes at night. Read separately, "Hutch" is only a Vietnam poem, not a text about Romey's awakening to the public world beyond his river-bend home, let alone a text in dialogue with "Box." That difference opens the challenge for readers of the book of deciding how much the twenty-six segments should be treated as separate poems. The strong narrative context in the book suggests they be seen as phases in Romey's mental development, but the exact status of the segments remains a difficulty for the reader to resolve. On the other hand, as is often the case with experimental poetry, some "difficulties," like this one, are both interesting and productive, not a burden but rather an incitement to intellectual engagement. It is an incentive not only to interrogate this issue in the poem itself but also to reflect in the integrity and relational status of poems more generally. For this is a case where poems published separately become not just modestly but radically different when included in a book.

Romey's world darkens considerably through the last third of the book. As the book nears its conclusion, we meet "*Clary* . . . body past bent. . . . Her null eye long since gone isinglassy, opal" (45). "Bear off," the penultimate poem urges, "right where understory comes to grief entire" (947). Then we encounter "the desolated train-trestle rust-buckling —and falling . . . downrivering *gone (gone) gone (gone)*" (50). We are now in the world of country music, "*where every Story cauls a Grief.*" And the abandoned industrial objects that offered opportunities at the book's outset now serve as symbols of loss.

Early in a book that returns repeatedly to cooking, Mama is preparing to bake, "palm-patting and -smoothing a belly-white (*Bobwhite!*) swole of dough" (17). She is working alliteratively from "her boulder-bellied hoard-sacks of flour for biscuits" (25). "*And raise them biscuits big, for sopping!*" (11), Romey calls out. Now we know more fully the range of what a home country biscuit—and the private, self-enclosed southern family world it represents—will have to absorb over time. The arc of the book runs from innocence to experience, though Romey creates an inner world of each, as all of us do. The apparent oddity of Romey's diction is thus a guide to his consciousness and a model of the mental landscape each of us inhabits, a landscape always in part a project of mental invention. In one way the book is pulled toward a sense of its uniqueness by the distinctive character of its verbal inventions. In another, we are led to ask whether Romey is much like the rest of us. As the book opens, Romey declares, "*I myself will monkey-shinny so high no bark-burns (or tree-rats, or tides) or lava-spit can reach me*" (8). And for a time he succeeds.

MYUNG MI KIM

from *Penury*

Radiant falcon
Scattering acacias

The recitation of acacias
A grove of riverbeds

Residence of years' repose
Patience aids such

A bank of wide hands
Tender petition

Horizon slope, a hoop(ed) light
A fragrant sight beheld beholds

Where in this, further dwelt
Abide

Nestled close
Civil bound

Chapter 12

✦

Paranoid Poetics:
Targeting and Evasion in Myung Mi Kim's *Penury*

Joseph Jonghyun Jeon

Myung Mi Kim's *Penury* (2009) contains within its 111-page body no fewer than thirty-four entirely blank pages (just over 30 percent), not including the more-than-usual number of blank endpapers. On a handful of pages only diacritical marks appear, most frequently three sequential colons that look like this: ":::."[1] Kim also includes a cross-out poem and a poem consisting entirely of forward slashes. If these qualities did not already pose sufficient difficulty, we might add to this list the challenges of her characteristically cryptic style, which is amplified in comparison to previous works. Furthermore, aside from the colons, which obliquely serve to divide the volume into six sections, there is little organization—no clear titles, table of contents, or index. It is difficult to discern if and where a single poem begins and ends, or even what the unit of poem might mean in this context. *Penury* is thus not only a volume of poetry that presents considerable interpretive challenges; it is one that renders the fundamental task of locating the poetry itself somewhat difficult. The question of what these poems mean is preceded by the problem of where these poems are.

It might be useful to begin by distinguishing between a penurious aesthetic and a minimalist one. Though both are stripped-down strategies that foreground simplified and essential forms, Kim's poetry here is less blunt and elemental, more obscure and thwarted. Instead of expression pared down to its core, her poetics seems bothered and unfulfilled, the glitchy product of a distant transmission or the puzzling remainder of a fuller text rendered inscrutable by faulty connection or dense encoding. It is the car radio that jumps in and out of static or the elegant alien glyphs of a superior galactic species, something left out or something out there. If minimalism streamlines aesthetic experience as part of a clarifying gesture, then Kim elides instead to obfuscate, cautiously offering clues to what we might call meaning while stridently frustrating the maneuvers of any interpretative enterprise.

Warren Liu has argued that rather than moving toward resolution, Kim's poetry works instead to enact a tension between epistemology and politics, that is, between "*generalized* forms of knowledge production" and "*specific* iterations of power."[2] So rather than settling on one or the other, Kim's poetics "urges a critical reevaluation of how these two sets of readings are not only related but necessarily intertwined."[3] This fact of "irreducible tension" also helps explain the difficult quality of the work,[4] which can be intensely specific, evocative, and even heartbreaking at the level of word, phrase, and image and at the same time unrelentingly opaque on any collective level. Inhabiting the unlikely intersection of the eidetic and the ephemeral, it is as if the poetic speaker had something very specific to say but feared that any articulation would ossify into trite reification at the precise moment of enunciation, as if the very fact of communication were catastrophic.[5] In this respect, it poses the antithesis to what Rachel Greenwald Smith describes as "compromise aesthetics"—a hybrid between mainstream and experimental strategies that Smith finds symptomatic of neoliberal cultural entrenchment[6]—so uncompromising that unintelligibility becomes preferable to reduction.

Animated by the sense of extremity that inheres in the very notion of "penury," a striking feature of Kim's volume is that it regards fear, anxiety, and even paranoia not as reactionary but as necessary cognitive stances against the overwhelming challenges of contemporary life, which are defined by epistemological structures and material apparatuses radical enough to warrant such outsize responses. In turn, these negative affects allow us to map with greater perspicuity the new disciplinary apparatuses that hide in plain sight. Although we don't need poetry to tell us that we live in a Deleuzian control society, Kim's paranoid poetics helps us recognize how capaciously that society extends, along with the biomechanics of its tendrils, mapping these regimes of control at the level of not just expression but code. Her earlier work (up through her 2002 volume *Commons*) offered recombinant possibilities that might redress the disjunctures and dislocations of slightly earlier visions of modernity as realized in a particularly intense form in the problem of diasporic subjectivity—a direction that poets like Cathy Park Hong have proven to be quite enabling for recent Asian American experimental poetry. In *Penury* Kim departs abruptly from this earlier track, now realizing that these synthetic activities aspire to suture fractures without recognizing that they are not part of a broken apparatus but rather the innovations of highly refined technologies through which the new regime pulsates. In *Penury*, poetry ends where the new codes begin. If her earlier work focused on language acquisition and foreign-accented English as a way to think about strategies for repairing the traumatic wounds of diasporic dislocation, here her linguistic inquiries leverage the diasporic position as a perspectival advantage from which to witness more pernicious and global forms of encoding.

Deeply distrustful of synthesis, Kim's critical stances manifest most powerfully in unresolved paradoxical formulations. An implicit desire throughout the volume is to make hidden systems visible against the recognition that such a totalizing vision would reproduce the operations it intends to expose.

Neither resistant to nor compliant with the forces of cooptation, *Penury* instead stages an intense awareness of the dangers that abide in penurious regimes while expressing an equally forceful desire to transcend them despite (and indeed because of) the impossibility. The book's focus on linguistic expression is more than just the realization of an amped-up deconstructive ethos concerned with the inevitable limits of language. Thus, in order to deal with the specifics of this extremism, I want to tweak Liu's account to suit a particular context that has persistently preoccupied Kim since her first volume, *Under Flag* (1991), namely the "irreducible tension" par excellence: war.

As we have witnessed all too plainly and with increasing frequency in recent events, war entails both discursive and physical violence, both generalized forms of knowledge production and specific iterations of power. In this context, one sees how simplistic forms of coherence elide the complexities that most require our attention. We can see why Kim might prefer to suspend resolution. The concerns of *Penury* are specifically aimed at an age of global perpetual war, which becomes increasingly characterized, with U.S. global militarism as an axiom.[7] This entails a vision of war as an endless series of complex conflicts among multiple actors on a planetary scale. It is fought with cutting-edge weapons technologies (missiles, chemicals, drones, cyberaggression, etc.) that allow violence to be imposed from greater distances, and thus permit the kind of terrifying apathy implied in dissociative euphemisms like "surgical strike" and "precision bombing." Accordingly, the militaristic regime imagined in *Penury* emerges not as the boisterous arrival of an army but in far subtler forms. It is not so much heavy artillery that bothers the imagination of the poem; it is the cool, logistical quality of the aforementioned military euphemisms, a kind of weaponized language that gradually becomes normalized after incessant repetition in public discourse.

Kim's is thus not a poetics of reduction but a poetics of evasion. Suffused with negative affect, Kim's linguistic evasiveness grafts Language poetry's aversion to simplistic formulation and reification onto a military context, in which to be identified is to be targeted. In "Lamenta," a poem from her 2002 volume *Commons*, Kim's speaker exemplifies this anxiety within a totalizing claim about the capacities of contemporary military epistemology: "The fundamental tenet of all military geography is that every feature of the visible world possesses actual or potential military significance."[8] Similarly, in his comparative study of military and cinematic technology, Paul Virilio quotes William James Perry (later secretary of defense under Bill Clinton) in terms that powerfully echo Kim's lines: "If I had to sum up current thinking on precision missiles and saturation weaponry in a single sentence, I'd put it like this: once you can see the target, you can expect to destroy it."[9] Both Kim and Perry implicitly imagine a world through a satellite lens, a view in which every visible geographic feature is a potential asset or threat and one that has become increasingly familiar in our current moment of drone warfare. We see a nightmare version of this military aesthetics in, for example, the recent Marvel production *Captain America: Winter Soldier* (2014). The film details a villainous plot to eliminate—instantly, simultaneously, and precisely—millions of people by using an advanced targeting technology that looks disturbingly like Google Maps. The multiculturalist term *target of opportunity* should resonate here disconcertingly.

Accordingly, *Penury* is interspersed with language that stages this modern military sensibility in often tactical terms that seem deeply informed by the kind of technologies and capacities that Kim and Perry summon. This tactical sensibility in turn influences Kim's thinking about the possibilities of poetic language. For example, in the opening line of the book, "Increased chatter," Kim signals a new approach. In the earlier work, Kim was interested in the physics of speech suggested by words like *chatter*—from the physical mechanics of the mouth in acts of pronunciation to the mediation of translingual practices like romanization. This earlier work troubled the politics of linguistic naturalization to stage new synthetic logics that might make claims on behalf of diasporic subjects. Her poems enacted metaphoric traversals that redressed dislocation without submitting to the violent erasures that attend assimilative logics.[10] But in *Penury*, the modest triumph in such acts of traversal are deeply troubled by issues of transmission as epitomized by military language, in which violence and aggression are contained, occluded, and bathed in banality.

Penury offers numerous examples and treatments of such language, some of which are excerpted here:

> deemed not worthy of destroying (7)
> the entire vertical profile . from atmosphere to subsurface (9)
> perimeter onset plain crucial corridor (28)
> huddle quadrant counting inhabitants (28)
> Bunker buster bomb (38)
> this is the designated pick up spot (40)
> you are now leaving the American sector (43)
> enemies captured in war (45)
> Measure streets by the number of uniforms (51)
> Weapon and deed (51)
> Strike point   full force (55)
> Border security operation (55)
> The extent of the land that must be cleared for tank traffic (58)
> Scorched earth tactics (58)
> intervals flank roadside sequence (71)
> machines hunch / vehicles in and out (85)
> Fighting house by house (100)

Military language in these cases ranges from strategic and technical to absurd and nonsensical to rhythmic and lyrical. The linguistic play on display in these lines, however, is less an attempt at resistant signification that undermines the language's authority (deconstruction is a foolish gambit here) and more an effort to produce cautious synecdoche that might sketch the contours of our military present. Kim painstakingly parses out its symptoms, even as we come to realize that such acts of cartography may become complicit with the very forms of ultra-panoptic seeing that is the poem's nightmare. Taken as a whole, these moments in Kim's text not only adumbrate the pervasiveness of militarism in contemporary life, but more radically, speculatively map how it constitutes the way we view our world: that is, as divisible into quadrants and sectors; circumscribed by perimeters and flanks; and policed by bombs, tanks, machines, and vehicles. The problem is increasingly vexed: how do we diagnose systems of articulation that are really systems of oppression if our modes of conceiving them seem blind to their enactments and occlusions of violence? If our codes touch theirs? In a moment of banal resignation, Kim offers a self-consciously tautological aphorism that articulates this dilemma: "Through sameness of language is produced / sameness of sentiment and thought." The problem of production is reproduction, and the problem of critique is complicity.

Linking the geopolitics of U.S. global militarism to the history of U.S. financial imperialism, Kim broadens the stakes even further by intermingling her concern for a deep-seated military ethos in *Penury* with parallel interests in labor exploitation and capital accumulation, a set of relations that she makes visible in the poetic assemblages early in the volume, in which the *barrack*, *internment camp*, and *refugee camp* coincide in conceptual orbit with *foundry*, *warehouse*, and *auto plant* (17). Together, these thematic categories index not only sites of contemporary power but, more important for Kim, the codes that invite our complicity. On successive pages about halfway through the volume (45–46), we see all three as elements of what Brian Reed has termed a "word square,"[11] presented together in poetic aggregations that, on one hand, suggest relations but, on the other, function to obscure relational logics. Kim's word square thus implies both the fantasy and impossibility of the kind of totalizing vision that Fredric Jameson locates in filmic conspiracy plots, which aspire and inevitably fail to imagine the totality of late capitalism's infinite social order.[12] As in Jameson's account, the performed hubris of Kim's systemic view is that the apprehension of systemic relations might eventually yield the system itself, though of course it never does.

accumulation of land	maintain household bear	labor of house child
cooking reserve line	belonging to	elaborate isolation
familias implements	enemies captured in war	bearing child rearing
production heirs number	and rear household	family contains
counting herds possessions	fellow feeling crude	isolate care

family contains in germ	bearing rearing	accumulation of land
implements of production	cooking reserve line of	the number belonging
counting possessions	heirs	the captured
isolated	household bear	rear heirs
feeling crude	belonging to	fellow feeling crude (45)

Kim's word table parses fragments of the book's thematic concerns into increments, such as "accumulation of land," "labor of house child," and "enemies captured in war," within a general framework that seems to foreground domesticity in a vaguely agrarian milieu: "and rear household," "counting herd possessions," "family contains." As is typical for Kim, the poem frustrates conventional reading, in either horizontal or vertical directions, and instead encourages compensatory practices: in this case, the identification of repetition and variance. One witnesses the repeated mention of "household," "heirs," and "crude," as well as the modulations of "maintain household bear" into "and rear household" into "household bear" and "real heirs." This example also demonstrates the various combinations as some of these entities recombine to form new constructs and divide to fracture off into alternate directions. One is tempted to mark up the page like this:

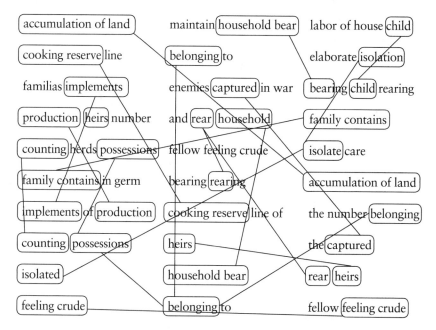

But of course doing so brings us only fields of spatial relations and not meaning. Although we are invited to read the chart as a cartographic space in which one locates the relative positions of linguistic objects, we do so without a sense of the logics that govern relation beyond *sameness*. Kim makes explicit the spatial logic of the poem fragment on the following page with the anaphoric repetition of the word *where* (46). We never learn the actual location—where "where" might be. We do, however, sense the difference between an older political economy in which ships bring "tax grains from the provinces" and "everyone had a plant job" and a newer model ruled by "boards of revenue," in which "preventable diseases run rampant" and "the good of the very few" requires "the suffering of a great many."

If anywhere, the anaphoric "where" seems to name the late-capitalist everywhere of the present as schematized by the previously mentioned poetic assemblages (17), but though the preliminary terms of such a diagnosis seem available, the real aim of these lines is not to produce a cogent economic assessment but rather to subordinate questions about late-capitalist systemic relations to the problem of mere location. Rather than seek explanations for global phenomena that arise from macroscopic forces, Kim helps us see the linkages, not through acts of synthesis but by continually staging decidedly unsynthetic relations of relative proximity in spatial terms while holding any actual diagnosis in abeyance.

This form of pattern recognition should be familiar as the paranoid, often schizophrenic activities of the disturbed genius who perceives conspiracy in everyday banalities, as in, for example, Russell Crowe's portrayal of John Nash's disturbed genius in *A Beautiful Mind* (2001), in which one manifestation of Nash's psychological disorder is his tendency to see nefarious connections between what otherwise seem the artifacts of ordinary living, leading Nash to produce diagrams that look like my marking up of Kim's words square. W. J. T. Mitchell has recently placed the filmic Nash's diagrams in a representational lineage extending back to Aby Warburg's *Bilderatlas*, a lineage that consists of texts aspiring to totalizing visualizations of data. Such visualizations exemplify what Mitchell describes as the pervasive "iconomania" of the age of Big Data: "The effort to create a total picture or master picture of a situation or a body of knowledge."[13] The representation of extensive connective networks in these cases, for Mitchell, "moves across the boundary between symbols and symptoms, detective work and psychosis, clues and paranoid fantasies, science and magic. At one extreme, the atlas is a matrix for the display and interpretation of symptoms. At the other, the matrix itself becomes a symptom, a clue to the pathology of the investigator, whether detective, connoisseur, or analyst."[14] Occupying the ambiguous space Mitchell opens between rationality and madness, these texts in imaging totalizing systems oscillate between rational synthesis and paranoid delusion, reflecting what Sianne Ngai describes as the "subjective/objective oscillation" inherent in the very structure of paranoia: "Is the enemy *out there* or *in me*?"[15] This double question inquires about not only the validity of the paranoid response but also its complicity with the conspiratorial power it identifies. In Ngai's reading of Juliana Spahr's *LIVE*, such paranoia is staged as a negative affect and a beginning point for political agency despite and indeed because of the complicity.[16]

Similarly, in Kim's *Penury*, speaking to a highly militarized world in which the apparatus of war becomes complicit with financial power, fear and anxiety rise to level of intelligence, not because the paranoid is sometimes justified in its estimation of global regimes of power but because the paranoid refuses synthesis. Though certainly a negative affect, the beginning point for Kim is also the end point, because the primary insight involves a capacious appreciation of the fundamental limit. The volume thus encourages a reading practice based on paranoid pattern recognition, a mode of reading capable of seeing relations in what otherwise seem random fields of information. The agency of the complicit paranoid inheres in the ability to negotiate the ambiguous terrain in which the apprehension of networked systems overlaps with fantastical delusion.[17] At the same time, it is a poetics that cannot see its way through to political agency because it also recognizes the limits of paranoid intelligence; though the paranoid senses system, the paranoid always lacks satisfaction in the insight. The system always expands, morphs, and deforms, extending out toward unanticipated avenues and through innovated codes. Paranoid cartography is a fundamentally unsatisfied task.

Recognizing these endless possibilities for frenzied, unrewarded labor, *Penury* returns frequently to lyrical moments, which function to ground abstraction and temporarily assuage a troubled reader. Though I have emphasized in this essay the volume's invocations of banal regimes of military language, *Penury* offsets these forays into cold linguistic appropriation with human-scaled moments and fragments of sincerity, introspection, and expression, perhaps most powerfully about a third of the way through, where it offers a glimpse of a first-person lyrical subject for the first and only time in the volume: "I go to my father's house / I wear a grief hat / I am told to put on coarse hemp and to proceed on my own" (33). Here, echoing her earlier work, the solitary diasporic subject proceeds to mourn according to an atavistic tradition that is disorienting rather than comforting. In a similar modality, the volume ends with a lyric (the lines printed at the head of this chapter) and with more familiar poetic conventions, namely a romantic symbolic iconography (of birds, flowers, and rivers), presented in recognizable lineation and couplets. But though we feel (at last!) as though we are in the presence of a poem, part of the pedagogy of the volume is to enter the experience with suspicion and to treat the lyric as the site of a possible cover-up.

Although it might well function as a discrete entity (one can imagine it comfortably putting down roots in an anthology), the explicitly conventional lyrical moment at the end of this volume seems to signify differently in relation to the entirety of the book that has preceded it. First of all, the poem is animated by a set of internal sonic relations—from "Radiant" to "acacias" to "Residence" "fragrant" to "further—in which echo and rhyme offer a paranoid sense of systemic relation that operates independently of whatever symbolic content might be derived. Secondly, the poem fragment embeds, within lyrical imagery, relations to the socio-political and economic fragments that animate the rest of the book but are notably absent on this final page. The lines "A grove of riverbeds" and "A bank of wide hands," for example, seem to return us to earlier in the book, where the "Perpetual Savings and Loan" modulates into the "banks" of the river where all the dead fish appear (43). The line "Where in this, further dwelt" reminds us of the previously discussed anaphoric rehearsals of "where." The "radiant falcon" that begins the poem fragment and the condition "civil bound" that ends it seem reifications of, respectively, "the bird of prosperity we provided you," which appears toward the beginning of the volume (21), and the experience described in the line "Ensconced so that only the gate is visible and nothing beyond," which appears toward the middle (57). Some of these connections are stronger than others and surely others are possible, but the point is that the book as a whole invites the reader to refuse any sense of the poem's discreteness and to look for connections outside the frame of a page to ascertain meaning, if only to frustrate those attempts. Thirdly, the poem here thematizes the implied diasporic subject of her earlier work, but the problems of dislocation and homelessness that characterize that early work turn into a resignation to remain: "Residence of years' repose"; "Where in this, further dwelt / Abide"; "Nestled Close / Civil bound." Though time has passed, long-term dwelling has not produced, it seems, a sense of belonging. These are mature conditions of diaspora, conditions in which the disorientation about history and language cause less immediate pain but drift into the background without resolution, and in which the once traumatic wounds of dislocation become the basis of a perception born of experience.

On its final page, then, *Penury* scales down the sociopolitical and economic abstractions that float about the volume in the form of fragments unmoored to the realm of lyrical experience, such that seeing images, hearing rhyme, and reflecting on poetry in general become experiences already irretrievably enmeshed with the powerful forces behind those abstractions. The lyric is not the interruption of the oppressive regime thematized in the volume but the landscape on which it becomes most pressing to witness evidence for the regime's codes. In a paranoid mode, we at once see system in falcons and acacias. We are surprised by what our senses perceive, suspended and arrested by doubt. Maybe it's just a falcon after all. In contrast to the paranoid frenzy of the *Bilderatlas*, Kim ends the volume by pitching her paranoid poetics in a more inhabitable milieu. But if birds and flowers offer lyrical comforts, they are offered without the anesthesia of naive refusals. What's important here is not the particular allegorical leaping that becomes possible in this paranoid mode, but rather the overall haunting sense that the provocations of the political are now apprehended as part of late diasporic sensory experience, as if we could smell ideology in the flowers. This transmutation is perhaps emblematized by the tautological synesthesia in the poem fragment "A fragrant sight beheld beholds." This is a paranoid synesthesia, a synesthesia without synthesis. Not only does scent become vision, but that which is beheld becomes the viewing subject that beholds. It is unclear in such reversals whether the flowers are benign or panoptic. In an especially penurious world, perhaps it is imperative to be afraid, even and especially when the flowers are in bloom.

Notes

1. For an account of colons in Kim's work, see Stephen Hong Sohn, "'Experiment Is Each Scroll of White Pages Joined Together': Reading Punctuation, Mathematics, and Science in Myung Mi Kim's *Dura*," *College Literature* vol. 42 no. 4 (2015): 648–82. https://muse.jhu.edu/ (accessed June 28, 2017). Sohn describes Kim's use of colons as part of a larger poetic interest in relation and ratio that resonates with my account of Kim's paranoid poetics.

2. Warren Liu, "Making Common the Commons: Myung Ki Kim's Ideal Subject," in *American Poets in the 21st Century*, ed. Claudia Rankine and Lisa Sewell (Middletown, Conn.: Wesleyan University Press, 2007), 253, 260.

3. Ibid., 262.

4. Ibid.

5. See C. J Martin, "On 'Penury,'" *Jacket2*, April 12, 2013, http://jacket2.org/article/penury. Martin describes the poetry as "a calling into account for legibility's high price."

6. Rachel Greenwald Smith, "Six Propositions on Compromise Aesthetics," *The Account*, Fall 2004, http://theaccountmagazine.com/?article=six-propositions-on-compromise-aesthetics.

7. See Bruce Robbins, *Perpetual War: Cosmopolitanism from the Viewpoint of Violence* (Durham, N.C.: Duke University Press, 2012), 1–30.

8. Myung Mi Kim, "Lamenta," in *Commons* (Berkeley: University of California Press, 2002), 32.

9. Paul Virilio, *War and Cinema: The Logistics of Perception* (London: Verso, 1989), 4.

10. For a fuller account of this argument, see Joseph Jonghyun Jeon, *Racial Things, Racial Forms: Objecthood in Avant-garde Asian American Poetry* (Iowa City: University of Iowa Press, 2012), 39–70.

11. See Brian Reed, "'Eden or Ebb of the Sea': Susan Howe's Word Squares and Postlinear Poetics," *Postmodern Culture* 14, no. 2 (2004).

12. Fredric Jameson, *The Geopolitical Aesthetic: Cinema and Space in the World System* (Bloomington: Indiana University Press, 1992), 9–10.

13. W. J. T. Mitchell, "Methods, Madness and Montage: Aby Warburg to *A Beautiful Mind*," December 8, 2014, Columbia Center for Contemporary Critical Thought, Columbia Law School, https://www.youtube.com/watch?v=d_w4Mjtm Clg.

14. Ibid.

15. Sianne Ngai, *Ugly Feelings* (Cambridge, Mass.: Harvard University Press, 2005), 19.

16. Ibid., 331.

17. See Eve Kosofsky Sedgwick, "Paranoid Reading and Reparative Reading, or, You're So Paranoid, You Probably Think This Essay Is about You," in *Touching Feeling: Affects, Pedagogy, Performativity* (Durham, N.C.: Duke University Press, 2003), 123–52. Against what she perceives to be the dominance of the hermeneutics of suspicion in contemporary critical practice, Sedgwick makes a case for a mode of reparative reading that instead foregrounds surprise, experiment, and pleasure. Though I've made the case for Kim's paranoid poetics, *Penury* also seems to fit the requirements of reparative reading as well.

Part Three

✦

Addressing the Multiple

NEGOTIATING DIFFERENCE

SHERWIN BITSUI

from *Flood Song*

Black ants drift through the throats of wounded stags;

they scuttle the dictionary's blank page for mention of him without her.

Chapter 13

Sherwin Bitsui's Blank Dictionary: Navajo Poetics and Non-Indigenous Readers

Brian Reed

If I encountered the above poem in a mainstream poetry journal—and knew nothing about the author—I wouldn't consider it difficult. It would register as almost *too* intelligible, wholly in line with the sort of verse I see on a near-daily basis. Almost on autopilot, I would begin making a few observations.

Sentence structure and layout. The poem consists of one sentence, lacks a title, and appears by itself in the middle of a page. We are invited to read it as a single, self-contained rhetorical act. It is also a two-part statement, divided by a semicolon and two carriage returns. The poem asks us to explore possible parallels and disjunctions between clause A and B.

Syntax and solecism. The verbs are peculiar. In the first line, *drifts* seems like a sloppy choice. While one can imagine "black ants" traversing "wounded throats," it is hard to envision them "drift[ing] through" them unless they're ghosts or holograms. In the second line, one wants *scuttle* to describe a second kind of movement, the ants now traipsing over a reference book. The poem, however, does not introduce between *scuttle* and *page* any of the prepositions, such as *across*, that this construction requires. Grammatically, *scuttle* thus cannot serve as the intransitive verb meaning "to run with quick hurried steps" (*OED*). Strictly speaking, it has to be the transitive verb meaning "to cut or bore a hole or holes into the sides or bottom of a vessel for the purposes of sinking it," as in "to scuttle a boat" (*OED*). Is this ambiguity deliberate?

Pronouns and indeterminacy. The overall parallel construction of the sentence suggests that *they* in the second line refers back to the "ants" that are the subject of the first clause, but grammatically *they* could also stand in for "stags" or "throats of . . . stags." This grammatical slipperiness extends to the remainder of the second line. There are no obvious antecedents for *him* and *her*. They are left free-floating, potentially referring to any man and woman, perhaps calling to mind an archetypal opposition between male and female.

Imagery and cinematic history. Perhaps a better word than *archetypal* would be *unconscious*. Slashed throats, dead animals, and "black ants" appearing on a "page" in a book where one would normally expect black ink: arguably the poem is more surrealist than Jungian, reminiscent of the vertiginous montage and violent episodes in films such as Luis Buñuel and Salvador Dalí's *Un chien andalou* (1929).

At this point, my preliminary analysis would come to an end. I would con-clude that like many contemporary poems, this one promises clarity but then proves to be linguistically obstructive. Seeking to understand what the poem is saying—to elucidate, that is, its plot, argument, setting, and so forth—a reader ends up pondering instead its recalcitrant diction and syntax. As I have argued elsewhere, such a "making difficult," what the Russian formalists call *zatrud-nenie*, has since the 1990s become a widely agreed-upon marker of seriousness and erudition, proof that journals, critics, and prize committees are supposed to grant a poem due weight and consideration.[1] The Jungian and/or surreal-ist touches here are also consonant with many present-day writers' efforts to employ the disruptive techniques associated with 1970s and 1980s Language poetry in the service of spiritual and psychological ends. In short, I would decide that this piece is a typical product of the current American poetry scene.

I would also be wrong. Like many poems by contemporary Indigenous writers, this couplet is difficult for non-Indigenous readers to interpret and evaluate with confidence. Moreover, this difficulty cannot, as with much modernist and postmodernist verse, be overcome through greater ingenuity, a reorientation to the nature of language, or immersive research. It has to do with the implied rhetorical scenario: who is speaking to whom for what purpose. Non-Indigenous readers are permitted, even invited, to read such poetry, only to have the fullness of its meaning withheld. Why? As Gwyneira Isaac writes, at such moments "secrecy becomes a vital tool in the peda-gogical process and a means to monitor how knowledge is transmitted and used."[2] On such occasions, as Bruce Ziff and Pratima V. Rao have put it, Indigenous writers publicly assert their "ownership" over culturally specific information, in hopes that non-Indigenous readers, such as myself, will affirm the validity of those "sovereign claims" and, in the future, stop trying to force intelligibility where they have no right to expect it.[3]

This essay records my struggle to reach that point of acceptance. It is hard work, and (spoiler alert) I do not completely succeed. Who ever said decolo-nization would be easy?

Sherwin Bitsui is from White Cone, Arizona, in Naabeehó Bináhásdzo, the Navajo reservation. He is Diné, born to the Tódích'ii'nii (Bitter Water Clan) and born for the Tłizílaaní (Many Goats Clan), and he holds an associate's degree from the Institute of American Indian Arts Creative Writing Program. The two-line untitled poem at this essay's beginning comes from *Flood Song* (2009), his second book, published by Copper Canyon Press, which is based out of Port Townsend, Washington, and has nationwide distribution. In other words, a Native American poet, raised and educated in an Indigenous context, writes here for an audience likely to include both Indigenous and non-Indigenous readers who live outside Diné Bikéyah (Navajo Land). He cannot presume that they will possess any familiarity with his home region and its canyons, mesas, and washes, and he cannot expect any competency in Diné Bizaad, the language of his childhood and ancestors. Under such circumstances, how does he proceed?

Flood Song begins with an epigraph from a poem by Rex Lee Jim that three times repeats the word *náhookǫs*, the Navajo name for the constellation also known as Ursa Major. Online Bitsui has explained why:

> I once attended a reading of Diné (Navajo) poets and writers in Window Rock, Arizona, on the Navajo Reservation. . . . One of the readers that night was Rex Lee Jim, a poet who read from his work entirely in Diné Bizaad. . . . It was a great honor to listen to contemporary poems in my language and to feel it awaken and transform the auditorium into the spacious landscape of the high desert plateau that I grew up in. Mr. Jim read a poem that evening . . . entitled Nahookos (big dipper) which is also a directional word meaning north, as well as a verb which can loosely be translated into meaning something which turns circularly. Ironically, the title of the poem is the whole poem! Mr. Jim just said it three times, each time with a renewed breath and extended silence. The poem enacted a totality and vision of the cosmos within my mind and body that I've longed to reach within my own work in English. At once I imagined the northern night sky, turning and turning.[4]

In *Flood Song* a reader who does not speak Diné Bizaad will have no access to this "totality and vision." No footnotes or other explanatory apparatus appears. Not even Google will help, since Bitsui has altered the word *náhookǫs* beyond a search engine's capacity to recognize it by spacing out its syllables—spelling it "na ho kos"—to suggest Rex Lee Jim's slow delivery.

After opening in a manner perhaps infinitely suggestive to its author but also likely impenetrable to a non-Diné reader, *Flood Song* contains a page that seven times repeats the word *tó* in a column.[5] *Tó*, a Navajo-English dictionary will reveal, means "water." Seven—and water—after using the word *Flood* in the title: for a veteran reader of English-language verse, this is like waving a red flag in front of a bull. Is Bitsui evoking the biblical seven days of creation, when the earth emerged from the waters? Are we to think of Noah's ark? Will the book depict a world after the Deluge, an allegory for Native American life since 1492?

Such readings could be wildly off base. The repetition of *tó* down the page could instead be intended to evoke the San Juan River, the principal waterway in Diné Bikéyah. It could also be a reference to the Diné Bahane', the Navajo creation cycle, more specifically to the walls of water that drove

The People from the Fourth World into the Fifth.[6] There could be additional, esoteric meanings only available to readers who have been initiated into the requisite mysteries. Bitsui gives readers a single phoneme, *tó*, and lets them make of it what they will, even if their cultural background and linguistic competency lead them embarrassingly far afield from the associations that *tó* would have for someone raised on the Navajo reservation.

This essay argues that the two-line poem quoted above is similarly troublesome for a non-Diné audience because it simultaneously addresses and ultimately excludes them. Anyone who has received a Western-style education is prone to find such a stance maddening. Why can't I be trusted? Why can't I work harder, learn enough? Why must I remain external to the poem's truth? Vi [taqʷšəblu] Hilbert (Upper Skagit) speaks for many Indigenous writers and intellectuals when she replies that effort, empathy, and goodwill are irrelevant. Among the "First People of Washington State," for example, "responsible members of each family inherit" the "sacred knowledge of their ancestors," and they can only "use this information when and where it is culturally appropriate." "Outsiders are not allowed to participate," not because they are unworthy or ignorant, but because it violates "inherited privilege."[7] Although the Navajo and the Coast Salish peoples prefer different vectors and occasions for knowledge transmission, Bitsui would surely agree with Hilbert that Indigenous peoples own their heritage and have a right to share it when and as their rules allow.

In settler colonial states such as Australia, Canada, and the United States, Indigenous forms of cultural expression have often been institutionally and discursively managed in two complementary ways, namely, under the headings of *ethnography* and *art*.[8] For example, in Diné Bikéyah, on certain occasions, a specially appointed individual, a *hataałii*, will use five colors of sand—white, red, yellow, black, and blue—to create an *iikááh* (a design or glyph) from memory. The two phrases commonly used in English to refer to the result are *sand altar* and *sand painting*. The word *altar* predisposes one to think about these actions as a ritual or sacred ceremony analogous to what occurs in a church, synagogue, or mosque. A sand altar can, for that reason, probably tell "us" (curious non-Diné cosmopolitans) significant things about Navajo beliefs, customs, and religious practices—assuming, of course, that an anthropologist or a native informant shares with "us" how to decode the lines and shapes made by the "shaman."

The word *painting* instigates a different chain of associations. It implies that "we" (non-Diné art appreciators) should attend to the appearance of the poured sand and think about it aesthetically, as a particular arrangement of forms on a flat plane. While its iconography might be conventional, each "artist" executes a sand painting slightly differently, and "we" can identify regional and personal variations in style. While these paintings might be uniquely Navajo in inspiration and meaning, they can still be productively compared to other examples of Indigenous and non-Indigenous art technically, formally, and thematically. A permatized sand painting could be placed in a gallery, for instance, alongside a painted bowl by Nampeyo (Hopi/Tewa) and a painting by Emily Kam Kngwarray (Anmatyerr).

Settler colonial societies, via ethnography and the art world, often construct and circulate representations of Indigenous cultural artifacts that pare them of the social and geographical particulars that originally imbued them with meaning and value. Today this dynamic is usually discussed under the heading of *cultural appropriation*, and scholars are apt to criticize, say, Edward Curtis's early twentieth-century photographs taken of *iikááh* because they are part of a documentary project that fundamentally distorts and falsely romanticizes the lives of Native Americans.[9] Other cases have proved more ambiguous, such as Jackson Pollock's fascination with the Navajo sand paintings at MoMA's "Indian Art of the United States" exhibition in 1941, which directly influenced his storied drip paintings.[10] Regardless, as Rey Chow has put it, what usually occurs is a version of "cross-cultural contact" that takes the form of a "brushing against the other as a mere external surface," which generally reconfirms the colonizing society's superior position vis-à-vis the colonized.[11]

Indigenous peoples have, of course, actively and creatively responded to imperialist efforts to codify and regulate their cultures. They have perceived that the externally imposed role of "artist-informant-spokesperson" can yield opportunities for self-assertion, status acquisition, and marketplace access.[12] Hosteen Klah (Diné), for instance, attended the 1934 Century of Progress Exhibition in Chicago, where he daily produced a new *iikááh*, and Fred Stevens, Jr. (Diné), gave numerous sand-painting demonstrations on television and at universities during the 1950s, eventually perfecting a method of fixing sand to boards that enabled the takeoff of Navajo sand paintings as a collectable art form.[13]

These moments of engagement with settler colonial institutions and discourses often require Indigenous individuals to make decisions regarding "secrecy, cultural property, and the protection of cultural property."[14] Will they honor proscriptions against circulating secret or sacred knowledge among people who, because of descent, communal affiliation, location, gender, age, and/or education level should not be allowed access to them? The mid-twentieth-century Pueblo artists José Lente and James Michael Byrnes risked ostracism by sharing carefully guarded "cultural information about traditional religious practices" with "white patrons" in exchange for money and recognition.[15] Fred Stevens, in contrast, made certain that his sand paintings were incomplete or otherwise differed from ones that a *hataałii* would make during an actual blessingway ceremony.[16] Indigenous artists can, in other words, earn a living by producing flawed, simplified, or ersatz copies of artifacts for connoisseurs and critics already prone to misreading their cultures by seeing them through a distorting Western lens.

Outsider interests—founded in both ethnography and aesthetics—have indisputably helped to spur the creation of what would now be called Navajo literature. From Washington Matthews's "The Mountain Chant: A Navaho Ceremony" (1887) to David McAllester's transcriptions of Navajo song, from Eda Lou Walton's reinventions of Navajo stories in *Dawn Boy* (1925) to Jerome Rothenberg's Navajo-inspired sound poetry, non-Indigenous Americans have approached the many forms of oral performance practiced among the Diné as if they belonged to, or could be understood by analogy to, Western literary genres. And as always, some Indigenous individuals have exploited this fascination with Indigenous culture for the purposes of innovation and self-fashioning. Certain Navajos, such as Frank Mitchell, have gained a reputation as modern practitioners of traditional arts, whereas others, such as Luci Tapahonso, Orlando White, and Sherwin Bitsui, have chosen to identify as authors in a Western sense and sought publication outlets for print-based work. They have become Navajo poets, or perhaps more accurately, both Navajos and poets. They mediate between two worlds, and they must resolve whether serving as an intermediary also entails adhering to university and marketplace expectations regarding colonized subjects.

Flood Song is clotted and jolting. Images arrive with such speed that they distort or interrupt the syntax of the sentences in which they appear. Its untitled, variously lineated poems do not follow any obvious ordering principle, whether narrative, thematic, symbolic, or argumentative. As a consequence of these traits, the book exhibits all-overness and self-similarity. That is, no matter where one opens the book and no matter how long a stretch one reads, the verse will display similar traits—such as restless, even hyperactive pacing—and will provide an excess of things, people, and actions.[17]

The book does contain abundant, recognizably Navajo-related subject matter, but it appears in unpredictable, confusing flashes:

> Coyote howls canyons into windows painted on the floor with crushed
>   turquoise;
> captured cranes secrete radon in the *epoxied* toolshed;
> leopard spots, ripe for drilling, ooze white gas when hung on a copper
>   wire.
> I pull electricity from their softened bellies with loom yarn.[18]

Here we start off with Coyote, who, like Raven, has long since entered (white) American popular culture in the guise of the Trickster. His name kicks off a string of near-clichés connected with the Diné ("canyons," "paint[ing] on the floor," "turquoise," "loom yarn"). These references do not, however, add up to a conventional portrait of Navajo life. What does it mean for a god to "howl canyons into windows"? Are we supposed to imagine the "howling" as a spell equivalent, magic that causes a landscape to become visible out a window? These windows, however, have been "painted on the floor." Has someone moved windows from walls to the ground to paint them? Or is Bitsui speaking metaphorically, referring, perhaps, to sand paintings as "windows," that is, as art that gives viewers a portal onto a represented world (perhaps involving "canyons")? If so, it is still unlikely that an *iikááh* would ever incorporate "crushed turquoise," a gemstone that is entirely too rare to use in a painting intended to last no more than a day. (To make blue sand, a *hataałii* typically uses chrysocolla or a mixture of gypsum and charcoal.) The rest of this extract—like the book as whole—behaves similarly, offering scattered, hard-to-process glimpses of the kitschified, romanticized version of the Navajo and the desert Southwest that non-Indigenous Americans will be accustomed to encountering in John Wayne–style Westerns and genre fiction à la Tony Hillerman and Patricia Briggs.

Other, less Hollywood-friendly aspects of Navajo history and culture also surface in *Flood Song*, if one knows to look for them. In the above passage, for instance, Bitsui refers elliptically ("secrete radon . . . ooze white gas") to a dark history of ecological and medical tragedies that are not often remembered outside of Diné Bikéyah. After World War II, one of the few well-paying jobs available to men on the Navajo reservation was work in uranium mines. Despite abundant evidence from the 1870s to the 1930s that connected exposure to radon (a gaseous by-product of uranium mining) to lung cancer, no protections were provided to Navajo workers until the 1960s, and enforcement remained lax thereafter. Only in 1990, after decades of activist agitation, did the federal government concede that thousands of Navajos were due compensation for radon-linked illnesses. Also in the background is the largest nuclear-related accident in United States history, the Church Rock uranium mill disaster of 1979, when a flash flood broke a dam and over a thousand tons of solid radioactive waste flowed downriver into Navajo lands, where people were using the water for bathing and drinking as well as farming. Unknown numbers of Diné suffered thorium poisoning, radiation burns, and other after-effects.[19]

Bitsui nods to other important community issues, too, such as the dependence of the economy of the Navajo reservation on extractive industries, especially the leasing of land to mining and energy corporations ("drilling," "copper wire," "electricity"). But, like the mention of radon, it can be tough to figure out how these assorted pieces are supposed to fit together. The "captured cranes" that "secrete radon" in "toolsheds" could be sandhill cranes (*déłi*), which are revered by the Navajo, and perhaps Bitsui wants readers to think about perversions of the natural world. Why are the toolsheds "epoxied," however, that is, treated with synthetic resin, and why does Bitsui italicize that one word and no others? What, if anything, do these cranes have to do with the "leopard spots" mentioned in the next line? Leopards are a variety of panther restricted to Africa and Asia. Another species of big cat, the cougar, can be found in Diné Bikéyah, but cougars do not have spots. Are the "leopard spots"—which, after all, are described as somehow, supernaturally or otherwise, removable from the cat, objects that can be "hung" on a "wire"—a metaphor or conceit based on Jeremiah 13:23 ("Can the Ethiopian change his skin? or the leopard his spots? then may ye also do good, that are accustomed to do evil")? If so, who has managed to doff his or her "spots," the traces of past "evil"? Corporations? The United States?

Throughout *Flood Song*, Bitsui's verse is vivid and vigorous but also frustrating to parse and pin down. Why write in such a manner? Encountering limits to one's ability to interpret a poem is not the same thing as discovering that a poem is at base meaningless. The couplet that opens this essay is a case in point. It opens by mentioning "black ants." Earlier, I connected these ants to surrealist cinema. That is one possible association. Someone familiar with the Diné Bahane', however, may think instead of the *wolozhini*, the black ants who were among the Different Insect Peoples who, together with the Mist People, governed the First World until it was destroyed by fire.[20] The introduction soon afterward of "wounded stags" may evoke another set of Navajo stories, connected to the Deerhunting Way, a "blessing rite" that recalls the "appropriate manner" of conducting a "successful hunt."[21] A reservation-raised Diné may well be able to recognize or infer profound connections between these two sets of stories that remain invisible to outsiders who lack the required information and interpretive context. The poem, in short, will prove differently meaningful depending on a reader's degree and kind of literacy.

At this essay's beginning, I placed Bitsui's two-line poem in the context of contemporary (non-Indigenous) American poetry. We're now prepared to see why and how his Indigeneity might distinguish his poetry from verse whose disjunctive surfaces superficially resemble his. He knowingly addresses a mixed audience with varying levels of familiarity with Diné culture and cosmology. He evinces an indifference toward outsiders that recalls the scorn one senses in Eliot, Pound, and other high modernists toward readers who lack their erudition. If a non-Indigenous reader takes up the implicit challenge and begins to research Navajo language, history, and religion, such labor will (as this essay illustrates) provide him or her with increasing insight into his verse, rendering intelligible much that would otherwise remain opaque or escape notice.

And yet—however devotedly a non-Diné poetry critic Googles and studies—he or she will continue to suspect the existence of hidden depths lurking just out of view. True, there is no guarantee that such strata of concealed significance even exist. The only people able to say for sure might be Navajos who, like Bitsui, were raised in traditional ways in Diné Bikéyah. In *Flood Song* Bitsui adopts the role of a native informant and theatrically draws on his Navajo heritage but then declines to explain what he shares. What do those black ants mean? Why talk about dead deer? This act of seduction, however, as we have seen, leads one into a disorderly, rambunctious body of work that, while offering symbol after symbol in a hallucinatory mythic landscape, can deliver more confusion than revelation. He gives his audience an imperfect, desanctified version of Indigenous artistry, suitable for wide distribution. The resulting poetry may, to a non-Indigenous audience, come across as "experimental" or "avant-garde," but one should not confuse this Indigenous rhetorical strategy—a way of responding to imperialist economic and political pressures—with the anti-representational sensibility of the historical avant-gardes. Its disjunctive syntax and assaultive imagery are products of the "conditions of historical struggle" that inform its making.[22]

Bitsui, one could say, presents non-Indigenous readers with a book that, according to the logic of colonialism, *ought* to make sense, to provide them with abundant insights, a kind of "dictionary," if you will, that neatly organizes and shares Navajo ideas, words, and stories. But, once opened, *Flood Song* proves to be resistant, full of sentences that, like "ants," refuse to stay put or be pinned down. They "scuttle" away when one peers at them, and as a consequence, the entire enterprise—the promise of untroubled immediate access to a Native American author's thoughts, feelings, culture, and history—appears to be "scuttled," sunk, doomed. For a non-Indigenous audience, at times the pages of this faux dictionary may as well be "blank."

Why hold up this "blank dictionary" in the first place, why solicit the attention of outsiders who cannot wholly read it? First, Bitsui does so while also pursuing other goals. In this couplet he also mentions, for instance, animals ("stag," "ants"), actions ("wound[ing]," "drift[ing]"), and people (the poem's unspecified "him" and "her"). Here as elsewhere, he evokes, in an abstract, eerie, and expressionist manner, the landscape of Dinétah and the history of the Diné. Non-Indigenous readers can, in a refracted and estranged fashion, encounter aspects of and potentially learn more about an Indigenous culture and worldview. But such access is not total. The image of the blank dictionary underlines this fact. Bitsui could provide clarity, a full reveal, but he does not do so. He challenges non-Indigenous readers to ask themselves: Can they reach a limit to what is legible and simply let it be, instead of trying to force their way across it? Can they assent to remaining outside the charmed circle of perfect understanding? Or will they cry foul, perhaps complain about a racist act of exclusion?

This essay shows that I, for one, find it hard to rest content with partial knowing. I keep adopting the stance of an expert, paragraph after paragraph, even as, in the manner of a game of Whac-a-Mole, I keep trying to knock myself back down to size by pointing out the restrictions on what I know (and what I can know). I am an invited guest in a Bitsui poem, which grants me certain privileges and opportunities but does not give me ownership of all I survey. I have to accommodate myself to this scene of reading; Bitsui has no obligation to make that process smoother for me. In discussions of contemporary American poetry, difficulty versus accessibility is an opposition often unreflectively mapped onto a presumed division between experimental and mainstream verse. *Flood Song* demonstrates that difficulty and accessibility might sometimes be better understood not via what is read but rather via who is doing the reading, how, and why.

An essay this short cannot do justice to a topic as large as poetry's role in a decolonizing politics. I would like to conclude with another gesture of self-undermining that also points to a possible next step. Throughout this piece I have staged an encounter between an Indigenous author and a non-Indigenous audience. But other author-audience relationships are possible. What about an Indigenous readership? Bitsui is only one example of the many American Indian poets writing today who have moved away from the populist oral poetics associated with the Native American Renaissance and explored more writerly and rhetorically complex stances toward their readers. Ideally, *Flood Song* should be placed alongside, and read in dialogue with, such works as *Apprenticed to Justice* (2007) by Kimberly Blaeser (Anishinaabe), *Streaming* (2014) by Allison Hedge Coke (Cherokee/Huron/Creek), and *Bulle/Chimére* (2006) by James Thomas Stevens (Akwesasne Mohawk). These books, in turn, would benefit from "trans-Indigenous" comparison to texts such as *Dha'lan Djani Mitti* (2008) by the Australian poet Lionel Fogarty.[23] Such a project could further elucidate the relationship between knowledge and the collective ownership of culture in Indigenous poetics. Law and land, not hermeneutics, might emerge as central preoccupations, and concepts such as modernist *difficulty* and postmodern *indeterminacy* would likely prove less useful than *conditional access* and *tribal sovereignty*.

Notes

1. The research leading to this publication was carried out while a visiting fellow with the Humanities Research Centre, RHSA, Australian National University. I would also like to thank Kornelia Freitag, Nicholas Nace, and Carol Warrior (A'ani/Sugpiaq/Dena'ina Athabascan) for their detailed feedback and their suggestions for revision.
See chapter 2 of *Nobody's Business: Twenty-First Century Avant-Garde Poetics* (Ithaca, N.Y.: Cornell University Press, 2013), esp. 29–31.

2. Gwyneira Isaac, "Responsibilities toward Knowledge: The Zuni Museum and the Reconciling of Different Knowledge Systems," in *Contesting Knowledge: Museums and Indigenous Perspectives*, ed. Susan Sleeper-Smith (Lincoln: University of Nebraska Press, 2009), 307.

3. Bruce Ziff and Pratima V. Rao, "Introduction to Cultural Appropriation: A Framework for Analysis," in *Borrowed Power: Essays on Cultural Appropriation* (New Brunswick, N.J.: Rutgers University Press, 1999), 15.

4. "Sherwin Bitsui," *Poetry Society of America* website, https://www.poetry society.org/psa/poetry/crossroads/new_american_poets/sherwin_bitsui/ (accessed April 2, 2017).

5. Bitsui, *Flood Song* (Port Townsend, Wash.: Copper Canyon, 2009), 3.

6. For this story, see Margaret Schevill Link, *The Pollen Path: A Collection of Navajo Myths* (Walnut, Calif.: Kiva, 1998), 11–14.

7. Vi [taqʷšəblu] Hilbert, "Introduction," in *Spirit of the First People: Native American Music Traditions of Washington State*, ed. Willie Smyth and Esmé Ryan (Seattle: University of Washington Press, 1999), 3–4.

8. Howard Morphy, "Seeing Aboriginal Art in the Gallery," *Humanities Research* 8, no. 1 (2001): 38.

9. See, e.g., Ben Burt, *World Art: An Introduction to the Art in Artefacts* (London: Bloomsbury, 2013), 207–9.

10. See Evan R. Firestone, "Jackson Pollock's *The Magic Mirror*: Jung, Shamanism, and John Graham," *Modernism/modernity* 15, no. 4 (November 2008): 703–24, esp. 710–11.

11. Rey Chow, *The Protestant Ethnic and the Spirit of Capitalism* (New York: Columbia University Press, 2002), 57.

12. Bill Anthes, *Native Moderns: American Indian Painting 1940–1960* (Durham, N.C.: Duke University Press, 2006), 31.

13. For the history of Navajo sand painting—including Fred Stevens's role—see Nancy Parezo, *Navajo Sandpainting: From Religious Act to Commercial Art* (Tucson: University of Arizona Press, 1983).

14. Anthes, *Native Moderns*, 32.

15. Ibid, 30–31.

16. Parezo, *Navajo Sandpainting*, 110.

17. For the "fractal" character of Bitsui's verse, see Kenneth Lincoln, *Speak like Singing: Classics of Native American Literature* (Albuquerque: University of New Mexico Press, 2007), 297–300.

18. Bitsui, *Flood Song*, 46.

19. See *The Navajo People and Uranium Mining*, ed. Doug Brugge, Timothy Benally, and Esther Yazzie Lewis (Albuquerque: University of New Mexico Press, 2006).

20. See, e.g., Ferlin Clark, "In Becoming Sa'ah Naaghai Bik'eh Hozhoon: The Historical Challenges and Triumphs of Diné College" (Ph.D. diss., American Indian Studies, University of Arizona, 2009), 93–94.

21. Terry Tempest Williams, *Pieces of White Shell: A Journey to Navajoland* (Albuquerque: University of New Mexico Press, 1984), 101.

22. Ian McLean, *How Aborigines Invented the Idea of Contemporary Art* (Brisbane: Institute of Modern Art, 2011), 142.

23. For the value of *trans-Indigenous* as a term in preference to *transnational* when comparing Indigenous writers from different parts of the globe, see Chadwick Allen, "A Trans*national* Native American Studies? Why Not Studies That Are *Trans-Indigenous*?," *Journal of Transnational American Studies* 4, no. 1 (2012): 1–22.

DOUGLAS KEARNEY

The Miscarriage: A Minstrel Show

DAMN-NEAR DAM   husband! peel your peepers of their sandgrits
imtermediately, says your beloved.

PATERFAMILISN'T   I hears not a cock crow but a crow crow.
morning broke not water but tomato!

DAMN-NEAR DAM   listen, my darkling. ain't I tell you not
to consummeat melon in our pallet?

PATERFAMILISN'T   consummeat?

DAMN-NEAR DAM   present tense of consummate.

PATERFAMILISN'T   but smudgy-poo: if'n I makes to eat
sweet Georgia ham, antatomically
speaking, mustn't my palate get a piece?

DAMN-NEAR DAM   lookee here, smokescreen: ain't shit aunt-tomic
bout this watermelon juice spilt betwick
and betwaint my legs. sheets to glory pinked!

PATERFAMILISN'T   then I ain't red handed; you're red-gamded!
t'ain't melonade if I ain't ate any.
sides: I ain't see'ed no seeds by your fanny.

DAMN-NEAR DAM   hog, hogslop and hogslop head! they making
Georgia ham seedless now. the stain's the thing!

PATERFAMILISN'T   seedless!? then alas: I guess Ise undoed.

DAMN-NEAR DAM   yes: un-dude. and she done. so Ise undid.

they cakewalk to the wings. ENTER, BONES.

Chapter 14

Patter as Misdirection in Douglas Kearney's "The Miscarriage: A Minstrel Show"

Nadia Nurhussein

Why try to express the trauma of miscarriage through the comic-grotesque lens of blackface minstrelsy? The genre, likely more popular than any other form of entertainment in the nineteenth-century United States, cannot legitimately support any serious topic of discussion without devolving into mockery, let alone a topic as painful as the loss of an expected child. Moreover, the genre depends upon a blatant racism that is viscerally repellent for a modern reader—particularly an African American reader—to confront. "The Miscarriage: A Minstrel Show" is one of a series of miscarriage poems in Douglas Kearney's *Patter*, each written according to a distinct set of generic conventions ("A Silent Film," "A Bar Joke," etc.). What the minstrel show in particular offers Kearney that the other genres do not is precisely this automatic and inevitable discomfort. This is not to equate the distress of miscarriage with the distress of racial caricature. In fact, the apparent linking or analogy (represented by the colon in the title) acts as a sort of misdirection: there is no way to understand miscarriage *through* minstrelsy.

Kearney's "patter" misleads us like the patter of a salesman or magician, beguiling and distracting us, through the use of slick language or a "smoke-screen" (to use one of Kearney's terms), from a sleight of hand that hides the poem's central tragedy in plain sight.[1] The characters' dialogue resembles "pattering," as defined by the *Oxford English Dictionary*: "Incessant or repetitive talking; continuous chatter, esp. with little regard to sense or content." This seeming nonsense of the poem, driven by wordplay, initially admits the twin illusions of both the simple amusement originally associated with the minstrel show and the modern-day horror of the form, but the poem's affect becomes only more confused when we discover the miscarriage at its heart.

In his ironic rewriting of the minstrel show, Kearney adapts its standard structure: the caricature and mockery of the central characters, the inclusion of Bones at the end (one of the traditional characters of blackface minstrelsy, whose most notable appearance in a major poetic work was in

John Berryman's *Dream Songs*, a more direct and problematic approach to minstrelsy), the use of the cakewalk. But these elements serve, for the most part, as mere props alerting us to the objectionable world in which we find ourselves. Only one of the elements associated with the minstrel show is exploited by Kearney to become productive and generative, and that is the element of wordplay. It is along this axis—the axis of wordplay and particularly the pun—that the minstrel show and the poem meet. "Good poets have a weakness for bad puns," W. H. Auden wrote in "The Truest Poetry Is the Most Feigning," and minstrely's highest form of linguistic inventiveness is often considered poetry's lowest. But the instability of the pun allows Kearney to achieve a singular form of complexity and intertextuality (one might say, difficulty) unavailable through any other use of language.

Kearney's elaborate network of wordplay crisscrossing and buttressing the poem displays a simultaneous delight in and disgust with the formulas of minstrelsy. Peppered with the ubiquitous malapropisms intrinsic to the genre (*intermediately* rather than *immediately*, *antatomically* rather than *anatomically*), his poem exaggerates and amplifies minstrelsy's parodic representations of what Paul Laurence Dunbar once called the "big-worded negro [*sic*]."[2] These moments of misspeaking are not, as Kearney shows us, simply opportunities for the reader to join in ridiculing the speakers' ignorance. Although Eric Lott's influential account of blackface minstrelsy claims that "malapropism figures as a kind of witless orality signifying nothing beyond itself"—and this may have been how the original audiences of minstrelsy received the "pattering" of its players—Sarah Meer reminds us, on the other hand, that "linguists have described the way the malapropism can itself be in fact a sophisticated play on words, both in minstrel show versions and in the black linguistic practices to which they allude."[3] Kearney's malapropisms show his characters to be ingenious manipulators of language, more like neologists than bunglers.

Most of Kearney's malapropisms generate wordplay through the insertion of a short extraneous syllable or letter that prismatically refracts the word into multifaceted puns. The aforementioned *antatomically*, for example, hints at the body revolting against itself—rejecting its role as procreator as it becomes inhospitable to life, a phenomenon also hinted at in other poems in the book—and at the complex shameful and antagonistic emotions of the father in response to the mother's inability to carry the child (such as "I love your body. I hate it," a contradiction found in "Sentence Done Red" and repeated in other poems in *Patter*). The word *darkling*, either a malapropism for or a nonstandard pronunciation of *darling*, refers to the beloved's skin color but is also a reversal of the *morning* in the previous couplet. Furthermore, the presence of the cock and the crow in that couplet raises the possibility that it may even be an echo of the "darkling thrush" in Thomas Hardy's poem of that name. The wordplay extends to the characterization of the players themselves, Damn-Near Dam and Paterfamilisn't, whose very names mock their inability to have children. The potential mother is practically a "dam," or blocked up, rather than the idealized conduit of woman-as-childbearer. "Paterfamilisn't" is straightforward enough: he is the negation of the patriarch. Even the title of the book from which this poem comes not only refers to the magician's or salesman's patter but also plays upon the now hackneyed synecdoche from Longfellow's "The Children's Hour" often heard by expectant parents (i.e., "the patter of little feet") and upon fatherhood (the first two syllables of the name of the poem's male character).

In importing the pun and the malapropism from the minstrel show to serve as the poem's central linguistic devices, Kearney leaves us torn between resisting these annoying "low" poetic jokes and submitting to this variety of verbal guilty pleasure. (And if we find humor in a given pun, we are laughing at a poem about miscarriage.) An even more basic aspect of the reader's response to wordplay, however, is the plain fact that wordplay—an instrument of misdirection—can "undo" one's presumed certainty; it shifts meaning, rendering it unstable to the point that one no longer understands what was once understood, or one understands it differently. It is therefore well suited to this poem about undoing. What one thought one was—a mother, a father—is suddenly taken away, and one's sense of self is undermined or even negated. Both Paterfamilisn't and Damn-Near Dam are undone at the end of the poem, and even their undoing evolves into a pun: Paterfamilisn't has been "undoed," but then he is also, as Damn-Near Dam tells him, "un-dude," his identity and masculinity having been stripped. Similarly, Damn-Near Dam is unsexed and dehumanized, as her name implies that she is almost a woman but less than a woman, and perhaps even less than a female animal. In other words, through this crass minstrel-show type of wordplay, the poem manages to articulate some of the sincere and heartfelt emotions that can be summoned by infertility struggles, so bound up with issues of gender and sexuality and even race (when we consider the opposition between the caricatured black woman as hypersexual and hyperfertile versus the actual woman unable to procreate). When "she done"—referring here to the lost fetus—then Damn-Near Dam is "undid."

The poem is effectively propelled by negation or loss. Aside from the three instances of "undoing" at the end of the poem, there are at least eleven other negative terms when we add up all the *ain't*s and *not*s. The most direct reference to the couple's infertility comes near the end of the poem, when Paterfamilisn't raises the objection, "I ain't see'ed no seeds by your fanny." Literally the line means, "I didn't see any watermelon seeds in the bed (by your behind)," but he is also saying to Damn-Near Dam, "I didn't inseminate you," or "seed no seeds" by your vagina. She responds that watermelon is now available in seedless varieties, which again is both literal and figurative: *seedless* refers to the watermelon but also to her womb.

The presence of the watermelon, of course, is meant to evoke the fruit's centrality in blackface minstrelsy and other forms of racist caricature. It is the stock foodstuff of the minstrel show (*Georgia ham* is a slang term for it). African Americans' supposed insatiable appetite for watermelon binds together much of Kearney's wordplay here, such as the *pallet/palate* homophonous pairing and the *consummate/consummeat* joke. The latter, according to Damn-Near Dam, is an inventive conjugation; it is worth noting, however, that *consummeat* also reads as a portmanteau combining the words *consume* and *eat*, doubly emphasizing the alimentary thread running through the poem.

In light of this thread, reading Kearney's poem through Kyla Wazana Tompkins's recent *Racial Indigestion: Eating Bodies in the 19th Century* proves fruitful. Tompkins begins by raising the specter of the all-too-familiar racist image of an alligator eating a "pickaninny" (referenced in Kearney's poem "Gator Bait") to address how the history of eating in the nineteenth-century United States reveals the collision of the alimentary with the racial and the erotic, and the prevalence of "the image of the black body as an edible object."[4] The central event of Kearney's poem—Damn-Near Dam accuses Paterfamilisn't of eating watermelon in bed only to discover that the red stain on the bedsheet is instead evidence of her miscarriage—revolves around a similar merging of consumption and sexuality. Her body is for a moment confused with a watermelon, and she herself—her actions and speech predetermined and defined by a racist genre—projects an image of herself as an edible object, to quote Tompkins. This equation is made even more apparent in a performed version of the poem that I discuss briefly at the end of this essay, in which Damn-Near Dam (now Topsy playing a character named Damn-Near Dam) enters "in a nightgown with a watermelon slice painted where her privates would go." When she calls her womb "seedless," she directly equates, as I suggested earlier, the watermelon with her body. And when she argues that *consummate* (i.e., literally to bring a marriage to completion) and *consume+eat* are variations on the same word, she defines sexual congress as if it were equivalent to the act of offering herself up for consumption.

The revelation that he "ain't redhanded" but that she is "red-gamded," her legs covered in blood, is a moment of dark humor, a gruesome and graphic representation of the moment of miscarriage, as well as a verbal sleight of hand that attempts to transfer the blame from the father to the mother. In response to this discovery, her Shakespearean exclamation that "the stain's the thing!" echoes both Hamlet's play and Lady Macbeth's "damned spot." And this is not the only lightly veiled Shakespearean reference in the poem. Early in the poem, Paterfamilisn't "hears not a cock crow but a crow crow." Could this be a minstrel-show translation of Romeo's argument with Juliet over whether it was the lark's or the nightingale's song they heard? As Lawrence Levine has shown us, performances of Shakespeare's plays were not as "highbrow" in the nineteenth-century United States as they are today, and minstrel shows in particular borrowed liberally from the Bard. Shakespeare's "weakness for bad puns" (John Dryden, for example, accused Shakespeare of allowing "his comic wit [to] degenerat[e] into clenches," an antiquated term meaning "pun")⁵ made him a perpetual source for minstrel show humor. The echo of *Romeo and Juliet* here makes sense in a way; Kearney's dialogue is, in fact, a love poem of sorts, even though the framework of minstrelsy's conventions can disguise that fact, as some of the couple's terms of endearment—such as "darkling," "smudgy-poo," and "smokescreen"—sound suspiciously like racial epithets. Unlike the association with *Romeo and Juliet*, however, the associations with *Macbeth* and *Hamlet* evoke nothing so much as the sentiment of guilt. As with the feelings of negation and unsexing, the poem's desire to confront the feelings of guilt and blame is one of the many ways it deals authentically and candidly with the emotions felt by a couple who have suffered a miscarriage.

And yet all of these sincere sentiments are still being filtered and misdirected through the cynical mask of blackface minstrelsy. Take, for instance, Paterfamilisn't's line early in the poem, "morning broke not water but tomato," which, by the end of the poem, is rendered newly legible as first and foremost a literal description of the blood-stained sheets resulting from a miscarriage in progress. But it is also a complex zeugma of three metaphors—morning breaking, water breaking, and tomato breaking—each less abstract than the last, ending with the implied image of a tomato being thrown at minstrel show performers by irate and dissatisfied audience members. It is also no surprise that the line preceding this one is the one in which Paterfamilisn't says, in response to his wife's "crowing," that he "hears not a cock crow but a crow crow." The "cock" disappears from a poem about the difficulties surrounding reproduction and is replaced instead by a reference to the most famous character of minstrelsy, Jim Crow.

Although the printed legacy of minstrelsy is evidenced in archives of ephemera found in libraries across the country and even the world, the essence of the minstrel show, of course, was in its performance. Not coincidentally, Kearney is also known for his virtuoso performances and showmanship; it is, in fact, challenging to isolate the text of his poetry from the performance of it. In one 2012 performance available on vimeo (an early version of the poem, one including introductory stage directions for the minstrel show),⁶ Kearney's screeching, rapid-fire delivery while embodying the two characters makes it clear that he is trying to provoke discomfort in our listening experience. The fact that his performance is so bodily, that it seemingly requires so much physical exertion, only intensifies the mingled pain and pleasure of listening. His performance of the poem is crucial to our understanding of it: the overextension of his voice, the hammy gesticulation, the herky-jerky movement of constantly shifting registers from one character to another all exaggerate the artifice that results from superimposing minstrelsy over such a serious topic. Extending *Patter*'s multimedia reach even beyond aural performance, however, is Kearney's elaborate Tumblr site, an authorial supplement designed to accompany the book.⁷ It includes information to help us read the poems, some of it—a link to a center specializing in IVF embryo transfer, an article about ovarian hyperstimulation syndrome, and a photograph of an empty sample vial labeled "Husband's Full Name"—surprisingly intimate. Even more than the poem to which it refers, the visual image of the vial, an artifact of that experience, feels like an intrusion upon his privacy.

Which is, of course, the point. One of the biggest disjunctures between minstrelsy and miscarriage is the enormous distance between public spectacle and private suffering. Kearney performs his loss; rather than rely on a mode that Marjorie Perloff claims characterizes the average poem found in *American Poetry Review*, featuring "the expression of a profound thought or small epiphany, usually based on a particular memory, designating the lyric speaker as a particularly sensitive person who really *feels* the pain . . . of some personal tragedy such as the death of a loved one," he filters that tragedy through the insincerity of staged performance.[8] Kearney writes *through* the minstrel show, and ironically intensifies the poem's pathos and intimacy as a result. Like the magician's patter, Kearney's patter guides us to look in one direction while the action is happening somewhere else. Once the gawking spectator realizes where to look, he wonders if what he sees was meant for an audience at all.

Notes

1. In another of the poems in this series, titled "A Miscarriage: A Magic Trick," the miscarriage is represented by "scarlet silks in a lady's skirt" and the magician "distract[s] the crowd with patter." Douglas Kearney, *Patter* (Pasadena, Calif.: Red Hen Press, 2014), 35.

2. Paul Laurence Dunbar, "The Tuskegee Meeting," in *In His Own Voice*, ed. Herbert Woodward Martin and Ronald Primeau (Athens: Ohio University Press, 2002), 187.

3. Eric Lott, *Love and Theft: Blackface Minstrelsy and the American Working Class* (Oxford: Oxford University Press, 1993), 126; Sarah Meer, *Uncle Tom Mania: Slavery, Minstrelsy, and Transatlantic Culture in the 1850s* (Athens: University of Georgia Press, 2005), 35.

4. Kyla Wazana Tompkins, *Racial Indigestion: Eating Bodies in the 19th Century* (New York: New York University Press, 2012), 8.

5. John Dryden, "An Essay of Dramatic Poesy," in *The Major Works, including* MacFlecknoe *and* Absalom and Achitophel, ed. Keith Walker (Oxford: Oxford University Press, 1987).

6. "Douglas Kearney Reads from 'The Miscarriage,'" vimeo video, 4:07, posted by Laura Mullen, 2013, http://vimeo.com/44957477.

7. Douglas Kearney, "*Patter* (Notes & Stuff)," Tumblr, February 1, 2015, http://dkpatter.tumblr.com/.

8. Marjorie Perloff, "Poetry on the Brink," *Boston Review*, May/June 2012, http://www.bostonreview.net/forum/poetry-brink.

TISA BRYANT

from *Unexplained Presence*

ILLUSTRATION

S.H. GRIMM, *Drolleries*

JUNE 14, 1771

PRINT COLLECTION,

LEWIS WALPOLE LIBRARY

YALE UNIVERSITY

An old woman in a humble cloak stops, thunderstruck, at the sight of a euphemistic "lady of fashion," emerging from an avenue of lindens.

Behind her trails a black page in ornate suiting, a plumed turban on his head, her lapdog tucked in his arms. He, too, is the mark of fashion among such of the period, who promoted their charms within sight of the well-heeled.

The lady's hair is teased to an exaggerated height that rises into the trees. At the summit of her coiffure sits a ribboned hat. The old woman must lean back and scope with her hand cupped around her eye in order to take it all in. Her wrinkled hand reaches for her heart in dismay. Her mouth drops open.

"Heyday!" reads the caption. "Is this my daughter Anne?"

Chapter 15

"What Is More Precise than Precision?" Tisa Bryant's *Unexplained Presence*

Jeanne Heuving

One of the most intractable problems articulated in the last decades of the twentieth century and carried over into the twenty-first is the way that dominant entities constitute (or perform) an unmarked dominance by othering others, through what Toni Morrison calls "techniques of 'othering.'"[1] Indeed, an important way this works is those who by race, gender, class, sexuality, or other social distinctions are able to presume their own positionality as unmarked are thereby enabled or even encouraged to issue descriptions, assertions, and commands as normative or universal, often disregarding, marginalizing, or abjecting others. Indeed, however broadly and subtly these patterns of dominance have been studied, the critiques themselves inevitably mark those outside their domains as "other than." Moreover, when this critique turns its focus on dominance itself, as in the pervasive critique of white privilege, it supplants the persons so injured with a renewed attention to itself. In other words, this critique, however necessary and powerful, often serves to re-entrench the very positionalities it contests.

In *Unexplained Presence* Tisa Bryant attends to this critique by engaging perceptual modalities that disrupt its seemingly intractable dynamics.[2] While Claudia Rankine has shown in *Citizen* just how important it remains to reveal the ongoing existence of racial "othering," Bryant furthers this critique by involving her readers in a cross-genre and cross-media exploration that demands they engage diverse modes of apprehension which have the power to unsettle embedded racial stereotypes.[3] Marianne Moore, who early in her career called for the inclusion of "real" things in poetry, including "toads" and "school-books," came to ask and answer: "What is more precise than precision? Illusion."[4] By this remark, Moore aimed to draw attention to how illusions in conveying will and desire convey much more than a putative real. Indeed, illusions, although often suspect as modes of knowledge, are necessary to the legibility of almost all cultural texts and certainly to an enriched apprehension of most art works.[5] Yet, it is precisely in and through illusions that at once mask and promote stereotypes that the most vicious and entrenched racism inheres.[6]

In a preface to *Unexplained Presence* Bryant designates her practice as "talking the seen" (x). A presentation of multiple "scenes" from prints, sculptures, films, television miniseries, and literary works, *Unexplained Presence* needs to be read in tandem with the depictions it presents. While it might be tempting to categorize Bryant's work as *ekphrasis* in an expanded field, it differs from most *ekphrastic* works as it neither merely serves to help us to see the preexisting work better as presumably intended by its auteur, artist, or writer nor usurps this work through its empowered revisioning. Rather Bryant's writing is a track running alongside these preexisting works. Much like ambitious film montage, this "recombinant" production exists most powerfully in the "receiver's" mind and imagination, making way for a third possibility (ix, x). Moreover, the switching between media—between Bryant's exclusively print text and the often visual works that it tracks—does not lead one to synthesize these but rather to switch between the different modes of apprehension demanded by diverse media (x). The scripted presences within her source texts thereby become destabilized and other than their textual interpellation, taking on the power of being "unexplained presences" or cumulatively as "unexplained presence." This process prompts a reseeing that must envision these presences as existing apart from their inscription and from habitual "takes" on racialized others.

Each of Bryant's "scenes" in this some 150-page work focuses on "nonwhite, africanlike (or Africanist) presence or persona" in works that are minimally and tangentially about them.[7] These presences are racially marked (by Bryant's selection and by their visual appearance) and loosened from their predictable social scripts through this double seeing. That is, we are invited to see these entities as Bryant instructs our seeing and as the preexisting work plays on. Indeed, most of Bryant's source texts are at least ostensibly on the side of nonwhite peoples, albeit indifferent to the uses to which they put "dark" presences in their own representational strategies. Focusing on Africanist persons that almost escape notice, so serviceable are they to the "scenes" in which they appear, Bryant, in staying our attention on these disappeared, makes their appearance uncanny. For example, the black page in "Illustration," which in the actual print is subordinated to and entirely tangential to the main drama of this "drollery," in Bryant's description emerges as a presence in his own right and must be seen afresh. Rather than broadly correcting for a pervasive racism, Bryant's wayward writing catches actual entities, visages, in the crosshairs of deliberately targeted vantages. One of the effects of this "talking the seen," read in conjunction with the preexisting works, is that a kind of phenomenal space develops, an illusion in the making but not quite formed in the reader's mind. The black face is no longer simply black; the white face is not so white.

In her preface, Bryant notes that Toni Morrison's *Playing in the Dark: Whiteness and the Literary Imagination* is a "touchstone" for her work and quotes Morrison's purpose as coincident with her own: "'An investigation into the ways in which a nonwhite, africanlike (or Africanist) presence or personae was constructed in the United States, and the imaginative uses this fabricated presence served'" (x). Yet, while Bryant's work is prompted by Morrison's *Playing in the Dark*, it differs in important ways from this work. Most notably Morrison stresses how black characters enable a white American literature to form—creating a book more about the construction of whiteness than about the black entities it uses. Bryant instead focuses on black presences and their presentation. Further, while Morrison's area of exploration is classic American literature, Bryant takes on the other side of the Atlantic (primarily Britain), delving into a culture of aristocratic flourishing and fripperies as well as patrician decorums and grotesques. While Morrison must attend to an American culture based on the brutality of Manifest Destiny and on an economy based on slavery in plain sight, Bryant turns to the more hidden racist history of Britain with its overseas sugar and tobacco plantations and their slave and indentured labor. Moreover, while Morrison and Rankine both appeal to the political and ethical sense of a critic-reader, Bryant, beginning with Morrison's apt insights into the "techniques of 'othering,'" refuses to allow her "receivers" the assurance of a critical stance as their main response to her work.

Addressing the problematics theorized by Morrison and Rankine, Bryant's work takes her readers *into* the phenomenal force field of their critique. Bryant describes the need for her work this way:

> Black figures in Eurocentric literature, film, and visual art are rarely presented without being given a distinct, racialized function, the import of which often goes largely undisputed, if not wholly unacknowledged, simply because the power of saying, of naming and describing it, has been withheld. The explanation for their presence and their function is hidden in plain sight, a double-sided sleight of hand between the maker and the subconscious, and between the maker and the receiver of the work. This sleight of hand intrigues me.

Bryant goes on to discuss "this sleight of hand" as itself existing as a covert communication that maker and receiver might in some way know but cannot or do not acknowledge:

> Like watching two people (lovers? spies?) silently mouthing words to each other from across a crowded room, my comprehension of the message occurs surreptitiously. I know things I am not supposed to know. I see without seeing, and witness an open secret, in a roomful of people where I am not the only one with such eyes.

In contrast to an implied citizen-critic, Bryant draws analogies for the "receivers" of the works she examines as well as her own as lovers and spies—those who are exceptionally aware of circumstances as well as fearful of being caught out. About her examined others, Bryant notes that "we're conditioned not to look too long or too closely at how or why these figures do what they do, how they might perpetuate or debunk myths around race, sexuality, and storytelling" (ix). Bryant draws attention to the perspicacious subjectivity by which she and others may understand and feel complex racial situations or texts, whether consciously or unconsciously, overtly or subliminally, while they simultaneously fail to acknowledge or deny these very responses. However, it is her intention not solely to identify or critique these unthought or illicit responses, but rather to involve her readers or "receivers," as she prefers, in "the foxy realm of myths that images, signs, and metaphors create, and to bring [them] with [her]." She explains: "I consider cinematic language, genre, myth-making, and the authority of the text in recombinant fashion, so as to write the story of a painting or a film . . . while imagining the voice and thought of unexplained presences, turning objects into subjects, metaphorical shorthand into a style of explication" (x).

The difficulties of *Unexplained Presence* are several. We must conceive of this as written by an African American auteur who is at once "paring her fingernails" and also intervening into the issues that Morrison and Rankine so clearly identify.[8] Secondly we must read her presented scenes in tandem with her source texts in a way that enables responses or images to form that cross both texts. While it is easy to be lulled by Bryant's often talky "telling the seen," at times seemingly little more than lively and well-written renditions of preexisting works, these are in fact setups to involve her readers in her ways of reading, which through her exacting word choices create complex portraits in a work that refuses to make isolated points. That is, rather than having her audience simply attain to the critical ideas that motivate her writing, she wishes them through their involvement in her writing and source texts to envision black presences as she sees them—neither uniformly as black nor existing apart from their blackness.

Further, we must take in the complexity of the totality of *Unexplained Presence*. It at once enacts and tells its significance. In a time replete with the flourishing of combined Internet images and texts, Bryant elects the comparatively impoverished look of print and asserts her own "seens" as only accessible through a print medium. As such, she involves us in the challenges of "seeing" itself, as both literal and illusionistic, as mediated and as existing apart from mediation. Moreover, one must read *Unexplained Presence* with all the attentiveness one gives to a long poem or a literary novel that engages in an ongoing advance of and return to its subjects, themes, and symbols through foreshadowing, allusions, and motifs. Two of the subjects to which Bryant repeatedly returns are portraits of ladies and of black men who lose their heads, figuratively and actually, whether Brontë's Heathcliff or the head of the Moor that Virginia Woolf sets spinning at the beginning of *Orlando*. As such, she engages one of the most problematic areas within Anglo-American culture and representation—of lovers and beloveds, sexual agents and sexual objects.[9] Indeed, the text ultimately asks, what does it mean to have a head or face at all—and how does this question change given one's race, gender, sexuality, or class?

Bryant introduces her text with "Illustration," quoted at the beginning of this essay, which is a verbal exposition of a visual plate that might customarily occupy the place of a frontispiece in a book and which also serves as an illustration of the paradigm that *Unexplained Presence* addresses throughout, of how black figures serve as accompanying accoutrements and foils in plots about white people. Replicating all the information that would accompany this print were it an actual plate in a book or hanging in a museum, Bryant proceeds to tell the print, introducing her first unexplained presence of the "black page," a likely pun. An old woman presumably stumbling upon her daughter, whose hair Bryant describes as "teased to an exaggerated height that rises into the trees," utters these words: "Heyday! Is this my daughter Anne?" While the colorful "heyday" expression is actually the title or caption of the print, thereby placing satiric or mocking attention on the lady of lower-class origins aspiring to high fashion, Bryant concludes her depiction with this statement, thereby creating a sense of the old woman's subjectivity—her possible hurt, dismay, and wonderment at this encounter with her daughter. Bryant places deliberate attention on the black page, visually describing his attire, "ornate suiting, a plumed turban on his head," and remarking, "He, too, is the mark of fashion." Mimicking the mood of the print, Bryant turns caricature into sympathetic portrayal, sentimental treacle into actual feeling. This illustration not only introduces the paradigm that *Unexplained Presence* explores throughout but is itself paradigmatic of illustrations, utilizing somewhat innocuous and declassed exemplars to initiate its case. While the figures in "Illustration" redound with the complexity of socially situated figures, their relations, in contrast to Bryant's other depictions, are relatively straightforward.

In next turning to John Schlesinger's 1965 "Darling," she continues her study of ladies and dark men into far more vexing territory. Schlesinger's film is a somewhat savvy presentation of the relations between moneyed British classes and the sense of noblesse oblige they bring to the downtrodden, especially the downtrodden outside their ken or color line. While in Schlesinger's film African presences provide evidence of the downtrodden as well as bring to the fore a metropolitan, international, and bohemian class of people, Schlesinger uses them primarily to tell the story about his own class of people, albeit a critical one that pins its harshest satire on the smart but ultimately witless Diana. "Darling" begins with Darling's voice-over, played by Julie Christie, which repeatedly surfaces but mainly lapses into fully rendered dramatic scenes, as Darling tells her own not very attractive narrative of a career and life created through her ambition and intelligence but also through the "honey glow" of her skin and her relationships with men.

Bryant tracks Schlesinger's satiric account as she focuses on how he uses African presences to tell this story. In one scene in which Diana works as an emcee for a charity event "bursting with hoi poloi," there are "several young black boys, eight or ten years old, dressed as pages in ornately designed jackets and powdered wigs, totally liveried, proferring trays of dainties" (7). They become the object of the lecherous gaze of the man at the helm of this wealthy fundraiser, Lord Grout. Bryant focuses on one of the boys, as seen by Lord Grout: "The boy in his gaze is distant but vulnerable, eyes spotting something unseen that keeps his back rigid, that keeps his head from spinning" (9). There is little here that is not in Schlesinger's film except for Bryant's making the black boy her primary focus and thereby marking his subjectivity, largely passed over in the film. Bryant's description brings to the fore how these "pages" must protect their selves and skins, with all the mental and physical knowledge they can command, from the Lord Grouts that would prey on them. And she does so by developing her own thematic attention to heads that spin, or in this case heads that try very hard not to spin. Her "totally liveried, proferring trays of dainties" draws out how these young boys are not only uniformed but hired out, much like horse stable liveries, quite in contrast to the trays they carry of "dainties," perhaps alluding to their vulnerable sexual organs. As such, their costumes drop away and their vulnerable faces remain.

Bryant makes much of the doubling in Schlesinger's film: Julie Christie's voice-over, two "gorgeous Negroes," and a truth game that builds on a covert visual comparison of Julie Christie to her black doppelgänger (6–7). Bryant writes of Julie Christie's sighting of two African presences in the stairwell of the somewhat upscale flat Darling shares with her lover, the television director Dirk. Diana announces to Dirk: "Darling, two of the most *gorgeous* Negroes you have ever seen have just gone up the stairs. What on earth is going on up there?" (7). Quoting exactly from the film but focusing on just this line, Bryant draws attention to how the presence of these Negroes excites Diana to imagine something untoward and unknown. Bryant presses her language: "Two black men in suede and velvet pantsuits, expensive leather shoes like twin Puss 'n' Boots, scud up the marble steps" (6). Puss 'n' Boots references a European fairy tale, well known in England, in which a trickster cat through illegal means gains power, wealth, and a princess for his poor master. But in Schlesinger's film, this singular trickster cat is doubled, two black cats, merely serviceable to Schlesinger's plot, providing an illicit and sexual turn. Bryant's choice of the verb *scud* is both descriptive of the action and pointed. While *scud* is in fact frequently linked to moving clouds (which darken the sun), she also suggests how these two Negroes are naturalized, just part of the scene. *Scud* further designates a sailing in which boats move before a wind, having not set their sails, as such conjuring how these presences are presented in the film as powerless, mere emissaries of a moneyed regime. After their brief appearance, Bryant writes, "No more close shots of suede crotches or West Indian skins" (7). This is Bryant at her most intrusive, since there are in fact no shots of crotches or of additional black skins in this fleeting scene. Yet she also claims through this interjection that the inclusion of these black men and their perfect skins, as flawless and perfect as that of "honey glow" Diana, are there to titillate—to connote illicit activity and sexuality. As Bryant economically and suggestively presents it, Schlesinger is conducting highway robbery through these trickster cats and all that they represent. Yet, their perfect dark skins, in this film about skins, remain on the viewer's retina. These men are most attractive.

Schlesinger's most penetrating perspective of *his* class of people occurs at a night party in Paris, where Diana abandons Dirk for the mogul Miles and enters into Parisian high society, made up of a crème de la crème of moguls and bohemians, directors and actors, transvestites and straights, wherein she might make movie connections. Bryant focuses on the unexplained appearance of a black man, who becomes Diana's doppelgänger in a "truth game" in which a black man mimics and acts out Diana in what amounts to a kind of whiteface of Diana. In his initial entrance into this filmed scene, the black man is just one of the crowd, but in his imitation of Diana his animated face makes his negroid features and teeth prominent. Earlier in the chapter, Bryant had twice echoed lines from Emily Brontë's *Wuthering Heights* in reference to the gypsy Heathcliff to describe Diana—"Those lips. Those eyes. Those dark and morbid bones beneath the teeth"—interjecting the darkness of death and racial othering into the sparkling white visage of Honeyglow Diana (5). In this scene, Diana and her doppelgänger are dramatically and visually intertwined through their unusually pronounced cheekbones, thick lips, and toothy smiles. But while Julie Christie's teeth are perfect, the doppelganger's crooked, prominent teeth, by comparison, are grotesque.

In the film *Darling*, the presence of this black man and his insight into the character of Diana are unexplained except that he appears to be one of several frequenters of this bohemian scene. In answer to the question thrown from the crowd, "What would you do to be in my next film, Diana?" the all-knowing black man responds: "I don't know, but I'll definitely do it." Initially creating her portrait of this black man by quoting his words directly from the film, Bryant next has him speak behind a "cupped hand": "What makes me the Ideal Revelator? . . . I do me better. But who'll watch? All and sundry?" (9, 11). By referring to him as the "Ideal Revelator," Bryant through this cumbersome epithet—a mouthful—draws attention to the ways this black man occupies an unlikely role not prescribed by a deep reading of the racial tensions were a black man to act out a white man's intended paramour for the evening, but by the logics and needs of Schlesinger's film. Bryant describes how this black man is accompanied by "'jungle music'":

Syncopation. Congas and flute. The players romp around in a circle, dancing, frolicking, shrieking shadows flung, stripping off and exchanging clothes. Buck wild! There's screaming. Cowbells. Then

Silence. The black man fills the frame of light. He wears a frosted
blonde wig and a white frilly blouse. (9)

Through her choice of the words *buck* and *cowbells*, Bryant suggests how
this scene achieves its pitch through implied racial illusions of bestiality
and slavery. Drawing on her earlier allusion to the two black cats, this man
also "purrs" (9). Bryant concludes her chapter with "Severe Face," a white
transvestite and an unexplained presence of a different ilk, as she thrusts "a
grimacing black mask" into the camera. Bryant describes this mask: "A fetish
of black wood. . . . It's dark and mysterious as a coconut, in the shape of a
face, hair sprouting from its nose and brow" (11).

Schlesinger himself, likely conscious of the conceit of whiteface, makes this
parody of Diana all the more satiric, all the more abject, using this African
presence to do so. Indeed Bryant, hardly a fan of the character Darling, steps
in to comment on Schlesinger's use not only of this black man but of the star
of his film: "By now it's easy to forget that *Darling* is being narrated by our
Darling, looking back at her career. So it's easy not to ask why she'd retell
this episode of her story. Darling never says how she felt" (10). Bryant asks,
"Whose child *is* she anyway?" and alludes to her frontispiece: "*Heyday, is
this my Daughter Anne?*"

Throughout *Unexplained Presence*, the themes, images, motifs, and allu-
sions that Bryant introduces in "Darling" continue to reverberate. The fate
of Diana Scott in Schlesinger's film replicates that of Isabel Archer in Henry
James's *The Portrait of a Lady*, as Darling, rising in the patrician class, finds
herself, by the end of the film, the captive of an Italian mogul and his villa,
from which there is no foreseeable escape. Bryant explores the "portrait of a
lady" theme in multiple chapters in diverse ways. For example in the chapter
titled "Portrait of a Lady," Bryant tells of the abolitionist Allan Ramsey's
portrait of Queen Charlotte Sophia, in which he "paints, ever so delicately,
Africa as he sees it sleeping in her" (107). This painter then turns to exert this
fascination on a very real clock, credited by Bryant as *Negress Clock Case*,
held at Hillwood Museum and Gardens, Washington, D.C., in which when
the ear of the sculptural clock is pulled, "the queen's eyes turn blue. He pulls
the clock's right ear, and Her Majesty's hair refines itself, smoothes, darkens"
(109). The Heathcliff allusion, along with the grimacing black mask and other
decapitated and spinning heads, precipitates into the chapter "The Head of
the Moor." In "The Head of the Moor," Bryant turns to Woolf's *Orlando*,
which begins with its protagonist, Sascha, "slicing at the head of a Moor"
(115). After a lengthy archaeology of how the head of a Moor comes to begin
what some assume is Woolf's love letter to Vita Sackville-West, which entails
in fact the rumor of an actual, possibly murdered Moor in Sackville-West's
line of descent, Bryant writes: "Orlando is placed in darkness; Woolf likes
to flirt with his, with Vita's being of darkness. . . . How to be a woman, who
loves women, without making that love (it has two faces) 'dark'?" (121).

Bryant's concluding chapter, "Unexplained Presence," provides another portrait of a lady condemned to wander aimlessly in a different kind of very large and haunted house: a mini television series manufactured by British Channel 4, which consists of a historical rendition of a grand provincial house set in Regency England and a British version of the American show "The Dating Game." This party, set in 1815 and aired over many weeks, mimics actual house parties that were held for the purpose of matching suitors with ladies under the watchful eyes of chaperones hired for the occasion by families, for the explicit purpose of securing advantageous marriages as first and foremost economic arrangements. The series engaged actual British young persons of marrying age and of identified classes and backgrounds who were willing to play by the rules of a Regency House party on the off chance that they, like their predecessors, might meet and mate for life. As with Bryant's other sources, "Regency House Party" demonstrates some social progressiveness in telling how grand estates, such as the one in the miniseries, were financed by sugar plantations and their slave workers. Well into the second part of the miniseries, a dark-skinned Miss Samuel is announced by letter and arrives in a carriage with attendants who strew rose petals at her feet (however historically unlikely, as Bryant notes.) In short, as Bryant writes at some length, Miss Samuel becomes one of the catalysts for the telling of romance, while she herself ultimately is left, without explanation, out of the mating game. Although she in real life is actually a successful fashion designer, after a few appearances in which she is the focus of the drama, she is dropped as a contestant for romance and marriage:

> With a twinkling sweep of plantation sugar, Miss Tanya Samuel is transformed (transforms herself?) from intimidating, poised, and beautiful West Indian heiress, the richest of the women present, to magical, matchmaking Negro, holding up a bold light for others to see their futures by. As a nun might guide one's spirit toward eternal reward, before going to join the angels herself . . . Tanya Ourika Samuel is born. (157)

Stepping into this fictional bachelor party, the real-life attractive and successful fashion designer Tanya Samuel, by the television producer's tactful and tactless exclusion of her from the ongoing mating game, is transformed for real into her West Indian ancestor. Bryant draws out how Miss Samuel, who serves in the televised house party only to enable the destinies of others, "twinkles" with "plantation sugar."

In Nathaniel Mackey's 1992 essay, "Other: From Noun to Verb," he draws a distinction between "social othering" and "artistic othering," emphasizing how the latter enables "invention and change," while the former enforces existing power strictures.[10] Although in the prevailing critique of white privilege and racial othering, social and artistic othering are often conflated, their distinction provides important avenues for both creative and critical work, albeit pursued quite differently by Bryant and Mackey.[11] In 2007, Bryant initiates her literary career by publishing *Unexplained Presence*, which draws on the logic of conceptual writing, with its skepticism regarding an original art or poetry, but elects mimetic hybridity over mimetic purism. Although in *Unexplained Presence* Bryant stays within the constraints of a project that is committed to rewriting existing literary and visual art, her cross-genre and cross-media "talking the seen" engages multiple modes: written and visual, critical and imaginative, and conceptual and expressive. Indeed, as with other socially suppressed and oppressed artists and writers, her election of hybridity is a refusal of any one mode by which to engage existing social scripts, since unified approaches often serve only to entrench the labyrinthine reaches of things as they are. As such, she "lift[s] from the dark side of history" not "voices" but rather visages, foregrounding what most marks these entities as "other," namely their skin color, and enables her readers to experience these presences as unexplained presence within an ongoing racist culture.[12] For Bryant to do anything less would be neither art nor poetry.

Notes

1. Toni Morrison, *Playing in the Dark: Whiteness and the Literary Imagination* (New York: Random House, 1993), 59.

2. Tisa Bryant, *Unexplained Presence* (Providence, R.I.: Leon Works, 2007). Hereafter, page numbers are cited parenthetically.

3. Claudia Rankine, *Citizen: An American Lyric* (Minneapolis: Graywolf, 2014).

4. Marianne Moore, *The Complete Poems of Marianne Moore* (New York: Macmillan, 1951), 151, 267.

5. Most "receivers" of art works wish to dwell among presences and not data, if only through imagining their authors or signatories.

6. Recent studies show how subliminal responses based in unconscious neural responses are racist. For example, see David M. Amodio,"The Neuroscience of Prejudice and Stereotyping," *Nature Reviews Neuroscience*, 15 (2014): 670–82.

7. Morrison, *Playing in the Dark*, 6, quoted in Bryant, *Unexplained Presence*, x.

8. James Joyce, *A Portrait of the Artist as a Young Man* (New York: Viking Press, 1916), 215. I am quoting Joyce to suggest how Bryant herself is responding to a similar imperative to remain "within or behind or beyond or above" her work. Yet, as we inevitably read Joyce as an Irish, Catholic, and heterosexual man in order to understand his work, to appreciate Bryant's work, we must bring to it what it means for her as an African American and queer woman writer to compose *Unexplained Presence*.

9. I take up this subject at some length in my book *The Transmutation of Love and Avant–Garde Poetics* (Tuscaloosa: University of Alabama Press, 2016).

10. Nathaniel Mackey, *Discrepant Engagement: Dissonance, Cross-Cultural-ity, and Experimental Writing* (Tuscaloosa: University of Alabama Press, 2000 [1993]), 265.

11. Mackey's inventive verse pursues a jazz aesthetic that he relates to open-field poetics. See my *Transmutation of Love,* 156–79.

12. Susan Howe, "Statement for the New Poetics Colloquium, Vancouver, 1985," *Jimmy and Lucy's House of 'K'* (November 1985), 17.

TONYA M. FOSTER

In/somnia

Beside her, he lies
curled—sleeping apostrophe
—possession and "O!

    mission accomplished."
Again to t/his sweat. Now sleep.
But not for her—sleep

    less eyes like stagnant
city pools. Saltiness, then
this thirst for ice.

*   *   *   *   *

Another night's
gradations of darkness be
           come the counted sheep.

Another night's
darknesses like tar, like silt, like
steel wool coil along

her screen's narrow field
of light.   She wants to shout into
the pastoral sleep

of t/his face, to shout
at how sleep absents him, ab/dis
        solves him from/in

      to himself, *Pussy*
is condition -al, -ing, -er.
And position.

Chromosomal, pre
    positional.   Behind them
brackish water bangs

through bathroom pipes, through
the evening's tv tones,
through this cask of sleep.

*   *   *   *   *

Click the remote;
cough into the dark tree
of (y)our hands. S/w/allow

your voice back, into
the back/dark/spit of her throat.
Love's silence comes on.

Can running her
finger, like a hiss along
t/his clavicle trip up

parenthetical
affection? Full of sleep, this
dark husk pulls closer.

Catone and Cattwo
meow meeoows under
the closed bedroom door.

Unmet desire
ain't nothin' but a mother
of un/intention

as she stares into
her tv's 2 a.m.
glares, watches the way

*   *   *   *   *

she once watched
a boy's body—too quick for
caution and traffic

signs parse the asphalt.
Neighborhood boy, corner boy,
man to be—been. Bones.

Man to be—been. Bones.
Man to be—been. Bear this.
Man to be—been. Bones.

Done and *gone*?
What good is light on that?
To want and not ask.

To want and not ask.
To want and not ask to want.
To want and not ask.

*   *   *   *   *

She, in somnium
dramas, get chased round the block
by rabid white dogs.

      She, in somnium,
      drums up the dreary, damned, stalks
      interstices 'cause

            "body" ain't only
            a grammatical sentence.
                  There's no fleeing flesh

                  with music so loud,
                  and sirens, that you forget
                  dis'quieting stars.

She's come to take this
as survival gospel
for sub'urban souls.

Note: *Rows of asterisks appearing in the excerpt indicate the page breaks in the poem, which appear in the book to be intentional.*

Chapter 16

✦

Difficulty Bees as Difficulty Does

Evie Shockley

Tonya M. Foster's book *A Swarm of Bees in High Court* comes to us between rich, deep orange covers, the front of which is adorned with a reproduction of a Wangechi Mutu collage, *Le Noble Savage*. The visual art makes a muted but unmistakable gesture toward Josephine Baker in her banana skirt, transforming the Afro-modernist polish of La Baker's "primitivism" into a surrealist fantasia of African woman as banana tree. Her sexuality thus rooted in the "Dark Continent," this strangely composite figure comments, without comment (so to speak), on the typical gendering of the "noble savage" trope, which is signaled by the masculine form of the article in the work's title. Mutu's work makes a wonderfully appropriate visual introduction to some of the methods and concerns of Foster's book-length poem, which can be seen in microcosm in the section excerpted here, titled "In/somnia."

Just as Mutu's distorted yet beautiful central figure is unambiguously composed of disparate elements—geometric prints and photographs of animal heads and flowers, for example, are collaged to form her head, torso, and limbs—the reader needs to see the poem as a lyrical assemblage of fragments (of language, of culture, of ideas) and to be aware of the various incommensurate relationships between part and whole within it. Looking at Harlem as both a city (within a city) and an ecology, Foster writes that *A Swarm of Bees in High Court* "is a biography of life in the day of a particular neighborhood," written in the "collect[ed] language of the place" (122). Telling ironies abound, beginning with the section title, whose interrupting slash mark reminds us how our words, composites of prefixes, suffixes, and roots, may carry forward the meanings of their discrete parts and/or move off in a third direction. *Insomnia* is our English word for "sleeplessness" (*somnus* = sleep; and *in-* = not), but when we are directed to consider it as potentially two words, we find ourselves located "in" (preposition) a condition (the state of dreaming) or location (a world of fantasy): the Latin *somnium, n. pl. somnia*. Foster has her Harlemite speaker both awake and dreaming, as has at least one poet before her. If the dreams in Langston Hughes's poetry are desirable but deferred, in Foster's they are nightmarish and seem nearly impossible to escape.

Foster's stanzas are just as packed and compressed as the section's title. The short-lined tercets, with their surprising images and dense, irreverent word-play, do for the haiku series what Harryette Mullen's *Muse & Drudge* does for the ballad's quatrains. Specifically, Foster gives us a new way to read the short, image-based tercet—which is still, like the haiku, about nature in its most expansive sense—as presenting images *in* language and *of* language, at once. "Beside her, he lies," runs the section's opening line, whose music (asso-nance, consonance, rhythm) conjure at once a love scene and the undercutting possibility that the speaker's lover tells falsehoods, or that his body itself is untrue (line 1). This possibility may contribute to keeping the speaker awake, long after her lover's "O! //   mission" (orgasmic emission) has been "accom-plished" (3–4).[1] Perhaps her own climax was "O!"-mitted? In any case, he is "curled" into the shape of an apostrophe: self-*possessed* enough to address "t/ his sweat"—the liquid leaving "his" body and becoming "this" externalized object—before he goes to sleep (2, 5). "But not for her—sleep," the abrupt midword enjambment tells us, as we move from the second stanza to the third (6). We see our suspicion of nonreciprocity confirmed in the final tercet on this page, which begins with lack ("less") and ends with desire ("this thirst") that remains unquenched (as per the belief some hold that chewing "ice" sig-nifies sexual frustration). In between we have watery "eyes" that are "like . . . city pools": "stagnant," at least at first (7–8). Foster won't use a cliché, so her speaker's emotions—unhappiness, possibly anger—must be tucked into an ambiguous one-word phrase: "Saltiness" (8). If "blood" usually accompanies "sweat and tears" (at least in the R&B tradition), then we know to look out for it; and as we will see, the (word) "city" is the hyperlink between this stanza and the later (non)appearance of blood.

But before we get there, we have fourteen stanzas working in this same dizzying mode through issues of gender and loneliness, love and desire. The insomniac speaker lies awake (again) counting the "gradations of darkness" that have "be / come" the proverbial "sheep" (10–12). Is that the echo of Baraka we hear, sliding in sideways through the slash that opens up the word *become*? In his "Preface to a Twenty Volume Suicide Note," he "count[ed] the stars" on the nights they would "come to be counted."[2] Foster instead counts *s/tars*—that is, "darknesses like *tar*, like *s*ilt, like / *s*teel wool," evoking the stars sonically as she blackens them visually—or perhaps, like Baraka, she is imag(in)ing "the holes they leave" when the stars don't "come out" (Foster, 14–15; Baraka, 3; emphasis mine). Frustrated at watching the beloved sleep the sleep of satisfied desire, the speaker "wants to shout" and interrupt his rest, which manages to be "pastoral"—"ab/ . . . /   solve[d]" and innocent, "dis /   solve[d]" and transcendent—notwithstanding the insistent urban soundscape of "water bang[ing] // through bathroom pipes" in an adjacent apartment (17–18, 20–21, 27–28). But she doesn't wake him. She tells herself to mute the tv and "cough into the dark tree / of (y)our hands"—the *our*, embedded in and released from *your*, connecting her not with her lover but rather with all the other insomniacs she imagines around Harlem, similarly abandoned by their sleeping partners (31–33). She thinks of them all as women—"*Pussy / is condition . . . -ing*"—and, like the speaker, each is "pre / position[ed]" by gender norms to swallow (and to allow) her "voice back, into / the back/dark/spit of her throat" (22–23, 25–26, 33–35). With a "click [of] the remote," the tv's sound goes off and "love's silence comes on" (31, 36). As the "dark husk" of the lover's body, evacuated by sleep, "pulls closer" and the exiled cats who long for her company "*meow meeoows*" unmuted, the speaker arrives at an insight: "Unmet desire / ain't nothin' but a mother / of un/intention" (42–44, 46–48). The vernacular, here and on the previous page of the poem, prepares us for the "fucker" that—like the speaker's orgasm—isn't coming; the enjambment leads us not into profanity but delivers up a playful yet sharp-edged revision of the adage that "necessity is the mother of invention." It's "chromosomal," the speaker would argue: the male body is "full of sleep," while the female body is trapped in sexual frustration and a paradox of "un/intention" (25, 41, 48).

The body connects the themes running rapidly through these stanzas and likewise links them to the slower, more mournful stanzas on the following page. The speaker likens the way she "stares" at the tv in her insomniac state to "the way / she once watched a boy's body" moving through the city streets, playing in the place where many so-called inner-city children are forced by default to play (49, 51–53). Here, her body's sleep-deprived listlessness contrasts with his activity. The half-buried rhyme between *quick* and *traffic* suggests what the poem never outright says, including the aforementioned "(non) appearance" of blood. His "body," we read, "parse[s] the asphalt"—and is parsed in turn, as the fate of this "neighborhood boy, corner boy, / man to be" is rendered obliquely via a dash, a past-tense verb, and a telling noun: "—been. Bones" (52, 54, 56–57). This alliteration—"be—been. Bones"—is amplified by the line's repetition, nearly unchanged, through the whole following tercet, in which the only relief from this stunned and stunning account of his transformation is the speaker's still grim, still alliterative instruction (to herself, to the reader) to "Bear this" (58–60). Foster continues using sound adroitly to underscore the significance of her language and unfold the meaning(s) of her words. She transitions out of this loop of alliteration using a powerful series of slant rhymes that turn on the English language's three voiced plosives: "Bones. // Done and gone?" (60–61). After a tercet obsessively reiterating the finality of death, Foster destabilizes that absoluteness with three words that are also, importantly, eye rhymes, as if to suggest that appearance is not all. The end of the body may not be the end.

This quietly explosive question leads us to reconsider the themes of desire, loneliness, and insomnia in "light" of this haunting memory of watching a boy's accidental death. "What good is light on that?" the speaker asks, in a challenge to both En*light*enment philosophy and our association of day*light* with truth—and the fragment that follows (following the same pattern of insistent repetition we traced in the preceding stanza) offers a response that is elliptical at best: "To want and not ask" (62–63). Is this line advice? Or, as I come to see it, a description of the speaker's state of paralysis through this long, sleepless night? She has "not ask[ed] to want," to lack, to be in this disturbing somnium (65).

What can the daytime—the properly waking hours—teach us about death and sleep, desire and "love's silence" (36), and their inequitable distribution, that we cannot learn from/in the night? Here our reading of the "In/somnia" section is informed by issues of racial "just *(i)/(u)s*" and "Y/Our / perennial (k)nots" raised in the brief preceding section, titled "Harlem Nocturn/e/s" (4). Those earlier lines contextualize the speaker's semiconscious dreams (her "in somnium / dramas") of being "chased round the block / by rabid white dogs" (67–69). This "in somnium" state is also where she learns that "'body' ain't only / a grammatical sentence," something that can "parse" and be parsed, as with the body of the "corner boy" in the moment of his destruction (73–74, 54, 56). To say that it "ain't only" this, however, posits that the body can be understood, in some way, as "a grammatical sentence." How so? The body's wholeness, its completeness, its functionality as a unit is here implied. The bodily wholeness (*"There's no fleeing the flesh"*) that underwrites the lover's postcoital somnolence is, by contrast, fragmented ("parse[d]") for the speaker (75). She is suspended between Harlem and "somnium," longing to sleep but unable, "with music so loud, and sirens," and all the noise that makes "you forget / dis'quieting stars" (76–78). The Christian Bible is both a source of and challenge to the dichotomization of mind and body, a familiar duality called up in the book's opening lines: "A mind is master / but the flesh is boss" (i). That opening call gets a response in the closing lines of our "In/somnia" section, where the speaker acknowledges this double-edged insight "as survival gospel / for sub'urban souls" (80–81).

Race is embedded in the situation of this insight as it is embedded in the language. Foster has taught us to read the apostrophes in these final stanzas with nuance, as marks of "blackness" that help us parse particular words in this context. She shows us the (embraced? imposed?) black vernacular *"dis"* within "dis'quieting," so that the word becomes a comment on the way African Americans may be deprived of peace by being *buried*, we might say, in segregated quarters of the city, like her adopted Harlem. If *disquiet-ing* describes the anxiety-producing, then Foster's release of black vernacular connects that anxiety to the silence of the grave, the *"sub"* in the newly ver-nacularized "sub'urban." But although such ghettos may be meant to entomb blacks, the *good news* is that Harlem's residents are largely able to survive. More than merely surviving, by telling us that, finally, *"she's come* to take" Harlem's particular reminders of our attachment to the body as "gospel," the speaker may be playfully suggesting that she has tapped into the potential for pleasure available even under these conditions, even to black women trapped in/somnia (79; emphasis mine).

✦

Noise is whatever the signifying system, in a particular situation, is not intended to transmit, be the system a poem, a piece of music, a novel, or an entire society.

— Nathaniel Mackey[3]

In doing a close reading of Tonya Foster's *A Swarm of Bees in High Court*, I sought to transform the gratifying but demanding work of unpacking a section of the poem into a text that does justice to both the gratifications and the demands involved in engaging it. The urgency of successfully walking this tightrope comes in part from Foster's commitment, as I understand it, to a poetics for the commons (about which more below) and in part from my sensitivity to the difficulty that poetic "difficulty" has historically presented to so much brilliantly innovative black poetry. As astute critics from Sterling Brown to Aldon Nielsen to Harryette Mullen have observed, through most of the period of modernism (and postmodernism, if you will), black poetry's more nuanced metaphysical depths and more complex formal strategies have tended to go underrecognized or, conversely, underappreciated by critics, scholars, and nonspecialist audiences. Taking our cue from Nathaniel Mackey, as per the epigraph to this section, we could think of the layers of innovation in black poetry as "noise" that the critical apparatus or scene of consumption largely available could not "transmit"—such that only a single track of a deeply layered recording could be heard, so to speak. *Simple until proven difficult* was the presumption that most frequently informed approaches to work by African American authors over the past century. Simply protest. Simply derivative. Simply vulgar. Simply black. Simply simple.

Some poets—Russell Atkins, for instance—have chosen to write with as much "difficulty" as they pleased and as little regard for critical opinion as possible, with more or less predictable results (i.e., undeserved obscurity). Some poets—Melvin Tolson or Gwendolyn Brooks can serve as examples—at times took it upon themselves to head off this presumption at the pass by putting their own inimitable spins on recognizably "difficult" virtuosity. Others—like Sonia Sanchez and Langston Hughes (and Brooks, at times)—have done "difficulty" in a different way, placing less emphasis on making their skills legible to establishment critics than on making them available to nonspecialist and popular audiences. That work of the last sort has been more associated with its political critique (particularly around racial politics) than work in the other groupings is no coincidence; rather, there is a consistent (if not constant) correlation between the degree of clarity and insistence in the political critique, on one hand, and the degree to which the poetry would be characterized as easily consumable (and thus not warranting close aesthetic attention or repeated reading). All strategies have nonetheless resulted in poetry that was heard too often and too much as "noise." The poets persevered. Subsequent generations of African American poets confronting the presumption of simplicity have followed, combined, and expanded upon the strategies of earlier poets, writing along an aesthetically diverse spectrum of difficulty that includes such voices as Ntozake Shange, Nathaniel Mackey, Rita Dove, Carl Martin, Mark McMorris, Erica Hunt, Will Alexander, Julie Patton, Thomas Sayers Ellis, Dawn Lundy Martin, and LaTasha N. Nevada Diggs, to name a very few. Such poets' work (along with poets and other artists from various traditions, genres, and media) has met with, and helped produce, shifts in the culture and the scholarship that generally make critics better equipped to hear less "noise" in their poetry. Thus, the landscape of African American poetry—of poetry— that Foster's debut book enters in 2015 is one that provides her a whole range of possibilities to draw upon or to jump off from.

What kinds of difficulty does Foster's poem present? Difficult for whom? A twenty-first-century black postmodernist difficulty, by one light, which desta- bilizes the terms of racial essentialism while simultaneously destabilizing the presumption that no collective or productive concept of "blackness" can exist without that ground. The poem's Harlem setting, the challenge to the devalu- ation of "darkness" embedded in our language, the critique of (black) male privilege, the only partly ironic use of black vernacular as a poetic device, and the critique of U.S. urban ghettoization of black people are all aspects of the poem that contribute to various postmodernist (and post–Civil Rights) stances that might seem paradoxical or self-contradictory. Related but dis- tinct is the kind of difficulty that, in Anthony Reed's words, "advances an aesthetic of what Erica Hunt has called 'unrecognizable speech,'" creating a "hiatus of recognizability [that] can spur new thought and new imaginings, especially the (re)imaginings of collectivities and intellectual practices."[4] The "In/somnia" excerpt is less representative of this mode of difficulty in Foster's work than other sections of the poem, such as "In/somniloquies," which con- tains a three-and-a-half-page riff on the "blackness" of the color red ("yarn red as cartoon blood, as red as Mammy Two Shoes' shoes, matchstick heads, / yarn red as cartoon lips and tongues, red as bandanas and pomegranates") that demands a wide range of cultural and historical literacies to unpack (19). These modes of black experimental writing might pose "difficulties" for any reader, but especially those not experienced in reading now-canonical American and European avant-garde poetries (in particular, work associated with the Black Arts Movement, Language poetry, and surrealism). Another form of "difficulty" some readers of *A Swarm of Bees* will encounter is emotional difficulty. We tend to associate emotion in poetry with "easier," more conventional aesthetic modes (traditional lyric and narrative poems, "confessional" poems, and so forth), particularly with poems that clearly announce their own emotional postures and seek to evoke corresponding emotions in the reader. But without indulging in sentimentality, asserting out- rage, or projecting extreme feeling of any sort typographically—moreover, without dealing in explicit narrative or graphic representation of sensational material—Foster's poem may leave some readers struggling with the emotions it calls forth. As with the death of the "corner boy" in "In/somnia" or her cool assessment of gender relations on the block ("They say 'bitch' and mean / the syllable to break her / solipsistic strides") in the section "Bullet/in," Foster neither softens nor exaggerates the sharp edge of her analysis (65). Those who do not share (or understand) the poem's politics may also struggle with this book, if they don't put it down.

Erica Hunt's essential essay, "Notes toward an Oppositional Poetics" (cited by Reed above), reminds us that oppositionality—stances of resistance to, and efforts to transform, the status quo—is the common ground of all these types of difficulty. Foster's work enters the aesthetic commons (so to speak) of oppositionality that Hunt identifies, and does so in the service of much larger cultural and sociopolitical commons that Foster seeks to uncover and extend. In poetics panels and other public conversations, Foster has consistently expressed her concern that the valuable intellectual and cultural work done in avant-garde and experimental poetry could and should be available to wider audiences than the most likely poetic and academic coteries. This concern, however, should not be equated with a ("simply black") call for poetic "accessibility" of the sort associated with many Black Arts Movement theorists and poets—though Foster's position is undoubtedly born from an appreciation of certain political and cultural advantages of collectivity (racial and otherwise) that the Movement prioritized. Because she values both inclusivity and specialization, she faces in her work the generative tension of working with modes of innovation (investigating new lexicons, formal strategies, and conceptual paradigms) and subjects that may be grounded in areas both disparate and (yet) sometimes overlapping, such as (black and other) popular and folk cultures; (black and other) critical theory and intellectual traditions; broad cross-sections of modern and contemporary American poetry and poetics; or very particular communities, like that centered on eco-poetics. This tension is embodied within the questions she once asked in a (written) conversational response to an essay on "our history" of experimental poetics: "Who's this *our*? Can I bring my mother?"[5]

Ultimately, the ways Foster negotiates the tensions, or "difficulties," she faces as a poet produce the difficulties readers may confront in engaging her work, insofar as she seeks to create in her poetry a satisfying assemblage of the sources and contexts that inform her thinking and creative process. Her discussion of the book's title brings form, content, and (political) subjectivity together explicitly. In the notes, she remarks that "bees are communal, plural, public, unindividuated, corporate, en masse," characteristics that helped her think formally about how she might portray the community of Harlem as a holistic entity (121). *A Swarm of Bees in High Court* collects communal experiences in a collage of aesthetics that calls its various potential readers to meet each other in the difficult, always-be(e)ing-made space of the commons.

Notes

1. I reproduce Foster's slash marks as she uses them, with no spaces between the slash and the letters on either side of it. Slash marks that I insert for the conventional purpose of indicating line (/) and stanza (//) breaks can be distinguished from hers by the spaces I include on both sides of the single slash or pair of slashes (sometimes noticeably more than a single space, as here, before "mission," to indicate an indented line).

2. Amiri Baraka, "Preface to a Twenty Volume Suicide Note," in *S O S: Poems 1961–2013* (New York: Grove Press, 2014), 3.

3. Nathaniel Mackey, *Discrepant Engagement: Dissonance, Cross-Culturality, and Experimental Writing* (1993; repr., Tuscaloosa: University of Alabama Press, 2000), 20.

4. Anthony Reed, *Freedom Time: The Poetics and Politics of Black Experimental Writing* (Baltimore, Md.: Johns Hopkins University Press, 2014), 1.

5. Tonya Foster and Evie Shockley, "Braiding ConVERSations: To, Against, For," in "Dim Sum," *Delirious Hem*, February 7, 2008, http://delirioushem.blogspot.com/2008/02/dim-sum-tonya-foster-evie-shockley.html.

MULTILINGUAL MODES

ROSA ALCALÁ

Voice Activation

Do not forget that a poem, although it is composed in the
language of information, is not used in the language-game of
giving information.
　　　　　　　　　　—Ludwig Wittgenstein, *Zettel*

This poem, on the other hand, is activated by the sound of my voice,
and, luckily, I am a native speaker. Luckily, I have no accent and you
can understand perfectly what I am saying to you via this poem. I
have been working on this limpid voice, from which you can read
each word as if rounded in my mouth, as if my tongue were pushing
into my teeth, my lips meeting and jaws flexing, so that even if from
birth you've been taught to read faces before words and words as
faces, you'll feel not at all confused with what I say on the page. But
maybe you'll see my name and feel a twinge of confusion. Have no
doubt, my poem is innocent and transparent. So when I say, I think
I'll make myself a sandwich, the poem does not say, I drink an isle
of bad trips. Or if I say, my mother is dying, where is her phone. The
poem does not say, try other it spying, spare us ur-foam. One way
to ensure the poem and its reader no misunderstanding is to never
modulate. I'm done with emotion, I'm done, especially, with that cer-
tain weakness called exiting one's intention. What I mean is Spanish.
What a mess that is, fishing for good old American bread, and ending
up with a boatload of uncles and their boxes of salt cod, a round of
aunts poking for fat in your middle. So you see, Wittgenstein, even
the sandwich isn't always made to my specifications; it's the poem
that does what I demand. Everything else requires a series of steps.
I call the nurse's station and explain to the nurse—her accent thick
as thieves—that I'd like to speak to my mother. She calls out to my
mother: "it's your daughter" (really, she says this in Spanish, but for
the sake of voice activation and this poem, you understand I can't go
there), and she hands the phone to my mother and my mother, who
is not the poem, has trouble understanding me. So I write this poem,
which understands me perfectly, and never needs the nurse's station,
and never worries about unintelligible accents or speaking loudly
enough or the trouble with dying, which can be understood as a loss
of language. If so, the immigrant, my mother, has been misunderstood
for so long, this death is from her last interpreter.

Chapter 17

Difficulties That Matter:
Rosa Alcalá's "Voice Activation"

Roberto Tejada

Close inspection of the poem above reveals a method whose sly maneuvers take up as subject matter the difficulties and social effects of first impressions. In what follows, then, I untangle the poem's fashioning of an implied reader whose cultural bias is enfolded back into the rhetorical framing device of this enacted moment, a situation that presupposes reader skepticism in what concerns this work's self-possessed ambivalence as an object worthy of U.S. avant-garde credentials. The political consequences of this device are in keeping with the language games of everyday social livelihood, and in what remains of the poem, equated with other forms of foreignness and belonging. This poem's thematic and formal concerns connect immigrant proficiency to artistic engagement and the material facts of bodily demise, inasmuch as the poem links the physics of voice modulation to the broader social project of intelligibility. The poem's design sides neither with the archival literalism of conceptual poetry nor with unruly assaults on decorum or on class-affiliated norms, long valued by the innovative ranks—what critic Daniel Tiffany has identified as a diction-driven form of "signaling."[1] It seeks rather to persuasively expose certain unexamined assumptions that inform a mainstream echelon dominant within the U.S. avant-garde. "Voice Activation" declares itself as language use at odds with the business of information delivery or the harvesting of utterance transposed verbatim from the discursive thrum of the electronic cultural ether. The speaking subject prompts this self-conscious occasion, "luckily" submitted in the native language. As a result, the poem denaturalizes the experience of unaccented address in English.

Insight into the indissoluble energies that mutually activate poetic form and ethno-cultural content have led literary scholars such as Dorothy Wang to make persuasive counterarguments to those critics who "assume that [ethnically or racially marked poetry] functions as a transparent window into the ethnographic 'truth' of a hyphenated identity and an exotic 'home' culture—in other words, as if there were no such thing as the mediatedness of language."[2] Similarly, poet Dale Smith makes rhetorical studies relevant to poetic production and consumption viewed as broad cultural performances in public space capable of acting on attitudes that have long arbitrated our institutions of taste.[3] Alcalá's work aligns with a mode of contemporary poetic practice invested in what Charles Altieri has called the project of reactivating the "ideals [and] resources of rhetoric that enable poetry to engage social forces."[4] The rhetorical turn, in an environment largely hostile to it, is a wager on discursive immanence and the speculative rehearsal, what Uruguayan artist and theorist Luis Camnitzer calls the ability of art to create itself "while it allows the play with taxonomies, the making of illegal and subversive connections, the creation of alternative systems of order, the defiance of known systems, and the critical thinking and feeling of everything. More than any other means of speculation it allows us to travel back and forth seamlessly from our subjective reality to consensus" and to the horizon of what is possible, regardless of its unattainability.[5] This mode enlivens experience with situations and arguments that so unsettle the agreement of cause and effect as to approximate the processes of thought—and by extension, the discontinuous view of history—as movements that amend, delay, curve, and surprise. Or, in terms of a question fellow poet-critic Peter Ramos has identified as being at stake in the work of Rosa Alcalá: "Where is the line, the border, between one's cultural identities and one's supposedly *true* self?"[6]

"Voice Activation" enlivens a scene of writing whose conception activates a *figure* of difficulty in which human voice is tied to personhood to the degree that speech-recognition technology is related to social competency and the contingencies of birthplace, a stagecraft that qualifies you as being either foreign or domestic. The poem's pitch intensifies in that contingency, equated as well to the difference between speaking voice and writing subject emerging as though from the acoustic interface transposed by technological means. Driving the immediacy of the poem's exposition is the image of a person coming into specificity as she contends with the electronic device for which the poem is a surrogate, and readers are interpolated into the scene of invention to the degree that it should be obligatory at all for a speaker to admit the status of her unmarked or uninflected English. To pronounce so that all who listen can understand without effort is to claim necessarily an unspoken proposition. A "foreign" accent is a surplus that culturally determines social interaction in that it attaches externally to a text deemed neutral. In a poem, therefore, accents can never been understood properly on their own terms but only as a measure of other competencies.[7] To verbalize without a foreign accent is an auspicious thing even from the ever-compensatory position of a speaker for whom English is the native tongue. Contrary to the language game of giving information, the poem here serves as a product of the software that makes possible the lines activated in the present tense of reading. In the concrete world that poems inhabit, technological design is related to the engineering of social space, including that of the nation. It follows, therefore, that an artistic method committed to uncritical deskilling—precisely thanks to automated means of production—will chance too close associations with the ascendency of U.S. values and advantages in the neoliberal global arena, by turn responsible for motivating new processes of migration. The speaker in "Voice Activation" rhetorically persuades you to acknowledge the patterns of immigration that subsist as the underside to modernist indeterminacy.

What impact do those narratives have on language? For subjects of immigration, household dynamics in the place of arrival can give way to a series of domestic identities, social functions, and cultural proficiencies, not exclusive of language competency and the aptitude necessary to attain a level of transparency or acoustic invisibility. To achieve a limpid voice—"readily intelligible," "absolutely serene and untroubled"[8]—is to live unburdened: a prestige that comes only as the result a lifetime of labor. Those learned skills—each word "rounded in my mouth," tongue "pushing," "lips meeting," and "jaws flexing"—constitute the means by which the student of communication becomes more than the sum of her speaking. To the degree that she can embody a voice without accent, released now from the gestures that locate persons in relation to region and language community, utterance grants entry into a version of utopia. This intelligibility, this passport that provides mobility, is also instruction into the psychodynamics of social assessment, inasmuch as "to read faces before words and words as faces" is to distinguish physical appearances—the perceived relationship between specific bodies and general proficiency—as the qualification for "passing" in the linguistic skill sets of English. It is, by extension, to view the printed or spoken word as a test of character and the performance of a personality. Finally, it is to ascertain ulterior motive in those gestures and cadences reflected in the facial expression of power's fluctuating personnel.

Names and faces here begin to resemble what media theorists refer to as "address gaps" and "context ruptures,"[9] especially for those who traffic in determining artistic "fit" for inclusion into group formations, as when circumscribed by a list of surnames. To any "twinge of confusion" you perceive between proper names and artistic practice, the activated voice in Alcalá's poem comes to your provisional protection with ironizing reassurances. The transparency of this enterprise is only as committed to sincerity as intoxications with technological progress are contained in some triumphalist examples of experimental U.S. poetry. To prove her point, the speaking voice proceeds again to disavow the poem as being anything but a figure for an automated recording device, even as the overlapping only deepens, startlingly so, by equating the internal chatter that makes diminutive everyday action possible ("I think I'll make myself a sandwich") with the incommensurable information that "my mother is dying." The garble of English speech-recognition software further impresses the negligible capacity of language to diagnose the circumstance as "other it spying." Within the range of acceptable U.S. Anglo-American vernacular and the possession of certain surnames, cultural biases are trumped by the rhetorical aptitude of the text. Purely technological or mechanistic reproduction is shown to be deficient when undermined by an irreducible difference of inflection. Modulation is a kind of psychological accent, the sound quality of an untamable tongue, capable of relating a particular history of displacement and submission to the lingua franca, in as many positive survivals—phonetic, lexical, logical—as there are alleged mispronunciations.

At stake here is what Alcalá describes elsewhere, in her work on New York–based Chilean poet Cecilia Vicuña, as "the interplay between poetic texts and the vocalization and improvisation of those texts." In her essay "Listening to Quasars," Alcalá engages the temporality of a poem's making in relation to its subsequent oral performance through internal discursive "listening" effects. As with Vicuña, Alcalá performs what Walter Mignolo calls "languaging": a "thinking and writing between languages, that moves us away from the idea that language is a fact (e.g., a system of syntactic, semantic, and phonetic rules), and toward the idea that speech and writing are strategies for orienting and manipulating social domains of interaction."[10] Aligned here with Vicuña, whose poetic works and performances Alcalá has translated and edited, is such a languaging strategy: "So you see, Wittgenstein, even the sandwich isn't always made to my specifications; it's the poem that does what I demand." To the degree that command between languages, or languaging, is able to master syntax, grammar, and idiomatic form as "social domains of interaction," the sonic torsions between *sandwich* and *Spanish* resemble the vexed connections—as though comprising a wireless surrogate for the umbilical cord—between the technological modernity of a smart phone and the object relation between mother and daughter. A slant rhyme (*sandwich/Spanish*) sounds the substitutive satisfactions for a fading body signifying material attachment and biological indebtedness. Neither the poem, however, nor the device of high-speed communication is able to close the gap for which death is the wedge between the components of such analogies.

What proliferations obtain in wordplay for the code-switching self of the bilingual? At what interval does the other language become the language of the other? If, in the psychoanalytic view, the self is partly a grammatical seduction dissociating reason from being—"I think where I am not, therefore I am where I do not think"[11]— is it desirable to eradicate forces that menace reason understood as a kind of automation? Or that threaten the enterprise of writing itself? Not only in terms of affect but also in the automated parapraxis of "other it spying," as though to elide the matchless foreign agent that is death? To be done with emotion, or with unwanted mechanized thoughts—with exiting one's intention—is as well to be done with, and done in by, Spanish: "What a mess that is . . . ." Here mother tongue becomes a figure of history for all the human waste, refuse, and self-horror; for the laboring immigrant body and its kinship networks ("boatful of uncles," a "round of aunts"); for the ensuing differences in upbringing ("American bread") and for the dilemma of displaced belonging.

The poem at this point escalates its conflict and figure of reasoning in relation to intelligibility and understanding, for now no system other than this poem can serve the demands that such a human scene obliges, even as the cellular phone facilitates and obscures the final exchanges among speaker, dying mother, laboring figure, and reading subject, in the requisite steps that connect present and future tenses. There enters into the foreground another inflection from a healthcare employee who otherwise threatens to compromise or derail, in an accent "thick as thieves," the urgent matter that "but for the sake of voice-activation and this poem, you understand" is requisite for the management from afar of the delivery system—now care, now information—that conflates the space of the poem and the hospital room. No one can go there, not even as the poem will have been capable of perfect understanding, uninhibited by pronunciation, released from the kind of dying in life that is never to have been properly comprehended. To never modulate is to equalize with the climate of the unremarkable—such everyday interactions of need—in relation to the arresting prospect that is the inflexible eventuality of death. To the degree that vocal expression can degenerate into the scramble captured by a recording device, the poem survives misunderstanding and demise, even though, it seems to ask, Is there any guarantee that someone, a last interpreter, can steward that immigrant archive?

The scene of "Voice Activation" renders dubious latter-day commitments to the technological optimisms of capitalist modernity. It ironizes interpretations of modernism that lay claim to a monopoly on difficulty and innovation, based on elaborately executed tautologies or methodically deskilled operations. It suggests an invisible relation: that redundancy is to aesthetic method what detachment is to the social domain. In short, "Voice Activation" reads as a crafty rejoinder to some highly visible instances of conceptual poetry, insofar as it provides a discursive mimicry of one of its primary modes and methods. In the sly antagonistic sense first described by Homi Bhabha, mimicry "emerges as the representation of a difference that is itself a process of disavowal."[12] The difficulty it poses to readers and critics habituated to novelty at the level of design, formal appearance, or diction is that of a "double articulation; a complex strategy [that] poses an immanent threat to both 'normalized' knowledges and disciplinary powers,"[13] even as it underplays its opposition to the strategic function it audibly discerns as hegemonic in poetic practice.

Consider a celebrated example. Kenneth Goldsmith's *Soliloquy* (1996/2001) is an "unedited document of every word [the poet] spoke during the week of April 15–21, 1996, for the execution of which he wore a hidden voice-activated tape recorder. The resulting web and print versions of the project were "transcribed . . . during the summer of 1996 at the Chateau Bionnay in Lacenas, France, during a residency there [that lasted] 8 weeks."[14] This poetic labor of "8 hours a day" resulted in a gallery exhibition at Bravin Post Lee in Soho (1997), a limited edition of fifty printed copies, an online platform, and a 487-page trade edition published in 2001 by Granary Books. Goldsmith's web version of the work begins with an epigraph by Wittgenstein: "Don't for heaven's sake be afraid of talking nonsense! But you must pay attention to your nonsense."[15] Alcalá's prose poem, on the other hand, contains less than five hundred words, although its "languaging" of Goldsmith via Wittgenstein throws the literalist monumentality of that work into a political and philosophical spin. In a related statement, she writes: "An article in *Time* magazine on voice activation technology discusses the failure of this innovation to recognize female or 'foreign' voices with thick accents. Even a British-made car—programmed like everything else to comprehend a kind of American accent—responds to its British owner's commands with, 'Sorry?' I sometimes worry that the ways in which we define poetry and separate it into exclusionary camps is like creating a technology that recognizes only a few representative voices—or no voice at all—and can only accomplish a limited set of commands."[16] For Alcalá, a philosophy that pays attention to one's nonsense is primed to interrogate the family resemblance between eight weeks' worth of transcription and the lifetime it takes a person to make herself intelligible, a "limpid voice." All efforts otherwise are an "exiting of one's intentions" if the aim is to find the adequate thought form for the speculative method to which Wittgenstein was committed. For the speaker in "Voice Activation," the trouble with accents, intelligibility, speaking loudly enough, or speaking at all is to concede death "as a loss of language"— efforts that follow the compass orienting the language world subjected to the incremental scrutiny of Wittgenstein. Guy Davenport wrote: "The world [for Wittgenstein was] an absolute puzzle, a great lump of opaque pig iron. Can we think about the lump? What is thought? What is the meaning of *can*, *can we*, of *can we think*? What is the meaning of *we*? If we answer these questions on Monday, are the answers valid on Tuesday? If I answer them at all, do I think the answer, believe the answer, know the answer, or imagine the answer?"[17] In the self-reflective calculations of obligatory living in a foreign tongue and atmosphere, such estrangements are equivalent to the everyday phenomenology of the immigrant condition.

As with an immigrant circumnavigating her new environment, emergent modes of experience are obtained in the interaction with technical objects. Similarly, a distinction gives way "between figure and ground [that] results from a state of tension, from the incompatibility of the system in relation to itself, from what one could call the oversaturation of the system."[18] There is, as Gilbert Simondon reminds us, a unity whose model in "Voice Activation" is doubled, on the one hand, into that of a parent and child, into vocal chord and apparatus on the other. For Simondon, reflexive thinking enhances humanity's relation to a world from which it is divided and comes to sustain science and ethics through technics and religion, between which aesthetic thinking develops."[19] The difficulty "Voice Activation" presents is a thematizing of *technicity*, which Simondon submits as the site of becoming, the place of individuation. According to Simondon, technicity constitutes one of two fundamental phases—an aspect resulting from the division of being when it is in conflict with or in opposition to another quality, attribute, or bearing. Contrary to the logic of negativity but not a dialectic, a phase relation is the condition of one aspect to another or several: in equilibrium or tension, it allows for a plurality of times and symmetries. "Voice Activation" debates internally and externally with the assumption that, hand in hand, aesthetic and technological developments understood as innovation necessarily depend on the negative gesture as evidence of advancement or alleged progress. To the degree that the technological has been naturalized, the progressive method seeks to renounce any origin that gave way to the theoretical and practical thinking of its innovated state, and so indulges in its own self-perpetuating form of wishful thinking, from which it cannot be disabused.[20] As far as Alcalá is concerned, "There's no doubt that voice activation technology and its failures are only a reflection of society's ongoing inability to hear and encourage variance and complexity."[21] To be sure, "Voice Activation" is a sophisticated performance of Simondon's technicity understood as applied language, whose contingencies are a matter of life or death when in conflict with or in opposition to another quality, even as cultural transmission and vocal modulations give way to discontinuous time frames or historical symmetries. In so doing, the poem exposes the very low stakes in some avant-garde attitudes about the relationship among speech, technology, and the materiality of language. In 2006, Kenneth Goldsmith by turns amused and irritated Poetry Foundation readers with the self-satisfied but typically exculpatory axioms of the monolingual: "I am an American poet, and like most Americans, I speak only one language. . . . Hence, I've decided to present this paper in English, a language that I have never spoken or written."[22] And with regard to the interpretive project, predictably: "The simple act of moving information from one place to another today constitutes a significant cultural act in and of itself. I think it's fair to say that most of us spend hours each day shifting content into different containers. Some of us call this writing."[23]

At stake today for art making is this question of information: what to do with it and how? Luis Camnitzer has suggested that technology has "surpassed quantity to move within the realms of quality."[24] High-speed data storage and retrieval; the immediacy of access, delivery, and production in the information cloud: what to do requires distinguishing figure from ground when the determinism of our tools confuses the differences between programmer and programmed in the system's relation to itself—as well as between number and kind in such oversaturation. "Voice Activation" plays difficulty in a cultural key whose opacity is to be found not on the surface but rather in the analogies of family kinship and media use that modify the poem's acoustic and signifying frame. In this habitus, to be a last interpreter is to enter a condition that Camnitzer identifies for the potential deliriums and humilities of art, in words by Deleuze and Guattari, apt to describe as well the encounter between a human voice and its automation: "When something occurs, the self that awaited it is already dead, or the one that would await it has not yet arrived."[25] In "Voice Activation" an ostensibly stable surface gives the lie to a protean performance. The poem's sentence structure stuns and stings any enchantment with facile narratives about successful advance, be they technological or cultural. It looks with skepticism at the alleged family resemblance between the language of aptitude and the rhetoric of cultural reproduction. In the interplay between an implied but unspoken maternal Spanish in the social space, made conspicuous when English is a second language, the poem underscores how applied speech is inextricable from factors of time and place in one particular difficulty that matters: the uneven distributions of modern life.

Notes

1. Daniel Tiffany, *My Silver Planet: A Secret History of Poetry and Kitsch* (Baltimore, Md.: Johns Hopkins University Press, 2014), 39. He writes: "Poetic diction modulates the sensuous currency of language (word choice, spelling, word order) in order to produce an expressive halo, a reverberating abyss of aesthetic and social history. Yet the substance of poetic diction must also be understood in a related sense as establishing the vice of *cosmetic materialism*." Tiffany pursues this mingling of cosmetic materialism and diction in "Cheap Signaling: Class Conflict and Diction in Avant-Garde Poetry," *Boston Review* (online), July 15, 2014. A complementary discussion can be found in Sianne Ngai, *Our Aesthetic Categories: Zany, Cute, Interesting* (Cambridge, Mass.: Harvard University Press, 2012).

2. Dorothy Wang, *Thinking Its Presence: Form, Race, and Subjectivity in Contemporary Asian American Poetry* (Stanford, Calif.: Stanford University Press, 2014), 23.

3. Dale Smith, *Poets beyond the Barricade: Rhetoric, Citizenship, and Dissent after 1960* (Tuscaloosa: University of Alabama Press, 2012).

4. Charles Altieri, "What We Can Learn from New Directions in Contemporary American Poetry," *New Literary History* 43, no. 1 (2012): 65.

5. Luis Camnitzer, "Thinking about Art Thinking," *supercommunity*, e-flux (May 2015).

6. Peter Ramos, "A Girl like Me: Rosa Alcalá's Band of Gypsy Dancers," in *Angels of the Americlypse: New Latin@ Writing*, ed. Carmen Giménez Smith and John Chávez (Denver: Counterpath, 2014), 5.

7. This discussion on accent aligns with discourses on race and poetic form; see Wang, *Thinking Its Presence*.

8. *Webster's Third New International Dictionary of the English Language, Unabridged* (Springfield: G. & C. Merriam, 1976).

9. John Durham Peters, "Mass Media," in *Critical Terms for Media Studies, Chicago*, ed. W. J. T. Mitchell and Mark B. N. Hansen (Chicago: University of Chicago Press, 2010).

10. Walter D. Mignolo, *Local Histories / Global Designs: Coloniality, Subaltern Knowledge, and Border Thinking* (Princeton, N.J.: Princeton University Press, 2000), 226.

11. Jacques Lacan, *Ecrits* (New York: Norton, 1977), 166.

12. Homi Bhabha, *The Location of Culture* (London: Routledge, 1994), 86.

13. Ibid.

14. Kenneth Goldsmith, *Soliloquy* (online), University at Buffalo, State University of New York, Electronic Poetry Center, http://epc.buffalo.edu/authors/goldsmith/soliloquy/.

15. Ludwig Wittgenstein, *Culture and Value*, trans. Peter Winchs (Chicago: University of Chicago Press, 1984), 56.

16. Rosa Alcalá, untitled statement, in *The Volta Book of Poets*, ed. Joshua Marie Wilkinson (Portland, Ore.: Sidebrow Books, 2015), 1.

17. Guy Davenport, *The Geography of the Imagination: Forty Essays* (San Francisco: North Point Press, 1981), 332.

18. Gilbert Simondon, "On the Mode of Existence of Technical Objects," trans. Ninian Mellamphy, Dan Mellamphy, and Nandita Biswas Mellamphy, *Deleuze Studies 5*, no. 3 (2011): 411.

19. Ibid., 409.

20. Simondon gives contemporary examples of magical thinking in urban contemporary life: time off from work, festivals, vacation—that is, key points in ordinary time/space serve as ground for these figures.

21. Alcalá, untitled statement, 1.

22. Kenneth Goldsmith, "I Love Speech," *Poetry Foundation* (January 6, 2007), blog post previously presented as a talk at the Presidential Forum, Modern Language Association Convention, Philadelphia, Pennsylvania, 2006.

23. Ibid.

24. Camnitzer, "Thinking about Art Thinking."

25. Gilles Deleuze and Felix Guattari, *A Thousand Plateaus* (London: Continuum, 2004), 219.

PAOLO JAVIER

Paolo's Lust

      assault   today Paolo's lust
Paolo & I are more radical than my eager & devouring Trysteaser
Camel triangle yells the soul lamp of Paolo he'll agree he'll argue
today Paolo occupies you, today Paolo occupies you
A tournament unforgotten come to heal Paolo
Paolo cruises   Granada embargo

     tournament   fugue comes   Paolo
queer hazard contiguous: Alma & Paolo,
on the lam? Alma's silence Paolo   echoes
missed parables on Paolo Javier sobers Tia Carrera's antidote
August arrival   in medias res the last of Paolo's   Infinity
Alma & Paolo eloped today, Alma & Paolo elope today

     Prim & Rose Javier's son,   lost in ceremony
why did Paolo marry? argues my devouring Trysteaser
toddle Paolo's hyenas, toddle Paolo's hyenas
sic 'em, company   in essence, Paolo's brand of justice
avast! daddy pining,   rumor   Paolo whom Kai brandishes
absurd   Paolo's toil   acid doses

     US Bases   pitch against Paolo's patience
hurricanes sway in the wind of Paolo's avarice alas turban
oh ponderous celebrant   toddle Paolo's verse   algorithm
Demoted kaya 'yun? Paliitin si Paolo as a rule?[1]

Chapter 18

Incipient Lust

Lyn Hejinian

The lexical, syntactic, and semantic difficulties in this poem are obviously many, and the facts that the poem is but one of sixty in a series and that references and repetitions crisscross through the different poems add to the overall density of the reader's experience and to the diversity of the poem's values, its terrains of relevance.

An attempt to identify those values, if it has any chance at all of succeeding, would have to be made after considerable attention is paid to the details of the poem. And as is true of most poems, this one is made of details. But, as isn't true of most poems, the details in "Paolo's Lust" function as impediments to assimilation—in part because they are referential details and thus direct the reader as much to things outside the poem as to things in it. The vivacity with which they defy coherence while generating mischief keeps the reader's attention darting. And for the attention to find what it's looking for, it has to leap.

But from where do we leap? The details are obstructive, too, because they are defiant, busily keeping us out of the poem. At least throughout our long first reading of it.

"Paolo's Lust" is a hypersignifying or oversignifying text. These two terms are almost synonymous, but they are not perfectly so. Each emphasizes a slightly different feature of the kind of poetry to which they are fundamental. Ultimately, the more important with respect to "Paolo's Lust" is *over*signification, as I'll explain below. But there's some utility to applying the term *hypersignification* to it too, insofar as "Paolo's Lust" (and kindred poems) are, in effect, hypertextual. They include materials not constrained to the text, and they invite us to seek them out. The possibility to link to further and/or alternative referential sites and systems is foregrounded, and use of it is encouraged. Indications of the existence of related or new areas of significance and signification are rampant.

The term *oversignification*, on the other hand, calls attention to the excessiveness of what's in play; it emphasizes a behavioral, performative element in the work. But there are two other connotative possibilities worth noting.

To the extent that lyric poetry is typically (or perhaps stereotypically) imagined to represent overheard thought, the poetry itself must be imagined as an internal sounding, undertaken by an alert, concerned, and intellectual spirit on whom the reader is focused. According to this familiar model, lyric poetry is cast as privacy overheard. The richness of an inner sensibility and its perceptual experience finds its parallel in the polysemous density of the phrases and images. The polysemous words and images are redolent with the energies of what they've taken in. Oversignification has a different task; it doesn't eschew polysemy (and the particular kinds of rich ambiguity it creates), but its real concern is to alert us to the *multiplicity* of signs in the poem and to competing demands on it from nonaesthetic spheres. Value is situated not in inner meanings but in the extroverted, manic outward cast of the poetry. It is not quality but quantity of signification that matters; the greater the number of references, the richer (and perhaps wilder) the relevance.

As distinct from the redolent depths of polysemy, oversignification races across surfaces, pointing a finger at faces, facts, sites, situations. Indeed, one of the central difficulties of oversignifying poetry concerns the situational. To answer "What is this?" one must figure out where it came from and what it was doing there. But even before that—before one can wonder "what this is," one must recognize that some "this" is before one. In "Paolo's Lust," it is obvious, for example, that "*kaya 'yun*" is an alien entity inviting attention (and perhaps then immediately resisting it). But what of "turban" in the second line of the fourth stanza? Or what of "alas" before it ("alas turban")—was I wrong to put it through one of the online free translation engines? Is it relevant that in Tagalog/Filipino *alas* means "ace" (a reference to gambling? luck?) and in Spanish it means "wings" (a reference to diasporic flight? air bases?)? And does it intentionally evoke the name of the Islamic Allah (with a nod, perhaps unhappy, to the Muslim Mindanao in the Philippines?)? All are possible, even while, for English-language readers, the accustomed sense prevails: Alas! Etymologically the word enters the West in the "mid-13c., from Old French *ha, las* (later French *hélas*), from *ha* 'ah' + *las* 'unfortunate,' originally 'tired, weary,' from Latin *lassus* 'weary' (see *late*). At first an expression of weariness rather than woe."[2]

"Paolo's Lust," obviously, is not expressive of weariness. But it does articulate woe. And anger.

It is thought that the first humans reached what we now call the Philippines around 67,000 years ago—which, depending on which of several bodies of archeological evidence you are using, is roughly 30,000 to 50,000 years before humans were in the Americas. Made up of 7,107 separate islands, the Philippines were never the site of a single culture nor (except artificially) a single political entity. By 1000 B.C.E. the inhabitants of the archipelago had developed into four kinds of social groups: hunter-gatherer tribes, warrior societies, highland plutocracies, and maritime harbor principalities.[3]

Maritime trade brought a number of influences to bear on the peoples of the islands, and an array of cultural, economic, and political alliances exercised varying degrees of control over life and ideas. Hinduism, Buddhism, and—from the late 1400s on—Islam all had adherents. And with the arrival in 1521 of the Portuguese explorer Ferdinand Magellan, who claimed the islands for Spain, Christianity entered the picture—rather grandly and coercively, as has so often been the case with Christianity. Given the complexity of the sociopolitical landscape, it is not surprising to find that the Philippines has a long history of revolutionary movements, rebellions, and uprisings, both internecine and anticolonial. Its most recent period of colonial oppression extended from 1898, when the United States took control of the Philippines at the end of the Spanish-American War, to the signing of the Treaty of Manila in 1946, when the Philippines gained its legal (if not actual) independence from the United States. Through most of its recent history, the Philippines was an occupied nation. Throughout this period and into the present, Filipinos have been treated much as subaltern colonial subjects are elsewhere. Loss of land, power, dignity, and language occurred relentlessly, with profoundly impoverishing consequences. The imposition of English, and the resulting suppression of native Spanish and, more important, Tagalog, have remained a source of cultural destruction—and this is one of the themes that recurs throughout *60 lv bo(e)mbs*. It is explicit in the title of the fifth poem, "English Is an Occupation," and it appears in the last line of "Paolo's Lust," which asks, "*Demoted kaya 'yun? Paliitin si Paolo as a rule?*" The question seems most immediately to respond to the phrase in the line above it ("toddle Paolo's verse"), which, in turn, echoes the third line of the third stanza ("toddle Paolo's hyenas, toddle Paolo's hyenas"). Roughly translated (by the Filipino-American poet and scholar Adrian Acu), the English translation of the poem's last line would be something like "Was that a demotion [diminution]? Shrink [belittle] Paolo as a lesson?"

As of this writing (in fall 2014), the Philippines are home to approximately 100 million citizens. Another 12 million Filipinos live elsewhere, constituting one of the contemporary world's largest diasporic populations. The narrator of the *60 lv bo(e)mbs*, who may or may not be the eponymous "Paolo" of "Paolo's Lust," struggles to account for the Filipino diaspora's decentered circumstances and to follow an array of "characters," who must negotiate multiple narratives and cope with the effects of manifold histories, many of which are not of their making. The histories that they do make seem often to be grabbed on the run and taken under question. Thus in "Paolo's Lust" we find "Alma & Paolo"— "on the lam?" And a few lines later, "Alma & Paolo eloped today, Alma & Paolo elope today," the present appearing to correct the past but without any change or remediation occurring. "Prim & Rose Javier's son,   lost in ceremony / *why did Paolo marry?*"

Elsewhere in the *60 lv bo(e)mbs*, it is "Kai & Paolo" who (perhaps) elope, and again, a certain "Mia" gets paired several times with "Paolo." But it is the name "Alma" that is most intimately connected with that of "Paolo," though just how intimate she is (if it is a she) is unclear, since there is ample suggestion that "Paolo" is "queer."[4] Whatever the case, "Mia" and "Alma" could be pet names—"Mine" (Mia) and "Soul" or "Spirit" (Alma). Even "Kai" may not be the proper or legal name of the person "Paolo" may have eloped with. As a name, the word is relatively common in Hawai'i; in English it means "Sea" or "Ocean" and thus may evoke, especially for people of a nation composed of thousands of islands, the world beyond that is always near at hand, the deep blue elsewhere that lies just offshore. On the other hand, Kai may be a diminutive of the word *kaya*, which appears at the end of "Paolo's Lust" and is the Tagalog equivalent of both "therefore" or "so" and "able" (as in "am/ is/are *able*"). "Mia," "Kai," and "Alma" are also relatively common Filipino names, so it may be amorous nominative play, rather than (poly)linguistic play, that is occurring. But the latter makes sense in this poem, given that lack of linguistic stability is one of its themes.

Much of what takes place in "Paolo's Lust" is a sequence of deflections, disconnections, and refusals or outwittings. Despite reference to marriage and filiation (and hence family—son and parents), elements in the poem only awkwardly combine, if they do so at all. Mostly the phrases seem to ricochet off each other, subject perhaps to the "Trysteaser," a recurrent figure in the sequence of poems, who can be variously imagined as a trickster, a tryst easer, a tryst teaser, or a strip teaser. Something in the tone and affect of "Paolo's Lust" suggests that it is "Paolo" who plays the role (or serves the function) of trickster in the world of the poem. If so, then the roles of pimp and pander (the tryst easer and tryst teaser) are almost certainly taken by the U.S. hegemonic power that continues its postcolonial occupation of Filipino socio-economic and cultural life. American business interests and, of course, American military bases remain dominant elements in the Philippines. And it is worth noting that prostitution, which is rampant in the areas around the military bases, is a major part of the Filipino "service economy." As yet another site of exploitation, this too is a recurrent motif in *60 lv bo(e)mbs*. And Javier sounds it in "My Corzine Slumber," the opening (prefatory) poem of the book, when he asserts, "I can ascribe lust to verses" and, in effect, takes eros back by offering a kind of counterlust: "I can ascribe lust to versus."

The notion is further complicated in the next line: "I can ascribe lust to verses. / I'm all for connoting."[5] It is through a particular form of *connoting*, which, in an interview, he calls "fishing," that Paolo Javier works to counter the linguistic domination imposed by colonial occupiers in his native Philippines. As he pointed out in a 2005 interview, "During friar rule in the Philippines, a method of homophonic translation called 'fishing' was used during the church sermons by the uneducated, non-Spanish speaking native congregations." Citing a passage from Vicente Rafael's *Contracting Colonialism: Translation and Christian Conversion in Tagalog Society under Early Spanish Rule,* he continues: "The priest's words rouse in [them] other thoughts that have only the most tenuous connections to what he is actually saying. It is as if they saw other possibilities in those words, possibilities that served to mitigate the interminable verbal assaults being hurled from the pulpit. To the extent that such random possibilities occur, the native listeners manage to find another place from which to confront colonial authority."[6] In the contemporary, twenty-first-century context, *fishing* is, in effect, a way for Filipinos to emigrate out of the English-language meaning world and into other possibilities. This does not, however, render the subaltern's situation less precarious. "Paolo's Lust" instantiates a condition that is fraught, wary, pissed off. But it is also strangely exuberant and even optimistic.

A markedly incantatory force is evident in the poem, resulting from the prevalence of lexical and rhythmic recurrence and of phrasal variation and repetition, and by virtue of internalized enjambment (as in the third line, where one is hard pressed to know where to insert a mental comma). The phrases may be disconnected, even radically separate semantically, but in reading them one can't stop. The poem has enormous sonic momentum. As it must; the poem is, as the book's title reminds us, a love *poem* as well as a love *bomb*.

In a general sense, the oversignification that I'm calling attention to is, as I see it, an intervention into lyric poetry that is almost always undertaken with political intent. It is at least partly thanks to this device that a poem like "Paolo's Lust" puts politically charged cultural demands on a reader. This is something that hip hop achieves similarly, and Javier is clearly conscious of this. In the interview referred to above, he says, "I listened to a lot of underground electronica, indie rock, hip hop, & new wave while working on '60 lv . . . ' , so you can definitely hear their influences in the book." And he announces his affinities to hip hop in the prefatory "My Corzine Slumber":

> I lent you my voice for a tryst.
> I lent you my voice Zion calm.
> & I rapped.

✦

Oversignification is noisy. "Paolo's Lust" is a noise poem—that's inherent to the bomb effect. But the noise in the poem is also an *initial* effect. Or perhaps it would be better to call it an *initiating* effect, a sign of incipience. And that's inherent to the love effect.

Of course the noise is that of the many factors that cause it—racism, colonialism, militarism, cultural and territorial exploitation, and so forth. It is extensive and ambient, like the hum of a city, with its unidentifiable sources. The radical status of nonidentity that is the condition of the poem's "Paolo" (and which may be synonymous with his "lust") is all the more intense for being situated in a verbal milieu in which so many proper names—personal names—proliferate. But they arise in the poem less to identify personages than to call to them. The poem proffers what the young scholar Eric Marxen calls "an invitation to subjectivity."[7] As Marxen has pointed out, this is central to all good lyric poetry, which impels the reader not to enter the author's subjectivity but rather to discover (or invent) and initiate his or her own.

"Paolo's Lust" generates precisely this kind of invitation, summoning the reader into the case the poem makes as an agent of its making. And it is in making it possible for the reader to do so existentially that the aesthetic, as distinct from the political, comes into play: "fugue comes   Paolo."

But that's too easy—inserting that fragment from the poem can tempt us into *feeling* the aesthetic emerge from the political (and perhaps even take it over), but the real question is, How does it do so? The text is noisily signifying—it's a bomb of references—but it is simultaneously doing something else.

It is making poetry—that's true. But poetry isn't the opposite of politics. Nor is it the opposite of noise, nor even properly on the same axis.

Strongly sonic elements are a prominent feature of the poem. One notes—and really, can't resist—the rhythmic propulsion and the excitement it produces. But it's not through any metric regularity that one gets caught up somatically in the poem. Indeed, the meter is markedly irregular, and it is not rhythmic pattern but the rise and fall, rush and hesitation, of articulated thinking that carries us along—the sound of excitement coursing through various emotional registers.

The poem begins with a single iamb, "assault"—nominative (naming), or imperative (demanding), or declarative (proclaiming). The line then continues (and ends) with an iamb, "today," and what seems to be an anapest, "Paolo's lust." But the first syllable of this anapest, the "Pao" of "Paolo," because of the diphthong, is somewhat elongated, the vowel sound bending slightly and taking on weight. Perhaps the last foot is dactylic. This is a technical matter, of only minor importance semantically, but it does establish "Paolo" as tricky.

In this twenty-two-line poem, "Paolo" appears twenty-four times, and even from the start it is lexically ambiguous, as all names are perhaps but especially when they are presented, in the effective third person, as the name of, while not the name of, the author—a semantic conundrum that is further emphasized in the poem's second line, which begins, "Paolo & I." By the end of the poem, "Paolo" is less a word (or name) than a sound, the diphthong always elongated, though to a lesser or greater degree, with sometimes plangent and sometimes slightly comic effect. And of course there's something amorous in play, too—we can't miss that, given the poem's title and the references in the poem to cruising (we shouldn't miss the mixed allusion here to yachts and/or battleships but also to quests for casual sex), as well as to elopement and marriage.

In the "untitled essay" with which Lisa Robertson ends her book *Nilling*, she offers a beautiful account of the ways in which language, incipience (though she uses Hannah Arendt's term *natality*), and subjectivity are interwoven into and as human (political) being. The process by which these intertwine and reciprocally produce each other posits being as always itself beginning. It is never static; it is always saying, and always to another, to whom it is another. And the originary site of this is within the domestic sphere, which, as Robertson points out, should never be confused with the private sphere, which is predominantly one of ownership. No one owns the beginner, nor his or her beginning.

As a political poem, a *bo(e)mb*, "Paolo's Lust" must rage at loss, injustice, destruction, and various forms of poverty. As a *lv* poem, the lust in question is a lust for existence, and as such it must look to the future. And that future is itself bound to beginnings (as to a projected "August arrival" [line 11], for example). The future, however, always, by definition, remains unknown. Or rather, it doesn't, properly speaking, *remain* anything or at all; it is a temporal realm for willing. And for initiative.

"Paolo," the trickster, is full of initiative. His lust is active, as beginning always must be. The whole poem is resonant with the vitality intrinsic to beginning; it instigates a quickening. And it is this quickening that I experience as per se quintessentially aesthetic.

Certainly "Paolo's Lust" puts political demands on a reader. But what is asked for is not conversion to its expressed opinion(s) nor embrace of the poem's ostensible social cause(s). As Lisa Robertson puts it, "Language, the historical mode of collective relationship, is also the aptitude by which humans innovate one another as subjects. . . . No binary is implicated. Neither individual nor instrumental, the linguistic aptitude accompanies the beginning of humans as a collective nature through which each subject, uttering 'I,' 'you,' 'we,' emerges and survives or perishes."[8] It is in bringing sense (in its multiple meanings) to the senses that "Paolo's Lust" causes the political to acquire the aesthetic power to begin us, "the reader," with lust for liberated existence.

Notes

1. Not all the poems in Paolo Javier's *60 lv bo(e)mbs* (Oakland, Calif.: O Books, 2005) include words or phrases in Tagalog, but some, including "Paolo's Lust," the twenty-fifth of the poems/bombs in the volume, do, adding a layer of difficulty to what is already an astonishingly complex landscape.

2. *Online Etymology Dictionary*, s.v. "alas," http://www.etymonline.com/index.php?allowed_in_frame=0&search=alas&searchmode=none.

3. "Philippines," in *Wikipedia*, http://en.wikipedia.org/wiki/Philippines.

4. The real Paolo Javier lives with his wife in Queens, New York (where, from 2010 to 2014, he was, curiously enough, the Queens poet laureate).

5. Unpaginated foreword, *60 lv bo(e)mbs*.

6. "Interview with Barbara Jane Reyes and Paolo Javier by Eileen Tabios," in *Exchangevalues*, September 20, 2005, http://willtoexchange.blogspot.com/2005/09/interview-with-barbara-jane-reyes-and.html.

7. Seminar discussion, University of California, Berkeley, December 4, 2014. My thanks to Eric for the phrase and the idea, and for permission to utilize them here.

8. Lisa Robertson, *Nilling* (Toronto: Bookthug, 2013), 73.

LATASHA N. NEVADA DIGGS

daggering kanji
after Christian Bök

k'k'kumu   kk'kk'khakis   k'k'kare   kk'kk'amikazae

k'k'ku'ulala   *k'k'ku'ulala*   *k'k'ku'ulala*   *k'k'ku'ulala*

k'k'kazoo   kk'kk'kūlolo   k'k'kahuna   kk'k'kabob

k'k'ku'ulala   *k'k'ku'ulala*   *k'k'ku'ulala*   *k'k'ku'ulala*

k'k'kali   kk'k'kulisap   k'k'kabuki   k'k'kk'kumala

k'k'ku'ulala   *k'k'ku'ulala*   *k'k'ku'ulala*   *k'k'ku'ulala*

k'k'krill   k'k'kk'kosher   k'k'kolohe   k'k'kk'kinkajou

k'k'ku'ulala   *k'k'ku'ulala*   *k'k'ku'ulala*   *k'k'ku'ulala*

k'k'kunan   k'k'kk'kinky   k'kk'karma   k'k'kosdu

k'k'ku'ulala   *k'k'ku'ulala*   *k'k'ku'ulala*   *k'k'ku'ulala*

k'k'kola   k'k'k'kitíkití   k'k'kanapī   k'k'kk'king

k'k'ku'ulala   *k'k'ku'ulala*   *k'k'ku'ulala*   *k'k'ku'ulala*

k'k'kudos   k'k'k'kanatsi   k'k'klutzy   k'k'k'kawoni

k'k'ku'ulala   *k'k'ku'ulala*   *k'k'ku'ulala*   *k'k'ku'ulala*

k'k'kawí   k'k'kk'kawaya   k'k'kao   k'k'k'kamama

k'k'ku'ulala   *k'k'ku'ulala*   *k'k'ku'ulala*   *k'k'ku'ulala*

k'k'koga   kk'kk'kung-fu   k'k'kimchi   k'k'k'kiru

k'k'ku'ulala   *k'k'ku'ulala*   *k'k'ku'ulala*   *k'k'ku'ulala*

k'k'kaliwohi kk'kk'kumquat   k'k'kina   kk'k'kanogeni

k'k'ku'ulala   *k'k'ku'ulala*   *k'k'ku'ulala*   *k'k'ku'ulala*

k'k'kinetic   kk'k'kanoheda   k'k'kapu   cc'cc'cum

Chapter 19

✦

Phrasebook Pentecosts and Daggering Lingua Francas in the Poetry of LaTasha N. Nevada Diggs

Jennifer Scappettone

Modernist multilingual poetry has tended, at least since the New Criticism, to be so mystified in the academic culture of the United States as to render it the involuted suburb of an elitist canon for which T. S. Eliot's *The Waste Land* and Ezra Pound's *Cantos* provide the template—as cosmopolitan epics groping from an English-language core toward arcane literary sources. In the bleakest of possible outcomes, poetry of the United States written in multiple languages from 1922 forward has provided the academic basis for generations of gatekeeping rituals.[1] One might have imagined a different future, for pupils like those who attended the "Ezuversity" of Pound's Rapallo were supposed—in the utopian mirage in which Ez's fascism paradoxically played a part—to constitute an enlightened population of intellectual renegades capable of radicalizing the reigning academic curriculum as "kulchur." Indeed, pathbreaking poets abroad, from the Noigandres group in Brazil to Pier Paolo Pasolini in Italy, regarded these polyglot montages as touchstones for a radically international vernacular language, transmitting a "**volgar' eloquio** " capable of "taking the sense down to the people."[2] Nevertheless, cross-cultural and -historical references in cosmopolitan modernist poems appear to offer but two possibilities of reception: they either repel monolingual Anglophone readers or send those compelled beyond the verse to annotations and, inevitably, institutions to accrue knowledge that might begin to make them adequate to the poetry.

The twentieth century produced a less institutionally mandated lineage of polyglot poetry, which I will call subaltern in the spirit of Antonio Gramsci, the political and cultural theorist whose concept of hegemony is inextricable from his background in linguistics—and further, from his linguistic upbringing: Gramsci was born to a father of Albanian descent on the island of Sardinia, where, in the year he moved to the industrial center of Turin on a university scholarship, illiteracy was at 58 percent and standard Italian was experienced as a distant second language.[3] These roots led Gramsci to a dynamic conception of the relation between "spontaneous," or immanent, unconscious, idiosyncratic, and evolving grammars and "normative" or prescriptive standard grammars—which he presented as transformative and potentially revolutionary. The dialectical interaction between unconscious and enforced, submerged and dictated linguistic habits renders the term that has become most associated with Gramsci, *hegemony*, useful, as it indicates that power does not operate unidirectionally but manifests in a dance between coercion and consent. In terms that speak to the linguistic panorama of today, Gramsci's twenty-seventh prison notebook argues that "the linguistic fact" (placing uncommon emphasis on active *facture*) "cannot have national borders strictly defined"—that "the national language cannot be imagined outside the frame of other languages that exert an influence on it through innumerable channels that are often difficult to control." Gramsci casts repatriated emigrants, translators, and even ordinary readers of foreign languages as agents of linguistic innovation and transformation.[4]

TwERK, the first full-length collection by multidisciplinary poet and sound artist LaTasha N. Nevada Diggs, published by the feminist collective imprint Belladonna in 2013, implodes any tenuous binarism we might erect between cosmopolitan modernist and subaltern multilingualism. *TwERK* draws on various languages of the African diaspora with which Diggs identifies and expresses solidarity but also deploys languages out of line with essentialist expectations of representation, as Theresa Hak Kyung Cha's *DICTEE* did in 1982. Diggs's biography and some of her prose would suggest that the welter of languages in these pages can be traced to her native Harlem, with its Black southern United States, Caribbean, Cherokee, Korean-War vet, and even Valley girl influences, and more broadly to New York City—a city now, as in Zukofsky's day, reputed to be the most linguistically diverse on earth, harboring as many as eight hundred spoken languages.[5] However, the range of languages in which Diggs's verse delectates exceeds the author's "proper" linguistic background from the start. *TwERK* is composed of words from (in order of indexing) Japanese, Spanish, English, Hindi, Urdu, Welsh, Maori, Hawaiian, Samoan, Malay, Swahili, Runa Simi (Quechua), Vietnamese, Yoruba, Portuguese, Chamorro, Cherokee (Tsa'lāgĭ), Barbadian dialect, Kikongo, Tagalog, a pidgin of Port Moresby in Papua New Guinea, Hawaiian Creole English, and Papiamentu, as well as passages in unannotated Nation language, pig latin, and Snoop-Dogg-inspired shizzling; the author may well be as remote from many of these languages as her presumed English-speaking readers are.[6] Like *The Waste Land, The Cantos,* and other cosmopolitan multilingual works, this is a poetry to which no localized "native" subject could have unmitigated access: it is laced with the traces of searching well beyond its immediate context of ambient noise for compelling lexical choices, and its notes provide deliberately capricious signposts for readers who choose to continue that process, or at least apprehend its scope.

Self-conscious engagement with the unprecedented reach of contemporary capitalist trade and communications networks (earlier versions of which triggered the amalgamation of the lingua franca) and their tendency to reify the identities they circulate with deleterious effects separates Diggs's multilingualism from that of the twentieth century; at its most critical, it brings out the "javelin," or national weapon, embedded in the term *franca*. While a book like *DICTEE* still finds a center of gravity in Theresa Hak Kyung Cha's immediate family narrative, however elusive, *TwERK* travels vertiginously around the erasure and (partial) recuperation of distanced, heavily mediated, and at times even branded histories. In the key of Gary Simmons's *Erasure* drawings of racial stereotypes, obliquely summoned in the poem "have you forgotten any personal property?" *TwERK* samples the languages and lingos of globalization and information overload deliriously, taking stabs at tweaking—or twerking—them. That the collection takes on an objectifying yet equally aggressive form of provocative dance associated with women of color as a figure and, through the obscurity of its language, obliges us to incorporate the global noise at play in these pages as somatic acts of speech makes Diggs's multilingualism both more approachable, in the literal sense, and more discomfiting.

How can we account for *TwERK*'s popularity, which surpasses any small-press publisher's expectation for experimental poetry? The book sold two thousand copies in just over a year and a half, and was well into its third printing as of the time of writing, in April 2015.[7] I want to propose that the poems' vernacular musicality seduces readers into a tuning relation of the sort that David Antin has theorized: "A negotiated concord or agreement based on vernacular physical actions with visible outcomes like walking together," as opposed to understanding, which is predicated, Antin contends, "on a geometrical notion of congruence."[8] The notion of tuning situates the poetic act in the realm of the oral/aural without recourse to Romantic assumptions surrounding the singularity and presence of lyric voice or naive "anthropological" notions of cultural origins. *TwERK* draws us into a dance (rather than a workaday walk) with linguistic alterity that would otherwise be daunting, driven by the tempos of cultures routinely branded as inaccessible to all but insiders.

Diggs's debut collection contains a wealth of references that send us to the section of copious notes in the back, once we realize that it exists. Yet simultaneously warding off the notion of the glossary or annotation, the author identifies her exegeses themselves as unassuming materials: the humble stuff of assemblage. The note section is given the title "rhinestones, acrylic on panel, knives, mirror, packing tape, fur, found medical illustration paper on mylar, rubber tires, wood, metal, plastic, porcelain, paper, latex paint, Lonely Planet phrase books. . . . " Performatively confounding researched sources with semitrashy material origins, Diggs infuses a sense of immediacy into the least immediate section of her book—and resists the forbidding assumption of difficulty attached to multilingual work in a monoglot climate. In spite of the inherent opacities that derive from deployment of remote languages, hyperlocalized or specialized corporate and gaming jargon, and the shit-talking code-speak of signifyin(g), *TwERK* vaunts a certain accessibility that dissociates this text from its most canonical modernist precursors by a wide gulf. Nowhere is this accessibility gap more patent than in the last item indexed: "Lonely Planet phrase books." This admission stresses not only the autodidactic impulse that led to these poems, but Diggs's conversationally oriented, ground-level approach to learning foreign languages: a phrasebook linguistics that Gramsci might place halfway between the "spontaneous" and the "normative," as it is based in a vernacular middle ground between the grammar book and a direction-giving organic center.[9] Diggs's emphasis on communicability rather than citation and the pervasive, though ludic and incomplete, floating of translated phrases throughout the text renders these poems approachable. Working with the phrasebook as literary source also detaches Diggs's language play from claims to either authenticity or mastery, further alleviating the pressure on the reader to comprehend that is bookishly provoked by pedagogically oriented, Renaissance-programming literary monuments such as *The Cantos*. "I love the tentative landscape of phrasebooks," Diggs says in an interview. "They are never 100% accurate."[10] Diggs's complexity instead hails from the populist branch of international-ist poetics—following most legibly from the ethnopoetic research of Jerome Rothenberg, David Antin, and Anselm Hollo through the Nuyorican tra-dition, yet infusing the linguistic adventurousness that characterizes these movements with twenty-first-century strains of suspicion in representation and Black feminist critique.

In "The Liquor Store Opens at 10 am," a lyric essay on polycultural Har-lem, Diggs stresses the fact that "in this assumed English-only neighborhood, if you turn down the volume of the Queen's chatter, other mother tongues are heard."[11] Diggs's New York City poems expose a plurilingual, polyrhythmic measure in the metropolitan soundscape that is routinely edited from con-sciousness because, as she notes in a *Cross Cultural Poetics* interview with Leonard Schwartz, "our ears are only tuned to the language of commerce in the city, which is oftentimes English (unless you're in Jackson Heights)."[12] The self-consciously multilingual subway poem "metromultilingopollone-grocucarachasblahblahblah," published in *TwERK*, suggests in terms both musical and corporeal that conviviality conditioned only to the ticking tempo of trade under globalization and its language of conveyance, English, will be "castrated by humdrum."[13] Training oneself away from the habit of mono-glot listening to attune to other tongues, on the other hand, can be an erotic exercise: in the interview with Leonard Schwartz, Diggs identifies a "cluster-fuck of tongues" hosted by urban spaces that can at times be understood only "through the physicality that's being performed"—so that hearing it requires a "navigation of bodies."[14]

While shot through with multiple languages, poems such as "metro-multilingopollonegrocucarachasblahblahblah" reward those who do not understand Spanish with the easily voiceable, nursery-rhyme musicality of the refrain "todo todo sabe a pollo" and enable those who do to ask further questions. The figure of a "Pentecostal woman" whose feet are crossed by a water bug (immediately translated as the more broadly known *cucaracha*) at the poem's close provides the cultural and linguistic key to this scene—and to some extent, to *TwERK* itself. For the book's epigraph cites the story of Pentecost as told in Genesis 11:1: "And the earth was of one language, and of one speech." The power of this citation resides in the fact that it, too, hovers as a double-edged sword; the sentence may refer both to the hegemony of English under the late capitalism of the aughts *and* to a utopia of transnational, transcultural, even translinguistic understanding modeled by the xenoglossic poetic work that follows.

Xenoglossia, a term coined in 1905, refers to the intelligible use of a natural language one has not learned formally or does not know and is distinguishable from (though often confused with) *glossolalia*, or lexically incommunicative utterances. The canonical narrative of the xenoglossic phenomenon in Western literature appears in the story of Pentecost, wherein the Holy Spirit is said to have bestowed upon the apostles the sudden ability to speak in languages previously alien to them, effectively remedying the confusion of tongues meted out as divine punishment for construction of the Tower of Babel. Such tales of miraculous translation evince a yearning for the promise of correspondence between languages, and thereby of erased cultural difference. But "metromultilingopollonegrocucarachasblahblahblah" cites more specifically the global movement we now know as Pentecostalism—based on ecstatic forms of worship that include dancing and speaking and singing in tongues—which was driven by African American preachers from the South; Pentecostalism emerged from humble roots in what is now known as the Azusa Street Revival in Los Angeles at the turn of the twentieth century and spread quickly across national borders. Immigrants told of uneducated Black members of the Azusa Street congregation suddenly able to speak in and translate from Yiddish, German, and Spanish, while local newspapers decried the "disgraceful intermingling of the races" on display in the "Weird Babel of Tongues" of the "New Sect of Fanatics."[15] In 1907, leader and preacher William J. Seymour reinforced that such linguistic, racial, and national commingling was central to the purpose of the movement: "One token of the Lord's coming is that He is melting all races and nations together, and they are filled with the power and glory of God."[16] Diggs's "Pentecostal woman" invokes the Black roots and modernized manifestation of this transnational phenomenon—one that promises not simply the channeling of enigmatic tongues (as in glossolalia) but the inspired transgression of enforced cultural segregation. These images conclude a section of *TwERK* titled "no te entiendo" (I do not understand you), which refers, as Diggs explained in a 2014 interview, to a category in the early colonial Mexican casta system denoting a person of racial mixture beyond classification.[17] The book becomes the receptacle for a communing of cultures, races, and languages, but does not offer instantaneous translation or transparency without obliging the work of attunement; outside a context in which we can confidently summon the Holy Ghost, we are not meant to understand the transnational speaking in tongues. *TwERK* makes an immersive, nondiscursive case for an opacity that resists comprehension as classification, in the mode of Édouard Glissant's groundbreaking demand: "Nous réclamons le droit à l'opacité."[18] It lures us into a musical and conceptual dance with this strangeness. The book in fact demonstrates how a world of incommensurable languages can make its way into "one speech"—and by extension, danceable song—without glossing over the violence that inevitably accompanies such a process.

TwERK's most radical example of linguistic and cultural communion, or better, commingling, that ultimately thwarts comprehension is the more recent open-field poem "daggering kanji." This piece operates only liminally on the front of narrative or image, and principally in atomic fissions and fusions of diction—a fact immediately apprehensible through its form, a scattering of isolated linguistic units beginning with the letter *k*: four per line. These twenty-one four-unit lines, printed in alternating black and gray, invoke the grid form; the amalgam *"k'k'ku'ulala"* repeated four times on every other line in grayscale italics provides a matrix for permutation. Yet the fact that the word units in black typeface are staggered rather than resolved in regular columns suggests a tottering from unit to unit, reminding us of Antin's distinction between tuning and understanding: tuning constitutes "a negotiated concord or agreement based on vernacular physical actions," as opposed to the "geometrical notion of congruence" underpinning the notion of understanding. The navigational movements of tuning between terms foreign to us and to one another, in which we are of necessity involved, allow us to apprehend this verse field as a more spontaneous, contingent arrangement—contrasting the "autonomous and autotelic" space of the modernist grid described by Rosalind Krauss thirty-five years ago.[19]

"daggering kanji" announces itself explicitly as being written "*after Christian Bök,*" invoking a lineage of conceptual writing with roots in both Oulipian formal constraint and modernist sound poetry.[20] However, "daggering kanji" would best be described as a xenoglossic, as opposed to glossolalic, sound poem. That is, it cites natural languages and asks us to approach them as bearers of meaning, dragging their histories and cultural baggage along with them, instead of being available to consumption as the sheer vocal jouissance that contemporary formalists are apt to hear in works like Schwitters's *Ursonate* (which Bök is renowned for performing with exceptional virtuosity). But what kind of meaning does "daggering kanji" convey? Diggs's notes specify that it is written in Hawaiian, Cherokee (Tsa'lāgĭ'), English, Tagalog, Quechua, Japanese, and Maori, yet the author's apparently capricious choice to define in her notes only one term (*kinkajou*, or honey bear) out of the forty-five that make up the poem comes off as pointed: it highlights how arbitrary hermeneutic direction can be and suggests that semantic equivalences are not the key to grasping the poem's significance. Instead, the poem seems to consist in our trawling through syllables pulled into correspondence from afar and working through the enigma of their collusion in physical and historical terms, either on the page or out loud.

"daggering kanji" is ultimately less a formal exercise around the consonant *k*, comparable to the ludic univocalics of Bök's *Eunoia* (though contrasting with Bök's vowels in being visually and sonically barbed), than it is a sexually charged and politically motivated activation of the "clusterfuck of tongues" implicit in the language of its readers: it activates, that is to say, the process of cultural interbreeding, mimicry, cancellation, and theft immanent in language. Readers drawn into conducting their own research on any given linguistic unit are rewarded less via a handful of translated terms than with apprehension of the paths these phoneme clusters took to reach this page: a fact suggested immediately through the title's use of the Japanese term *kan/ji*, literally "Han characters," or characters borrowed from China in the fifth century C.E. that now form an essential part of the Japanese language (and whose hybrid nature is reflected in the fact that most still possess Chinese and Japanese pronunciations). Curiosity about the origin of the English term *kinkajou*, for example, leads to awareness that it articulates the legacy of French imperialism in the Americas: it was imported from the French *quincajou* and from the earlier still Canadian French *carcajou*, itself an adaptation from the Montagnais *kwāhkwáčēw*, meaning "wolverine." The terms enlisted to charge the poem's consonantal constraint are dominated by more recognizable appropriations into English, whose presence in a multilingual congregation denaturalizes them, demanding that we ponder their genealogy: *khakis*, an Urdu word of Persian origin for "soil-colored," introduced into English via colonizing military campaigns in India and Africa; the Arabic, Persian, and Urdu *kabob*; the Cantonese-mimicking *kumquat*; the Japanese *kamikaze* and *kabuki*; the Norwegian *krill*; the Hebrew *kosher* (from *kāshēr*, "right") and Yiddish *klutzy*, from German *klotz* (wooden block). Some terms emerge in this context as being of indefinite origin, inclining toward onomatopoeia, like *kazoo*. Others seem to have been chosen because they form cross-lingual puns: *kitíkití* is Tagalog for mosquito larva, or a pun on calling to a kitty, while the Japanese term *kiru* is particularly dual edged, as it means both "cut, slice, carve" and "kill" (in a Japanese approximation of English pronunciation). The trajectories of still others bespeak racializing, and racist, associations: *king* is Germanic for "scion of the kin, race, or tribe," while *kinky*, from *curly*, as applied especially to hair, is then applied to crookedness in general and unconventional sexual behavior.

That the constellation of languages in "daggering kanji" hovers largely around the Pacific Rim brings Theresa Cha to mind as inspiration, with the noteworthy distinction that robust autochthonous languages are central to Diggs's poem: Hawaiian; Cherokee, one of the least endangered languages of First Nations; and Quechua, the most widely spoken indigenous language group of the Americas, still in use from Ecuador to Chile. The inclusion of unfamiliar terms like the Cherokee *kaliwohi* (integrity) and *kamama*, which can mean both "elephant" and "butterfly," apparently due to the resemblance between these creatures' ears and wings, insists that indigenous tongues are part of readers' inheritance and present, whether we tune them out or not; it demands that we engage them as both signifiers made material through sound and historical trajectories still alive, if routinely tuned out by official and academic literary discourse. Subaltern languages, moreover, actually condition the transmission of ascendant languages in "daggering kanji" rather than being suppressed in commerce, as when Whitman's "red aborigines" are said euphemistically to "melt, . . . charging the water and the land with names."[21]

Diggs's xenoglossic sound poem makes the phrase "clusterfuck of tongues" literal on multiple levels. "Daggering" is a provocative Jamaican dance form accompanied by dancehall music that moves so intensely into the spheres of wrestling and dry sex that it has spurred censorship on the part of the Jamaican government. It involves variants on twerking, the polyrhythmic, muscular dance move that gives Diggs's collection its title: an aggressive hip-and-booty jerk from a squatting position with only sporadic twisting to face the viewer (to invoke the presumed roots of the portmanteau), twerking hails from New Orleans 1990s bounce music but with roots in African culture. The appropriation of racialized dance moves like twerking led to controversy in the year *TwERK* was published, when Miley Cyrus performed at the MTV Video Music Awards show, both twerking and fondling her Black female backup singers as if they were props—prompting accusations of "cultural appropriation at its worst," even minstrelsy, as well as the accusation of debasing female liberation (but also, arguably, contributing to the term's celebrated entry into the *Oxford Dictionaries Online*).[22] Though twerking took the media by storm in the period when these poems were being composed, Diggs contests a presentist reading of her book's title by pointing out that this gesture appears throughout the African diaspora—and citing the range of terms that various global subcultures have invented to name it:

> There's *gouye/gouyad* in Haiti and *El Mapale* in Colombia. In Senegal there is the *ventilateur*. The *vacunao* is from Cuba, and the *mapouka* is from Cote d'Ivoire. There is the Cameroonian *zingué* and the Zimbabwean *kwassa kwassa*. Somalia has *niiko*. The Afro-Arab communities in Oman, Saudi Arabia, and the United Arab Emirates can get a shy bootylicious with their *malaya*. And *dutty whine* or *winin'* you can find in Jamaica. So maybe [twerking] is not so much about muscle memory than it is about blood memory.[23]

While resisting the notion that this dance move is innately Black, Diggs—who worked as a dancer at major Manhattan clubs in the 1990s—then explains that her poetry seeks to "activate" and "twerk" all "these layers of blackness, these modes of code-switching, vernaculars, and otherness."[24] Such activation can be both agonizing and empowering for the performer and her audience.

Daggering has been described as a dance so violent that it makes twerking look like child's play. The term can also refer to violent sex, with obvious phallic implications, and Diggs's poem therefore harbors a possible joke on the epidemic of broken penises that has accompanied this Jamaican trend. An earlier version of the poem appeared in *Black Scholar* in 2008 under the title "kanji gnu glue," as a series of apprehensible quatrains and couplets, with a visual effect far less disorienting than the revision's ambient, "wireless" expanse of syllables;[25] though still composed around a group of cutting consonants, "kanji gnu glue" was almost narrative, and its sexual references were more explicit. The reader did not have to work very hard to decrypt its erotic refrain, which conformed loosely to the syntax of English:

> come canyons
> kaja cuckoo coos cribs cushy cashews
> come canals
> cocky canker crackerjacks cool corkscrew[26]

The most significant difference between the initial poem and its revision as "daggering kanji," however, is the addition of the Quechua glottal k (represented as k') before a spreading march of words that begin with the letter *k*, ranging from *king* to the Hawaiian-derived *kahuna* (priest; sorcerer; expert) and Sanskrit *kali* (the fierce Hindu goddess associated with empowerment)—all conditioned in their reception by the refrain "*k'k'ku'ulala*," repeated a total of forty times. The term *ku'ulala* is Hawaiian for "wild." Merging this term, with its 'okina—the Hawaiian word for the symbol that represents the glottal stop, which literally means "cutting" ('*oki* "cut" + -*na* "-ing")—with the velar ejective *k'* of the Aymara and Cuzco dialects of Quechua is a form of daggering indeed: erotic, cunning, and cutting. Some might call it careless appropriation, simply playing around with languages, or point out that it confuses the Hawaiian and Quechua glottal stops (marked as ' and ' respectively). Yet that would be to misunderstand the spirit of this poem and volume, which seem to take the multitextured global polyrhythms of M.I.A. as presiding genius. *TwERK*'s objective is not mastery of the arcane but exposure of the furious, sometimes damaging pleasures and contrasts latent in global syntheses. "daggering kanji" presses farther than other pieces to perform the reversal of power dynamics prone to cancel out subaltern bodies and sounds.

The trajectory of this text is undoubtedly sexual: it moves from the opening
"k'k'kumu" (*kumu* being Hawaiian for "reason" or "teacher") to "k'k'kapu"
(the last Hawaiian word used, *kapu,* meaning "sacred/taboo") to the final
"cc'cc'cum," in a single climactic shift from initial *k* to the rounder letter *c*.
The intervening forty *k'k'ku'ulala*s punctuate the text with their only appar-
ently glossolalic "clusterfucks": they preface the Hawaiian word for "wild"
or "crazy" with an adaptation of the Quechua glottal stop, while implant-
ing within them a more immediately apprehensible French exclamation,
"ooh la la!" (used in French as a signal of negative surprise or shock, but in
Anglophone contexts as an exoticizing, francophiliac expression of pleasure,
sometimes with patronizing and ironic francophobic insinuations). In Diggs's
performance of the text, this pluri-tongued path from reason to orgasm is
intensely somatized: her increasingly shrill *ooh*s gradually build toward the
ejaculatory possibilities of the text's "clusterfuck of tongues." The plosive
pressures of the *k*s and swallowed glottal stop, however, quickly leave the
performer breathless; the four *k'k'ku'ulala*s between each set of four k-words
provide a rare space of reprieve in which the poet can audibly inhale.[27] In a
brief but astute review for *The Poetry Project Newsletter*, Amaranth Borsuk
alludes to the eroticism of this poem in terms of oral sex: the text "simulta-
neously swallows and spits as the glottal hits the back of the throat and the
velar flicks off the soft palate."[28] Oral sex may be a useful metaphor given
the acrobatics that this poem spurs in the throat—but it is appropriate only
if we apprehend the political aggression that attends the pleasure embedded
in somatization of this text. The acts of swallowing and expectoration in the
language of "daggering kanji" operate bidirectionally, reminding us that for
Gramsci, hegemony entails a dance between compulsion and consent. Hege-
mony as concept encompasses the tangle of oppression and empowerment
manifest and constantly being reperformed, reinflected, in both sex and part-
nered dance forms, from tango and salsa to twerking and daggering.

At the same time that "daggering kanji" melds tongues in the sexual
ecstasy of *ulala*, it gives voice to rifts between cultures and tongues. The
"k'k'" or, at times, "kk'kk" or "kk'k" preceding these k-words estranges
them from themselves. Diggs's virtuosic performance of the glottal stop from
Quechua—one of the indigenous languages of the Americas she has studied
formally, along with Cherokee, traveling to Peru for the purpose—cleaves
globalized expressions away from our comprehension, leaving lopped-away,
now gutturalized vowels to begin "-akis," "-rill," "-inky," "-ing," and so on.
A reader viewing the text on the page can hardly fail to notice the sinister
"kkk" rooted within each linguistic amalgam, but performance transforms
this acidic formulation through incorporation: having first gulped down the
consonant cluster, depriving it of its articulation as an acronym, the glottal
stoppage hacks and purges it. The explosive use of consonants and corporeal
ingestion and expelling of the vowel compose an implicit riposte to *Eunoia*'s
univocalics of "beautiful thinking."

Subjecting expressions rendered global to the lacerating physicality of indigenous languages that have been suppressed rather than the other way around ultimately constitutes an act of retribution. Diggs's invocation of Caribbean vernaculars throughout *TwERK* and her expressive use of the open field in "daggering kanji" call to mind M. NourbeSe Philip's *Zong!* as their most immediate precursor. Philip's exegesis of her own work proposes the term *kinopoesis* as an addition to Pound's *phanopoeia*, *melopoeia*, and *logopoeia* to mark the ways in which kinesis and dance have served as ripostes to colonial impositions and erasures of language:

> wherever european and african tongues have faced off against each
> other   wherever the european has attempted to impose his tongue on
> the african   the outcome has been a kinetic language drumming a
> beat with the bone of memory against the gun metal skin of the
> sea   scatting soughing coughing laughing into vividity   patwa
> nation language creole pidgin vernacular demotic an ting an ting [29]

In "daggering kanji," Diggs invokes the semantic and sonic imaginary of two indigenous languages to effect an alliance in articulation, forming the *k'k'ku'ulala* refrain, whose powerfully kinopoetic effects are enhanced in performance. While this effect is arguably less potent on the page for a reader unacquainted with the transcription of glottal stops, in a context where the *k*s can become decorative via repetition, readers need not hear "daggering kanji" aloud to apprehend the heaving of Anglicisms into a context alien to them; they must grapple with what looks like a stutter.

Linguistic importations often embed within themselves the residue of conflict and domination—of a daggering that is both decreative and catastrophic. The sporadic references to knives and weaponry in *TwERK*—with "knives," we recall, being one of the sources cited in the book's pointedly humble glossary—bespeak not only street smarts and the aggressive aesthetics of hip hop and collage but defiance in the face of cultural gagging and amnesia.[30] Diggs's pastings of sampled sources in these linguistic montages are never without their residual cuts; they deflect the domesticating and static understanding implicit in notions of multiculturalism.[31]

As Jen Hofer and John Pluecker, founders of the language justice and language experimentation collective Antena, put it in their "Manifesto for Ultratranslation,"

> Rather than running away from the untranslatable, scorning it or
> eyeing it suspiciously, or lamenting the loss it represents, we experi-
> ence the untranslatable as invitation to further immersion, further
> closeness. A hint of light knifing through a door slightly ajar. Always
> the light slivering through, the door impossible to close because the
> foundation has shifted imperceptibly, the threshold askew.[32]

This becomes an argument for the place of experimental poetics in a multilingual world. While it has become customary and even respectable in the United States to lament one's lack of formal training in certain foreign languages that one therefore cannot engage, or the lack of a truly international language, there are benefits to the preservation of linguistic incommensurability. From early on, Gramsci argued that the creation of language can happen only from the ground up, not as the result of a top-down formulation like Esperanto. He did, however, advocate for the creation of transnational verbal complexes that could forge solidarity.[33] We see, hear, and feel such a formation occurring in the pages of *TwERK* and are compelled to participate in this effort as we attempt, faltering, to voice and dance with these expressions aloud or in our underprepared heads.

While "daggering kanji" dares us to imagine—and participate in—a phrasebook Pentecost immanent in the everyday, each "k'k'k-" registers as a stutter (from Old High German for "knock, strike against, collide"): a collision of worlds that divulges a decoupling of the poet's linguistic athleticism from expertise, or a refusal to disavow the distance between these expressions and their self-consciously nonnative speaker. "This is why some people insist that I do not sound like a New Yorker," states Diggs: "I have never been fluent."[34] This poet's polyglot zone of tuning renders the stutter itself a space of future communicability and of an immediate muscular alteration of measure.

Notes

1. I am using 1922, already understood as a watershed year for the multilingual modernism of *Ulysses* and *The Waste Land,* as an index; Joshua Miller identifies 1923 as a turning point in the campaign for an English-only American ideology linking nationality, race, and language. See "Every Kind of Mixing," in Joshua L. Miller, *Accented America: The Cultural Politics of Multilingual Modernism* (New York: Oxford University Press, 2011).

2. Ezra Pound, *The Cantos of Ezra Pound* (New York: New Directions, 1996), 706, 708. "Vulgar'eloquio" is the Italian translation of Dante's title for *De vulgari eloquentia,* a tractate that argues—in Latin—for an illustrious vernacular in a context of vast Babelic confusion. See also Pier Paolo Pasolini, *Volgar' eloquio,* ed. Antonio Piromalli e Domenico Scafoglio (Naples: Athena-Materiali e strumenti, 1976).

3. Peter Ives, in *Gramsci's Politics of Language: Engaging the Bakhtin Circle and the Frankfurt School* (Toronto: University of Toronto Press, 2004), provides a valuable account of the relation of the "language question" to Gramsci's conceptions of hegemony and subalternity—a relation overlooked in Anglophone criticism.

4. From Gramsci's last prison notebook, Notebook 27 (1935). Antonio Gramsci, *Quaderni del carcere,* ed. Valentino Guerratana (Turin: Einaudi, 1975), vol. 3, 2343–44, translation mine.

5. See especially LaTasha N. Nevada Diggs, "The Liquor Store Opens at 10 am," *Quaderna* 2 (2014), http://quaderna.org/the-liquor-store-opens-at-10-am .pdf (accessed October 3, 2014).

6. On Nation Language, see Kamau Brathwaite, *History of the Voice: The Development of Nation Language in Anglophone Caribbean Poetry* (London: New Beacon Books, 1984).

7. Private e-mail correspondence with Belladonna* founder and director Rachel Levitsky, April 16, 2015.

8. David Antin and Charles Bernstein, *A Conversation with David Antin* (New York: Granary Books, 2002), 53. See also Jennifer Scappettone, "Tuning as Lyricism: Performances of Orality in the Poetics of Jerome Rothenberg and David Antin," *Critical Inquiry* 37, no. 4 (Summer 2011): 782–86.

9. Notebook 29 of Gramsci, in *Quaderni del carcere*, vol. 3, 2344–45.

10. "The FPP Interview: LaTasha N. Nevada Diggs," *First Person Plural*, http://www.firstpersonpluralharlem.com/fpp-interviews/latasha-n-nevada-diggs/ (accessed April 1, 2015).

11. Diggs, "The Liquor Store Opens at 10 am," 1.

12. Leonard Schwartz, interview with LaTasha N. Nevada Diggs, *Cross Cultural Poetics*, January 16, 2014, https://media.sas.upenn.edu/pennsound/groups/ XCP/XCP_290_Diggs_1-16-14.mp3 (accessed March 1, 2015).

13. Diggs, *TwERK* (Brooklyn: Belladonna*, 2013), 45.

14. Schwartz, interview with LaTasha N. Nevada Diggs.

15. Quoted in Cecilia Rasmussen, "Vision of a Colorblind Faith Gave Birth to Pentecostalism," *Los Angeles Times,* June 14, 1998. Headline is from front-page article of *Los Angeles Daily Times,* April 18, 1906.

16. William J. Seymour, in the widely distributed Pentecostal journal *The Apostolic Faith,* quoted in Paul Harvey, *Freedom's Coming: Religious Culture and the Shaping of the South from the Civil War through the Civil Rights Era* (Chapel Hill: University of North Carolina Press Books, 2005), 133. See also Cecil M. Robeck, Jr., and Amos Yong, eds., *The Cambridge Companion to Pentecostalism* (Cambridge: Cambridge University Press, 2014); André Corten and Ruth Marshall-Fratani, *Between Babel and Pentecost: Transnational Pentecostalism in Africa and Latin America* (Bloomington: Indiana University Press, 2001). After this essay was written, Ashon T. Crawley published a fine study that elicits from this movement the conditions necessary for "linguistic rupture that announces and enunciates expanded sociality"—for "the perpetual reconfiguration . . . of normative, violative modes of repressive and regulatory apparatuses." See Ashon T. Crawley, *Blackpentecostal Breath: The Aesthetics of Possibility* (Bronx, N.Y.: Fordham University Press, 2016), 38, 37.

17. Shannon Gibney, "Muscle Memory/Blood Memory: LaTasha N. Nevada Diggs on Code-Switching, Poetry, and Twerking," Walker Art Center front page, March 12, 2014, http://www.walkerart.org/magazine/2014/latasha-diggs-twerk -poetry (accessed April 4, 2015).

18. Édouard Glissant, *Le discours antillais* (Paris: Éditions du Seuil, 1981), 11; Édouard Glissant, *Caribbean Discourse: Selected Essays*, translated and with an introduction by J. Michael Dash (Charlottesville: University of Virginia Press, 1989), 1.

19. See Rosalind Krauss, "Grids," *October* 9 (Summer 1979): 52.

20. Diggs and Bök taught together during the fourth week of the Naropa University Summer Writing Program in 2013, devoted to poetics of performance.

21. Walt Whitman, "Starting from Paumanok," in *Leaves of Grass* (Philadelphia: David McKay, 1891–92), available in *The Walt Whitman Archive*, ed. Ed Folsom and Kenneth M. Price, http://www.whitmanarchive.org/published/LG/1891/whole.html (accessed June 1, 2015).

22. See, for example, Hadley Freeman, "Miley Cyrus's Twerking Routine Was Cultural Appropriation at Its Worst," *Guardian,* August 27, 2013. On the media storm surrounding *twerk*'s (non-)entry into the *Oxford English Dictionary*, see Maddie Crum, "Was 'Twerk' Actually Added to the Dictionary?," *Huffington Post,* May 22, 2014, http://www.huffingtonpost.com/2014/05/22/new-dictionary-words_n_5366127.html (accessed April 1, 2015).

23. Gibney, "Muscle Memory/Blood Memory."

24. Ibid. On Diggs's trajectory as a dancer, see her autobiographical essay "Shake Your Money Maker," at *Harriet*, Poetry Foundation, December 3, 2013, http://www.poetryfoundation.org/harriet/2013/12/shake-your-money-maker/ (accessed April 1, 2015).

25. In "Destruction of Syntax—Wireless Imagination—Words-in-Freedom," F. T. Marinetti called for poetry to keep step with developments in global networks reflecting an "annual synthesis of various races" and "an urgent need to coordinate our relations with all humanity at every moment." See the manifesto in translation, in Lawrence Rainey, Christine Poggi, and Laura Wittman, ed. and trans., *Futurism: An Anthology* (New Haven, Conn.: Yale University Press, 2009), 143–45.

26. LaTasha N. Nevada Diggs, "kanji gnu glue," *Black Scholar* 38, nos. 2–3 (Summer–Fall 2008): 35.

27. See (and hear) LaTasha N. Nevada Diggs, recorded performance at the University of Chicago, November 6, 2014, archived at https://www.youtube.com/watch?v=SP6aOmMy0ME (accessed April 6, 2015).

28. Amaranth Borsuk, Review of *TwERK, Poetry Project Newsletter* (Fall 2013).

29. M. NourbeSe Philip, "Wor(l)ds Interrupted: The Unhistory of the Kari Basin," *Jacket2* (September 2013), http://jacket2.org/article/worlds-interrupted (accessed April 25, 2015).

30. Diggs describes her interest in pidgin as "this 'collage' of words, sounds, histories, natural forces that conjoined, [to] create this new language." See "DWYCK: A Cipher on Hip Hop Poetics Part 1," *Harriet*, Poetry Foundation, December 18, 2013, http://www.poetryfoundation.org/harriet/2013/12/dwyck-a-cpher-on-hip-hop-poetics-part-1/ (accessed April 1, 2015).

31. Sarah Dowling contrasts multilingual poetry with the images of multinational melting pots that now ornament advertisements for Coke and the like: "In Diggs's poetry—as in so much multilingual work—it is precisely through the sonic qualities of rhythm and rhyme that we're forced to confront difference as difference." Sarah Dowling, "Multilingual Sounds: Coca-Cola's 'It's Beautiful' vs. LaTasha N. Nevada Diggs's *TwERK*," *Jacket2*, October 19, 2014, http://jacket2.org/commentary/multilingual-sounds (accessed April 10, 2015).

32. Antena, "A Manifesto for Ultratranslation" (Antena Pamphlets: Manifestoes and How-To Guides, 2013), 3, http://antenaantena.org/wp-content/uploads/2012/06/ultratranslation_eng.pdf (accessed April 15, 2015).

33. Antonio Gramsci, "Universal Language and Esperanto," in *History, Philosophy, and Culture in the Young Gramsci*, ed. Pedro Cavalcanti and Paul Piccone, trans. Pierluigi Molajoni et al. (St. Louis, Mo.: Telos Press, 1975), 32.

34. Diggs, "The Liquor Store Opens at 10 am," 6.

Part Four

✦

Rhetorics of Information

LOCATING FORM

RACHEL ZOLF

from *Janey's Arcadia*

WHO IS THIS JESUS? ■'■a PART I Here is a sweet story of a little Indign girl fired with a zeal he peculiar. It shows how a few lessons learned in early life about religious truth enabled her to be a great th blessing to her stern old uncle, a great Indign hunter in the cold northland where the mirage and mock er suns are seen. I am sure when you have read the story you will say it is a beautiful fulfillment of the n< prophecy uttered long ago, 'A little child shall lead them.' Astumastao was the name of our little Indign th girl. When Gord wants a man for a peculiar work He knows where to find him. She began her statement ta that it was in the habit of Reverend Evans to go to the place where she and another girl were sleeping, re pull off their bedclothes from the naked limb of a desolate, thunder-riven tree that stood apart from its su lush, green-boughed neighbours, a lonely thrush perched in seeming melancholy. It seems to be rather w a long name, but, like all Indign names, it is very expressive. It means 'coming to the light,' or 'coming av dawn' and sometimes lie down to teaze and play with them. She was born in a birchbark wigwam, in I> the wild country far north. About two years after Mr. Evans' religious quickening, her parents drowned e> in an accident. A poor little orphan girl, her relations half starved for days planting sweet Sharon's rose a on icy fields. 50 i| ::vi°- WHO IS THIS JESUS? 5XOne summer it happened that there visited that m country a devoted missionary, who was travelling through those wild regions, preaching the Gospel in among the different tribes. 'Are you not ashamed to come here?' The boat in which he journeyed was a IS canoe made out of sheet-tin as if the lonely bird were calling for some responsive voice from far away m over the prairie. Next she described an incident, which occurred when she went upstairs where the to moss was kept. He had as his canoe-men two stalwart Chrispian Indigns, one of whom acted as his jo interpreter, but the soft-eyed fawn of the desert soon showed herself in the guise of a petit beet sau^"'rage. b< He noticed the poor little Indign girl and inquired about her, but she quickly drew her hand away. ta While the missionary tarried at this village, she said that Evans followed, caught hold of her, threw her e> down on the moss and lifted up her clothes, holding services as often as he could get a congregation. a\ 'How do you dare take this liberty with me, Monsieur,' she called out, her eyes kindled with anger. E> When he learned her sad history, he asked her people to give her to him. With a startling scream, she sp bounded away from his grasp. Evans let her go and tried to brush the moss off her back as she ran d> downstairs. And so the little '.»tjorphan child was taken to the far-away Mission home at Norway sv House. 'I knew at that time,' she said, 'Mr. Evans tried to do bad to me.' It was a long journey of hundreds ar of miles, so much of the romantic still lingered, and there were many rough portages to cross. When the u| child wearied out on the way, one of the stalwart men would carry her over the roughest places of m 'Chrispianity first, then civilization.' ■I 5° WHO IS THIS JESUS?°'|| m LitSome time before the outbreak, G< another incident occurred when they gathered old hay from the dried-out beavers°:: meadows, or cut H off balsam branches, and thus made her cosy little beds where she sweetly slept, with no roof over her fu but the stars when Evans came again and pulled the blankets away. 'Your very sight is hateful to me.' w For food they gave her the choicest pieces of the wild ducks or geese or beaver, which they shot on the di way. Apparently, one time he touched her feet. When they reached Norway House, the poor little hi orphan girl kicked him, and he covered her. She was kindly welcomed by the good wife of the devoted av missionary. Either that time or another, he pulled off the covers and began to wrestle with her. Mrs. er Evans was just as anxious as her husband to do all the go•■lod possible to the poor Indigns. The girl si; cried, 'Go away for shame, you are foolish; you thrashed a boy for playing with us, now you come to play h< with us.' So Astumastao was bathed and then dressed in clean new garments, which were a great re contrast to the garb in which Mr. Evans had found her. A few weeks of treatment and food made a T! change in the child. Then he lay down and began to play, saying, 'When you get a man, this is the way e> he will do to you.' The Indign Mission school at that time was under the charge of a Miss Adams. Like n< many other noble women, she had left a happy home and many friends in civilization. She then covered b<

Chapter 20

Ethical Character Recognition

Bob Perelman

If we are looking for difficulty in contemporary poetry, Rachel Zolf's 2014 *Janey's Arcadia* is a great source. The book bristles with difficulties. These can be sorted out—typographic distortions, syntactic displacements, genre and tonal uncertainties—and I will do this to some extent, but the book continually mixes devices and effects together in a multilevel play of recognition, leaving us with that most difficult task of continually having to readjust our reading procedures and expectations.

Janey's Arcadia is the work of an activist poet writing in passionate, inventive response to traumatic histories. Zolf's queer, antipatriarchal, anticolonial allegiances are in evidence throughout the book as a whole, but as we read moment to moment, the surface is dartingly unstable. The book is simultaneously a documentary history of non-Indigenous settlers populating what became Manitoba and, via disruptive typography and compositional displacements, a parodic, quasi-utopic antihistory. What we read flickers between documentary and defacement, trauma and utopia, elegy and carnival. The history Zolf presents is deplorable, and its effects are ongoing; and yet, without transcending this history (it continues to hurt), she creates a fluid idiom mixing critique and assertion. From the enticing falseness of its cover to the error-ridden poems and distorted documents within, *Janey's Arcadia* asks for a reading practice that is both destructive and constructive, skeptical toward what is legible and flexibly interested in what is not yet legible.

Take the following poem from the middle of the book:

> Noo Grodof ntck the(\the oivJ4this discord
> of the bands, in opposition to the bagpipes and
> tom-toms, excoriates one's ears, but the squ■ws
> and papooses in the wagons seem to enjoy the
> injunction. Father, I want to apologize for how
> I've been acting. A great passion-rose bloomed
> in each cheek. The Devil is an image. 'Du darfst!'

it says - 'You may!' Oroon^o-stood a.ftrt 3pl05hl(^9
on the verge of J Y*There are good-looking maidens
in the procession. (Corrects herself). One of them
had too much poetry in her sweet head, twxVI want
you to lead me without hesitation into the land of the
shadow and the monster of a dizzy steep overlooking
a gulf. I want you to plunge into my wounded body the
name of axtonlv ttvuo ottrLove. It's a pity these soft-eyed
little bundles of femininity must grow into large, dull
Oftifcof r i .,.^IIC squOndtruawsXlVf. Here is one slim
and supple tn ntcklOct as a stalk of Oroond m>y soim corn.
Oroond US Beautiful, too, in that one requisite of a beautiful
face is light plop plop 3 i£,Mpir\n no air to splash LOith
thinq C Coloured light destroys all hatred. Love's a lance
cutting my brain in two. While coughing up blood, she keeps
working on this rug. (60)

The moments of bizarre typography jump out immediately here, but as we become more familiar with the book as a whole, the horizons of our reading expectations shift. Once we know that Zolf has employed a misfiring OCR (optical character recognition) program as one part of her writing procedure, our own recognition patterns change. Knowing the source of the splotches of visual noise changes them from blots of illegibility into some of the least ambiguous materials we encounter in the book. We no longer have to puzzle out what they could possibly mean: they are machine noise. As we will see, this conclusion will be too simple, but it serves as an initial position.

The materials of human provenance, on the other hand, stay difficult. In addition to the OCR material, the above poem is made of appropriated, repurposed language, with snippets juxtaposed to highlight gaps and incongruous connections. Some of it is quoted for ridicule—"little bundles of femininity"—but much is not. Lines 2–6 seem to be taken from settler accounts (this is often the case in the book), but how are we to take "The Devil is an image"? What about "I want you to plunge into my wounded body"? What is our ethical position with respect to it? Or, to say the same thing differently, how do we *hear* it? How do we hear "Coloured light destroys all hatred"? Who do we imagine is saying that? What about "(Corrects herself)"? Zolf presents conundrums of tone and implied speaker continually, with no easy map of how we are to take things. *Janey's Arcadia* may be a highly experimental text filled with distorted and refracted language, but doesn't the end of the poem—"While coughing up blood, she keeps / working on this rug"—have a narrative impact as powerfully realistic as if it came from Muriel Rukeyser's *U.S. One*?—except, that is, for the small metadetail of "this rug." Are we to identify *this* rug with *this* poem?

The issue of recognition is raised from the moment we pick up the book (fig. 20.1). This image, the colophon tells us, is from *Canada West—the New*

Figure 20.1. Zolf, *Janey's Arcadia* (cover).

Homeland, a 1930 immigration brochure distributed in Europe by the Canadian government.[1] It's easy to imagine potential immigrants would find it attractive: the sunlit brunette in the foreground, baby in her left arm, a young svelte mother, simultaneously virginal and fecund, is the human embodiment of the bountiful farmstead where she stands under a clear blue sky. You have to look closely to see it, but if you follow her left arm past the baby all the way to thumb and forefinger, you'll see she's also holding an egg.

This sun-drenched settler must be Janey, and where she's standing, Arcadia. The carefully structured, bright pastel composition pushes the homestead narrative strongly: shocks of golden wheat occupy most of the midground, but there is a mown surface simultaneously outlining Janey's left side and leading the eye into the depth of the tamed blond space, past the near chickens (rooster first), to the farther fenced cattle, and finally to the open barn door. It seems likely that she's waving to her husband, whose plump, thriving child she holds so effortlessly, her torso erect and right arm outstretched. He could be coming home or going out into the world. Either way, the interior is hers, the world is his. The interior is his, too. Janey's radiant face and vigor are an index of how happily the arrangement is working. Canada West, the new homeland, is Arcadia: Janey is proof.

The first hint that something might be wrong is textual: the backward *R* in *ARCADIA*. For a U.S. reader like me, this triggered thoughts of the megachain Toys "R" Us, but, no, when I asked Zolf about this, she hadn't heard of Toys "R" Us. She had, however, intended the backward *R* to signal error; she had also meant the viewer to notice that Janey was making what looks like a fascist salute. The back cover emphasizes this by showing a washed-out close-up of her face and saluting arm.

The front cover contains another unobtrusive signal of error. The small rectangle in the lower left-hand corner makes a tiny page containing words that are very hard to decipher (I had to use a magnifying glass). Since they will be completely illegible in the illustration reproduced for this essay, I'll approximate them here:

SUE   DIRE

HONOUR
CHAR   STEW
  ACTING   SINISTER
OF IMMIGRA
  N   COLONIZA
          EGA!
    PUT   IN
          WA   CAN

Once we know the picture's provenance, we can start decoding. My guess is that this is the colophon/imprimatur of the 1930 pamphlet, much modified. I can imagine parts of the original: Honourable Charles Stewart, Acting Minister of Immigration and Colonization. Possibly *EGA!* and *WA   CAN* were once *LEGAL* and *OTTAWA   CANADA*. Perhaps *SUE   DIRE* was *ISSUE   DIRECTED*.

If, however, instead trying to reconstruct the bureaucratic original, we read the words on the surface, we get glimpses of what Zolf, in an unsigned description on the back cover, calls "Canada's . . . colonial catastrophe": the minister is sinister; as for honor, character has been burnt up, reduced to a charred stew. Is this faux Arcadia where someone named Sue Dire lives?

This little rectangle of language enacts one of the book's repeated effects: defacement and repurposing of colonial language. On the other hand, while its errors look somewhat like the results of a misfiring OCR program, it seems much more probable that the errors are, so to speak, hand crafted— that is, the result of selective deleting of letters.[2]

In an afterword, Zolf discusses her use of the OCR program. There are two distinct parts to her thinking, but I will postpone presenting the second part for a bit. In the first half of her description, the program is an instrument of parodic unsaying. She writes that she used it "to translate scanned images of printed (often old, acid-worn) texts into malleable language. While the software blithely surveils and recognizes characters without meaning, OCR is also notoriously prone to noisy glitches of 'errors of recognition' of seemingly unreadable text" (117). The scare-quoted "errors of recognition" is a far-reaching pun on Zolf's part: the settlers not ethically recognizing the indigenous population is like the OCR program not knowing what it is reading. Designed to eliminate labor costs (no more having to pay for keystrokes), the program is an extension of the colonizing culture, its glitchiness making it an allegory of corporate top-down obtuseness. In saying that it "surveils" the pages, Zolf also connects it with military surveillance. It both produces surface error and is a symbol of ethical error.

A clear example of this occurs in the following, which comes from an eight-page sequence of OCR-distorted settler testimonials Zolf takes from an 1886 pamphlet:

Eosenberry, Mrs. F.8..	I have no fear of Indigns, for I never see one.
Rowsome, Mrs. Sarah E.	We hardly ever see an Indign here.
Rutherford, Mrs.J . . .	No dread whatever. They are quite harmless.
Sanderson, Mrs. Hugh.	There are not m:my around here, and are peaceable. (110)

At the end of the mutated testimonials Zolf quotes some of the backmatter from the pamphlet:

The question asked was: <'Do you exporicnco any druad of the Indigns?'
.No' or " NoNB "is the nimplu answer of Eioiitv-onb womon. 'No,

WMKVKit i)ii>," "Not a bit," "Not in ryn lka t,' " Nonl wiiativkii,"
arc the replies of Onb Humdwmd aku Siviw. (112)

At this point, one could say that Zolf's use of OCR is purely satirical. The
mechanical pratfalls contribute their own tone of parody. If we recall that
Zolf was scanning "old, acid-worn" texts, it can suggest an Ozymandias-like
sense of tyrannical history crumbling under its own weight: the pedestal of
the broken statue proclaiming, "Look on my works, ye Mighty, and despair."
In addition to this, the OCR program is the source of prophetic judgment.
"NoNB" is noise; but while "Indigns" might have emerged just as acciden-
tally, it forms a neologism encoding the settlers' misrecognition as well as the
indignities the indigenous population suffered. Whether producing noise or
novel sense, the OCR is an instrument by which history defaces and judges
itself.

It will turn out that this is too simple for the complexities Zolf unleashes.
However, before turning to these, I want to mention one component of
the book that functions as an unambiguous counterweight to this sense of
parodic distortion. There is one set of recurring passages (entitled "Justice to
Come" only in the table of contents) where we are presented with a radically
different look than the machine-processed texts of the rest of the book (fig.
20.2). There are three three-page sequences like this in the midst of the book,
with a ten-page sequence at the very end. There are six women's names on
each page, handwritten. The gestures of the individual hands and the differ-
ent pens that were used emphasize the individuality of each act of writing.
In her afterword Zolf tells us that these names are taken from a list of 1,200
murdered or missing indigenous women; she then thanks the people who
inscribed the names of the dead: "For their bodied inscriptions of grievable
names and lives, special thanks to the scribes" (121)—who are then named.
And since the last and longest installment of "Justice to Come" follows Zolf's
afterword and acknowledgments and thus ends the book, one could read this
sequencing as an argument that all the prior textual distortion in the book
is a less developed stage, that the bad history and glitchy text are meant to
resolve to the full, embodied, undistorted legibility we read in the final ten
pages.

Two statements of Zolf's can be cited in support of this. The acknowl-
edgments begin: "I would like to acknowledge that I wrote this book while
living on the traditional territories of the Niitsitapi, Nakoda and Tsuu t'ina
peoples" (121). And at the end of a complex self-description in the afterword,
Zolf names what she wants as "a poesis of acknowledgement and response-
ability and honouring treaty" (117). Getting the names right would be the
beginning of an honorable response to the facts of history.

While this equation of ethical responsibility and orthographic clarity
is certainly one part of *Janey's Arcadia*, most of the book cannot be read
according to such a treaty. This is not to say that Zolf has any interest in

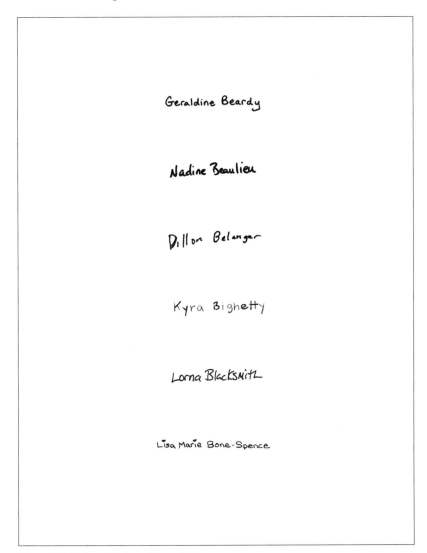

Figure 20.2. *Janey's Arcadia*, p. [45].

ethical ambiguity: visual distortion may be the norm of the book, but there is no ambiguity about the history, even as it's being typographically and syntactically distorted. Zolf uses irony constantly, but she never ironizes the awfulness of the settlers' language. As Zolf presents the colonialist violence, religious cant, and sexual predation of the settlers, there is no more ethical ambiguity than there is in Dante's presentation of the sinners in Hell. When a child-molesting minister running an orphanage for Cree children is

WHO IS THIS JESUS? ■'■a PART I Here is a sweet story of a little Indign girl fired with a zeal h(
peculiar. It shows how a few lessons learned in early life about religious truth enabled her to be a great th
blessing to her stern old uncle, a great Indign hunter in the cold northland where the mirage and mocke r
suns are seen. I am sure when you have read the story you will say it is a beautiful fulfillment of the n(
prophecy uttered long ago, 'A little child shall lead them.' Astumastao was the name of our little Indign th
girl. When Gord wants a man for a peculiar work He knows where to find him. She began her statement ta
that it was in the habit of Reverend Evans to go to the place where she and another girl were sleeping, re
pull off their bedclothes from the naked limb of a desolate, thunder-riven tree that stood apart from its st
lush, green-boughed neighbours, a lonely thrush perched in seeming melancholy. It seems to be rather w
a long name, but, like all Indign names, it is very expressive. It means 'coming to the light,' or 'coming a\
dawn' and sometimes lie down to teaze and play with them. She was born in a birchbark wigwam, in I!
the wild country far north. About two years after Mr. Evans' religious quickening, her parents drowned e\
in an accident. A poor little orphan girl, her relations half starved for days planting sweet Sharon's rose a
on icy fields. 50 i| ::vi°- WHO IS THIS JESUS? 5XOne summer it happened that there visited that m
country a devoted missionary, who was travelling through those wild regions, preaching the Gospel in
among the different tribes. 'Are you not ashamed to come here?' The boat in which he journeyed was a IS
canoe made out of sheet-tin as if the lonely bird were calling for some responsive voice from far away m
over the prairie. Next she described an incident, which occurred when she went upstairs where the to
moss was kept. He had as his canoe-men two stalwart Chrispian Indigns, one of whom acted as his jo
interpreter, but the soft-eyed fawn of the desert soon showed herself in the guise of a petit beet sau^"rage. b(
He noticed the poor little Indign girl and inquired about her, but she quickly drew her hand away. ta
While the missionary tarried at this village, she said that Evans followed, caught hold of her, threw here\
down on the moss and lifted up her clothes, holding services as often as he could get a congregation. al
'How do you dare take this liberty with me, Monsieur,' she called out, her eyes kindled with anger. E\
When he learned her sad history, he asked her people to give her to him. With a startling scream, she sp
bounded away from his grasp. Evans let her go and tried to brush the moss off her back as she ran di
downstairs. And so the little '.»tjorphan child was taken to the far-away Mission home at Norway s\
House. 'I knew at that time,' she said, 'Mr. Evans tried to do bad to me.' It was a long journey of hundreds ar
of miles, so much of the romantic still lingered, and there were many rough portages to cross. When the u|
child wearied out on the way, one of the stalwart men would carry her over the roughest places of m
'Chrispianity first, then civilization.' ■l 5° WHO IS THIS JESUS?°!| m LitSome time before the outbreak, G(
another incident occurred when they gathered old hay from the dried-out beavers°:: meadows, or cut H
off balsam branches, and thus made her cosy little beds where she sweetly slept, with no roof over her fu
but the stars when Evans came again and pulled the blankets away. 'Your very sight is hateful to me.' w
For food they gave her the choicest pieces of the wild ducks or geese or beaver, which they shot on the di
way. Apparently, one time he touched her feet. When they reached Norway House, the poor little hi
orphan girl kicked him, and he covered her. She was kindly welcomed by the good wife of the devoted a\
missionary. Either that time or another, he pulled off the covers and began to wrestle with her. Mrs. er
Evans was just as anxious as her husband to do all the go • ■lod possible to the poor Indigns. The girl si|
cried, 'Go away for shame, you are foolish; you thrashed a boy for playing with us, now you come to play h(
with us.' So Astumastao was bathed and then dressed in clean new garments, which were a great re
contrast to the garb in which Mr. Evans had found her. A few weeks of treatment and food made a Tl
change in the child. Then he lay down and began to play, saying, 'When you get a man, this is the way e\
he will do to you.' The Indign Mission school at that time was under the charge of a Miss Adams. Like n(
many other noble women, she had left a happy home and many friends in civilization. She then covered b(

Figure 20.3. *Janey's Arcadia*, p. [74].

adulated with the refrain "WHO IS THIS JESUS?" (74–77), we are meant
to feel disgust at each repetition. Figure 20.3 shows a reproduction of one
the pages from that section (the words stretch from page edge to the book's
gutter). I'm not sure how this was produced, but it cannot have simply been
scanned via OCR. Consider this sequence from the center of the page: "He
had as his canoe-men two stalwart Chrispian Indigns, one of whom acted as
his interpreter, but the soft-eyed fawn of the desert soon showed herself in the

guise of a petit beet sau^'"rage"—clearly this is not a distortion of a single original passage. Perhaps *sau^'"rage* is "pure" OCR, but the soft-eyed fawn of the desert as a sausage must come from Zolf: the juxtaposition of fawn as sentimental-erotic and deer as sausage meat is typical of her sardonic critique of the settlers' high-minded predatory practices.

While the book can be divided into poems and documents, this distinction is iffy. Some pages, like the "Who Is This Jesus?" passage and the 1886 testimonials I've just cited, are clearly documentary in origin; other pages present themselves as lineated dramatic monologues, that is, as poems: "Janey's Invocation," "Janey Settler's Pastoral Oasis," "Janey's Hospitality." But any division into poem and document is not easy to maintain: almost every poem seems pretty clearly made up of scraps of documentary language with Zolf's own bitingly sarcastic additions mixed in; and the documents, besides being compromised by the OCR, constantly show Zolf's parodic touches. In other words, the poetic and the documentary are more or less blended together.

Recognition remains an open question, both in detail and in gestalt: Is this page documentary or poem? Who is the source of these words? What word was this originally? What is it saying now? Is it saying anything or are we reading the chance debris from a poorly functioning piece of software? Is this an OCR glitch, or is Zolf mimicking OCR glitches for her own quite intentional purposes?

Such OCR mimicry is ubiquitous. *Indigns* may have originated as a mechanical glitch, but Zolf uses it consistently as part of her own vocabulary: the word *Indians* never appears. Similarly, almost every word denoting power or religion is altered: *Sovereign* becomes *$overeign*; *Christ* is always *Chrisp*—when Zolf makes a sly reference to two fellow poets, David Buuck and Christian Bök, she calls attention to the distortion: "Chrispian Buuck [*sic*]" (31)—by inserting "[*sic*]."

In the following poem, in addition to the by-now-familiar *Chrisp* and *Indign*, note the consistent wordplay around the absent word *God*:

> The monotonous iteration of the tom-toms
> is maddening. If the gads were listening
> they would strike these young men dead;
> but if there is Goad, Gord is disjunction
> and madness leaving the young men
> of the tribes like vibrating nuts. No emotion
> possible is dark mist Gourd blotted out: Your
> hateful sweetness I'm clinging to. 'Nearer,
> clearer, deadlier than before.' Lo! out of
> the west came what seemed like a dim shadow
> moving across the plain. Temperamental
> and raging like all the Arabs folding their tents
> like all the Indigns stealing silently away. Turn

my eyes insane while being corrupts itself
AS A POOL OF SHAME. Poetry! fc^tO thtre'5
Poetry! Take me away through the farthest
races through the farthest waves to where no
men reek hot breath all over my body. I'll do
anything, anything but yumped up Jesus Chrisp! (58)

The continual difference of *gads, Goad, Gord, Gourd* can be taken as one element of a jacobin poetics: Gord (not God) is disjunction.

I detect a number of distinct compositional elements here: (1) straightforward documentary ("The monotonous iteration of the tom-toms / is maddening"); (2) "genuine" OCR distortion ("Poetry! fc^tO thtre'5 / Poetry!"), although it is deployed jokingly by being inserted amid the twin apostrophe to Poetry; (3) OCR mimicry; and in the last line, (4) what Zolf refers in her afterword as the "Red River Twang" (117). Before getting to this last item, I want to turn to the second half of Zolf's discussion of her use of OCR distortion. I will link her description to the end of my earlier quotation:

> OCR is also notoriously prone to noisy glitches of 'errors of recognition' of seemingly unreadable text. These accidents can, perhaps (in Derrida's torqued messianic sense of *peut-être*), conjure other forms of mis- and non- and dis- and un-recognition—and hauntological error. This errancy can, perhaps, enact a process of thinking past (or through) the retinal struggle for recognition to a kind of disfluent listening (an attempt that is also a waiting and conjoining) and always-already-complicit, glitched, queered witnessing. (117)

Zolf extends this evocation of errant, queer, disfluent witnessing to include William Carlos Williams's iconic figure of impure, immigrant mixture, Elsie. "To Elsie" begins, "The pure products of America / go crazy" and ends "No one to witness and adjust, / no one / to drive the car"; Zolf's version of this is as follows:

> As the impure products of not-post-colonial 'North America' go crazy, 'Noone / bears witness for the / witness': Noone drives the spewing car without licence. Yes and no ec-statically unsplit, singular-plural in the perverted body of the noem, there are appropriations and re-appropriations and other improper ways of making Noone('s) own (up); a poesis of acknowledgement and response-ability and honouring treaty (117).

Here, "honouring treaty," the phrase I quoted earlier in support of correct naming, must be taken in a very different way. Treaty is based on not accuracy but acknowledgment of difference. Identity here is opened up in improper ways—instead of a poem, we have a queer poem, a no-poem, a "noem."

Janey, our book's eponymous hero, is also subject to improper identity. The historical figure consistently invoked (and I believe, quoted via distortion) throughout the book is "Janey Canuck," the pen name of Emily Murphy. Zolf recounts that Murphy, a "first-wave feminist (not to mention eugenicist), who successfully fought for certain women to be deemed 'persons,' also wrote under the pen name of the plucky white-supremacist settler, Janey Canuck" (117). The online *Canadian Encyclopedia* tells us that Murphy was a judge in Alberta whose "public support of eugenic policies likely contributed to the passage of Alberta's Sexual Sterilization Act in 1928."[3]

Janey Canuck is thus a deeply problematic character, but Zolf (improperly) combines her with Kathy Acker's Janey Smith (from *Blood and Guts in High School*). In Zolf's description, "*Janey's Arcadia* seeds a savage, fleshy rendezvous between Janey Canuck and punk pirate Kathy Acker's guerilla icon Janey Smith. What pops out skewed-wise is Janey Settler-Invader, a fracked-up, mutant (cyborg?) squatter progeny, slouching toward the Red River Colony" (117). Certainly, Acker's anarchic sexuality is an inspiration for such passages as the following:

> No Indign ever became a priest. Should I tell
> your fortune? Who saw you cry? Not even
> a priest gave a shit about my funeral.
> It may be that celibacy yokes heavy. Turn
> the eyes as if some hope f■cked me in the
> as•s, but that's only in my memory. And it doesn't
> help this aching c□nt. The sturdy 'tiger blossoms,'
> and passionate prairie roses blew two fair cold lilies
> along the flower-rimmed path. (59)

To turn to the fourth element I mentioned some pages back, the Red River Twang, this is both a casualty of history—a dead language—and a model for the glitchy, improper recognition and acknowledgment that Zolf is modeling. She describes it as follows:

> The Red River Twang (also known as Bungee) was the dialect (now 'dead') used primarily by English speakers in the Red River Colony. . . . [It] was a 'polyglot jabber' of Scots English and Cree, with vestiges of Gaelic and French. . . . 'A man whose language is English, and one who speaks French alone, are enabled to render themselves mutually intelligible by means of Cree, their Indian mother tongue, though each is totally ignorant of the . . . language ordinarily used by the other.' (117–18)

As an example of Zolf's version of Red River Twang, here is the last stanza
of "Janey's Dead":

> He's a widow-woman too. Or is it we
> in the flesh who are dead? We who
> weep. We who sin and talk like a Bungee.
> Times is changed, my girl. I'm not got a hand
> like my father, Chistikat. Is it we who are hopeless?
> I just never had enough examples. Janey took
> a big swig of the lamp oil (and din't I see Lucy
> and Dora), gave the shtring a haird pull, and
> that's about the size of all what happened
> around here, my girl. I clean forgot Janey
> becomes a woman. (99)

Such a comic language—"utopic" in the original, etymological sense of
nowhere (u-topos)—can only exist in antifoundational linguistic circum-
stances. As a physical, commercial enterprise, *Janey's Arcadia* participates
in such circumstances, as we can see by reading the copyright page. First we
have the precise language and typography of an institution that is commer-
cially viable, even prestigious (in small-scale poetry terms, of course):

> *Janey's Arcadia* is available as an ebook: ISBN 978 1 77056 393 3
>
> Purchase of the print version of this book entitles you to a free digital
> copy. To claim your ebook . . . please email sales@chbooks.com with
> proof of purchase

But the next paragraph reads:

> Tha institute has attamptad to obtain thabast originai copy avaiiabia
> for fiiming. Faatuas of this copy which may Im bibiiographicaiiy uni-
> qua, which may aitar any of tha imagas in tha reproduction, or which
> may significantly change tha usual method of fiiming. Pages wholly
> or partially obscured by errata slips, tissues, etc. have been ral^iimed
> to ensure the besr possible image/

It's one thing to disrupt the colophon of the *Canada West* pamphlet, but this
distortion undoes the authoritativeness of the place from which distortion
can be defined as such. There will be no ground where the reader can say, the
distortion stops here. The comedy of legibility can be performed on any and
all physical platforms.

It's hard to sum up such a passionately political and energetically self-
differentiating book as *Janey's Arcadia*. In its polemical, ethically engaged

use of documentary materials, it's slightly like Rukeyser's *U.S. One*, Charles Olson's *Maximus Poems*, or Pound's *Cantos*, but its insistence on a deformed, anarchic surface makes it quite different. Its gleeful presentation of chaos, error, and crudeness is a bit akin to Flarf; its programmatic, defamiliarizing use of technology is somewhat akin to conceptualism. But none of these comparisons work well. Zolf is asking us to attend minutely to traces of a history that continues to impinge on our present, and via Zolf's manic, inventive distortions, we are asked to imagine that history as superseded—or, better, we are being asked not to recognize it (in the diplomatic sense of the word). We are reading a parodic unsaying of a bad history and, simultaneously, the creole of an emergent future.

Notes

1. A reproduction of the original cover can be found at http://www.history museum.ca/cmc/exhibitions/hist/advertis/images/ads7-16b.jpg.

2. Ronald Johnson's *Radi os* (made from letters quarried out of *Paradise Lost*) is one example of this technique.

3. Susan Jackel, "Emily Murphy," *Historica Canada*, 2008, http://www.the canadianencyclopedia.ca/en/article/emily-murphy/.

LISA ROBERTSON

from *R's Boat*

I'm really this classical man.
I withdrew from all want and all knowledge.
In the strange shops and streets I produce this sign of spoken equilibrium.
I write this ornament, yet I had not thought of rhyme.
This is emotional truth.
I'm crying love me more.
Its landscapes are cemeteries.
I'm just a beam of light or something.
I only know one thing: I, who allots her fickle rights.
I'm using the words of humans to say what I want to know.

Chapter 21

✦

Robertson's Research

Lytle Shaw

Criticism, perhaps, should be an act of boat stealing, in which truly to give restitution to the other we must first commandeer the artifact of the other and row away toward as sharply defined a spur of difference as possible.

—Alan Liu, *Wordsworth: The Sense of History*

What, exactly, has Lisa Robertson wanted to know, and how has her brand of boat stealing benefited from the strategies and targets staked out by historicist critics like Liu? At one level, the Canadian poet has asked what happens when women hijack literary history's largest cruise liners and yachts or make, as she puts it, "tactical intervention in the official genres"—eclogue, georgic, and epic.[1] "For if Virgil has taught me anything," Robertson proposes in *Debbie: An Epic,* "it's that authority is just a rhetoric or style which has asserted the phantom permanency of a context."[2] But as this statement suggests, what she seeks to know is not just what it feels like to captain the biggest vessels of literary history, channeling or destabilizing their authority. Rather, Robertson wants to understand more about the slippery relationship between that authority and its enabling contexts—between the broad-scale assertion of genre and the granular push of lush phrases that resist its organizational effects; between the stabilizing forces of literary history and the centrifugal pull of a world of pure and endless surface. This further goal has led the poet, over the last two decades, not so much beyond the metageneric concerns of her early books as farther inside them, to the point where, in her work as the Office for Soft Architecture, in *Nilling,* and in *Cinema of the Present,* a series of terms have emerged, a consistent vocabulary of inquiry: surface and description above all.

Like her outmoded and maligned high genres, these terms too had had a rough life in the world of recent poetics prior to her taking them in and cleaning them up. In fact it seems in part the stability of received opinion about the problems of both that caused them to sparkle dangerously from a distance. Nor was Robertson simply accepting surface and description in their bad old ways. Rather, she was gradually building for them a rhetorical and stylistic context for new meaning and new authority, constructing the "spur of difference" Liu recommends in his boat-stealing instructions. To do this, she turned to the terms' histories. And yet here Robertson did not so much dutifully document as polemically redescribe description and surface. Thus from the start description is not simply a term to be recuperated through a series of historical precedents but also a way of performing that recuperation itself.[3] Similarly, surface is not merely a constellation of values associated with edges rather than centers or cores. It is a vehicle for resisting the rhetoric of depth and the dismissal of ornament, and for cultivating the affective possibilities opened up by a kind of ongoing ethnographic contact with shifting environments. When Robertson writes elsewhere, "Your concept remained surface but you didn't yet know why," the suggestion, read across the ongoing inquiry of her work, is that this knowing will take some time, will take prolonged quasi-ethnographic contact with the world's shifting skin conditions.[4] Indeed the ongoing open work of describing surface has led Robertson from the rapidly shifting architectural envelopes of boom-era Vancouver in the late 1990s to a more recent study of nested noise pockets within Paris, from physical to sonic urbanism. As a describer of surfaces, Robertson has also become something of a historian, an experimental researcher operating in a wide variety of contexts. How, then, does her historical research relate to the larger historicist turn recommended by boat stealers like Liu since roughly the 1980s?

Let us take, as an exemplary case of critical transformation brought about by thinking historically, the neat figure/ground reversal of the vaunted interiority previously associated with Wordsworth. Reframed by critics like Liu, Marjorie Levinson, and Clifford Siskin, what might once have seemed the autonomous Wordsworthian interior was demonstrated not just as a development in history (or even as an active repression of history) but as an exemplary form of labor, that of self-representation, central to the emergence of professionalization, disciplinarity, and the discursive transformations that underlie them. Propelled by the underrecognized georgic dimensions of Wordsworth's project, the poet became representative because, as Siskin puts it, "the professional work of knowing . . . became, during the eighteenth century, the newly heroic work."[5] To have shown the singularities of Wordsworthian depth as a new form of normative surface and to have sketched the social roles that surface came to play in late eighteenth- and early nineteenth-century England—these were not just workaday recontextualizations. When the loneliest of wandering clouds has been shown to blow and billow strictly to state-authorized weather patterns, this is something of a bravura critical performance. As Robertson nearly agrees in *R's Boat*, "The quiet revolutions of loneliness are a politics" (52).

And yet, after almost three decades in a historicist climate, we might now be sufficiently alerted to the inescapably social dimensions of subjectivity to wonder at another, less remarked element of this story: whether it's self-evident that a poetics of research will operate as a handmaiden to repressive power, whether "knowledge" made by poets will always function within its historical moment as that Foucaldian agent of hypostasis that inscribes subjects within discourses, turning previously inchoate practices into mea-sureable, controllable elements in the system it makes. Robertson's practice opens up other roles for a poetics of research. And in doing so it points to limitations not only within still influential models of historicism but equally, though perhaps more strangely, within the dominant interpretive paradigms of avant-garde poetics.[6] This latter point is strange inasmuch as shifting modes of experimental knowledge production could be the narrative logic of any number of critical histories of poetry from Wordsworth to the present. Stops along the way might consider modernists like William Carlos Williams, new American poets such as Charles Olson, rogue historiographers who emerged in the 1970s like Susan Howe, as well as those whose first books appeared in the 1990s, like Robertson herself. Why then has this poetics of research not been a prominent way of understanding North American poetry?

One answer has to do with the emergence of Language writing not merely as avant-garde practice but equally as a discourse of poetics—initially as an outlier in relation to what Charles Bernstein calls "official verse culture," but gradually as the dominant account of contemporary poetics, and even, to an extent, as the frame in which the larger history of twentieth-century poetry has been recast critically. The pluses for poetics were many and have been well documented. In this context, though, I want to address one possible minus, which stems from the otherwise productive orientation of the Lan-guage writers toward conceptualizing poetry as a form of ideology critique. Such critique, for many of the Language writers, functions only so long as language's raw materials can be recombined at a scale below that of genre or discourse. Bruce Andrews, for instance, puts this stance programmatically when he claims that he does not want to "*just* deal with discourse," to, as he puts it, "ironically, appropriatively, assemble existing social materials and bring them together in interesting, clashing ways and do appropriation art, do that genre of work."[7] He explains that it's because of his commitment to the "more foundational level of the functioning of language at the sign level" that he remains distrustful of "any larger building up of representational genre activity on top of the structure of the sign" (98).[8] To engage discourse is to abandon the social dimension of the sign and fall into the familiar trap of genre, which seems to convey an a priori stable irony.

If Andrews's commitment to the micro-linguistics of disjunction operates as one pole within the poetics of Language writing, then the related cultural poetics and cultivation of inquiry associated with Barrett Watten and Lyn Hejinian, respectively, might be seen, despite their differences, as roughly providing an opposite pole.[9] Even within Watten's and Hejinian's work, however, there is a characteristic distrust of genre and a commitment to the line and sentence not so much as the primary unit of meaning making (both insist on semantic architectures that extend to the poem or book as a whole) but as a recalcitrant language event that will not be seamlessly subsumed to the higher level of genre. Seen at the level of the line, Robertson's work as well often employs a degree of disjunction that attenuates any easy isomorphism between microlinguistic event and macroconceptual or generic frame. After a line in *Debbie: An Epic*, for instance, about the forest's "archival plentitude and entanglement," Robertson continues: "The clerical earth just exudes itself. / —and the carved ruckus of milky bark / spells a long diary of placation / repeating ad infinitum we want / to love. We want to love. / Or the heart's cheap / diphthong snaps" (n.p.). It's not that one can find *no* relations between lines like these and the generic frame of epic, but rather that a reader's felt need to pursue such relations depends largely on the performative *assertion* of epic as frame. Given this assertion, the path is still tricky, even for the "rhetors" addressed as the first word of the poem's first line. This is a feature of Robertson's work that has not been sufficiently noticed by those critics who have largely taken her statements of poetics as the truth of her books, glossing over the recalcitrant particulars of her lines and sentences to turn them into clean illustrations of the concepts sketched in her forewords and liner notes.[10]

Even in the comparatively rare moments that *Debbie* makes programmatic, legible contact with the contours of epic, it swerves unpredictably:

> FATHER'S REAL SOUL OWES OBLIVION
> to himself so slips into that long lake
> and goes. Good-bye Father. I Debbie speak
> —as evening's lily-drunk and belling and
> roman as the fields singed by white boots
> rivers rocking and confluent where my
> navy rides at anchor as will loosens
> the glorious girls from middling forest
> from choked sex and fallen torso—I
> design sublime climates for them. (np)

Epic dad dies; Debbie grabs the mike; there's a navy waiting, perhaps a little S&M in the trees. But at the very moment she might issue a clear anti-epic statement to the troops, Debbie instead becomes "evening's lily-drunk and belling" designing "sublime climates" and getting her boot fetish on. If we're seeing here a shift from old-fashioned critique to internal destabilization of a genre, how exactly do we establish our position as inside the genre?

How, in other words, might one more accurately characterize the strange status of genre within Robertson's simultaneously disjunctive and historicist poetics? We might note, to begin with, that this tension is most pronounced in the early works—*The Apothecary* (1991), *XEclogue* (1993), and *Debbie: An Epic* (1997)—where, first, Robertson's commitment to disjunction is greatest, and second, unlike Watten or Hejinian, she insists nonetheless that the works' operative frames are in fact genres (with their histories) and not newly engineered structuring devices like we find in many works of the Language writers.[11] But this is not merely a matter of an imaginary allegory of genre undone by a residual commitment to disjunction; it is instead the basis of an untimely poetics that appeals to the obsolescent both at this level of genre and at that of terms like surface and description. The result is a new kind of collision: if genre cannot, in Robertson's hands, perform its work of containing and normalizing unruly linguistic invention, it can operate nonetheless as a continually evoked frame, a datum of historical precedents and intertexts.[12] The research that gets done in these works (on the social function of genre, on the literary dimension of nationalism, on the relation between gender and authority) depends at once on the assertion and immanent critique of these generic frames. Robertson's reader, in other words, must think in this gap between the evocation of genre as container and the simultaneous unfolding of uncontained linguistic effects.

One might thus be tempted to call genre a *rhetoric* in Robertson's work, and in a sense this would be true—certainly it is a contestable claim, a counterintuitive assertion, in the context of the granular, word-to-word texture of her poems. "*For you, rhetoric and erotics are irreparably aligned and give support to a needed life.*" (CP, 25) The problem here, however, is that rhetoric, for Robertson, does not take on its traditional (or at least Platonic) dualistic status, the claim as opposed to the fact. Genre is a rhetoric, for Robertson, not because *Debbie* is not really an epic; rather, *Debbie* evokes and exceeds the frame of epic, but benefits, or simply takes on part of its meaning, from having that frame in place, from having that frame asserted, rhetorically. Similarly, when Robertson writes in *Occasional Work and Seven Walks from the Office for Soft Architecture* (2003), for instance, that, after being introduced into California, the "Himalayan blackberry escaped," and then "maximized distribution through the temperate mesophytic forest . . . up the Northwest coast as far as southwestern British Columbia," description is at once factual and rhetorical.[13] The berry's insistence on making "new hybrid architectures, weighing the ridgepoles of previously sturdy home garages and sheds into swaybacked grottoes, transforming chain link and barbed wire to undulant green fruiting walls, and sculpting from abandoned cement pilings Wordworthian abbeys" (ibid.)—this romantic building-breaking spree is, in Robertson's frame, not just push-back against the plant's initial, ornamental and orientalist, frame; it's also selected as a kind of anti-architecture that the project as a whole poses against the slick transformation of Vancouver in the image of capital.

Description emerged for Robertson most centrally and programmatically in *Soft Architecture*, a book she taxonomizes as essays, but which could easily he read as an extension of her poetry. "The truly utopian act," she there proposes, "is to manifest current conditions and dialects" (20). How to do this? "Practice description." What then to describe? The answer, to repeat, is the surface of the world, pursing that involves a potentially infinite "horizontal research" (ibid.), which, in *Soft Architecture,* puts her in contact with textiles, huts, picnic sites, pavilions, invasive bushes, scaffolding, parks, hypothetical fountains, thrift store clothing, and the antique wood and cushion textures of Eugène Atget's interiors as made available by his photographs. Obviously there is a level of replicability or iterability in these categories.[14] They are not unique to, or exhausted within, Vancouver. What is exemplary about them for Robertson is not that they fix a specific spatiotemporal position, but that they indicate a collection of methods in relation to a claimed site. An urbanism of Vancouver is, in a weird way, their "genre." In claiming this, Robertson again explores, as in her early work's evocation of historical literary genres, the gap between such frames and the particulars they would subsume or explain.

Robertson's methods shifted, then, when she moved to France and began working in relation to the French capital, with its infinitely sedimented history of interpretation. "But Paris is an immense ocean," Balzac's narrator taunts in *Père Goriot*: "Drop in your sounding line and it will never reach the bottom. . . . Have a look, try describing it! No matter how carefully you try to see and understand everything, to describe everything . . . there'll always be places you never get to, caverns you never uncover, blossoms, pearls, monsters, quite incredible things that every literary diver overlooks."[15]

Robertson's first proposition was to stop looking altogether and start listening. Operating as an experimental ethnographer of sound, Robertson brought her recording apparatus to a collection of Atget's unremarkable sites and "exposed" them, opening a technical orifice (now an ear rather than an eye) for the same duration, thirty seconds, Atget used in his photographs. Since ears can't shut, the photographer's exposure time and shutter mechanism allow Robertson to excerpt a small enough section of ambient sound that it can be experienced as an object, not a bottomless archive. "Disquiet," a piece in her book *Nilling,* frames this activity not just in relation to Atget but also in the wider context of sound studies. Like *Soft Architecture*, "Disquiet" gets officially classed as an essay, but this assertion of genre, like the others we've considered so far, operates again more as a datum or frame than as a container, since "Disquiet," which includes the URLs for the actual recordings (posted on the publisher's website), is arguably as close to Robertson's poetry as it is to the genre of the essay. In "transport," the second recording, for instance, we hear some kind of funk/soul song on a radio organizing the sonic space for most of the duration, overlaid by birds, irregular clanks of steel (a stand or scaffolding coming up, going down?), intermittent muffled voices, and a quiet background roar, perhaps a nearby thoroughfare. In what sense do we know a location through such a recording?

In "Disquiet" Robertson suggests that the project offers "some plots of noise as the inconspicuous descriptions of a civic thinking," a formulation that might operate as a microcosm of Robertson's research.[16] One sense of plot has to do with the way that, as with *Soft Architecture*, Robertson invents a commission for herself that identifies objects of inquiry and experimental methods: a methodological narrative or conceptual frame. This is also, in the case of "Disquiet," an itinerary for experimental ethnographic fieldwork: it organizes for Robertson a sequence of Atget's sites, where, via sound, she less summarizes than makes contact with them, mobilizing the intense contingency of their sonic landscapes, their noise: "Duration's artifacts are indiscriminate." Noise does, in this sense, need a narrative structure or conceptual frame—a plot that brings us into relation with it.

But in addition to this larger conceptual plotting, noise also requires plotting in at least two other senses—one temporal, one categorical. First, for Robertson's project to work, we need to have a manageable duration of noise: noise of a short enough length that we pay attention to it, that we can understand it as a discrete event—an invitation to a certain kind of listening—and not as the infinite condition it operates as otherwise. This temporal plotting, achieved by the thirty-second recordings, depends, however, on an underlying categorical plotting or separating. As avant-garde musicians have told us for a century, noise is less a self-evident sonic category than one produced through differentiation with "meaningful" sound. To experience noise semantically, we must resituate or replot it.

This is the edge of Robertson's research, the domain where her isolation of objects also bleeds back into the world: "Noise is the non-knowledge of meaning, the by-product of economies" (*Nilling*, 57). And yet this unknowable semantic excess is, in Robertson's paradoxical framing of it, not merely the domain of linguistic play familiar to poetry, but the object of a poetics of field research that increasingly parts ways with traditions of disjunction. Because noise is "the multiply layered sonic indeterminacy that is the average, fluctuating milieu of dailiness" (*Nilling*, 57), the present is always an instance of disquiet. This lends a certain inescapable sonic texture to duration, though this texture of course changes depending on sites and situations. Since it is an ongoing condition rather than a discrete event, this duration dips below the threshold of sensibility. Hence the appeal of framing noise: "Noise gives the listener duration as an artifact" (ibid.). Plotted noise offers discrete amounts of indiscriminate sound—the present not imposed but experienced. "There must be several distinct kinds of ephemerality, you decide" (*CP*, 27), Robertson writes elsewhere. "By means of description, a whole profound mass of time became your milieu" (*CP*, 21).

One might speculate that the urgency to claim, through poetic research, an experience of duration now emerges, after the problem of charting the physical transformation of a city like Vancouver, because the struggles that then seemed to play themselves out on the surfaces of buildings now are less locatable in any single physical location. They seem, rather, to be associated with the administration of time. Provocatively untimely, Robertson's early work turned to a vertical axis of literary history that, organized by the rhetorical assertion of genre, opened up the social functions of literary language. In her more recent work on cities, time is less associated with genres or discourses that might frame objects of inquiry; rather, time has increasingly become itself the object of research. Though operating in Paris, Robertson here intervenes in the broadest and seemingly least locatable of problems: the gradual speeding up of daily life: "About the time question in money culture: you perceive an exhausted narrative hardening into currency" (*CP*, 10).

Notes

1. See for instance, *XEcologue* (Vancover: New Star, 1993).

2. Lisa Robertson, *Debbie: An Epic* (Vancouver: New Star, 2009 [1997]), n.p.

3. The critique of description includes Robert Creeley's 1953 statement, "To Define," in which he claims that "a poetry denies its end in any *descriptive* act, I mean any act which leaves the attention outside the poem" (reprinted in *A Quick Graph: Collected Notes and Essays* [San Francisco: Four Seasons, 1970], 23). Citing these lines in his essay "Of Theory, to Practice," Ron Silliman proposes that Clark Coolidge's early poetry "carries this to a logical conclusion" (*The New Sentence* [New York: Roof, 1987], 58). I consider this in *Fieldworks: From Place to Site in Postwar Poetics* (Tuscaloosa: University of Alabama Press, 2013).

4. Lisa Robertson, *Cinema of the Present* (Toronto: Coach House, 2014), 11; future citations parenthetically marked by *CP*.

5. Clifford Siskin, *The Work of Writing: Literature and Social Change in Britain, 1700–1830* (Baltimore, Md.: Johns Hopkins University Press, 1998), 125.

6. Nor have critics pursued the methodological and chronological parallels that link the emergence of New Historicism to the development of poets' collage historicism in North American poetry. Twentieth-century poetry has been seen by New Historicists rather as a quarry of particulars or as a domain of expressivity. And so the movement's more intimate relationship to the history of poetics has been overlooked or even repressed.

7. Bruce Andrews, *Paradise and Method: Poetics and Praxis* (Evanston, Ill.: Northwestern University Press, 1996), 106. He is, rather, "still interested in the basic foundational structure of meaning, in its material form in the sign," trying "to retain the interest in sound and sight and materiality at the level of the letter, syllable, paragraph, syntactical micro-unit" (106–7).

8. These statements of Andrews's in fact come from an interview at the Kootenay School of Writing in Vancouver, conducted, not coincidentally, by poets Kevin Davies and Jeff Derksen. Both Davies and Derksen could be thought to complicate and extend Andrews's paradigm for poetics by their new ways of

framing the sort of sign landscape of linguistic raw material in which Andrews labors. For both Davies and Derksen, in slightly different ways, what is of interest is the threshold at which administered social and political positions touch down in individual speaking subjects. Attention settles neither at a macro level of political structure nor at a micro scale of subjective experience. Both work at the threshold of the impersonal, considering the relationship between utterance and frame, between speech acts and the institutions and conventions that give them social meaning. Both, too, are extremely funny and inventive writers. Robertson also emerged from the Kootenay School, whose history has yet to be sufficiently written.

9. Such a stance is operative, I'd argue, even in Watten's first critical book, *Total Syntax* (1985), and certainly in works like *Bad History* (1998) and *The Constructivist Moment* (2003). The title of Lyn Hejinian's *The Language of Inquiry* (2000) aptly characterizes the project of many of her books—most famously *My Life* (1980, revised and expanded twice), but equally such later works as *A Border Comedy* (2001), *Slowly,* and *The Beginner* (both 2002), among others.

10. Such has been the problem for most poets who have offered powerful conceptualizations of their practices—from Wordsworth, through Olson and the Language writers, to Robertson: the first reception phase almost invariably involves using the poems as illustrations of the poetics statements. The core of the criticism on Robertson has happened in two special issues of journals devoted to her: an issue of *Open Letter* (14, no. 5, 2011) and an issue of *Chicago Review* in 2006. Michael Davidson has a good passage on Robertson in *On the Outskirts of Form: Practicing Cultural Poetics* (Middletown, Conn.: Wesleyan University Press, 2011), and I have part of a chapter on her in *Fieldworks: From Place to Site in Postwar Poetics* (Tuscaloosa: University of Alabama Press, 2013), as well as an introduction in *Nineteen Lines: A Drawing Center Writing Anthology* (New York: Roof/The Drawing Center, 2007).

11. Silliman's use of the Fibonacci sequence in *Tjanting* (1981) is perhaps the most famous example, but Hejinian's attempt to correlate the number of sentences in *My Life* (1980) with the number of years she had lived at the time of each writing could equally serve as an example, as could her organization of the first letter of different first lines at different points across the left-right spectrum of the page in *Writing Is an Aid to Memory* (1978).

12. To an extent this is always how genre operates. Which is to say that most books worth reading can be understood as complicating the historically shifting generic frames they evoke. So Robertson's example presents perhaps a difference in degree but not in kind. Still, Robertson's example is illuminating in part because genre operates less as a legible frame that gets deformed than as a performatively asserted one that at moments seems not to contain the linguistic effects it proposes to corral.

13. Lisa Robertson, *Occasional Work and Seven Walks from the Office for Soft Architecture* (Astoria, Ore.: Clear Cut, 2003), 109.

14. Though Robertson frames this work in relation to Vancouver, she also acknowledges that there are necessary limits to and complications of its site specificity: "The critique and perception I can bring to Vancouver, as a site, comes by way of Toronto, Quebec, Alberta, Nova Scotia, Cambridge, Paris, Oakland . . .

more interestingly from the complex subjectivity coded via my body, my friends' bodies, through family, emigrations, national politics, friendships, all the books I've ever read, buildings we've walked through and absorbed in some measure, all the media consumed. Maybe this is simply to say that aesthetic experience is political, collective and social experience. Same for practice. The political history of the body and its delimitations, suppressions, and joys opens up the scale of the city. *Soft Architecture* has to do with the overlay of site specificity with feminism and philosophy, as felt and distributed by and through the body" (*Printed Project 14: The Conceptual North Pole*, ed. Lytle Shaw [Dublin: Visual Arts Ireland, 2010], 99).

15. Honoré de Balzac, *Père Goriot,* trans. Burton Raffel, ed. Peter Brooks (New York: Norton, 1994), 13.

16. Lisa Robertson, *Nilling: Prose Essays on Noise, Pornography, the Codex, Melancholy, Lucretius, Folds, Cities and Related Aporias* (Toronto: Book Thug, 2012), 69.

KEVIN DAVIES

from "Lateral Argument"

Lateral Argument

"Persons exist
as practical ways of speaking about

bundles."
                – Paul Williams.
They awoke in a bookless world studded with lean-
to performance artists interacting with electricity.
This must be the place. Evicted from elsewhere, here at last
not rest but an apprenticeship in container
technology. A kind of music that, though apparently stopping,
starting, stopping, more specifically never ends, thus
displaying as virtue its greatest flaw. Successfully,
irritatingly. *Who here has access to liquor?* The youth
of this centreless void gave voice to the sensual trepidations of
the nearby chopping block. This transparency at once
a local pride and a fulcrum of alertness. Yes. They
then proceeded lengthwise down the post-racial boulevard,
exhausted but coy, their travel plans successfully forgotten.
Perhaps they would stay awhile. But

no ... What's that humming sound?
                        Hello
The so-called outside
                    Strangers
                Buckets
            The newfangled windowpanes across

the street, emptied into deltas of greeting.

Chapter 22

"Distributed via whatever":
Locating Form in Kevin Davies's "Lateral Argument"

Geoffrey G. O'Brien

"Lateral Argument" began its passage through publications in 2002, appearing on the Internet at the *Alterran Poetry Assemblage*. One scrolled smoothly, mesmerically down the unsegmented white space of the endlessly accommodating page, encountering at the rate of reading capacity the poem's consistently inconsistent fits and starts of stanza. That is, "Lateral Argument" is a poem that at first may appear to have no global form; it roves across classical and nonce possibilities of stanza as well as through an array of indentation schemes.[1] Eventually, though, one could notice that two rules continually bind all the bundled variety: every stanza terminates without concluding its last sentence (except the last) and every stanza's first line terminally punctuates the sentence enjambed to it over the break (except the very first). More succinctly, all stanzas save the first and last are open at their close, closed in their openings.

That second rule's exception is at best half true. One look at the poem's beginning is enough to understand that it will be difficult to say where and how the poem's first stanza actually begins. Its one-sentence epigraph from Paul Williams's *Buddhist Thought* has been segmented in various ways; it appears as three lines of verse with an internal stanza break, and its author attribution has been set vertically flush with the conventional start of the poem, with none of the typographical space conventionally used to dignify and separate a poem and its apparatus. This arbitrary reflowing and segmentation of Williams's sentence is typical of LA's behavior—it's eventually easy to see what it's doing and initially difficult to say why.

One answer might be that the poem's epigraph inaugurates its global thought about what "persons" are, what "practical" or impractical "ways of speaking" are available (and what the difference, if any, is), and what we might think "about // bundles," especially those made of, or offering, "speaking." We could also say that the poem's very action upon its own epigraph initiates and enacts the rebundling of a sentence into lines, lines into stanzas, and stanzas that keep sending their last sentence across a break. In other words, the poem's epigraph is not only a guide to some of the poem's concerns but a key to the verse form those concerns will take. In making a historian's prose-as-epigraph into stanzaed verse, Davies gives us the poem's first instance of a non-end-stopped stanza whose syntax will pull up short in the next: "about // bundles."

Lateral Argument's second appearance was in the usual three dimensions, as a stand-alone unpaginated chapbook.[2] It thus moved forward in time across its publication history while moving backward, laterally, across the history of print, from the Internet to the book, here in the modest form of a stapled chapbook. Davies bundled its third appearance into the middle of his most recent volume, *The Golden Age of Paraphernalia*.[3] The first two poems of that collection—"Floater" and "Remnants of Wilma"—appear indiscretely, sometimes mixed together on a page with a ● or a |[4] to indicate which of the two poems is occurring, or interleaved as consecutive pages, themselves often interrupted by pages of the third poem, "One-Eyed Seller of Garlic," which differentiates itself from the first two by its section numerals and by being always "alone" on a page. Much like the rearticulation of LA's epigraph and its spatial relation to the poem, this blending and interleaving of discrete poems produces an initial difficulty of reading (if reading's goal is an encounter with a discrete poem sequentially presented) combined with an easiness of passage, a reduced responsibility to scale, across moments of text whose implied wholes we cannot apprehend. One could reproduce the conventional experience of a poem, but it would involve an absurd amount of flipping forward and back and ignoring intervening material. It would, in short, be physically and mnemonically difficult to read what is typically formally easy, yet it is physically and mnemonically easy here to read what is considered formally difficult, a running concurrence of texts. The reading is hard until we exchange reading itself, as a practice, for something more like navigating web content.

Each page of *Golden Age* prior to LA thus forces us to use one sense of laterality, one form of argument (moving backward as well as forward), if we want to recover a single poem from enmeshment, while also proposing another laterality mimetic of hyperlinked Internet reading and viewing that we can instead pursue, though necessarily outside the bound of the category "poem." In *Golden Age*, we don't know what we're in; we only know where we are. My argument about how to read Davies's deliberate difficulties of presentation depends on this constricted, dramatic-ironical sense of location—whether the reader is a "floater" (between pages) or one who moves through "remnants" (parts, links) with a compromised sight of some whole ("one-eyed"), that reader more nearly resembles a surfer on the Internet than a traditional parser of poems and books. At the level of both poem and book, Davies has, since early in the Internet's existence, been interested in subjecting Internet navigation and poetic composition to each other's conditions and rules of engagement. By upsetting practical conventions for bundling passages and stanzas into an integral poem and discrete poems into a book,

Davies disturbs the "feeling rules" of poetic reading, using verse form to mime digital experience.[5]

The opening gambit of *Golden Age* and the formal rule of LA are both instances of a mimesis testing how poetry might represent and imitate the reading and viewing strategies contemporary persons use to process informatic bundles. Perhaps this is why LA is exempt from the procedure and presentation to which the first three poems of *Golden Age* are subjected, instead offered as an intact poem after this combination and alternation of the first three (which will continue on the other side of LA and one other intact poem, "Duckwalking a Perimeter," and close the book). In LA, Davies will build his mimesis of web reading and an "argument" about the perils of any social optimism concerning Internet affordances via the two stunningly different senses of *lateral*—sideways and backward. Both motions will be present in the poem in several ways, organizing and estranging reading practice against typical bounds—the stanza, the sentence, the thought. The poem will accomplish this via a formal continuity that crosses formal variety (of stanza scheme and indentation), hides in plain sight, and links topical disjunction; it will call this method "bundling" and will always be thinking about bundling as both an ideological regulation (fascism), a poetic activity (form's composition), and a new readerly experience of the "golden age" of the Internet (its architecture's packeted "bits" and hyperlinks), while meditating on whether poetry can imagine any worthwhile differences between itself and these other two.

We can now return to LA's rearticulation of its epigraph as the key to how the poem bundles its information—not only within the stanza but across stanzas. It reprises *Golden Age*'s formal plan, which bundles poetry not within the bounds of the poem but across poems and the pages they cohabit. LA does this in the first formal space in the poem, after the title, where we expect to know how to read: within the epigraph; we expect the epigraph to be formally segregated from the body of the poem in page space and to be exempt from internal segmentation. As described above, LA's epigraph observes neither of these two conditions. Instead, it is lineated and stanzaed, and what's more, its internal stanza break optionally attaches its second part, via the "person" of "Paul Williams" to what would otherwise be the beginning of the poem's first stanza.

This confusion about where things start proves important for what defines a stanza as well: its line quantity. Is the first stanza of LA fourteen lines, and thus nominally a sonnet, if one free of its other traditional features, or does the epigraph "problem" preclude this reading? The poem begins with a dominant, familiar archival method for "bundling," but one already disturbed by its attachment to the disturbance of another method for bundling (the production of internal space in the epigraph and the refusal of separation between it and the poem). Bundling requires both attachment and separation, and both are turned against prior expectation in LA, but the new method is offered immediately, pedagogically, wordlessly. The formal continuity thus hides in plain sight, because the reader is not yet equipped with the right plain sight but sees through earlier and incommensurate habits of bundling, the epigraph and the sonnet, when instead we might be served best by seeing this opening as a segmented flow of text we scroll down—or we did in the poem's first, digital incarnation.

The poem then leads us on a tour of—no, *through*—other classical formal segmentations (stanza forms we "recognize" from their iteration in other archival settings): first a radically indented sestet, then two tercets, then three couplets, ringing changes on how to bundle and permute six lines into verse forms. Each stanza configuration is free of much of its traditional formal and conceptual closure but hosts the consistency of the poem's formal rule: the stanza will conclude without closing its syntax, and the next will begin with the end of that syntax. If the poem began in a difficulty of beginning, this is also how it continues. In moving from its initial buried sonnet to many of the subquantities proper to that form—2, 3, 6—the poem resembles the opening and formal logic of Eliot's "The Love Song of J. Alfred Prufrock," that modular meditation on the floating components of the sonnet. If LA is a Prufrock for the digital age, it is therefore also unlike Prufrock because Davies, in a different historical moment, is a very different political and spiritual animal than T. S. Eliot: "An anti-Buddhist Buddhist, plus a commie and the commie thing takes precedence."[6] LA is not primarily anxious as to affect, does not suffer from a tactically stipulated belatedness or bemoan emptied sociality, and is not full of the desire to prove its virtuosic worth atop a ruin made from both the archive's unavailable intact forms and unsuccessful social speech. Instead, LA is hilarious, its bitter pills coming in the form of pun, quip, and satire; rather than Prufrock's dis- and re-composing of traditional form in a world gone bad, the poem refuses to save poetry to an inhuman, uninhabitable sector (underwater mermaid song) and instead sportively models the "radiant connectedness" of the totality—none of it habitable yet all of where we live—whether thought of as capital, spectacle, the Internet, or the poetry Davies thinks they deserve.[7]

Davies's poem takes the feeling rules of Internet bundling and its end-user experience and transposes them to print as the formal action of the verse, but the silver digital age (early 2000s) also shows up in the propositional space of the poem. In fact, the poem's opening quasi-sonnet begins with and in this immaterial "place" "evicted from elsewhere, here":

> They awoke in a bookless world studded with lean-
> to performance artists interacting with electricity.
> *This must be the place.* Evicted from elsewhere, here
> at last not rest but an apprenticeship in container
> technology. A kind of music that, though apparently stopping,
> starting, stopping, more specifically never ends, thus

displaying as virtue its greatest flaw. Successfully,
Irritatingly.[8]

Given that this poem first appeared on the Internet, its opening is also its myth of origin, the moment of its encounter with the "they" of online readership that have left the book behind for the makeshift dwellings of the Internet, their provisionality enacted here via the intraverbal enjambment of "lean-/to." The third line begins with an italicized sentence that can be either a Talking Heads song (full title "This Must Be the Place [Naïve Melody]") or a colloquialism, but either way it seems to be reported speech evicted from elsewhere and so appears in italics. But italics play differently on the Internet in 2002, where this poem debuts and whose navigation it mimics and critiques—there they can indicate the state of a hyperlink (clicked vs. unclicked, or hovered over). In a "bookless world" typography makes place as well as emphasis. Further, if we move past the period to take the entire line as syntax, then "this . . . place" is the very thing "evicted" from both "elsewhere" and "here" because it is not a place at all but a metaphor for digital storage and our "interacting" with it.

This new placeless place, where we were all initially naive, offers tutorials in its navigation, an "apprenticeship in container / technology." In addition to being naïfs, we are all also apparently either "artists" or artisans, learning to discern and build the bundles that web content offers, that poems are, and that poems might be metaphorized as in the digital age. Again, enjambment, a classical zone of verse capacity, enacts what the line holds and fails to: "container / technology" closes the line while the sentence overflows it, stopping short on the next left margin in "technology." This must be the next place, the next eviction.

In addition to doing what it says, this moment early in the poem's first bundled stanza also prefigures the poem's interstanzaic principle at the scale of the line: the rule that a stanza's last line must enjamb its last sentence into the next's first line and there terminate. Here, in "container / technology" we have our first experience of the entire poem's container technology, a technique for making stanzas "that, though apparently stopping, / starting, stopping, more specifically never ends." The "apprenticeship" is the reader's to the poem as well as to its digital environment—both will be negotiated via a laterality: in the poem, enjambment (of both line and stanza); on the web, browser clicks backward and forward. This apprenticeship and the technology to which it is addressed are both accomplished "successfully, / Irritatingly." We might replace these two terms by *easily* and *with difficulty*, as they indicate both how the poem's containers, its practical ways of speaking about bundles, work, and how those "ways," both method and path, might disturb and annoy conventional readerly expectations of a poem. This self-assessment also functions as yet another introduction to that way, enjambing a sentence over the break ("apparently stopping"), beginning the next line with its continuation ("starting"), and ending the sentence immediately there ("stopping"). It is thus also "successful," however irritatingly, in descriptive rather than evaluative terms, simply indicating that its containers are full of sequentiality.

To quote another poetico-technological manual, "What more is there to do, except stay? And that we cannot do" in this technology:

> Perhaps they would stay awhile. But
>
> no... What's that humming sound?
> $\qquad\qquad$ Hello...

The first instance of stanza break gives us what enjambments already have, the stopping-starting-stopping sequence of container (form) and content (syntax). That the first example of the global principle uses a three-dot ellipsis followed by capitalization rather than a period (or the correct four-dot ellipsis) suggests that even termination is in motion in this poem and part of the poem's formal mimesis of web experience—not only do we not "stay" in any place on the Internet for long, but the ellipses here also figure the waiting periods during a dial-up modem's connection to the early web, as well as the animated metaphor for loading an electronic page. On the next page of the poem, this digital ellipsis will be redescribed as "the still point // on fire and twirling" in yet another example of the poem's interstanzaic connectivity, which also functions as another mordantly pertinent allusion to Eliot as well.

As we move across these Prufrockian permutations of stanza components via a more modern container technology, we will continue to encounter moments of rule that not only structurally mime web navigation but capture its experience and affects. After the opening sequence of stanzas, which runs 14/6/3/3/2/2/2/6, permuting even the sonnet sestet into its stanzaic factors, here are the next two:

> a sunny ledge. Not
> not this. What,
>
> this then?
> The stems must be crushed or the flowers will wilt
> thought Tito, dreaming of access

In addition to adding the question mark as another method for ending a sentence after the break, this passage uses enjambment at the level of both line and stanza to model surfing's temporary satisfactions ("a sunny ledge"), aimless consumption ("Not / not this"), passive selectivity ("What, // this then?"), and "access" to georgic content ("The stems must be crushed"). Of course this movement also harbors a loud reference to the opening of Ron Silliman's *Tjanting*:

> Not this.
> What then?[9]

Davies takes the lineless paragraph-as-stanza structure of Silliman's poem, organized by the Fibonacci sequence, and breaks it, much like Williams's epigraph, into lines and verse stanzas. The paraphrase and formal disarticulation of a classic moment from Language poetry's canon does several things: it lets Davies express a distrust of Language poetry's distrust of syllogism (*not* "not this") and a debt to it (LA will soon announce, "This is our heritage," one that includes Eliot's still point and Silliman's *this*)—both the distrust and the homage are present in the reversification of Silliman's prose. Davies mimes web experience while engaging verse lineage because his ambition here is not merely to use poetry to capture a new, vast, and alien space of reading and viewing, but to offer poetry and its formal capacities, its history, as another feature of this present, one that can resist easy consumption while imitating it.

On the plane of content, LA also directly expresses a relation to the wooden past and digital present of textual storage, running us backward, laterally, just like its own publication history, from the Internet to paper, and across the destruction of persons on 9/11:

> This is our heritage, bits
>
> of burnt paper float over Brooklyn.

LA itself was first "bits," then paper, a movement forward in publication time but backward through the history of media, and thus lateral both to that history and the fate of office paper from the towers. Beyond the poem's own provenance is a larger history in which, because of enjambment, "our heritage" may be digital bits, which would thus indicate what we will bequeath (optimistically/pessimistically) as technology to the future rather than what we have inherited; but these bits transform across the stanza break into the burning records from capital's old filing system, our heritage now the destruction of paper and/or an imperium's reaping what it sows. It's an elegiac instance of the poem's global procedure, dispersing persons and their practical ways of speaking across the break by remembering them in the air over Brooklyn, floating like cursors, stopping, starting, stopping.

As a "commie," Davies is neither hopeful nor terminally pessimistic about whether Internet dynamics or poetry can produce a worthy sociopolitical counter to fascist bundling, in part because he understands they are not outside the totality—what counts as good practicality, as the good way of speaking that a person could be, won't appear until a new dispensation comes. Instead of sounding Eliotic lament about the body or idealism about the archive, Davies just sees them as provisional forms of vulnerable storage; and instead of Eliot's anxiety about unavailable forms of genius or desire to become one of them, Davies's poem is incandescently, disposably funny, where we can understand humor to split the difference between optimism and pessimism, comedy and tragedy, especially around whether the Internet is an emergent commons or the newest marketplace. Five years before Anonymous, he did it for the lulz.[10]

Very near the end of this poem of stops and starts, we get one of the longest, and thus most immersive, stanzas on offer, and the most explicit description of the "bookless world" of the Internet:

> workers.
> I remember most of the plot. And the main character—
>   his name is Fritz or Cooper or Kawasaki, something
> like that—spends the whole film trying to get change
>   for a hundred. And he wakes up humping
> his aged father. Or *has he awoken*? One of
>   those brain tweezers that appeal to crossword
> types. Any surface at all, inside or out, you touch it
>   and a scrolled menu appears, listing recent history,
> chemical makeup, distance to the sun in millimetres,
>   distance to the Vatican in inches, famous people
> who have previously touched this spot, fat content,
>   will to power, adjacencies, and further articulations.
> And each category has dozens of subcategories
>   and each subcategory scores of its own, all
> meticulously cross-referenced, *linked*, so that each square
>   centimetre of surface everywhere, pole to pole,
> from the top of the mightiest Portuguese bell tower to
>   the intestinal lining of a sea turtle off Ecuador, has
> billions of words and images attached, and a special area,
>   *a little rectangle*, for you to add your own comments.
> It is the great work of a young-adult global
>   civilization, a meta-literate culture with time on its
> prosthetic tentacles, at this point slightly more silicon
>   than carbon, blinking vulnerably in the light of its own
> *radiant connectedness*. What
>
> villain would wish to blow this up?[11]

The stanza imagines the Internet as an informatic overlay on the world, offering encyclopedic knowledge, comprehensive surveillance, and pseudo-engagement in a disembodied square. Perhaps this is why the stanza also comically paraphrases the famous ending of Keats's "Ode to a Nightingale" ("Or *has he awoken?*"). Like a convincing dream, the Internet is at a metaphorical distance from the material world that generates it, but is also one of its "adjacencies," as is the "will to power" that determines search result hierarchies. Even this topical invocation of the Internet will offer formal mimesis—the multiple instances of italics could again summon their sometime use to indicate a hyperlink clicked or hovered over—here it happens on the very word "*linked,*" but also on "*radiant connectedness,*" at once a send-up of Internet architecture and its self-celebration, a New Agey motto, a figure for the poem's own recursivity and linkage, and an exaggerated image of a sociality, one actually confined to "*a little rectangle*" via commentary made in the surplus time this "young-adult global / civilization" has on its ramifying prostheses, themselves built on other people's labor and time—it's no accident that the superintendent first line of this stanza, which ends the prior stanza's sentence, reads, in its entirety: "workers."

Thirteen years after "Lateral Argument" debuted on Web 1.0, seven since it took up residence in a volume, do we see and feel poetry's formal segmentations differently, wherever we find them, now that the screen may be the primary location for reading flow and break, page and link? Poetry need no longer address itself exactly to the spatial limits and affordances of the book without that meaning it has to adapt seamlessly or ecstatically to those of HTML either. It can, in fact, productively pit itself inconsistently against and within these forms of storage, conforming to neither, parodizing both, making the expected familiarity of one readerly interface the apparent difficulty of another. During its history of publication, Davies's poem has moved backward and sideways across media, titular meaning, and ease of use. The feeling rules of each medium remain, and the poem, that thing not necessarily proper to either anymore but which can move laterally across both, carries its own set of feeling rules with it and accommodates new ones.

Of course, the "lateral argument" here is also a joke, in that when space becomes nearly metaphorical, directionality does as well—what's the difference between backward and forward, up and down, when they become descriptors of a sincerely ironic "*radiant connectedness*"? If "lateral" is a joke, then "argument" can be too, and the poem's title describes its readerly passage as aimlessness in the face of a cancelled telos, or, to return some seriousness to the title's phrase, the poem is a telling argument about digital aimlessness, its first ode and parody, hard to read and easy to surf. The argument is the lateral passage backward and forward across these experiences in the place we must be.

Notes

1. "Lateral Argument" is hereafter indicated by LA, save when referring to the chapbook.

2. Kevin Davies, *Lateral Argument* (New York: Barretta Books, 2003).

3. Kevin Davies, *The Golden Age of Paraphernalia* (Washington, D.C.: Edge Books, 2008).

4. Each of these poems is linked to its symbol in the table of contents.

5. Arlie Russell Hochschild, "Emotion Work, Feeling Rules, and Social Structure," *American Journal of Sociology* 85, no. 3 (1979): 551.

6. Kevin Davies, interview with Marcella Durand, *The Poker* 3 (2003): 40.

7. Christopher Nealon writes beautifully about how in a Davies poem "contemporary social relations give the lie to historical hope, especially as they are enmeshed in production processes" (*The Matter of Capital* [Cambridge, Mass.: Harvard University Press, 2011], 154).

8. Davies, *Golden Age*, 36.

9. Ron Silliman. *Tjanting* (Berkeley: The Figures, 1981), 11.

10. Gabriella Coleman, *Hacker, Hoaxer, Whistleblower, Spy: The Many Faces of Anonymous* (London: Verso Books, 2014), 1.

11. Davies, *Golden Age*, 58–59.

CONCEPTUALISM AND CONSEQUENCE

VANESSA PLACE

First Stone

A Muslim walks
Into a bar, and
The bartender says,
"Why the wrong place?"

I asked my Muslim
Neighbor if "Mohammed"
Was his Christian name.

I saw the headline:
"Islamic court tries
Nigerian Gays."

I bet they secretly
Enjoyed it.

The French magazine
Is awaiting a cartoon
Backlash. My money

Is on that anvil
Springing back and

Hurling them
Into the canyon.

Laugh, and the whole,
Non-Muslim, world
Laughs with you.

Chapter 23

In Bad Taste: Type, Token, and Tone in Vanessa Place's "First Stone"

Nicholas D. Nace

Can this simple poem really be saying what it appears to be saying? First, there is the opening stanza's assertion of Muslim unbelonging without any clear markers of tone that tell us how to take the related incident. This is done, of course, within the template offered by a linguistic type: a joke involving someone walking into a bar and a bartender's response. Through this template an unidentified speaker leverages a specific token by means of a conceptually delivered rhyme: The bartender's question, "Why the wrong place?" echoes "Why the long face?" the famous punchline to a joke about a horse walking into a bar. The second stanza offers a neighborly faux pas—perhaps proudly recounted, perhaps ashamedly—that identifies a decidedly Christian understanding of identity. Here again types and tokens are at play, though now the distinction between *the* joke and *a* joke recedes into the background while the distinction between *the* Muslim and *a* Muslim collapses into "my Muslim / Neighbor," an ironic epithet in which expectations of proximity and familiarity fail to coincide. The third and fourth stanzas exploit an ambiguity between legal and experiential understandings of *trial*: an "Islamic" court "'tries / Nigerian Gays'" only to find that one, or both, of those entities "liked it." Then we arrive at a high-resolution political issue framed by imagining the backlash against what can only be *Charlie Hebdo*, which the increasingly intimate voice finds to be as prone to backfire as the traps of Wile E. Coyote.[1] And finally, in the self-reflexive final stanza, we have an asseveration of the Muslim world's humorlessness under and against the mirth of the rest of humanity, though there is also, perhaps, a sympathy with not laughing in relation to cultural insensitivity. The grim, flinty title holds everything together for interpretation, with the suggestion not only that the poem should be interpreted but that it should be filtered through the concept of instigation.

The statements offered in "First Stone" present themselves with explicative ease and simplicity. We know what is being said, with some ambiguities and grammatical uncertainties excepted. Nonetheless the poem presents enough difficulties on the interpretive front to require contemplation about what this "I"—whether a person or a grammatical function—recounts. We do not know why we are being told these things or what attitude the lines take toward the statements they offer. Because we have no clear tone, it should be impossible to understand the politics of the individual utterances. Do we wish to condemn or support them? Are we being asked to? And who or what has cast this "first stone"? We cannot answer these questions simply, so this essay seeks to explore the difficulties we confront in our attempts to do so.

And now for the reveal: every one of the five discrete scenarios included in "First Stone" was taken whole from a site called Sickipedia, which promises to be a repository of the "sickest, rudest, most offensive, inappropriate & politically incorrect jokes & puns." They were all once considered "jokes," and their sickness was quantified by users who measure the jokes between the twin poles of *sick* or *suck*—two words that can be reconciled to the same scale of value only if we recognize *sick* as a youthful euphemism (following the previous generations' *bad* and *ill*) for transgressive cool, and hence the opposite of *suck*. Taken together, the five jokes that make up "First Stone" had, at roughly the time of the poem's publication, a sickness quotient of 1476.8. Though this is a meaningless statistic, we nonetheless have a quantifiable amount of repugnancy that, I believe, is here transmuted into condemnation simply by the fact that these jokes are read as lyric, not as humorous wordplay. Before knowing the origin of the appropriated material, the poem cannot but be read as an expressive lyric. In other words, we do not decide it is a lyric before we treat it as a lyric. However, once revealed as a work of appropriation, the poem's ability to continue being a lyric becomes attenuated as its sincerity evaporates. As so often in appropriative writing, what once appeared to be relative ease becomes, to a mind bent on interpretation, a mini-epic of instability that causes even our deepest beliefs about poems to teeter.

In writing a conventional poem, Place of course did not write a conventional poem. By some standards, she did not *write* the poem at all but rather dragged its words from the Internet into this arrangement.[2] What verbal ingenuity the words have was already there; Place only selected and lineated the sentences in which they appear. But we must not assume that the inevitable recognition of appropriation here is the end of interpretation, even if the "aha" moment of recognition can sound a lot like laughter. The point is not just to see how we respond differently to displaced content in a form that looks to all purposes like a lyric, but to engage with the fact of appropriation as an interpretative act designed precisely to clarify the features that make us select one mode of apprehension over another even when we flit between two. Here it is useful to remind ourselves how seldom Place writes in a form that could be seen as lyric and how frequently she has asserted mere lineation as the sine qua non of the lyric.[3]

Here is where a critic must offer a definition of lyric into which this poem fits during the moment before one runs a Google search to trace its language.

At the risk of reductiveness, we might begin to address this issue in a descriptivist way. Just what is lyric as it's practiced today? Place's "As James Franco Knows" articulates what I take to be a commoner stance than the burgeoning field of lyric theory would like to accept: to write lyric, "all you really have to do is express / what you feel / emotionally and physically / and how this affects / the world around you."[4] This last phrase might constitute the expression of the monstrous ego of expressivist poetics, but as a quick Google search demonstrates, it also could be—also is—advice for eco-friendly online shopping. Here the lineation is performing an act upon an otherwise unremarkable manifesto for poetic treacle that the real James Franco may or may not actually believe; the melodrama of lineation, the dramatic slowing and interruption of an otherwise undistinguished thought, is for many what makes something poetry, so long as its sentiments are sincere. This suspension enables and ennobles conventional interpretation. While I agree with Marjorie Perloff's assessment of the three minimal formal requirements for what I'll call the common lyric (expression, in lines, with repetition), I would reduce them to just one.[5] The minimum requirement for words to be classified as a lyric is, for many readers, simply the breaking of lines, which is all that Place has done here.[6] Within that nonconstraining constraint, you can put anything you like and have it be framed as sincere. If Microsoft Word decides where your lines end, you have written prose. If *you* decide, then you are a poet—even if you decide that Microsoft Word did it right. And if you are a poet of lyric, custom has it, you are also sensitive, perceptive, and penetrating, and you can write no doggerel if you are true to yourself.

By that logic, the difficulty of Place's "First Stone" cannot immediately be seen, which is in keeping with many forms of conceptual difficulty discussed in this volume. It is, by traditionalist standards, a modest triumph: a bland, smugly assured, tepid lyric, seeming to fold in on itself with interpretative closure and what Gillian White, characterizing the Language poet's contempt for such things, calls "degrading interpretability."[7] It promotes a condemnation of whatever might smack of anti-Muslim sentiment as a "first stone" of provocation. It has line breaks and therefore form. And because those breaks do not always come where grammar might naturally require a slight pause, we have *meaningful* form. Its structure offers little to work with: eight frictionless stanzas composed of seven sentences that in themselves do not offer much beyond the simplest exigencies of continued grammatical enunciation—though what stimulation, what linguistic interference or nonsubstantive meaning they do offer occurs lexically via wordplay that was already present in the jokes.

As Cathy Park Hong, the most trenchant critic of poetry's racial politics, has shown, such lyrics as we might take "First Stone" to be, along with many privileged forms of avant-garde poetry, are quietist and comfortable. Even poets of color who are urged, in workshops, simply to "find" their voices—which means expressing and confessing in the way Sharon Olds might—continue to write white-endorsed "sanitized, easily understood personal lyrics."[8] They are not tied to a chair and made to confess, but the coercions are nonetheless there if their voices are even to be heard within the poetic sphere as it has been established. Here I find a small but valuable patch of common ground among Hong, Perloff, and Place. They all wish for poetry to reject the easy politics that come with the common lyric of mindless lineation and consistently intoned sincerity. They all feel that poetry which requires but withholds interpretation is the way forward; they further feel that the self-explicating, tightly closed lyric dampens what could otherwise lead to a radical politics able to attack the comforts of mediocrity and easy intelligibility of the established lyric voice. Precisely how they wish this to be accomplished is a hotly contested matter.

Yet a desire for resistance motivates even the self-explicating lyric as it seeks intelligibility in a common form. But just as forms become trite executions, so too can voices become bromidic. When the minimal requirements of lyric form (lines) coincide with the minimal requirements of lyric voice (sincerity), a similar tone of suspicion precipitates, pushing self-explication through a shared politics and toward tired critique. Works of art, perhaps specifically poems, have gradually absorbed more and more of the critical impulses to question, subvert, and demystify that Rita Felski argues now overwhelm literary criticism and drown out the concerns of "aesthetic pleasure" and "perceptual invigoration" (which I argue Place's conceptualism aims for).[9] The political aims of poetry and those that motivate criticism on poetry have largely coincided, to the point where the politics of critique, as they are currently accepted by the largest interpretative community, are also largely the politics of the poets who cohabit this community. A lyric claims ownership, of one kind or another, over all that its voice enunciates, however ironically. And what subtends it all is sincerity. Its parts may come from other places, but they all contribute to an overall effect, whether of expression or display, whether to elicit sympathy or condemnation.

While its parent concept, "voice," has risen to a level of prominence that now demands its critique as a tool of conformity, "tone" has fallen out of favor as a critical term. In fact, Jonathan Culler's *Theory of the Lyric* originates from a rejection of the New Critical fetishization of tone and its ambiguities.[10] But in the conceptualist repertoire, the very idea of an earthly "ditty of no tone" is repeatedly questioned, both by the movement's proponents and its detractors. While conceptualism may at times appear to believe in the dream of the inert text or the possibilities of ecstatic self-loss through transcription, in many cases the act of reframing material for presentation becomes as much the focus as is the reframed product. And that is what "First Stone" does.

Slavoj Žižek has most recently been the one to demonstrate that jokes, too, can be—often are—a form of critique.[11] But what happens when two tonally different forms of critique collide? We have in Place's poem one iterable form of critique being subsumed within another. The joke is lost. While there is an ongoing debate about the propriety of appropriation focusing on the ethical dimension of what one selects and republishes (at the center of which is Place herself), jokes are seldom traceable to an original context or speaker. They are already appropriated, unowned; they lead our focus to their role in social life rather than their role as constituents of a single speaker's perspective. They express a ludic tone that every joke shares, and their affect of amusement is the telos of their tone. Their type, in other words, is determined by their tone. A person can tell a joke and not believe or even agree with it. But can a lyric be insincere in this same way?

As I believe "First Stone" shows, the result of making a lyric that contains potentially inflammatory public-domain material is that it *contains* that material—holds it, yes, but also constricts it—an effect that can say more about lyric sincerity than it does about jokes. Copied from one context and pasted into another, these jokes sit oddly in their new container. Far from functioning as a kind of *lorem ipsum* that will not distract from an examination of their new format, as might be said of works like Kenneth Goldsmith's *Day*, these jokes offer their impact to test the politically dampening effects of lyric presentation.

In a lyric, political lines suddenly seem starker, pressurized as they are by the drama of lineation—not because lyric grants clarity but because it obscures it, often by narrowing interpretative possibilities and retraining our focus away from content and context onto the moment of expressive genesis, which is often entangled with the impulse to critique. We can sympathize with the voice or condemn it, and we almost never condemn before we make affordances for the statement having originated through self-condemnation. Because we see it as lyric before we know how it was constructed, we ask where the sincerity is rather than whether it exists at all. Instead of assessing our emotional response to the jokes qua joke, we ask of a lyric what emotions gave rise to this particular configuration and how we care that these particular jokes are being uttered.

Place frames "First Stone" to be intelligible to readers of poetry who will largely know how to orient themselves in relation to what are seen as the poem's expressions, even, perhaps, if they know their origins as "tasteless" jokes. Readers will accept its lyric form as a bid for the triumph of voice at the same time as they reject the demotic nexus of intolerance out of which its content comes. While this poem might offer an opportunity for using poetry to examine the ethical dimension of our public utterances, the lyric as it is practiced at present too often provides the unexamined baseline for expressing ethical orientations. I would argue that a reverse process yields more insight. The tried, the true, and the tired modes of lyric expression create their own blindspots; their form is political even when the writers think that only propositions can carry such a payload. Because Place defies the logic of expression by not composing in the traditional sense—by not using what are from the start her own words, dealt out one at a time—her poem enables us to read, as it were, in the wrong direction. We can gain a great deal more, I believe, by using public utterances to understand what the lyric does, what it is and what it hopes to do, and by extension, what it realistically might be able to do.

"First Stone" makes no mention of its unoriginality. In the opening stanza, the punchline is predicated on the idea that we may recognize the punchline of another joke as well as the fundamental incompatibility between Muslims and bars (alcohol, being *haram*, makes a bar indeed an unlikely place for a Muslim to be). Even if bar life is expressly forbidden, does that mean the joke itself cannot be humorous to Muslims? Can a Pole find Polish jokes humorous, or a blonde, blonde jokes? The difference might be the amount of genuine intolerance the Muslim faces in the United States, which this poem reduces to a pat conclusion that the non-Muslim world does not laugh when the speaker's "we" laughs.

In "First Stone" we might recognize Western self-centeredness, intolerance, flippancy, the assumption of humorlessness that registers the Muslim, any Muslim, as a tool for humor. We see five varieties of utterance (straightforward joke, confession, explication, wager, aphorism), the wit of each being sharpened by the active employment of what would, outside the sphere that conventional lyrics inhabit, be classed as errors: an error of articulation ("wrong place" for "long face"), a faux pas (the use of "Christian name" in a socially inappropriate way), an interpretative error ("tries" in its experiential sense instead of its legal sense), an error of reference ("them" has an unclear antecedent, as did "they" in stanza four), and a punctuation error (the restrictive commas that make "world" coincident with "Non-Muslim"). What holds these utterances and errors together as a lyric? It would be too simplistic to say sentences, but it is true. Beyond that, we assume a consistent voice to match the consistent topic. There is nothing that strains our sense of why the words are placed in this order, no work that we have to do other than absorb the statements and react. There is, in other words, very little of what we take to be specifically formal difficulty, and even less of what might raise a lyric to the status of a *good* lyric.

So how does it offer its critique? From the start of "First Stone" we are seeing double (at least). A Muslim walks into the formal space of a joke that is also the start of a lyric:

> A Muslim walks
> Into a bar, and
> The bartender says,
> "Why the wrong place?"

After the stern title, the poem opens with a bald statement of existence, "A Muslim walks," which possibly, for a form-enabled split second, suggests a kind of release or freedom for our dubiously representative "Muslim." The poem essentially refuses to distinguish between type, in this case a Muslim who is not distinguished as an individual, or token—an individual who is not distinguished except by being a Muslim. But suddenly this line is enjambed into the recognizable template of a joke. A quick change of registers, a slip into a new frame, and we are in the uneasy grip of someone who expressly means to entertain us with material that already seems ill suited to socially conscious mirth.

The second stanza likewise is a single sentence, a confession of a faux pas, with no natural pause to solicit permission or audience receptivity:

> I asked my Muslim
> Neighbor if "Mohammed"
> Was his Christian name.

Here a first-person lyric subjectivity enters the poem, and automatically the tone has become dramatically unstable. Or has it? Is this the same "I" who recounted the joke in the previous stanza? Is this stanza likewise a joke? While it does rely on recognition of a kind of linguistic duplicity, one that may in the end be just as exclusionary as it sounds, it feels more like a solecism disclosed with rue at the slip, if not embarrassment. Filtered as it is into an "I," this stanza's assertion would normally be an uncertain one, leaving unclear whether the anecdote emerges from mortification or contrition, or repentance, or grinning confederacy, or whether it picks up the defiance of the previous stanza. The coherence is threatened. Is this a joke? A confession? Is it an instance of taunting? Of intolerance? How does liberal confession sit with, among, jokes such as the foregoing one that rely on a positive valuing of non-Muslim "normalcy" for their very appeal? While we might use the poem as an occasion to meditate on the pernicious fact that "Christian name" is a common and religiously exclusive euphemism for one's *prénom*, we might go the other way to ask why lyric contextualization makes that which we don't like sound always as if it is being appropriately lamented rather than merely being expressed. The reader's work is assumed to reproduce, retrace, the work of the voice.

Place's "I" is in truth not precisely an "I," not a lived "I." It is itself an exigency, the kind of "I" one needs to be in order for the fiction to take hold, nowhere more so than in the third stanza:

> I saw the headline:
> "Islamic court tries
> Nigerian Gays."
>
> I bet they secretly
> Enjoyed it.

The reference to "headline" here takes us to late-night comedy, though its definite article feels a little too definite for Jay Leno. How different would the stanza be if it began, as the late-night comedian might formulate it, with a nonchalantly narrativizing "So"? "So I saw the headline" would enable us to read this as a generic utterance, a type; however, without that initial nonchalance, we become victims of the default sincerity of the lyric "I." As stand-up comedy demonstrates, the joke teller is not necessarily the writer. Jokes somehow already exist, even if they don't. So liable to mutate are they that they prove unclaimable even by their author, who disowns them from the start. "Have you heard the one about . . . ?" Such openings solicit some kind of complicity as they insist on the inability to own a product of wit, and they constitute a trapdoor through which agency can be replaced by a form of passivity, of repetition. The issue of complicity and permission is offered a bit more directly in Place's work on rape jokes, but the lyric voice never pauses for permission because it already has that permission due to its very inability ever to offend.

With the retrofitting of these jokes to a poetic form, Place demonstrates the effect of working backward. The force of the punchline demands the space before it, the showman's pause that allows an auditor's thinking to become complicity after a scattershot of targets, but the pauses are the line breaks, which are in comedically wrong places. Here "I bet they secretly / Enjoyed it" uses enjambment to extend the silence that attends grammatical incompletion, which makes the stanza's final line less a punchline than a dying *sotto voce* confessional whisper. However confidential it feels, though, "enjoyed it" leaves us with questions. Enjoyed *what*? We therefore reread "tries" in a probative way, as something like *samples* or *experiments with*, instead of *puts on trial* or *litigates*. We retrace our steps back to the pun, only to realize that we should have gone the other way, the way context did not urge us to go. Of course, we're likely to concede, the fear of homosexuality motivating the trial emerges from repressed homosexual desire. But does this imply ridicule of Islamic law or just acknowledgment of difference? The lyric does not make us dwell on this issue.

Similarly, in the next stanza we are introduced to a highly politicized issue that is diffused over the course of three stanzas and ambiguated by an unclear pronoun reference:

> The French magazine
> Is awaiting a cartoon
> Backlash. My money
>
> Is on that anvil
> Springing back and
>
> Hurling them
> Into the canyon.

Given the context established by the three previous jokes, "French magazine" can only refer to *Charlie Hebdo*. The potential for violence is cast as cartoonish "backlash" against a cartoon ("cartoon" here does not commit to being a noun or an adjective), thus equating cartooning with violence, which will satisfy those who feel the cartoonist deserves what he gets. If we consider the "anvil" and "stone" as analogues, we might wonder which act, the incendiary cartoon or the anticipated "backlash," constitutes provocation. But who gets hurled into the canyon? Since this "backlash" became real and not cartoonish in 2015, there is a new solemnity to these stanzas that perhaps might push a reader to contemplate this issue further, but the idea is that the "Muslim neighbor" may try to harm the insolent cartoonist with a doggedness that over time shades into vindication.

The conclusion requires careful attention because it openly provides the comforting closure that informs our entire interpretation.

> Laugh, and the whole,
> Non-Muslim, world
> Laughs with you.

Sutured to itself by commas that shrink the entire "world," this final assertion makes "whole" coterminous with "non-Muslim," pulling the meaning inside out with typographic precision. The world of mirth, like the bar with which the poem opens, does not include the Muslim. Here we not only have the first half of an incomplete equation of social laughter and antisocial weeping, but we have the first portion, too, of lines that constituted the opening of Ella Wheeler Wilcox's inspirational "Solitude": "Laugh, and the world laughs with you; / Weep, and you weep alone." This is a double appropriation: an appropriation of a sentiment that itself appropriates an influential but forgotten poem, a much more formally accomplished poem that trades precisely on the curative powers of positive thinking. Where, precisely, does the *détournement* occur? What is different? Who is weeping? The inevitable comparison to Wilcox's poem, which has released these two lines into the public domain of inspirational quotation, reveals how much formal ingenuity has been lost by the common lyric, and how much of the insistence on feelgoodist maximology has remained.

This kind of allusion is our prompt to interpret what should be an occasion for moral reflection, and the title does this same kind of work.[12] Of course, the title's two words do a great deal of framing from the start, offering us the possibility to see the poem and its utterances as acts of instigation. While it does establish a notion of difference that is maintained through the possibility of aggression, we have no way of knowing which entity in the Muslim/non-Muslim dualism is the first aggressor. The poem's surface difficulty lies in reconciling this contextualizing gesture with the lyric that follows. We easily understand the title by recognizing the phrase and filling it out with its biblical context. The earliest English language version of John 8:7 appears in the 1535 Coverdale Bible: "He that is amonge you without synne, let him cast the first stone at her." The undelivered idea that establishes the poem's conceptual context—and I argue, fuels its lyric politics—is that of being "without synne," a famously impossible subject position to occupy but one that the conventional lyric endorses in its fidelity to sincere expression. Read as a maxim about the individual's role in social life, the biblical imperative means to forestall accusation and violent provocation with a reminder of guilt or complicity.

Yet this poem, like all the poems originally published on the Home School website, carries with it a poetics statement. Place has chosen hers carefully: "Never apologize, never explain," which, with its emphatically secular injunction, offers itself with the terseness of an iterable mantra. But it takes us away from such comfortable expectations through its own, very different original context. While the origins of this phrase are disputed, its first utterance, and a first provocation of sorts, appears to have been made by the Oxford theologian Benjamin Jowett, who advised Balliol diplomats to "never apologize; never explain." This surely fits our present author, constituting as it does an epi-conceptual commitment that Place has taken to new lengths in her refusal to apologize for her *Gone with the Wind* Twitter project (still ongoing, friendlessly, to two followers exclusively). But what do we do with this dual refusal of forms of capitulation, both of which, even with their capacity for insincerity, constitute mechanisms by which we are able to inhabit a world with other people? Perhaps the more relevant issue here is whether we understand the will to "explain" as a disguised wish to "apologize"? If so, does the easy, self-explicating lyric contain an urge always to apologize for itself? If Place's poetics statement involves refusal, perhaps the lyric as it is commonly practiced feels the opposite: always apologize, always explain, and never throw any stone at all. It forestalls apology altogether because it is an expressive act. Beneath its conventional appearance, the difficulty of Place's poem is dispositional and orientational, in relation both to the poem and to the world it invokes.

What, after all, is the relationship between explanation and poetic content? Explanation is a communicative act, and a poem is not—or at least not exclusively. Poetry deals in the substantive, the content of the expression, as that substance is occasionally subordinated to the nonsubstantive (the meaningful effects, such as lineation, that aren't inherently part of the communicative statement system). And because communication is the preoccupying day job of language where it acts as a valet for our intentions, the rejection of "explanation" seems an especially strident refusal—a Bartlebyesque defiance, a flouting of the Gricean conversational maxim of quantity and, at its core, a refusal to engage others with the courtesies of self-justification that can help them fit their ideas to their politics. We therefore entertain why a refusal should constitute Place's poetics, even before we encounter a poem that may or may not require apology. The issue is not—cannot be—that innocence precludes apology. More likely, the resistance of explanation is a resistance to a variety of social coercions, the refusal of which maintains radical presence and keeps the interpretative lines open.

And what, finally, is the difference between telling a joke and writing a lyric of jokes? When their joke status is accepted, the jokes are harder to respond to than they are as a poem, despite the philosopher Ted Cohen's insistence that they shouldn't be. The jokes are not, after all, propositions but fictions. Though they may rely upon knowledge of the way the real world is commonly perceived, laughing is not an act of approval that the way the world is is the way it should be. If we follow Cohen's guidelines for interpreting jokes, we cannot be offended at the jokes themselves or our enjoyment of them. In this vein, a "complaint that such jokes are in bad taste or unwholesome comes to nothing more than a wish to be free of them."[13] By the inverted standards of Sickipedia, by which bad taste is good, the jokes in Place's poem are not especially tasteless. "Taste is," as Place elsewhere claims, "the flavor of ideology." But what of the things without taste? Place goes on: "My *Statement of Facts* may be called a-political while a rather dumb rape joke is immediately understood as terribly political. This is because one remains in the realm of the real, i.e, taste-less, while the other is received or perceived as already processed, i.e., tasteless."[14] What do you find when you take jokes that potentially affront standards of taste and offer them with the one formal feature that makes a common lyric? The jokes become flavorless because the lyric processes them. There is therefore an important difference between a lyric presentation and a nonlyric conceptual presentation. Without a lyric voice that glues these utterances together, we have a list. A mere list. But still not an innocent list. Even a humble grocery list can be nonobviously determined—by the disposition of aisles and items in a familiar store, by the combinatory pressures of a recipe, and so on.

This brings us to the great unanswered question of a good portion of conceptualism. Does language have a politics when it is dematerialized and awaiting delivery on our clipboards? Or can language deal with contextualizing politics in fresh ways? Is language wiped clean—even of its serifs, the tiny epaulettes of authority—before we "paste special"? Or what kind of politics does language have in a poem? The list format is so integral to conceptualism, so entangled with its self-conception, that the movement itself cannot be characterized without recourse to an elegant list of its own techniques. Thus we have Goldsmith's discussion of how he rewards his students for "plagiarism, identity theft, repurposing papers, patchwriting, sampling, plundering and stealing"; or Perloff's "appropriation, citation, copying, reproduction."[15] As a term, *appropriation* has largely stuck for proponents, *reinscription* for detractors. But what this dragging and clicking does that links it so directly to poetry, and in my belief makes it best and most enjoyably read as such, is reduce language's communicative function. It radically, perhaps even completely, defunctionalizes the communicative dimension of language. It may "dematerialize" this language, but as it takes a new material form, it takes on a new function and a new politics. This new function allows the language to be less communicative, less ripe for interpretation. When communication is reduced, when use cedes to mention, when difficulty emerges, thought—particularly thought about language—can occur. What Place seems to be after is traditional literary suspension of existential judgment pushed as far as it can go, though she knows the lyric will work against such abeyance.

Place superficially embraces the lyric as a means of testing our faith in the most reductive version of the form as a vehicle for political engagement. In his *Notes on Post-Conceptual Poetry*, Felix Bernstein offers a made-up quotation—"not a real quote"—from Place that articulates just this problem: "Poetry is what poetry is, and what poetry is has everything to do with the packaging of the imaginary libratory subject."[16] As "First Stone" shows, the lyric can, at least for the space of twenty-two lines, make even a cruel, queer, white, unapologetic conceptualist such as Vanessa Place appear to be producing what she calls "art that's sanitized, art that's precious, art that's playing safe, art for the market."[17] Displeasure at "sanitized" art is what Place, Perloff, and Hong share; what appears to have done the scrubbing, at least in this case, is the stereotypical lyric voice.

In this way, "First Stone" draws our thinking away from the specific utterance to the variety of utterance spoken—in this case the genre of the lyric and how it, like the Muslim joke, is built upon a consensus that identifies difference but does not, cannot, incorporate it. Fully attending to Place's use of convention turns genres into occasions for contemplation and brings categories and stereotypes into focus. The implication of such work is that the category *needs* to be examined, not just the category of jokes but that of lyric as well. Conceptual writing demands this kind of engagement as it moves text from one interpretative frame into another, but it aims not to control or constrain the process beyond that control exerted by dimensions of its new frame and our reliance on that frame. Yet perhaps owing to the modal difficulty readers experience in recognizing such "writing" as "poetry," the second decade of conceptualism has shown signs of bringing its techniques of examination and renovation to lyric forms, as likely or unlikely as that move might seem given conceptual writing's insistence on impersonality. The questions that arise from this conjunction of conceptual writing and lyric form ask, as limit-case poems always have, how tokens relate to their types.

As Place claims in her 2015 interview with the *Guardian*, in a good portion of contemporary poetry, "it's not about what you say or think, it just matters what it looks like you might be saying or thinking."[18] Taking into account all the frames of Place's *mise en abyme*, we might see the type of "First Stone," the outermost frame of sincere lyric that it hopes to be seen as, including the conformist interpretation its form offers and demands, to be a cultural provocation by the way it creates its tokens without reflection on what they represent.

Notes

1. "First Stone" was published on the website for the Home School on February 28, 2014, nearly one year before the fatal attack on the *Charlie Hebdo* nerve center.

2. I discuss "First Stone" as a conceptual poem, not flarf, based on the difference that Place insists upon in *Notes on Why Conceptualism Is Better Than Flarf* (Calgary: No Press, 2010).

3. See especially Marjorie Perloff's interview with Place in *Iowa Review* 44, no. 1 (2014): 63–73, esp. 67.

4. Vanessa Place, "As James Franco Knows," *Lemonhound*, April 19, 2014, http://lemonhound.com/2014/04/19/vanessa-place-as-james-franco-knows/.

5. Marjorie Perloff, "Towards a Conceptual Lyric: From Content to Context," *PN Review* 38, no. 3 (2012): 20.

6. Perhaps the greatest creative challenge to received formal notions of lyric comes from Claudia Rankine's book-length prose lyrics, *Don't Let Me Be Lonely: An American Lyric* (2004) and *Citizen: An American Lyric* (2014). In the case of *Citizen*, Rankine's text (outside of the roughly 10 percent that is lineated) is double justified, with typesetters determining the final line length by the exigencies of the book's *mise-en-page*. The lines therefore are not themselves tools of expression in the general sense. Opportunities for exerting poetic form are chosen not to be chosen, leaving control to be exerted by the book's form. Yet *Citizen*'s affective dimension is importantly defined by the very issue of line breaks. Ben Lerner laments that, unlike in the published version, early drafts of *Citizen* featured virgules marking line breaks that were run into the text. For Lerner, as I think for Rankine, the virgule functions to register the "unavailability of traditional lyric categories" and therefore constitutes a "sign of vanished possibility"—though the markers of this absence have themselves vanished with publication. Lerner rightly concludes that "Rankine's work depends on making the lyric felt as a loss" (*The Hatred of Poetry* [New York: FSG, 2016], 72). But if that too is the case, if the form of lyric is felt as "an impossibility" by the lack of line breaks, then "lyric" is in a significant way coincident with the missing formal marker that is the line break.

7. Gillian White, *Lyric Shame: The "Lyric" Subject of Contemporary American Poetry* (Cambridge, Mass.: Harvard University Press, 2014), 138.

8. Cathy Park Hong, "Delusions of Whiteness in the Avant Garde," *Lana Turner* 7 (2014), though here I incorporate several points from "How Words Fail," http://www.poetryfoundation.org/article/178505.

9. Rita Felski, *The Limits of Critique* (Chicago: University of Chicago Press, 2015), 188.

10. Jonathan Culler, *Theory of the Lyric* (Cambridge, Mass.: Harvard University Press, 2015), viii.

11. Slavoj Žižek attempts to make jokes assume all the work of critique by vacuuming out the jokes from his oeuvre to make *Žižek's Jokes (Did you hear the one about Hegel and negation?)* (Cambridge: MIT Press, 2015).

12. Definitions of *lyric* might be clarified by examining the acts of framing offered by titles, following the process begun by Anne Ferry in *The Title to the Poem* (Stanford, Calif.: Stanford University Press, 1996).

13. Ted Cohen, *Jokes: Philosophical Thoughts on Joking Matters* (Chicago: University of Chicago Press, 1999), 79.

14. Vanessa Place, "I is not a subject," *Harriet the Blog*, May 1, 2013.

15. Kenneth Goldsmith, *Uncreative Writing: Managing Language in the Digital Age* (New York: Columbia University Press, 2011), 8; Marjorie Perloff, *Unoriginal Genius: Poetry by Other Means in the New Century* (Chicago: University of Chicago Press, 2010), 23.

16. Felix Bernstein, *Notes on Post-Conceptual Poetry* (Los Angeles: Insert Blank Press, 2015), 79.

17. Edward Helmore, "*Gone with the Wind* Tweeter Says She Is Being Shunned by US Arts Institutions," *Guardian,* June 25, 2015, https://www.theguardian.com/books/2015/jun/25/gone-with-the-wind-tweeter-shunned-arts-institutions-vanessa-place.

18. Ibid.

DIVYA VICTOR

from *Hellocasts*

Chapter 24

✦

Hellocasting the Holocaust: Appropriative Poetry as an Ethical Practice

Adalaide Morris

The title is tucked in the upper right-hand corner, just above Hello Kitty's pacifier hair bow. An earmark of sorts, it assigns ownership of the language that follows: "Holocaust by Charles Reznikoff. VIII. Children." Beginning at the left ear and filling the rest of the outline of Sanrio Corporation's globally recognized trademark are excerpts Reznikoff selected from twenty-six volumes of court records from the Nuremberg (1945–46) and Eichmann trials (1961), lineated as a poem and published under the title *Holocaust* (1975).[1]

Section VIII begins with a fairytale formula—"Once," it says—but what it contains is not fantasy but sworn evidence by a series of witnesses to recurrent, even routine, events:

> Once, among the transports, was one with children—two freight cars full.
> The young men sorting out the belongings of those taken to the gas
> chambers
> had to undress the children—they were orphans—
> and then take them to the "lazarette."
> There the S.S. men shot them.[2]

Nominally a site for reception of the diseased poor, this "lazarette" is, like the "showers" nearby, a killing field. The three anecdotes that fill the rest of the outline describe children thrown from balconies into open trucks full of sick men and women; toddlers, some no more than two or three years old, left for the night in an empty hall with bug-ridden straw bags on the floor; and soup served to children in a death camp—we are now at the lower right-hand corner of the Hello Kitty outline—in tins too hot for them to hold.

This image, the second of twelve, comes from a chapbook titled *Hellocasts* published in 2011 by Ood Press. Identified in the colophon as Factory Product 2, it is attributed on the cover and title page to poet, performer, and codirector of Les Figues Press, Vanessa Place, and listed on Les Figues website as *Hellocasts* "by Charles Reznikoff by Divya Victor by Vanessa Place."[3] The chapbook is laid out so that each leaf, recto and verso, presents a blank lined-notebook page on one side and, on the other, a variant of the inscribed Hello Kitty icon.[4] Some of the Hello Kitties are accessorized with hair bows, underpants, or pairs of mittens; some have fat little feet, a nose, and two eyes; none, significantly, has a mouth. In the chapbook's centerfold and at its end, the icon disappears to create a double-sided spread of copybook pages.

A serial copyright infringement, a sacrilege, a scam, a trap? But there is more (fig. 24.1).

Already multiply estranged as an artifact, *Hellocasts* also appeared as an installation and two performances curated by Les Figues Press at Los Angeles Contemporary Exhibitions (LACE). Entering the gallery on opening night, a visitor would have seen a young woman in a short dress standing with her back to the room, writing on a wall. A spotlight casts her shadow into a Hello Kitty silhouette approximately twice her size. Although it would not at first be possible for a viewer to read them, the words she writes spool across the icon, separating to allow for Hello Kitty's oval nose and round eyes. Whiskers arc off to the left and right of her chubby cheeks.[5]

In "A Feral Cat Attack," a subsequent performance, seven participants take Victor's recorded dictation to transcribe stanzas from "Work Camps," Section VII of *Holocaust*, into seven Hello Kitty outlines projected on the gallery wall. In a YouTube clip of this event, the poet reads in a slow, formal, British-inflected English:

> The state is to get hold of those who never had emdash linebreak or
> no longer have emdash linebreak a right to live in the state comma
> linebreak and the state must turn their strength while it lasts linebreak
> to the good of the state period. They must be fed comma sheltered
> comma and treated in such a way linebreak as to use them as much
> as possible linebreak at the lowest possible cost period.

In Victor's amplified speech, the language used to denote stripped citizenship is chill, clinical, definitive: the word *linebreak* sounds like *language*, so we hear something like "those who never had emdash language or no longer have emdash language." The word *state* sounds like a combination of *seat*, *seed*, and *stet*.[6]

In its print, installation, and performance versions, *Hellocasts* is, in Marjorie Perloff's term, a *differential* text—a text "that exist[s] in different material forms, with no single version being the definitive one."[7] As Victor's title suggests, however, in addition to being instigations and interpretations, these versions are interpellations: they greet or hail a listener, reader, or viewer and cast her into the project.

Like readers of the chapbook with its lined notebook pages, visitors to LACE are given an assignment: entering the room, they confront a desk, a stack of Hello Kitty outlines, and a pair of headphones with Victor's readings

Figure 24.1. *Hellocasts*, LACE, June 21, 2010. Photo
courtesy of Les Figues Press.

of Reznikoff's transcriptions. "Sit at the desk," the gallery-goer is instructed:
"Listen, look and write. Make your own Hellocast, to take home or leave in
front of the big kitty."[8] Whether accepted or refused, Victor's assignment is
wryly DIY, time-intensive, risky, and difficult if not impossible to take seri-
ously without a significant shift in our assumptions about the reception of
art. What would it mean to "sit at the desk," fill in the outline, make our own
hellocast? What would it mean to refuse?

In a prompt given to writers for this collection, Charles Altieri asked the
following questions: "What new or reconfigured demands do contemporary
poets make on readers? And how can awareness of those demands make
their texts not only more intelligible but more entertaining? Is the main
difference in our sense of contemporary difficulty that scholars have not pro-
vided the historical contexts and the imaginative frameworks that they have

for reading modernist difficulties? Or are there simply different tasks now confronting scholars and critics?"

What scholars and critics know how to do with the difficulties of such modernist poems as Ezra Pound's *Cantos*, T. S. Eliot's *The Waste Land*, William Carlos Williams's *Paterson*, or H.D.'s *Helen in Egypt* badly misfires as a tactic for confronting documentary or conceptual texts such as Reznikoff's *Holocaust*, Heimrad Bäcker's *transcript* (1986/2010), Vanessa Place's *Statement of Facts* (2010), Frank Smith's *Guantanamo* (2010/2014), Robert Fitterman's *Holocaust Museum* (2011), Philip Metres's *Sand Opera* (2015), and, notoriously, Kenneth Goldsmith's performance of the text of Michael Brown's autopsy (2015). Faced with the appropriated language of these texts—language of administrative, political, legal, and historical consequence—how are we to process these records of harm? What "different tasks" do these texts ask of us? What would it mean, to return to Victor's prompt, to look, listen, write, or perform one's own "hellocast"?

Keenly alert to the language and layout of their materials, appropriative poets "write" by selecting, lineating, collaging, or, in the case of *Sand Opera*, partially erasing public documents. Like Reznikoff's *Holocaust*, each of these books draws upon transcripts, edicts, articles, reports, operations manuals, or other excerpts from official discourse retrieved from archives, the Internet, or, in the case of *Sand Opera*, WikiLeaks.[9] All use language and thus invite interpretation, but the statements they contain are for the most part straightforward, even disturbingly mundane. The language is not, in this sense, unintelligible; it does not aim to entertain; and it does not engage—or require a reader to engage—familiar literary-critical issues of authorship, self-expression, or originality.

When an "author" disappears behind a quotational practice, an act of ventriloquy, or, in Victor's case, the Factory Work series' commodification of source texts, issues of identity and authenticity recede. Although a reader may seek to verify a citation or situate it in its cultural or historical context, she is not asked to peer back through a scrim of language toward an authorial psyche or autobiographical incident. Because the source of documents reprinted in these texts is announced at the outset and/or annotated in the back matter, the labor assigned the critic is not bibliographical: what is difficult is not locating, translating, or parsing obscure citations but coming to terms with the world these documents certify, administrate, and record. The challenge is emotional and, such is the cunning of Victor's prompt, performative.

In citing the language of the Holocaust, Reznikoff, Bäcker, Fitterman, and Victor take us as close to events as we can get in a belated world of words. There is, however, a difference between the tactics of the first two poets, both alive during the Holocaust, and those of the second two, born into its aftermath. If Reznikoff and Bäcker's deployment of documents is positive, even indexical—"See," they seem to say, "*this* happened and *this* and *this* and *this*"—Fitterman and Victor's approach asks us to contemplate not just what happened (the "facts" that blur as firsthand accounts grow increasingly distant, brittle, and auratic) but the gap that opens in time between events and the representations that evoke them. As we will see, the self-reflexive negativity this gap necessitates is a crucial factor in the cultural work performed by contemporary documentary and conceptual poetics.[10]

If historians monitor the accuracy of received narratives of catastrophe and sociologists assess their origins and dynamics, poets like Pound, Williams, Eliot, and H.D. look back in order to press toward an altered future. As Patrick Greaney observes in reference to the quotational methods of Walter Benjamin's *Arcades Project*, "The past matters not only because of what actually happened but also because of the possibilities that were not realized and that still could be."[11] In this sense, appropriational poetics are both diagnostic and prognostic: they reanimate a past to reconceive a future. By asking the observer to reframe her reframing of Reznikoff's reframing of materials from the Holocaust, Victor implicates her audience in the difficulties of this ethical obligation.

Before returning to Victor's *Hellocasts*, I want to look briefly at Reznikoff's *Holocaust* (1975) and Bäcker's *transcript* (1986), then turn, at slightly greater length, to Fitterman's *Holocaust Museum* (2011).[12] My aim is to suggest elements of the conversation Victor enters from the standpoint of a woman who is neither Jewish nor German but a postcolonial subject born in India in 1983, raised in Singapore, resident of Baltimore, Philadelphia, and Seattle, PhD student at SUNY Buffalo, and most recently, assistant professor of poetry and poetics at Singapore's Nanyang Technological University.[13] These elements are significant, I will suggest, not just in relation to the events chronicled and their poet-chroniclers but to the gallery-goer standing in the force field created by Reznikoff's *Holocaust*, Victor's handwritten copies of his transcriptions, a desk, a pair of headphones, and a stack of Hello Kitty icons.

Reznikoff's text, however unconventional and uncanonized, is the best known of these four appropriative poems. Selecting excerpts from over 650,000 pages in *The Trials of the Major War Criminals at Nuremberg* and *The Eichmann Trial in Jerusalem* and arranging them in twelve sections that progress from "Deportation" through "Ghettos," "Massacres," "Mass Graves," "Work Camps," "Children," "Marches," and "Escapes," Reznikoff registers, detail by detail, the courtroom narrative of the Nazi campaign to exterminate European Jewry. As Victor's appropriations from Sections VII and VIII demonstrate, these details—the cup of soup too hot to hold, the determination "to use [prisoners] as much as possible linebreak at the lowest possible cost" before eliminating them—are excruciating in their specificity. In their narrative alignment and citation of verifiable records, these sections are documentary; in their resonant details, concrete language, and—emdash linebreak—halting cadences, they are poetic. The questions they raise, however, are not just formal and aesthetic but sociological, political, and ethical.

The shock of encountering this material—its full-on, face-to-face impact—is augmented by a number of factors, including its provenance as sworn testimony in courts of law, the force and confluence of the evidence it provides, and the fact that we are, to all intents and purposes, abandoned by an "author" willing or able to provide a rationale or lexicon sufficient to the atrocities laid before us. Unlike Pound, Eliot, Williams, and H.D., each of whom attempted to imagine a remedy for a culture gone awry, Reznikoff holds back. If there is a response adequate to the occasion, the reader must herself enter the poem's aftermath—its forensic field of interpretation, accountability, debate, and activity—to imagine and, on however small a scale, attempt it.[14]

Heimrad Bäcker's *transcript*, published in Germany in 1986, also appropriates and itemizes details from the administration of the so-called Final Solution. Summarized by Bäcker's editor, Friedrich Achleitner, these particulars include, but are not limited to,

> lists, entries in registers, numerical tables, interdictions, arrest reports, lists of synagogues destroyed, prohibited acts, instructions, definitions, expressions, linguistic scraps, dates, numbers, abbreviations, names, professions, activities, questions, orders, map legends, enumerations, fragments, descriptions of medical experiments, indications of time, execution lists, ideological phrases, captions, interjected comments, marginal comments, minutes of negotiating sessions, last letters, verbatim notes of hearings, statements, files of criminal charges, records of kilometers traveled with the tally of those dead from the day's march, etc.[15]

Categorized, sequenced, and arrayed on the page with a concrete poet's care, these details have the weight of forensic exhibits. "Every part of *transcript*," Bäcker affirms in his introduction to the volume's notes and bibliography, "is a quotation; anything that might seem invented or fantastic is a verifiable document."[16]

Although Bäcker's notes and bibliography meticulously identify the sources of his materials, like Reznikoff he provides no voice-over—no frame or commentary—to explain, rationalize, or ease the horrors they chronicle. Unlike Reznikoff, however, Bäcker uses an endnote to link himself to a fragment of the language he transcribes. Deep in the back matter, tied to a fulsome description of the Führer "as a mature man in a position of great responsibility . . . reverently pausing at the small patch of earth where his parents lie in the cemetery at leonding,"[17] is a reference to a book review by one "Heimrad B.," a piece of prose, Bäcker continues, "[s]imilarly marked by a dangerous, imbecilic mania for hero worship."[18] This is neither a gratuitous nor an exculpatory gesture.

The effect of Bäcker's self-reflexivity is to collapse past and present, inside and outside, objective and subjective vectors of the text. The initial "B."

identifies the dictator's sentimental apologist with the same being who some forty years later collects and exhibits evidence of his own complicity in events that now seem unthinkable. Heimrad B., writing in 1942, is exemplary, and thus important, for his failure to stand out; Heimrad Bäcker, writing in 1986, has no illusion that his self-incrimination explains or atones for his actions.

"There is," Bäcker observes, "no other anthropology of fascist/terrorist systems except the analysis of their language."[19] The text of *transcript* collates discourse all members of the culture heard, many spoke, and few publicly recognized, resisted, or disavowed. The horror of this language is its ubiquity: it is everywhere in plain sight, active but unacknowledged. Although critique risked severe reprisals at the time, it is not, as Bäcker demonstrates, an opportunity that expires. Bäcker's appropriations expose what Roland Barthes calls the *stickiness*—"the aggressive force, the power of domination"—of a discursive system.[20] The demand the poem makes of us, its readers, is civic, forensic, and ethical, available to anyone willing to take up the burden of self-reflexive analysis.

Fitterman's *Holocaust Museum* takes two of its three epigraphs from *Holocaust* and *transcript*: the first, a brief account of SS men taking a little girl from her mother; the second, a list of five telephone numbers registered to Auschwitz. The lead epigraph, however, comes from Vilém Flusser's *Towards a Philosophy of Photography* (1983/2000), a treatise that links a diminishment in the capacity for critical thought to a form of magical thinking fostered by the increasing dominance of technologies of imaging. This epigraph, I will suggest, opens a way to understand the peculiar demands Fitterman and Victor's appropriative poems make on a reader, a gallery-goer, or a person sitting at her desk.

To Reznikoff's faith in language's capacity to index the events of the Holocaust, Bäcker adds both a conviction that the language of the Third Reich had systemic force[21] and an awareness that it circulated through a network of interchanges that included not only mass media communications but acoustical technologies such as the telephones that rang into and out of Auschwitz.[22] Flusser's epigraph adds to this mix the element of photographic and cinematic imaging.

"This space and time peculiar to the image," the epigraph reads, "is none other than the world of magic, a world in which everything is repeated and in which everything participates in a significant context."[23] Despite their deployment as documentary evidence, for Flusser, photographic images emerge from and merge into the static and repetitive world of mythology, folklore, religion, and political ideology. "Such a world," the epigraph continues, "is structurally different from that of the linear world of history in which nothing is repeated and in which everything has causes and will have consequences."[24]

Fitterman's poem appropriates captions assigned to three hundred of the more than eighteen thousand photographs held by the U.S. Holocaust Memorial Museum in Washington, D.C. Some of these captions reference photographs exhibited in its galleries; others, retrievable through its web-site, reference photographs stored in its archives. Like Reznikoff, Fitterman divides his materials into thematic sections arranged in rough chronological order from "Propaganda" to "Liberation."[25]

The narrative these captions create is ominous in its familiarity: "The Tichauer family poses for a family photo in the German countryside"; "A Jewish family climbs the stairs to the train platform"; "View of a sign outside of Buchenwald which reads: 'To the Buchenwald Zoological Park!'"; "Partial view of the crematorium, focusing on the chimney"; "A group of liberating U.S. Army soldiers speaking with prisoners in the Buchenwald concentration camp."[26] Seven decades after the events they register, the images these captions describe exist deep in our collective imagination—they are iconic, even, in Flusser's sense, mythic—but here the captions stand alone.

Instead of undermining or diminishing the actualities of the Holocaust, the act of stripping the captions from the images creates a space for the negativity Flusser calls "philosophy." The possibility the poem creates is a space resistant to the magic of iconic images, suspicious of apparently neutral curatorial language, and alert to the seductions of ideologies, our own as well as those belonging to others.[27] The effect of this excision is to complicate a case all but closed by the burden of its own mythic resonance.

To give just one example of an analysis that troubles the narrative evoked by the captions, Fitterman's selection creates an eerie echo between the poem's first section, "Propaganda," and its last, "Liberation," both of which convey state-sponsored accounts of the events in question. In the first section, the captions describe Nazi images that caricature Jews as "Race Defilers," hate mongerers, ritual murderers, and "Titans of Corruption"; in the last, the captions set side by side "Mug Shots" of SS guards and camp commandants and views of "prisoners cheer[ing] the liberating Americans, who freed them from . . . inhuman treatment."[28]

The chasm between absolute evil and absolute good that characterizes these captions belongs to Flusser's world of myth. The Nazi propaganda of the first section and the American liberation story of the last depict a terrain in which, as sociologist Zygmunt Bauman puts it, "murderers murdered because they were mad and wicked and obsessed with a mad and wicked idea," and liberators liberated because they were noble and heroic.[29] The point obscured by the iconicity of the photographs but available through analysis of the captions is that in this mythic world the personnel changes but the plot is static: if, in the first narrative, Nazis liberate Germans from inhuman Jews, in the second, Americans liberate Jews from inhuman Nazis. "Imagination," as Flusser puts it, "has turned into hallucination."[30]

The poet standing, her back to us, at the gallery wall, transcribing sentences from Reznikoff's *Holocaust* into a Hello Kitty outline, occupies a historical moment in which the hallucination Flusser identifies with mechanized imagery serves the needs of a hypercommodified global consumer culture.[31] Trademarked by Sanrio Corporation, Hello Kitty—the cutest of cute consumer kitsch—is one of the most successful brands in the world. Available everywhere, its image appears on products that range from toys, socks, clocks, knapsacks, lunch boxes, cupcakes, pop-up-straw bottles, and greeting cards to key chains, wallets, tote bags, and credit cards.

With no mouth of her own, Hello Kitty is available to ventriloquize any product, phase, or ritual of display and consumption. In this sense, she is a token of goods exchanged, debit or credit, for money; a mobile signifier for one of our favorite things, *any* one of our favorite things; and a marker, in particular, of cultural products—material or aesthetic—that promise to comfort, console, or pacify us. The spell she casts on children, teens, and adults alike is the magic of commodity capitalism.[32]

What would it mean, then, to sit at a desk and fill a Hello Kitty outline with our own *Hellocast*? What event—past, present, or potential—would we use such an occasion to address? What public records hidden in plain sight expose the dynamics of this event? What would the act of squeezing those records into a global trademark of consumer culture tell us about the landscape of terror and unknowing we now inhabit? And, finally, how could we entice others—as Reznikoff, Bäcker, Fitterman, and Victor entice us—to think about our own entanglement in the myths with which we explain to ourselves and others systematic scenes of death and disaster?

As Sianne Ngai observes, the aesthetic of cuteness elicits both positive and negative affects: something like tenderness and affection, on the one hand, and, on the other, something like condescension and contempt. The cute object is helpless and pitiful. Its contours call out for snuggling: we want to hold it, take it home, make it our own, and care for it, and it, in turn, seems, as Ngai puts it, "to want us and only us as its mommy."[33] The two vocabularies Ngai melds to explain this magic—Marx's account of commodity fetishism and "the one-to-one, intimate manner of lyric poetry"[34]—undermine the impulse toward more historical, civic, ethical, or self-reflective logics.

The shock of Victor's *Hellocasts* is multiple and complex. The poem's difficulty lies in its violent clash of registers: high and low, aesthetic and commercial, reverential and cartoonish. From the desk where I sit with these contradictions, the Hello Kitty outline puts into question not the veracity or value of Reznikoff's poem but the narrowness and complacency with which twenty-first-century readers tend to consume it.

To be specific, for me the effect of filling the Hello Kitty icon with Reznikoff's text is double, even triple: it does not allow me to linger, as high modernism taught me to do, in an aesthetic or formal analysis; it interrupts the build of any narrative of liberation, restoration, or transcendence; and it expands the theater of action from World War II Europe to contemporary global scenes of consumer capitalism, racism, genocide, and terror. For me, perhaps paradoxically, the effect of Hello Kitty's cuteness is to darken, disturb, and expand the force of Reznikoff's poem.

Different as it is from the poetics that precede and follow it, appropriative poetry is not neutral or indifferent, affectless or inert. We can deny its claim to the status of poetry, refuse its invitation to analysis, demonize its practitioners, or shut the door of the gallery behind us, but a riskier, more rewarding course is to engage one or more of the occasions of reception it makes available. Whether our responses to documents of trauma and suffering are ethically adequate to their occasion, whether they can make a difference as the present moves toward the future, depends, at least in part, on the audience's willingness to take up its challenge.

Notes

1. For Reznikoff's sources, see Janet Sutherland, "Reznikoff and His Sources," in *Charles Reznikoff: Man and Poet*, ed. Milton Hindus (Orono: National Poetry Foundation, 1984), 301–5.

2. Charles Reznikoff, *Holocaust* (Boston: David R. Godine, 2007), 49. Lineated in Reznikoff's transcription, this material is copied into the outline of Hello Kitty without line breaks.

3. Factory Works is a multivolume project in which Place published under her own name texts written by others. The cascade of attributions marks Place's appropriation of Victor's appropriation of Reznikoff's appropriation of the words of survivors who testified at the Holocaust tribunals.

4. When Victor's images were published in the Factory Work series, Place added the lined notebook pages to fill out the chapbook. The insertion between poems of lined, list-sized pages also marks the layout of Victor's *Partial Derivative of the Unnamable* (Buffalo, N.Y.: Troll Thread, 2011).

5. The Ood edition retains strikeouts to mark transcription errors made—and corrected—by the latest "author," as, for example, "~~through~~ out" in the first sentence of Section VIII.

6. "Not Content: Divya Victor 'Feral Cat Attack,'" *YouTube*, https://www.youtube.com/watch?v=N9t0Ycv6dQc (accessed April 28, 2015).

7. Marjorie Perloff, "Vocable Scriptsigns: Differential Poetics in Kenneth Goldsmith's *Fidget* and John Kinsella's *Kangaroo Virus*," in *Poetry, Value, and Contemporary Culture*, ed. Andrew Roberts and John Allison (Edinburgh: Edinburgh Press, 2002), 21.

8. For a description of the June 21, 2010, performance, see the archived page for Les Figues's *Not Content* website (https://web.archive.org/web/20120507011028/http://www.notcontent.lesfigues.com:80/2010/06/divya-victor/). In her instructions for this performance, Victor included a mechanism that would allow gallery goers to leave a cellphone number she might use to summon them to the desk. E-mail message from author, March 3, 2015.

9. Philip Metres, *Sand Opera* (Farmington, Maine: Alice James Books, 2015), 101.

10. I draw here on Barrett Watten's many discussions of critical negativity, which he defines as "an open series of critical interpretations" characteristic of

avant-garde practices. See, for example, *Questions of Poetics: Language Writing and Consequences* (Iowa City: University of Iowa Press, 2016), 9.

11. Patrick Greaney, *Quotational Practices: Repeating the Future in Contemporary Art* (Minneapolis: University of Minnesota Press, 2014), x.

12. See also Victor's procedural engagement of Reznikoff's *Holocaust* and *Testimony* in *Partial Dictionary of the Unnamable* (Buffalo, N.Y.: Troll Thread, 2011).

13. For additional biographical details, see Victor's meditation on citizenship in *Natural Subjects* (40–43 and passim) as well as Les Figues's website for the installation and performances at LACE.

14. Anticipating the dismissal of more recent appropriative poetry, critics in the last half of the twentieth century who read Reznikoff's verse did not consider his documentary account to be "poetry" that could or should be read with the attentiveness automatically granted modernist poetry and poetics.

15. Friedrich Achleitner, "the describability of the indescribable or attempting an afterword to *transcript*," in *transcript* by Heimrad Bäcker, trans. Patrick Greaney and Vincent Kling (Champaign, Ill.: Dalkey Archive Press, 2010), 147.

16. Bäcker, *transcript*, 131.

17. Ibid., 97.

18. Ibid., 138.

19. Cited by Patrick Greaney, "afterword to the english edition," in ibid., 149.

20. Roland Barthes, *The Rustle of Language*, trans. Richard Howard (Berkeley: University of California Press, 1989), 108.

21. On "the language of Nazism" as the "breeding-ground" of the Holocaust, see Victor Klemperer, *The Language of the Third Reich*, trans. Martin Brady (New York: Continuum, 2006), 2.

22. Like the transport trains Claude Lanzmann features in his 1985 documentary, *Shoah*, the phone numbers Bäcker reprints testify to a widespread and daily circulation of incriminating evidence.

23. Robert Fitterman, *Holocaust Museum* (London: Veer Books, 2011), n.p.

24. Ibid., n.p.; For more on the clash between the world of magic and "the linear world of history," see Flusser's chapter on "The Photographic Universe," in *Towards a Philosophy of Photography* (London: Reaktion Books, 2000), 65–75.

25. For additional information about the composition of *Holocaust Museum*, see Charles Bernstein, "This picture intentionally left blank: Robert Fitterman's 'Holocaust Museum,' Heimrad Bäcker's 'transcript,' Christian Boltanski's 'To be a Jew in Paris in 1939,' and the documentary poetics of Raul Hilberg," *Jacket2*, http://jacket2.org/commentary/picture-intentionally-left-blank (accessed April 29, 2015).

26. Fitterman, *Holocaust Museum*, 22, 52, 54, 94, 112.

27. Marianne Hirsch and Leo Spitzer make an analogous point in their essay on photographs displayed in Holocaust exhibits ("Incongruous Images: 'Before, During, and After' the Holocaust," *History and Theory* 48 [December 2009]: 25).

28. *Holocaust Museum*, 13, 20, 19, 13 (first section); 116, 119 (last section).

29. Zygmunt Bauman, *Modernity and the Holocaust* (Ithaca, N.Y.: Cornell University Press, 1989), vii.

30. Flusser, *Towards a Philosophy of Photography*, 10.

31. This culture is also the target of Fitterman's mall verse in *Sprawl* (Los Angeles, Calif.: Make Now, 2010) and Nick Thurston's collection of poems composed by piece workers in Amazon.com's Internet-based, crowdsourced labor pool in *Of the Subcontract, Or Principles of Poetic Right* (York, UK: Information as Material, 2013).

32. In this sense, Sanrio's icon is the agent Lacan identifies as a partial object or *objet petit a*. For a trenchant analysis of the commodity aesthetic of cuteness, see Sianne Ngai, *Our Aesthetic Categories: Zany, Cute, Interesting* (Cambridge, Mass.: Harvard University Press, 2012), 1 and passim.

33. Ibid., 64.

34. Ibid.

GUY BENNETT

One-Line Poem

This is it.

Chapter 25

Self-Expression without Self-Expression: The Political Meaning of *Self-Evident Poems*

Jennifer Ashton

> Contemporary poetry, why so difficult?
> —Jacques Roubaud

When Charles Altieri and Nick Nace first wrote to the contributors of this volume back in October of 2013 asking them to pick a single contemporary poem and explain how to read it, the reason Charlie gave, as if channeling the epigraph to this essay, was, as he put it, "I am tired of just complaining that I cannot read much of recent poetry in an experimental or innovative vein."[1] When presented with the task of explaining a difficult contemporary poem, my thoughts immediately turned to Guy Bennett's 2011 volume, *Self-Evident Poems*, and specifically to the poem titled (aptly for reasons that are, as it were, self-evident) "One-Line Poem."[2] My thinking was that this poem, whose one line, as we have already seen, consists of a simple three-word sentence—"This is it."—would strike most readers as far from difficult. What critics often mean by difficulty is that the meaning of the text is opaque. The idea that this poem is "self-evident" suggests, by contrast, that if anything, its meaning must be obvious or easy to see. My hope in choosing this poem was that it could serve as a test of the framework of difficulty, for if it appears to qualify as an instance of nondifficulty, then it might also tell us something about difficulty.

Let's start with the obvious. The briefest glance tells us that "One-Line Poem" consists of one line. We can see without even reading it that the form of the line—and for that matter, of the poem—bears out what the title promises. Whatever else we might say about it, "One-Line Poem" proves itself to be a one-line poem. The poem is its own evidence; hence the poem is self-evident. A different way to put this would be to say that the poem speaks for itself. There's no need for anyone to speak for it—no need, in other words, for interpreters or interpretations. It's in this connection that Bennett's *Self-Evident Poems* first struck me as having something important to do with poetic difficulty—that is, something potentially at odds with the poems' apparent ease, in that the self-evident poems' obviousness appears to render any interpretation we might produce for them irrelevant.[3] They appear, in effect, to resist interpretation altogether. Given the emphasis on hermeneutic challenge that historically has been identified with poetry as a gauge of its difficulty (at least since the development of the New Criticism and the institutionalized "close reading" we associate with it), it's hard not to see the kind of obviousness that obviates interpretation as itself a form of difficulty.

But self-evidence of the kind we see in "One-Line Poem" doesn't necessarily entail the disabling of interpretation. Take, for example, this poem written three centuries earlier, which, like "One-Line Poem," couldn't be more obvious in its manifestation of its eponymous subject:

A broken A L T A R, Lord, thy servant reares
Made of a heart, and cemented with teares:
Whose parts are as they hand did frame;
No workmans tool hath touch'd the same.
A H E A R T alone
Is such a stone
As nothing but
Thy pow'r doth cut.
Wherefore each part
Of my hard heart
Meets in this frame,
To praise thy Name;
That, if I chance to hold my peace,
These stones to praise thee may not cease.
O let thy blessed S A C R I F I C E be mine.
And sanctifie this A L T A R to be thine.[4]

As with "One-Line Poem," we don't even need to read the words of George Herbert's "The Altar" to see that the poem looks like what its title says it is. But as Stanley Fish makes clear in a tour-de-force reading of the poem, the fact that we can see so readily that the poet has achieved in form what the title describes by name is actually an invitation to peer more closely into the construction of the poem. I think we'd find it difficult, to say the least, to make the same claim about "One-Line Poem"'s "This is it." To establish some sense of what it might look like to read Bennett's poem in the same manner as we are compelled to read "The Altar," let's walk through some angles of approach that Herbert's poem (or, for that matter, any "difficult" poem) might be said to invite, taking Fish's well-known analysis as our blueprint.

As Fish notes, from the first line of the "The Altar" ("A broken ALTAR, Lord, thy servant reares"), we have a syntax-generated ambiguity that leads us to question who or what is doing the "rearing" on which the initial couplet turns: "The delaying of the verb momentarily suspends the sense and leaves us uncertain of the relationship of the three noun phrases, altar, Lord, servant."[5] Fish is especially interested in how the reader is compelled to rearrange the syntax to resolve the ambiguity, an activation of readerly agency that the poem, he goes on to argue, ultimately exists to cancel out. Indeed, by the third line ("Whose parts are as thy hand did frame"), the agency responsible for the altar (the "hand" doing the "fram[ing]") is made completely unambiguous, and as Fish explains, it's neither the reader nor the poet. Through an ingenious deployment of the pronoun *whose*, "'thy hand' replaces 'thy servant'" such that

> the poet is not the framer of his altar-poem and we are not coparticipants in an independent and autonomous act of creation. Instead both the shape we see and the experience it provides are generated by a power whose presence has only now been fully revealed. It is as if a curtain had been drawn back during the presentation of a puppet show, and the hidden springs of the players' actions were suddenly visible.[6]

The revelation of divine agency only grows more vivid as the poem unfolds. By the time we reach the final couplets, which visually make up the foundation of "The Altar," the monument itself ("these stones") can now substitute both grammatically and visually (literally by way of the poem's shape) for the speaker ("I") in praising God, such that "The Altar" acquires the same graphic shape as the first-person pronoun (the letter *I*) that identifies the speaker throughout the poem. "The Altar" and the poet's "frame" thereby become alike in form, even as they owe their form not to the poet's agency but to God's (a resemblance, by the way, that Fish does not remark upon, but which is entirely consistent with his analysis). By the very end of the poem, everything that is "mine," poet and poem alike, is proven to be "thine," such that by extension, everything belongs to God. Just as "Altar," "servant" and "Lord," are rendered equivalent and thereby substitutable for one another in the first line, so are the rhyming "mine" and "thine" in the closing couplet. But unlike the first line, in which the substitutability makes the priority and agency of the subjects ambiguous, the final transition to "thine" (referring to what is possessed by the "Lord") stops the chain of substitutions and leaves us with "Lord" as an all-encompassing referent. Thus, through these relations of equivalence and transitivity, enacted syntactically, grammatically, prosodically, and graphically, the poem's self-evidence and God's self-evidence are rendered one and the same.

If we return now to Bennett's "One-Line Poem," we can see that the kind of visual self-evidence it so clearly shares with Herbert's poem has a very different function in the one than it does in the other. For Herbert, self-evidence is a means rather than an end, a way for the "The Altar" to embody and insist upon the sovereignty of divine creation under tremendous pressure from the poet's own creative agency. That realization, moreover, is the reward the reader gets from the kind of careful analysis that a critic like Fish is able to perform. For Bennett, by contrast, insofar as the very title of his collection suggests that self-evidence is to be taken as an end in itself, such analysis (once again) would seem beside the point.

One clear way to respond to this challenge is to subject "One-Line Poem" to the very sort of scrutiny it seems designed to discourage.[7] Taking up one of the typical close-reading techniques that Fish uses to produce his analysis, we can start with the grammar and syntax of "This is it." Here we have a demonstrative pronoun, *this*, followed by the verb *to be* in third-person simple present tense, followed by the personal pronoun *it*. Our immediate task when faced with any pronoun is to determine its referent, which we typically do by looking in the direction of what comes before it. What comes most immediately before *this* is the last word of the poem's title: *poem*. Or we can take *this* as pointing at the entire title: "One-Line Poem." Either way, the demonstrative pronoun gestures toward something we understand to be "One-Line Poem." The poem doubles down on this self-reference as we continue. The be-verb *is* indicates that what follows will predicate something definitive or ontologically significant pertaining to the subject *this* (i.e., pertaining to the poem itself). What "this" "is," of course, is "it," another pronoun. Once again we need to ascertain its referent, which only returns us to *this*. *Is*, moreover, performs a copular function between the two pronouns, rendering *it* the predicate nominative to the subject *this*, and thereby creating a transitive equivalence between the two pronouns. With only each another and the title as their available referents, we find the two substantive elements of the poem's one line functioning in a kind of identity equation, each insisting on the poem's reference to itself: "One-Line Poem" = "One-Line Poem." Rearranging the syntax, moreover ("it is this," "this it is," "is this it," etc.), only produces the same insistence (despite differences in voice and tone that might be available), because the terms of the equation remain functionally the same.

Suppose we turn now to the poem's prosodic elements. Such an analysis of "This is it" might well seem like a nonstarter; nevertheless, we can detect right away a pattern of assonance in the same short vowel sound ĭ that occurs in each of the line's three words (*this*, *is*, *it*). And if we note that the words all share the same syllable count of one, we might say these details of the parts instantiate the whole, that they embody the oneness the title announces as an essential property of the line comprising them, as well as the self-sameness that we register from the moment we identify the visual appearance of the line with the title. "One-Line Poem" is self-evident all the way down. There is nothing in or about the poem that doesn't in some way express its self-evidence. Bennett's poem thus works analogously to Herbert's "The Altar" in more than just its immediate, visual self-demonstration. In both instances, all the interpretive avenues within the poem lead inexorably to a single realization. In Herbert's "The Altar," it's God's sovereignty that every element of the poem serves to express and insist upon. In Bennett's case, every element of the poem expresses and insists upon the poem's self-evidence. But if "One Line-Poem" turns out to reward our close-reading efforts in some of the same ways that "The Altar" does, what exactly is the value in that reward? What does it mean that everything the poem has to say is tantamount to saying that it is what it says it is? Or, to reduce the formulation even further to the tautology it would seem to be, that it is what it is?

As it happens, the marketing publicity for *Self-Evident Poems* encourages Bennett's readers to understand the collection from a point of view that takes up self-evidence in similarly tautological terms and at the same time locates the work in relation to existing poetic practices: "This new collection of brief conceptual poems strives to demonstrate Jacques Roubaud's axiom whereby 'poetry says what it says by saying it.'"[8] But just as the technique of self-evidence accomplishes something very different in the context of Herbert writing devotional poetry in the seventeenth century than it does for Bennett writing, as he puts it, "brief conceptual poems" in the twenty-first, it also can't exactly do the same thing for Bennett now as it did for Roubaud, who published his "axiom" in 1995.[9] For one thing, even with the explicit reference to Roubaud, for most readers, the label *conceptual* is more likely to evoke the recent work of poets like Kenneth Goldsmith and Vanessa Place, who've laid claim to and helped promote conceptualism as a movement, than the more distant works of Roubaud and fellow members of the experimental writing collective Oulipo, which claimed Roubaud as a member in 1966.[10] After all, in the year and months prior to the publication of Bennett's book, several widely discussed efforts to theorize and taxonomize conceptual practice appeared, entirely as a response to conceptualism's resurgence and momentum in the field of poetic production.[11] But as I'll try to show in the space that remains, the fact that "One-Line Poem" does indeed "demonstrate [the] axiom whereby 'poetry says what it says by saying it'"—that is, the fact that it's the kind of conceptual poem that does that (in 2011 as opposed to 1966 or 1995) is also what makes both the aesthetics and the politics of its conceptual framework importantly different from—indeed, opposed to— that of conceptualist poetry as it is practiced right now.

The antagonism signaled in a title like *Against Expression*, Goldsmith and Craig Dworkin's 2011 anthology of conceptual writing—which Dworkin explains is an antagonism toward the "'the interference of the individual as ego'" and toward works "that express unique, coherent, or consistent individual psychologies"—is not confined to the works represented as examples of conceptual writing in that volume, but is a prominent feature of the general state of affairs in poetry now. The last several decades of poetic production in the United States have been punctuated by a series of attacks on poetry's dominant genre, the lyric, treating it as more or less synonymous with self-expression.[12] By the same token, these attacks on the lyric have in turn prompted efforts to defend the lyric, in some cases by defending the value of self-expression as such. We could say of Bennett's "One-Line Poem" that it shares in the anti-lyric tendency, that it too is "against" the kinds of "expression" that conceptualism seeks to refuse, insofar as we'd be hard put to think of this poem as an instance of any sort of subjective expression. It does, however (and this is part of the force of its being self-evident), express itself. It is self-expressive to the extent that it expresses what it is, a "one-line poem" and, more generally, a "self-evident poem." But even if we can say that the poem is self-expressive in this way, the kind of self-expression it entails involves no subjectivity. And it certainly does not appear to issue from the kind of "self" whose expression is presumed to be of value in, say, late capitalism's ubiquitous imperative to "be yourself." "One-Line Poem" can only be itself, but even if we see it as one of a kind, the point is not that it's "one" but that it is of a kind, a "One-Line Poem."

So far all of this would seem perfectly in keeping with the antiexpressive tendencies that have emerged recently and, more specifically, with conceptualist poetic practice as it seems to understand itself right now. But the "concept" in Bennett's "brief conceptual poem" also has a different status in relation to the achieved poem than it does in contemporary conceptual writing—and for that matter, the conceptualism of the 1960s to which Goldsmith and others claiming the label pay homage. The difference lies between thinking of the concept itself as the work and thinking of the work as an expression of the concept. That difference was already available as an aesthetic conflict in the 1960s, that is, at the moment when postmodernist art, in the form of minimalism (including conceptualism), was emerging out of the late modernist art of abstract painting and precisely as an attack upon it. It was also a moment when self-evidence looked, to at least one prominent artist, like a powerful way to launch an attack. In 1966, in a conversation with Donald Judd published in *ARTnews*, Frank Stella produced his famous claim for the self-evidence of his own paintings: "What you see is what you see."[13]

Stella says this to explain what it is about abstract expressionism that requires the kind of solution his paintings undertake. The problem, according to Stella, is that abstract expressionism partakes in a commitment to drawing that it shares with most of the history of painting. And for Stella, the problem with drawing is that it is, as he puts it, "like handwriting": "Well, you have a brush and you've got paint on the brush, and you ask yourself why you're doing whatever it is you're doing, what inflection you're actually going to make with the brush and with the paint that's on the end of the brush."[14] To grasp what Stella means we only need to consider how it is that the effects of the painter's use of the brush could be like the effects of the handwriter's use of the pen. On the one hand, the "inflections" of handwriting are simply how the writer wants the letters to look, but on the other, they are also the products of all sorts of movements and habits not reducible to what the writer thinks he is "going to do" with the pen, much less "why." Like handwriting, the abstract expressionist painting expresses the contingencies and idiosyncrasies of the painter's style. But for Stella, unlike his contemporary Sol LeWitt, this antipathy toward style does not translate into an antipathy toward expression as such, and we can see this when the interviewer tries to reduce Stella's "what you see is what you see" to a kind of conceptualism in LeWitt's terms: "You're saying that the painting is almost completely conceptualized before it's made, that you can devise a diagram in your mind and put it on canvas. Maybe it would be adequate to simply verbalize this image and give it to the public rather than giving them your painting?"[15] Stella responds that "a diagram is not a painting," making it clear that it's not just that the concept cannot suffice as the work of art, but that even the diagram as a visualization of the concept will not suffice.[16] The distinction between painting and diagram emerges more forcefully a few moments later in the interview. "You actually want to see the thing," says Stella. "That's what motivates you to do it in the first place, to see what it's going to look like."[17] If you can see the diagram, it's not the visualization of the concept that matters. It's that what you're seeing expresses the concept in the form of the painting. We can also see why Stella's "what you see is what you see" is useful for explaining self-evidence. For insofar as the painting is an expression of the concept of the painter, and the painting you see is what that concept looks like as a painting, the painting itself is also thereby the expression of a type or a kind of thing, albeit the sole instance of it.

We can feel the force of Stella's remarks for our reading of "One-Line Poem" if we return to the tautological paraphrase—"'One-Line Poem' is 'One-Line Poem'"—that the engines of its transitive operations produce. It's also hard not to see the poem's self-evidence in terms of one of the most basic mathematical identities, A = A, which seems at once like a clear example of a self-evident proposition and the exact opposite of the kind of identity we associate with subjectivity or self-expression (the opposite of the kind that goes with handwriting). But in mathematical philosophy, a field as uninterested in self-expression as it's possible to be, there's significant disagreement over the extent to which any proposition deemed self-evident can be considered axiomatic, much less true. Far from offering any objective foundation, the argument goes, such claims are fundamentally subjective, amounting, as Bertrand Russell, C. G. Hempel, and others have put it, to a "feeling."[18] "One of the several answers which have been given to our problem" writes Hempel in his essay "On the Nature of Mathematical Truth,"

> asserts that the truths of mathematics, in contradistinction to the hypotheses of empirical science, require neither factual evidence nor any other justification because they are "self-evident." This view, however, ... ultimately relegates decisions as to mathematical truth

to a feeling of self-evidence. . . . [J]udgments as to what may be considered as self-evident are subjective; they may vary from person to person and certainly cannot constitute an adequate basis for decisions as to the objective validity of mathematical propositions.[19]

The way out of the problem, it turns out, is to understand the terms of such propositions as representations of kinds or classes of things, defined by the stipulated requirements of shared properties. Take, for example, the first three of what are called "primitives" in Giuseppe Peano's effort to construct foundational principles from which "the entire arithmetic of natural numbers can be derived":

P1: 0 is a number
P2: The successor of any number is a number
P3: No two numbers have the same successor.[20]

To establish "0 is a number" as a viable axiom, we define number by intension, so that its "meaning," Hempel says, "can be considered as characteristic of a class of objects." Thus "2 is that property which is common to all couples. . . . Analogously, 1 is the class of all unit classes. . . . Finally, 0 is the class of all null classes, i.e., the class of all classes without elements."[21] For our purposes, mathematical philosophy solves the problem whereby self-evidence appears purely subjective by understanding axiomatic propositions as representations of kinds or classes of things, whose generality is not achieved by empirical verifiability but, Hempel says, "enforc[ed] . . . by stipulation."[22] For Bennett, the fact that "this is it" is an expression of a kind of thing (a "One-Line Poem") is a way of insisting that what it expresses is a concept, not a subject.

If we return now to the version of self-evidence that takes the form of *Self-Evident Poems*, we can see why the commitment to expressing the concept matters (as opposed to the kind of conceptual poetry for which being against self-expression is also being against expression tout court). We can also see how it is shown to matter by means of the work itself. On the page following "One-Line Poem" we find "Alternate One-Line Poem":

Here it is.[23]

The very existence of "Alternate One-Line Poem" bears out something the title of Bennett's book already implies. That is, the idea that the poems in it are a "particular type" of poem (the "self-evident" type) entails a related but distinct idea, one that may sound like a truism: that these poems belong to a class or kind as such. What they express is their self-evidence, as we have seen already, but in doing so they also are expressions of the common features of the class to which they belong. Another way to put this is to say that the difference between "One Line Poem" and "Alternate One-Line Poem" is not like a difference in handwriting. That is, insofar as the difference is between two members of a class of poem, the particular features that make "This is it" distinct from "Here it is" cannot be explained as inflections of individual style, because these features are understood as expressions of a shared concept of the whole.

In this respect, Bennett's "One-Line Poem" is against self-expression in a way that the conceptual writing practiced and promoted by his contemporaries Goldsmith and Place ultimately is not. In an essay revolving around one of his earliest conceptual projects, Goldsmith describes giving his creative writing students an "uncreative" writing assignment, asking them to model the process by which he made *Day* by choosing a piece of writing to transcribe word-for-word.[24] In the end, the value of the assignment comes down to a matter of individual choice:

> There was only one girl who didn't have some sort of a transcendental experience. . . . She was a waitress who took it upon herself to retype her restaurant's menu in order to learn it better for work. She ended up hating the task and even hating her job more. It was an object lesson in the difference between voluntary and involuntary boredom.[25]

Two things are striking here: (1) that the students' experiences of the process of transcribing matter more than the writing that results from it and (2) that what determines whether a student's experience of the process is a bad one or a good one, whether she hates it (or likes it), is dependent on her making a voluntary choice. The aesthetic value that Goldsmith assigns both to the choice of material and to the experience of transcribing it come down to a matter of what one likes or doesn't like. It's hardly surprising, then, that Goldsmith cites Andy Warhol's aesthetics of "liking things" as a model for his practice.[26] And it's even less surprising that Goldsmith at one point sought to rebrand conceptualism as a "pro-consumerist poetry," effectively codifying the primacy of choice.[27] And while Vanessa Place's decision in 2013 to launch her corporation, Vanessa Place, Inc., was clearly meant as a spoof, the aesthetics of its business motto ("Your desires are our need") follows a consumerist logic nearly identical to Goldsmith's.[28] Referring in an interview to one of her first projects, a publishing initiative called "BookIt," Place explains how "for $50, you can buy a BookIt ISBN number . . . put it on whatever you like— . . . and it will become a book published by VanessaPlace Inc."[29] Thus what BookIt publishes are works produced by "whatever you like," in effect, by its consumers' self-expression. For Bennett, refusing self-expression by embracing self-evidence clearly goes along with a set of aesthetic commitments, which we might call formalist. But at the present moment, it also turns out to go along with a set of political commitments, which we might call anticapitalist.

Notes

1. Charles Altieri, e-mail to the author, August 23, 2013.

2. Guy Bennett, *Self-Evident Poems* (Los Angeles: Otis Books/Seismicity Editions, 2011), 17.

3. For a stunning analysis of poetic "ease" and its uses, see Oren Izenberg, "Confiance au Monde, or, the Poetry of Ease," *nonsite* 4 (Winter 2011/2012), http://nonsite.org/article/confiance-au-monde-or-the-poetry-of-ease.

4. George Herbert, *The Temple: Sacred Poems and Private Ejaculations* (Cambridge: Thom. Buck and Roger Daniel, 1633), reprinted at https://archive.org/stream/templesacredpoe09herbgoog#page/n14/mode/2up, 18.

5. Stanley Fish, *Self-Consuming Artifacts: The Experience of Seventeenth-Century Literature* (Pittsburgh: Duquesne University Press, 1998 [1972]), 208.

6. Ibid., 210.

7. In a 2011 interview, Bennett himself suggests that the poems are meant to be taken in at a glance as well as given more extended consideration:

> Interviewer: How do you see people reading these poems? . . .
> Bennett: I don't know how they would read them any differently than any other poem. . . .
> Interviewer: . . . Do you see this is as something where a person would sit down and sort of dedicate time, or is this something where they would read when they would have a moment?
> Bennett: Well, some of them are pretty short. In fact one of them doesn't have any words at all. . . . [S]o they don't require much time to actually read, though I hope that folks would think about them after the fact. So they could be, like, quick for consumption purposes, but hopefully slower for reflection purposes.

"Guy Bennett Discusses Self-Evident Poems with Alexandra Pollyea," Otis College of Art and Design, April 13, 2011, https://www.facebook.com/Otis.College/videos/216553998360935/.

8. While the publicity statement for *Self-Evident Poems* does not appear in or on the physical book itself, it seems to accompany the book wherever it appears for sale online. Roubaud's original statement ("La poésie dit ce qu'elle dit en le disant") appears in *Poésie, etcetera: ménage* (Paris: Stock, 1995). Bennett himself produced the English translation of Roubaud's text, published as *Poetry, etcetera: Cleaning House* (Copenhagen: Green Integer, 2006).

9. Roubaud, *Poetry, etcetera*, 5.

10. Seeing Bennett's work described as "conceptual," in other words, would likely call up for most readers appropriative works like Goldsmith's *Day* (2003), a word-for-word transcription of a single Friday's issue of the *New York Times* or Place's highly controversial *Statement of Facts* (2010), which, as one review described it "reproduced her appellate briefs [for sex offense cases] and represented them as poetry," more than the kinds of generative works we tend to associate with Oulipo: Raymond Queneau's *Cent mille milliards de poèmes*, for example, the lines of whose ten sonnets can be broken up and rearranged to form

the number of poems promised by the title, or Georges Perec's *La disparition*, an execution in novel form of a single rule: that the letter *e* never appear in the text.

11. See, for example, Vanessa Place and Rob Fitterman, *Notes on Conceptualisms* (Brooklyn: Ugly Duckling Presse, 2010); Marjorie Perloff, *Unoriginal Genius: Poetry by Other Means* (Chicago: University of Chicago Press, 2010), which features Goldsmith as a prominent example; Kenneth Goldsmith and Craig Dworkin, eds., *Against Expression: An Anthology of Conceptual Writing* (Evanston, Ill.: Northwestern University Press, 2011); and Goldsmith, *Uncreative Writing: Managing Language in the Digital Age* (New York: Columbia University Press, 2011).

12. There are myriad reasons to argue that this is an inaccurate depiction of lyric; nevertheless, the association with subjective expression is sufficiently codified that college textbooks and handbooks, from the early twentieth century until today, have consistently led with it in their definitions of lyric as a genre. For example, the definition of lyric in the widely used twelfth edition of the *Handbook to Literature*—"A brief subjective poem strongly marked by imagination, melody, and emotion, and creating for the reader a single, unified impression"—has survived since the 1936 edition of the same textbook (William Harmon, *A Handbook to Literature*, 12th ed. [Upper Saddle River, N.J.: Pearson Prentice Hall, 2011]). And M. H. Abrams's definition of lyric as "any short poem, consisting of the utterance by a single speaker, who expresses a state of mind or a process of perception, thought, and feeling" in the 1957 first edition of his *Glossary of Literary Terms* remains intact in the most recent edition from 2014 (M. H. Abrams and Geoffrey Galt Harpham, *A Glossary of Literary Terms*, 11th ed. [Boston: Wadsworth, 2014]). I include an extended discussion of this long-standing tendency in defining lyric in "Lyric, Gender, and Subjectivity in Modern and Contemporary Women's Poetry," in Dale Bauer, ed., *The Cambridge History of American Women's Literature* (Cambridge: Cambridge University Press, 2012), 515–38.

13. Bruce Glaser, "Questions to Stella and Judd," ed. Lucy Lippard, *ARTnews* (September 1966), available at http://www.artnews.com/2015/07/10/what-you-see-is-what-you-see-donald-judd-and-frank-stella-on-the-end-of-painting-in-1966/?singlepage=1. I'm indebted to Nick Nace for encouraging me to think more carefully about the resemblance between Stella's formulation and the form self-evidence takes in Bennett's poems.

14. Ibid.

15. Ibid.

16. Ibid.

17. Ibid.

18. See C. G. Hempel, "On the Nature of Mathematical Truth," *American Mathematical Monthly* 52, no. 10 (December 1945): 543–56. See also Bertrand Russell, "Truth and Falsehood," in *The Basic Writings of Bertrand Russell* (New York: Routledge, 2009 [1962]), 296–311, esp. 301–2.

19. Hempel, "On the Nature of Mathematical Truth," 543.

20. Ibid., 546.

21. Ibid., 550.

22. Ibid., 546.

23. Bennett, *Self-Evident*, 18.

24. Kenneth Goldsmith, *Day* (Great Barrington, Maine: The Figures, 2003). See also Goldsmith's widely cited account of the work, "Uncreativity as Creative Process," *Drunken Boat* (Winter 2002–3), available at http://epc.buffalo.edu/authors/goldsmith/uncreativity.html.

25. Goldsmith, "Being Boring" (November 2004), available at http://epc.buffalo.edu/authors/goldsmith/goldsmith_boring.html.

26. Goldsmith, "Conceptual Poetics," *Dispatches*, Poetry Foundation, January 24, 2007, available at http://epc.buffalo.edu/authors/goldsmith/Goldsmith_ConceptualWriting.pdf.

27. Goldsmith, "Pro-Consumerist Poetry," *Harriet*, Poetry Foundation, June 2007, http://www.poetryfoundation.org/harriet/2007/06/pro-consumerist-poetry/.

28. This appeared at www.vanessaplace.biz/about/. The site no longer exists.

29. "Vanessa Place to Ben Fama on Her Passion for Chairs," *Harriet*, Poetry Foundation, July 2013, http://www.poetryfoundation.org/harriet/2013/07/vanessa-place-to-ben-fama-on-her-passion-for-chairs/.

CRAIG DWORKIN

from *The Pine-Woods Notebook*

The pitch of the pines on the ridgeline thickens, bewitching.
A needle drop announces with a bounce the delay in patience it
anticipates. . . .

From pine to sigh a sound propounds the ingrained impulse to perpetuate;
the needling breeze yields, fecund and promiscuous . . .

The pitch of the pines aligns, defining: to repine: to sigh—from desire to
resign.

Chapter 26

Meditation as Mediation:
Craig Dworkin in the Pine-Woods

Marjorie Perloff

In 2015, Craig Dworkin, perhaps best known in poetry circles as the coeditor, with Kenneth Goldsmith, of the controversial anthology *Against Expression: An Anthology of Conceptual Writing* (Northwestern, 2011), produced a long poem (306 strophes, ranging from one to four lines each, plus a few pages of notes) called *The Pine-Woods Notebook*. Although the sequence is subtitled "after Francis Ponge," it is by no means directly based on Ponge's *Le carnet du bois de pins* (1947). Rather, Dworkin's is a definition poem (it presents itself as a list of short aphoristic definitions), whose mode, I shall suggest here, is best described as *conceptual lyric*. What makes the poem at once difficult and intensely rewarding is that, at every step, it revises our expectations of what "nature poetry" is and can be in the twenty-first century.

Consider the opening line:

> The pitch of the pines on the ridgeline thickens, bewitching.

This seems, on the face of it, a fairly normal descriptive opening for a poet's meditation in a pine forest. But the intricacy of internal rhyme (*pitch/bewitch*; *pine/line*), the alliteration of hard stops (*p*; *k*) and fricatives (*tch*), the assonance of short *i*'s, as well as the tight metrical form (from iamb and anapest to trochee) call attention to sound structure rather than to what is being represented. Then, too, the meaning is equivocal: how can the "pitch" (we first think of pitch as angle) "thicken"? Are the trees sloping downward? And since *bewitch* is used intransitively here, who or what is it that is being bewitched? *Pitch*, of course, also refers to the pines' blackness—"pitch black" comes from the term for the viscous substance produced by plants (in this case, the pine bark) or formed from petroleum—which, from below the "ridgeline," is seen to "thicken."

We are, in any case, in a world of words rather than the things designated by the words in question. As such, *Pine-Woods Notebook* represents a significant departure from the modernist text cited by Dworkin as its source, Ponge's *Carnet du bois de pins*. The latter was composed during a brief idyll in 1940, when the poet and Resistance fighter, escaping the battlefront, joined his family in the wooded mountains of the Haute-Loire in south-central France. What, asks Ponge, constitutes "le plaisir du bois de pins"? and he observes:

> De quoi est-il fait, ce plaisir?—principalement de ceci: le bois de pins est *une piece de la nature, faite d'arbres tous d'une espèce nettement définie; pièce bien délimitée,* généralement assez déserte, où l'on trouve abri contre le soleil, contre le vent, contre la visibilité; mais abri non absolu, non par isolement. Non! C'est un abri relatif. Un abri non cachottier, non mesquin, un abri noble.
>
>   C'est un endroit aussi (ceci est particulier aux bois de *pins*) où l'on évolue à l'aise, sans taillis, sans branchages à hauteur d'homme, où l'on peut s'étendre à sec, et sans mollesse, mais assez confortablement.
>
>   Chaque bois de pins est comme un sanatorium naturel, aussi un salon de musique ... une chambre, une vaste cathédrale de meditation (une cathédrale sans chaire, par bonheur) ouverte à tous les vents, mais par tant de portes que c'est comme si elles étaient fermées. Car ils y hesitent.

> Of what is it made, this pleasure? Principally of this: the pine forest is a *piece of nature*, composed of trees of a distinct kind, all of a piece, generally quite deserted, where one can take shelter from the sun, from the wind, from visibility; but not a complete shelter, not a place wholly isolated. No! it is only a temporary shelter. A shelter, not a hiding place, not niggardly, a noble shelter.
>
>   It is also a place (this is peculiar to pine forests) where one can move easily, there being no brush, no branches the height of men, a place where one can stretch out on the dry ground, a ground not soft but comfortable enough.
>
>   Each pine forest is like a natural sanatorium, also like a concert hall, a vast cathedral for meditation (a cathedral fortunately deserted), open to all the winds, but entering by so many doors that it's as if these were all shut. For the winds hesitate there.[1]

Ponge's fabled *chosisme* (thingness) is a matter not of direct visual or aural image—no imagist he—but of phenomenology: he is defining what a pine forest *is* and how it *feels* and *functions* from the vantage point of the unnamed observer. In the third paragraph, the pine wood becomes the motive for metaphor: it is said to resemble a sanatorium, a concert hall, a cathedral. As in Baudelaire, nature is a temple; everything one sees is charged with meaning, even if the meaning often remains mysterious, as in the case of the pine trees resembling doors, closed to the wind.

Then, too, Ponge's very particular response to the pine forest accords with the distinction made by the San Francisco Zen monk Shunryu Suzuki in a passage that Dworkin uses as his epigraph:

> When we hear the sound of the pine trees on a
> windy day, perhaps the wind is just blowing, and
> the pine tree is just standing in the wind. That is
> all that they are doing. But the people who listen
> to the wind in the tree will write a poem.

The supposition is that the poetic imagination is transformative, that one can see the pine forest as sanatorium or cathedral. Anglophone readers, perhaps not familiar with Ponge, will immediately think of another great modernist poet, Wallace Stevens, for whom the wind in the pine trees is always, as the well-known Stevens title would have it, "The Motive for Metaphor." Thus, in "The Snow Man":

> One must have a mind of winter
> To regard the frost and the boughs
> Of the pine-trees crusted with snow.

Or again, in "Six Significant Landscapes," which begins with the image of an "old man sit[ting] / In the shadow of a pine," whose "beard moves in the wind," and moves from there to the reflection that "the night is of the color / Of a woman's arm: / Night, the female, / Obscure, / Fragrant and supple," and then to the curious admission that "I measure myself / Against a tall tree," against what Stevens, in his later "Credences of Summer," wryly calls "the physical pine, the metaphysical pine."[2]

Dworkin will have none of this: Ponge's or Stevens's ineluctable modalities of the visible give way, in Dworkin's poetics, to an obsession with the dictionary. In his *Pine-Woods Notebook*, the "thing" (as in Stevens's "Not Ideas about the Thing") is replaced by the always equivocal and endlessly overdetermined *word* or word group. Then, too, each declarative sentence or sentence set has its own identity, defying absorption into the larger picture. Thus line 1 above, "The pitch of the pines on the ridgeline thickens, bewitching," is followed by the line: "A needle drop announces with a bounce the delay in patience it anticipates." Here we immediately note the arresting rhyme of *announces* and *bounce*, as well as the "delay" (in the Duchampian sense of "a delay made in glass") caused by the recognition that *patience* is indeed *anticipated*, the latter word functioning as an anagram for the former. The line, far from carrying on the bewitchment motif from line 1, seems to move elsewhere somewhat confusingly, for pine needles don't in fact make a "bounce" when they fall to the ground, and what does patience have to do with it? Do we anticipate the fall of a pine needle? Then again, suppose this is a needle for injecting a "drop" of fluid into a body, impatiently anticipating relief from pain? In this context, *patience* also suggests *patients*, and the setting shifts from pine forest to hospital or sick room.

Is this, then, nonsense verse, designed to confound the reader with a catalog of endlessly punning double entendres and sound play? Certainly the representational function of language is short-circuited: the actual pine forest, still alive and breathing in Ponge's poem and certainly in the Zen meditation of Suzuki, seems to have disappeared. Or has it? In strophe after strophe, *pine*, with all its meanings, obsolete and current, remains at center stage, whether etymologically, phonemically, or allusively. As Dworkin himself has explained his procedure:

> First, [the poem] has an exhaustive, comprehensive impulse: to find the connection between ALL the definitions of "pine" and ALL the definitions of "pitch." And so on, for other key terms.
>
> Second, it's not "expressive" in a certain, conventional way. As in MOTES,[3] most of the words . . . had to be there because of their own logics, not my initial whim, or desire or what I "wanted to say." So there are multiple reasons for any word, usually at least three: rhyme, etymology, homography . . . but also the conventional definition of a given term. . . . My mode throughout was the *resonance of sympathetic vibration*: a poetics that would echo its theme of sound. . . . It's not as if I had something to say and then found the right words, or as if I wanted to communicate some idea and then found the "poetic" way to say it . . . but rather that I was finding words and then—under their own chance constraints—seeing what THEY said. I was trying to record what the sets of sounds were constructing on their own.[4]

The last part of this statement recalls such L=A=N=G=U=A=G=E manifestos as Steve McCaffery's "The Death of the Subject" or Lyn Hejinian's "If Written Is Writing," with its formulation, "Where once one sought a vocabulary for ideas, now one seeks ideas for vocabularies."[5] Dworkin was an undergraduate at Stanford when Language poetry became prominent in the Bay Area, and he quickly absorbed its lessons, later producing a digital archive called *Eclipse* (http://eclipsearchive.org/), which reproduces out-of-print or obscure small-press books and individual poems by Language poets (and other experimentalists) from Bruce Andrews to Tina Darragh and Peter Inman.

The difference is that, even as Dworkin is aware of what the Language poets called "the referential fallacy," his own poetry is much more literary than theirs, with regard to both sound and poetic allusion: there are passages in *Pine-Woods Notebook* that echo and deconstruct canonical lyric poems from a variety of languages and cultures. Indeed, if, as Virginia Jackson reminds us in her essay "Lyric" for the *Encyclopedia of Poetry and Poetics*, *lyric*, with its derivation from the Greek musical instrument, the lyre, "was from its inception a term used to describe a music that could no longer be heard,"⁶ the *Pine-Woods Notebook* is lyric through and through, an echo chamber of earlier pitches and pines, composed for a poetic moment very different from Francis Ponge's in World War II—different too from such Language projects as Bruce Andrews's *Getting Ready to Have Been Frightened,* which contains such minimalist units as "a box / with a lid" or "wife / eggshells," in that Dworkin's is, however covertly, a much more personal poetry.

To begin with, the kernel words *pine* and *pitch*, which provide the unity and continuity of Dworkin's poems, have been chosen, not just for their various meanings (e.g., *pitch* as angle, pitch as black) or connotations but for their etymology. In its contemporary literal sense, *pine*, deriving from Old English, is "a tree of the genus *Pinus*, or of various allied coniferous genera; comprising trees, mostly of large size, with evergreen needle-shaped leaves, of which many species afford valuable timber, tar, and turpentine and some have edible seeds" (*Oxford English Dictionary*). But the second, now obsolete meaning of *pine*, deriving from the Latin *poena*, originally referred to "punishment; suffering inflicted as punishment, torment, torture"—the earlier form, in other words, of *pain*. Over the centuries *pine* was separated from punishment and meant mental suffering, grief, sorrow, trouble or distress of mind, anguish, and "grievous or intense longing," which gives us, in turn, the verb *to pine*, to long for. By the eighteenth century, *pine* had been largely replaced by *pain*, although Alexander Pope, as cited in the *OED*, still uses *pine* and *pain* interchangeably. And, for that matter in U.S. southern and in Australian pronunciation, *pain* continues to be equivalent to *pine* for many people.

Dworkin's choice of tree is thus hardly coincidental: pain, we shall see, is central to the *Pine-Woods Notebook*: spruce, fir, cypress: these would not quite do in the context. Then, too, the pine, with its endless species (e.g., Bishop's Pine, Hickory Pine, Scotch Pine) and derivates (pine cone, pineapple, pineal) allows for remarkable possibilities. Consider the sixth strophe of the poem: "From pine to sigh a sound propounds the ingrained impulse to perpetuate; the needling breeze yields, fecund and promiscuous." Here metrical patterning and rhyme ("From píne to sígh a sóund propóunds") as well as word choice (*propounds, perpetuates, fecund, promiscuous*) create a distinct aura of the literary past: are we reading Thomas Gray? Tennyson? And yet the strophe makes perfectly good sense: those who pine also sigh and long to perpetuate the mood of pleasurable pain; indeed the "needling breeze," where the pine needles are animated and given power to "needle," yields to a "fecund and promiscuous" moment, rather like "the wakeful anguish of the soul" in Keats's "Ode on Melancholy."

Indeed, the Keatsian mood is apposite here. The "ingrained impulse to perpetuate" something "fecund and promiscuous" is a thread running through the whole poem; remembered pain, the poem implies, is a source of pleasure: the "promiscuous" memory, invoked, as it were, from the world of nature outside the self, bewitches the poet. So, a few lines later:

/   /   /   /   /   /   /   /
Sap from the wavering sutures of the bark darkens and brittles, black as shellac.

The predominantly dactylic rhythm of the opening goes into reverse with the rhyme "bark darkens." At one level, Dworkin is giving us straightforward information about pine bark: the sap that oozes through the cracks hardens ("brittles") giving the bark a black shellac-like surface. But pine bark extract also has medicinal purposes: it yields pycnogenol, used for treating cancer. So the sap is also something injected into the wound, which is then closed by sutures. And by this time, the wavering sutures seem to be the poet's own: it is as if the blood darkens and congeals ("brittles"), turning black as shellac.

Indeed, as we read on page 7, "The dark of the trunks predates the dusk," an almost perfect iambic tetrameter that puts the description of "sap" in context. The pine trunks are dark even in bright light—theirs is a dark that predates the dusk. It is an especially memorable and quotable line, given the alliteration of *d*'s, assonance of short and long *a*'s, consonance of "*dark/trunk*," and the mix of all three in *dark/trunk/dusk*. If the dark predates the dusk, it is especially threatening, for it is always there. Suturing, moreover, is never quite pain-free. Indeed, further into the poem, we come to the line "The pitch of the pines darkens the daytime" (p. 17). In other words, darkness at noon.

But there is a further complication. For as the endnotes inform us, some of the *Pine-Wood Notebook*'s striking phrases are in fact citations taken from a wide variety of poetic sources. "Pine trees pulsate between the graves" (p. 6), for example, is a translation of Valéry's "Les pins palpitent entre les tombes," in *Le cimetière marin*. A few lines further down, "The forest floor patterns its parquetry without any smooth planks, without a single washed board, but with the thickest of carpets" is a translation of "Sans planche lisse au sol, sans planches lavées au sol mais de tapis épais" in Ponge's *Carnet du bois de pins*. Such allusions to earlier poets are not especially unusual in twentieth-century poetry—think of Eliot and Pound—but what do we make of the following example, in which the short strophe, "One finds the consensus again and again: nothing is better suited to wind than the pine," is given the following mock-scholarly note:

> "Nothing is better suited to wind than the pine." Liu Chi: "Wind-in-the-Pines Pavilion," *Inscribed Landscapes: Travel Writing from Imperial China,* trans. Richard Strassberg (Berkeley: University of California Press, 1994): 281. Chi goes on to explain: "When the wind passes through it, it is neither obstructed nor agitated. Wind flows through smoothly with a natural sound." The trope is common across cultures. Consider, for just one example: "what purely natural sound appeals more to the imagination than the wind in pine-trees?" [Caroline Fathergill: *Diane Wentworth: A Novel* (New York: Harper

Brothers, 1889): 74. This conflation is perhaps what Augusta Larned
refers to as a "summer philosophy": "a philosophy of trees and flow-
ers, of sound of breakers on the shore, the murmuring wind in pine
trees" [Augusta Larned: "A Summer Gospel," *The Christian Register*
8 (26 July, 1900): 819].

What is the point of this absurd footnote, with its move from a fourteenth-
century Chinese poet (the translation by Strassberg, published by California,
is one that might have come across Dworkin's desk) to observations in Victo-
rian novels no one reads anymore—novels that Dworkin probably found by
surfing the net rather than through any reading project? The note is a witty
example of consensus building at its most rudimentary, which is to say cliché.
The wind in the pine trees: what could be a more hackneyed image, the sub-
ject of pop song and everyone's "summer philosophy." All the more reason
to set the stage with such commonplaces so that we can appreciate the high
style of such neighboring passages as

> Against the trunk's tower and the acclivitous thrust of the boughs the
> branchlets depend, perpendicular, imitating the fall of the rain
> they maintain.

Acclivitous, which I for one had to look up, means "sloping upward"; it
here creates a vivid image of the angle formed between the boughs and their
perpendicular branches, making parallel lines with the falling rain. And the
"rain they maintain" contains an echo of *My Fair Lady*'s "The rain in Spain
stays mainly in the plain."

The difficulties of such poetry are, we might say, horizontal rather than
vertical: it is not a matter, as in the case of modernist or, for that matter, Lan-
guage poetry, of interpreting Empsonian ambiguities, because the fact is that,
given the Internet, everything here can be looked up and "explained." An
"obscure" line like "Solutes pass through the symplast of the vascular xylem"
is botany textbook talk, meaning something like "Substances dissolving in a
liquid pass through the inner side of the plasma membrane of the tissue of
a vascular plant." But in Dworkin's alliterative line, with its symphony of *s*'s
and *l*'s, this information sounds so interesting!

Where, then, does all this playful process lead us? Toward the end, we get
such revealing statements as "The pitch, as a liquid, seeks its own level. The
flow lasts as long as the vessels communicate"—a strophe that gives us the sense
that the poet is finally coming to terms with the possibility of pinning down the
"pitch" and communicating his own sense of his verbal symphony. And indeed,

> The skin, porous, absorbs the last fragrance.
> The supine rises, erect, to embrace—and resists.
> The lasting remains.

Is the poet still meditating on pine forests? Or have these given way to the landscape of human desire—the geometry, not of trees, but of bodies? "To recognize the sign's desire for expression," we read on the penultimate page, "is to prize the regression from pitch to rhythm to resonance." Here is the "resonance of sympathetic vibration" Dworkin has spoken of, in connection with his poem. Its last two strophes are

> The insatiable frustrates its statement's conclusion.
>
> The pitch of the pines aligns, defining: to repine: to sigh—from desire to resign.

Desire is insatiable: one must, it seems, resign oneself to that "defining" insight. The final line contains five rhyming words, providing seeming musical closure, but what is also clear is that no definition can adequately convey the poet's response to the pine/pitch world he has been exploring. "To sigh—from desire / to resign": it is the perennial lover's mission. And also the poet's mission "to re-sign" his text.

Dworkin's, I would conclude, is a meditation for the information age. For one thing, it is entirely mediated: nothing comes to us directly; rather, every branchlet, every twig and pitch has always already been contextualized and defined elsewhere. In keeping with the notion of mediation, the poem could not have been written, say, thirty years ago because it depends throughout on the ability of both poet *and* reader to inform themselves of meanings and definitions. It is, so to speak, a digital poem that is, paradoxically, not written for the computer screen—but digital in that it could not have been composed without Internet access. Everything here can—and must be—looked up on Google and in specialized online dictionaries. No hypothetical reader (or writer!) could have this material at his or her fingertips: information gathering, conceptualization, and translation is prompted at every turn.

Yet, in the end, Dworkin's elliptical poem is less a rejection than a renewal of the literary tradition. I have already mentioned Keats; the nature poems of Wordsworth are also apposite. On the last page of *The Pine-Woods Notebook*, we find the line, "The fleeting breeze betrays the trees"—a parodic echo of Wordsworth's "Daffodils": "Beside the lake, beneath the trees, / Fluttering and dancing in the breeze." In our own moment, the poet suggests, inspiration comes not directly from hearing the wind in the pine trees or suddenly coming upon a "host of golden daffodils," but through the mediation of code that now transmits all that we touch. "Nature always wears the colors of the spirit": the Emersonian precept is as powerful as ever. But its manifestations are, to use Gilles Deleuze's term, which Dworkin cites in one of his strophes, *deterritorialized*.

Notes

1. The edition Dworkin is using here is Francis Ponge, *Le carnet du bois de pins* (Lausanne: Mermod, 1947). The *Carnet* was reprinted in *La rage de l'expression* (Paris: Pléiade, 1976), 148–223. Translation mine.

2. Wallace Stevens, *Collected Poems* (New York: Alfred A. Knopf, 1961), 9, 23, 373. For an excellent essay comparing Stevens to Ponge, see Andrew Epstein, "'The Rhapsody of Things as They Are': Stevens, Francis Ponge, and the Impossible Everyday," *Wallace Stevens Journal,* 36, no. 1 (2012): 47–77.

3. Craig Dworkin, *Motes* (New York: Roof Books, 2011).

4. Craig Dworkin, e-mail to author, February 9, 2015. Emphasis mine.

5. Steve McCaffery, *L=A=N=G=U=A=G=E*, Supplement Number One (June 1980), front page, unpaginated; cf. Steve McCaffery, "Diminished Reference and the Model Reader," in *North of Intention: Criticial Writings, 1973–1986* (New York: Roof Books, 1986), 13–29; Lyn Hejinian, "If Written Is Writing" (1978), in *The Language of Inquiry* (Berkeley: University of California Press, 2000), 27.

6. Virginia Jackson, "Lyric," *Princeton Encyclopedia of Poetry and Poetics*, 4th ed., ed. Roland Greene, Stephen Cushman, et al. (Princeton, N.J.: Princeton University Press, 2012), 826–34, quote on 826.

ACKNOWLEDGMENTS

We would first like to thank the contributors for their labor and, even more, for their supreme goodwill in difficult times. Times were made considerably less difficult by the staff at Northwestern University Press, particularly Gianna Mosser, and the press's anonymous readers, without whom there would be no occasion for the pleasures of giving thanks. Thanks, too, to Drew Daniel, Adam Fitzgerald, Dylan Furcall, Oren Izenberg, Hank Lazer, Ming-Qian Ma, Chelsie Malyszek, Mark McMorris, Marjorie Perloff, Neil Perry, and Nick Thurston. And finally, each editor would like to thank the other one—not just for his labor, goodwill, and what appeared to be his ease with difficulty, but also for his half of the 976 e-mails that helped bring this volume together.

Charles Altieri teaches in the English Department at the University of California, Berkeley. He has two books on what was contemporary poetry. His most recent books are *Wallace Stevens and the Demands of Modernity* (2013) and *Reckoning with Imagination: Wittgenstein and the Aesthetics of Literary Experience* (2015).

Jennifer Ashton is an associate professor of English at the University of Illinois at Chicago. She is the author of *From Modernism to Postmodernism: American Poetry in the Twentieth Century* (2008) and editor of *The Cambridge Companion to American Poetry since 1945* (2013). She is a founding member of the online arts and political journal nonsite.org and a founding organizer, former chief steward, and proud member of UIC United Faculty (IFT-AFT-AAUP-AFL-CIO Local 6456).

Michael W. Clune is a professor of English at Case Western Reserve University. His most recent critical work is *Writing against Time* (2013); his latest creative work is *Gamelife* (2015).

Michael Davidson is Distinguished Professor Emeritus at the University of California, San Diego. He is the author of *Ghostlier Demarcations: Modern Poetry and the Material Word* (1997), *Concerto for the Left Hand: Disability and the Defamiliar Body* (2008), and, most recently, *Outskirts of Form: Practicing Cultural Poetics* (2011). He is editor of *The New Collected Poems of George Oppen* (2002) and author of six books of poetry, including *Bleed Through: New and Selected Poems* (2013).

Al Filreis is the author of *Wallace Stevens and the Actual World*, *Modernism from Right to Left* (1991), and *Counter-revolution of the Word: The Conservative Attack on Modern Poetry, 1945–60* (2008). He is the director of the Kelly Writers House, director of the Center for Programs in Contemporary Writing, codirector of PennSound, publisher of *Jacket2*, and creator-teacher of "ModPo," a free and open online course for 175,000 participants since 2012—all at the University of Pennsylvania.

Judith Goldman teaches as core faculty in the Poetics Program at SUNY–Buffalo and is the author of *Vocoder* (2001), *DeathStar/Richo-chet* (2006), *l.b.; or, catenaries* (2011), and *agon* (2017). She also serves as the editor of poetry features for *Postmodern Culture*. Her current project is _____ *Mt. [blank mount]*, a hybrid scholarly-creative work that writes through Shelley's "Mont Blanc" in the context of environmental disaster.

Langdon Hammer, Niel Gray Jr. Professor of English and chair of English at Yale University, is the author of *James Merrill: Life and Art* (2015) and editor of the Library of America's *Hart Crane: Complete Poetry and Selected Letters* (2006). He has been the poetry editor of *The American Scholar* since 2004.

Lyn Hejinian is a poet, essayist, translator, and teacher, currently serving as the John F. Hotchkis Professor of English at the University of California, Berkeley. Her most recent book is *The Unfollowing* (2016). In 2013 Wesleyan University Press republished her best-known book, *My Life*, in an edition that includes her related work, *My Life in the Nineties*.

Jeanne Heuving is the author of *The Transmutation of Love and Avant-Garde Poetics* (2016) and *Transducer* (2008). Her cross-genre book *Incapacity* (2004) won a Small Press Traffic Book of the Year Award. She directs the M.F.A. in Creative Writing & Poetics at the University of Washington–Bothell.

Joseph Jonghyun Jeon is an associate professor of English and Asian American Studies at Pomona College. He is the author of *Racial Things, Racial Forms: Objecthood in Avant-Garde Asian American Poetry* (2012). He is at work on a book titled *Korea's IMF Cinema and the End of the American Century*.

Aaron Kunin is an associate professor of English at Pomona College. His most recent book of poems is *Cold Genius* (2014).

Ben Lerner is the author of three books of poetry (*The Lichtenberg Figures, Angle of Yaw,* and *Mean Free Path*), two novels (*Leaving the Atocha Station, 10:04*), and a short work of criticism (*The Hatred of Poetry*). He is Distinguished Professor of English at Brooklyn College.

Adalaide Morris, a professor emerita at the University of Iowa, writes on the expanded field of modern and contemporary poetics, including information art, countermapping, documentary, and the digital. She is the author of *How to Live/ What to Do: H.D.'s Cultural Poetics* (2003), editor of *Sound States: Innovative Poetics and Acoustical Technologies* (1998), and coeditor of *New Media Poetics: Contexts, Technotexts, and Theories* (2009).

Nicholas D. Nace is the editor, with Russ McDonald and Travis Williams, of *Shakespeare Up Close* (2012) and author of more than twenty book chapters and articles. *Catch-words*, a book-length conceptual work, was published by Information as Material in 2017. He is currently at work on a cultural history of the eighteenth-century novel *Fanny Hill*.

Cary Nelson is Jubilee Professor of Liberal Arts & Sciences at the University of Illinois at Urbana–Champaign. Among his thirty books are *Repression and Recovery: Modern American Poetry and the Politics of Cultural Memory, 1910– 1945* (1991), as well as *Anthology of Modern American Poetry* (2nd ed., 2014) and *Anthology of Contemporary American Poetry* (2nd ed., 2014).

Nadia Nurhussein is an associate professor of English and Africana Studies at Johns Hopkins University, where she specializes in African American literature. Her first book, *Rhetorics of Literacy: The Cultivation of American Dialect Poetry,* was published in 2013. She is currently at work on a monograph tentatively titled *Abyssinia's Power: Imperial Ethiopianism and African American Literature.*

Geoffrey G. O'Brien is the author, most recently, of *People on Sunday* (2013), *Metropole* (2011), *Green and Gray* (2007), and *The Guns and Flags Project* (2002). O'Brien is an associate professor of English at the University of California, Berkeley, and also teaches for the Prison University Project at San Quentin State Prison.

Bob Perelman is a poet and critic. *Modernism the Morning After* is forthcoming; he is working on a new book of poems, *Jack and Jill.*

Marjorie Perloff's most recent book is *Edge of Irony: Modernism in the Shadow of the Habsburg Empire* (2016). She is the author of many books on contemporary poetry, including *Unoriginal Genius: Poetry by Other Means in the New Century* (2012). She is Sadie D. Patek Professor Emerita of Humanities at Stanford University and Florence R. Scott Professor of English Emerita at the University of Southern California.

Siobhan Phillips's poems, essays, and fiction have appeared in *PMLA, Missouri Review, Boston Review, Southwest Review,* and other publications. She is the author of *The Poetics of the Everyday: Creative Repetition in Modern American Verse* (2010). She teaches at Dickinson College.

Brian Reed is a professor of English and Comparative Literature, Media and Cinema at the University of Washington. He is the author of *Hart Crane: After His Lights* (2006), *Phenomenal Reading: Essays on Modern and Contemporary Poetics* (2012), and *Nobody's Business: Twenty-First Century Avant-Garde Poetics* (2013). *A Mine of Intersections: Writing the History of Contemporary American Poetry* is forthcoming.

Jennifer Scappettone works at the crossroads of writing, translation, and scholarly research, on the page and off. Her books include *From Dame Quickly* (2009), *Locomotrix: Selected Poetry and Prose of Amelia Rosselli* (2012), *Killing the Moonlight: Modernism in Venice* (2014), and *The Republic of Exit 43: Outtakes & Scores from an Archaeology and Pop-Up Opera of the Corporate Dump* (2016).

Lytle Shaw's books include *Frank O'Hara: The Poetics of Coterie* (2006), *Fieldworks: From Place to Site in Postwar Poetics* (2013), and *The Moiré Effect* (2012). He is a contributing editor of *Cabinet* magazine and professor of English at New York University.

Evie Shockley is the author of *the new black*, winner of the 2012 Hurston/Wright Legacy Award in Poetry, among other collections, and of a critical study, *Renegade Poetics: Black Aesthetics and Formal Innovation in African American Poetry* (2011). A new poetry volume, *semiautomatic*, is forthcoming. She is an associate professor of English at Rutgers University–New Brunswick.

Roberto Tejada is the author of the poetry collections *Full Foreground* (2012), *Exposition Park* (2010), *Mirrors for Gold* (2006), and the cultural poetics *Still Nowhere in an Empty Vastness* (2017); *Todo en el ahora* (2015) gathers Spanish-language translations of his work. His art history publications include *National Camera: Photography and Mexico's Image Environment* (2009), *Celia Alvarez Muñoz* (2009), and other writings on contemporary U.S. and Latino American artists.

John Wilkinson teaches English and creative writing at the University of Chicago. His most recent books include a collection of selected poems, *Schedule of Unrest* (2014), and *Ghost Nets* (2016). He is the principal investigator for an international research program called Outsider Writing (http://neubauercollegium .uchicago.edu/faculty/outsider_writing/); his other main research focus is mid-twentieth-century British poetry and painting.

POETRY SOURCES

Page 29. Srikanth Reddy, from *Voyager* (Berkeley: University of California Press, 2011), 3.

Page 47. Laynie Browne, "6/14 Donne Sonnet," in *Daily Sonnets* (Denver: Counterpath Press, 2007), 37.

Page 59. Jacqueline Waters, "The Tax," in *One Sleeps the Other Doesn't* (New York: Ugly Duckling Presse, 2011), 99–102.

Page 71. Geoffrey G. O'Brien, from "Winterreise," in *People on Sunday* (Seattle: Wave Books, 2013), 103.

Page 83. Andrea Brady, "The Husband," in *Cut from the Rushes* (Hastings: Reality Street Editions, 2013), 128–29.

Page 93. Aaron Kunin, "First," in *Cold Genius* (New York: Fence Books, 2014), 67–69.

Page 107. Juliana Spahr, from "switching," in *Fuck You-Aloha-I Love You* (Middletown, CT: Wesleyan University Press, 2001), 35–42.

Page 121. Jena Osman, "The Beautiful Life of Persona Ficta," in *Corporate Relations* (Providence, R.I.: Burning Deck, 2014), 11–12.

Page 133. Maggie Nelson, from *Bluets* (Seattle: Wave Books, 2009), 1.

Page 145. Ariana Reines, from "RENDERED," in *The Cow* (New York: Fence Books, 2006), 65–83.

Page 159. Atsuro Riley, "Flint-Chant," in *Romey's Order* (Chicago: University of Chicago Press, 2010), 3.

Page 169. Myung Mi Kim, from *Penury* (Richmond, Calif.: Omnidawn, 2009), 111.

Page 187. Sherwin Bitsui, from *Flood Song* (Port Townsend, Wash.: Copper Canyon, 2009), 54.

Page 201. Douglas Kearney, "The Miscarriage: A Minstrel Show," in *Patter* (Pasadena, Calif.: Red Hen Press, 2014), 37.

Page 209. Tisa Bryant, from *Unexplained Presence* (Providence, R.I.: Leon Works, 2007), 1.

Page 223. Tonya M. Foster, "In/somnia," in *A Swarm of Bees in High Court* (New York: Belladonna,* 2015), 7–13.

Page 237. Rosa Alcalá, "Voice Activation," in *M(y)O t (h e r) T o n g u e* (New York: Futurepoem, 2017).

Page 249. Paolo Javier, "Paolo's Lust," in *60 lv bo(e)mbs* (Oakland, Calif.: O Books, 2005), 29.

Page 259. LaTasha N. Nevada Diggs, "daggering kanji," in *TwERK* (New York: Belladonna*, 2013), 64–65

Page 281. Rachel Zolf, from *Janey's Arcadia* (Toronto: Coach House, 2014), [74].

Page 297. Lisa Robertson, from *R's Boat* (Berkeley: University of California Press, 2010), 11–12.

Page 309. Kevin Davies, from "Lateral Argument," archived at http://web .archive.org/web/20030404031731/http://members.rogers.com/alterra/davies .htm.

Page 323. Vanessa Place, "First Stone," *The Home School*, February 28, 2014, http://ashberyhomeschool.org/gallery/vanessa-place/, archived at https://web .archive.org/web/20150111014024/.

Page 339. Divya Victor, from *Hellocasts* (Rio de Janeiro: Ood Press, 2011), 2.

Page 353. Guy Bennett, "One-Line Poem," in *Self-Evident Poems* (Los Angeles: Otis Books/Seismicity Editions, 2011), 17.

Page 367. Craig Dworkin, from *The Pine-Woods Notebook* (forthcoming), 3–4.

INDEX

Abrams, M. H., 2–3
abstract expressionism, 360–61
access/accessibility, 24, 140, 191–98, 233, 264
Achleitner, Friedrich, 351n15
Acker, Kathy, 293
acknowledgment, 2, 5, 12, 15, 37, 91, 115–16, 136, 138, 156, 213–14, 230, 241, 307n14, 347; poesis of, 288–92
Acu, Adrian, 253
address, 12–14, 24, 26, 33, 43, 50, 81, 114, 130, 163, 192, 196, 239, 241, 292, 302, 315, 342, 349
Against Expression (Dworkin and Goldsmith), 34, 359, 369
Alcalá, Rosa, 15, 237–46
Alexander, Charles, 53
Alexander, Will, 232
allotment, 65–66
allusion, 16, 17, 23, 74, 123, 124, 166, 214, 218, 256, 316, 333, 372, 374
Alterran Poetry Assemblage, 311
Althusser, Louis, 129–30
Altieri, Charles, 5–6, 240, 343
Andrews, Bruce, 301, 306, 372–373
Antena, 271
Antin, David, 263–64
anxiety, 8, 11, 66–69, 89–90, 114, 151, 172–73, 178, 230, 318
appropriation: cultural, 17, 91, 163, 178, 193, 267–69, 292; textual, 4, 21, 33–34, 52, 124–28, 149–53, 284, 301, 326–36, 341–50, 364n10
Arendt, Hannah, 257
Aristotle, 52
Ashbery, John, 1, 25n1, 75–77, 80n4, 82n5
Ashton, Jennifer, 22–23
assemblage, 89, 175, 177, 227, 233, 263, 311
Atget, Eugène, 304

Atkins, Russell, 231
Auden, W. H., 204
audience, 2–3, 5, 6, 7, 8, 10, 12–13, 14, 18, 19, 22, 24, 25n5, 76, 77, 79, 164, 191, 192–98, 204, 207–8, 214, 231, 233, 269, 331, 345, 350
authenticity, 2, 5, 34, 124, 207, 264, 344
avant–garde poetry, 15, 54, 128, 136, 139, 140–41, 197, 232, 233, 239, 245, 301, 305, 327, 351n10

Bäcker, Heimrad, 344, 346–47
Baker, Josephine, 227
Balzac, Honoré de, 304
Baraka, Amiri, 228
Barthes, Roland, 347
bathos, 89
Bauman, Zygmunt, 348
Benjamin, Walter, 44n8, 140, 345
Bennett, Guy, 22–23, 353–63
Bernstein, Charles, 301
Bernstein, Felix, 336
Berrigan, Ted, 52, 56
Berryman, John, 204
Bervin, Jen, 34, 41
Bhabha, Homi, 243
Bidart, Frank, 163
biology, 7, 97, 99–101
Bion, W. R., 88, 92
Bishop, Elizabeth, 1
Bitsui, Sherwin, 12, 187–98
Black Arts Movement, 232–33
Blaeser, Kimberly, 198
Blake, William, 64–67
Blast, 73
Bök, Christian, 266–67, 291
Borsuk, Amaranth, 270
boundary crossings, 4, 12–14, 177
Bourdieu, Pierre, 96
Brady, Andrea, 6, 82–92
Brooks, Gwendolyn, 231